PEERLESS

WISCONSIN FILM STUDIES
Patrick McGilligan, series editor

PEERLESS

Rouben Mamoulian,
Hollywood, and Broadway

Kurt Jensen

THE UNIVERSITY OF WISCONSIN PRESS

The University of Wisconsin Press
728 State Street, Suite 443
Madison, Wisconsin 53706
uwpress.wisc.edu

Gray's Inn House, 127 Clerkenwell Road
London EC1R 5DB, United Kingdom
eurospanbookstore.com

Copyright © 2024
The Board of Regents of the University of Wisconsin System
All rights reserved. Except in the case of brief quotations embedded in critical articles and reviews, no part of this publication may be reproduced, stored in a retrieval system, transmitted in any format or by any means—digital, electronic, mechanical, photocopying, recording, or otherwise—or conveyed via the Internet or a website without written permission of the University of Wisconsin Press. Rights inquiries should be directed to rights@uwpress.wisc.edu.

Printed in the United States of America
This book may be available in a digital edition.

Library of Congress Cataloging-in-Publication Data

Names: Jensen, Kurt (Writer on film), author.
Title: Peerless : Rouben Mamoulian, Hollywood, and Broadway / Kurt Jensen.
Other titles: Wisconsin film studies.
Description: Madison, Wisconsin : The University of Wisconsin Press, 2024. | Series: Wisconsin film studies | Includes bibliographical references and index.
Identifiers: LCCN 2023040957 | ISBN 9780299348205 (cloth)
Subjects: LCSH: Mamoulian, Rouben. | Motion picture producers and directors—United States—Biography. | Theatrical producers and directors—United States—Biography.
Classification: LCC PN1998.3.M3205 J46 2024 | DDC 791.4302/33092 [B]—dc23/eng/20231204
LC record available at https://lccn.loc.gov/2023040957

A version of chapter 13 was originally published as "What Did Mamoo Do? The Rouben Mamoulian Papers and *Oklahoma!*" in *Studies in Musical Theatre* 4, no. 3 (December 2010), by Intellect Press.

Correspondence from Oscar Hammerstein II used by permission of the Trust and under the Will of Oscar Hammerstein II and Hammerstein Properties LLC.

For

MICHAEL SRAGOW, who said, "Write it yourself," and
LEE LAWRENCE, who said, "Yes, do that," and
KRISTINA ARRIAGA, who reminds me that I never walk alone.

Contents

Introduction: Enjoy the Journey	3
1 Tiflis to New York	10
2 Catfish Row	34
3 From Eugene O'Neill to Burlesque	47
4 Finding Elissa	60
5 Those Darn Cats	66
6 Isn't it Romantic?	83
7 Dietrich and Garbo	93
8 In Which Anna and Miriam Star	108
9 My Colored Brainchild	119
10 The Folks Who Live on the Hill	134
11 Golden Holden	150
12 Mon General Zanuck	158
13 A Bright Golden Haze	177
14 Otto and Ethel	192
15 A Real Nice Clambake	201
16 Come Rain or Come Shine	217
17 Found in the Stars	231

18 Mamoulian Marches On	246
19 Breathtaking Cinemascope	262
20 Perfidy and *Bess*	270
21 Dulce et Decorum Est Cleopatra Mori	283
22 Leavin' Time	299
Acknowledgments	311
Notes	315
Bibliography	343
Index	351

Illustrations

A painting of Mamoulian's grandmother Kato Bobo, a spinner of tales	13
Mamoulian family portrait (1915)	15
Mamoulian in Kew Gardens, London (1922)	19
Vladimir Rosing and Mamoulian at the opening of the fall term of the Eastman School of Music (September 1923)	25
Mamoulian at the Theatre Guild acting school in Scarsdale, New York (spring 1927)	32
Jack Carter as Crown taunts the residents of Catfish Row during the hurricane scene in *Porgy*	41
Mamoulian, Joan Peers, and Helen Morgan on the set of *Applause* (June 1929)	52
Mamoulian, Sylvia Sidney, and Gary Cooper filming a scene from *City Streets* (February 1931)	69
Fredric March as Mr. Hyde and Miriam Hopkins as Ivy in *Dr. Jekyll and Mr. Hyde* (1932)	74
Maurice Chevalier and Jeanette MacDonald sit still for the focus puller during filming of *Love Me Tonight* (April 1932)	86
Marlene Dietrich as Lily with her statue in *The Song of Songs* (1933)	98
Greta Garbo, John Gilbert, and Mamoulian on the set of *Queen Christina*	102

The famed Garbo close-up that ends *Queen Christina*	103
Garbo photographed by Mamoulian in Taos, New Mexico (January 1934)	106
Virginie Mamoulian played a mute prisoner in *We Live Again* (1934)	112
Mamoulian, Nigel Bruce, and Miriam Hopkins on the set of *Becky Sharp*	117
Luigi Pirandello, Mamoulian, and George Gershwin in front of the Alvin Theatre (September 1935)	121
Caricatures of Lawrence Langner, DuBose Heyward, and Theresa Helburn	130
Mamoulian with William Saroyan in Hollywood (1935)	135
Nino Martini and Ida Lupino in *The Gay Desperado*	136
Mamoulian with Elizabeth Patterson and Irene Dunne in *High, Wide and Handsome*	141
On the set of *Golden Boy*	152
Tyrone Power and Linda Darnell in the robing room of *Blood and Sand*	165
Gene Tierney, Mamoulian, and Henry Fonda aboard John Carradine's yacht on Catalina Island (December 7, 1941)	171
Celeste Holm performs "I Cain't Say No" in *Oklahoma!*	179
The finale of *Oklahoma!*	188
Russell Collins as the Starkeeper tends to his sky in *Carousel* (April 1945)	212
Mamoulian and Azadia Newman shortly after their wedding (February 1945)	215
Mamoulian and Mickey Rooney on the high school graduation set of *Summer Holiday* (1946)	224
Todd Duncan and Leslie Banks in *Lost in the Stars*	235
Herbert Coleman and Judson Rees in the "Big Mole" number in *Lost in the Stars*	243

Georges Guétary and Nanette Fabray in *Arms and the Girl* (1950)   247

Stunt rider Russell Forehead and Shane leap from Mark Antony's barge during Mamoulian's night shoot of *Cleopatra* (November 1960)   284

Lord Louis Mountbatten, left, and Prince Philip visit the set of *Cleopatra* (November 1960)   292

Elizabeth Taylor's costume test for *Cleopatra* (December 1960)   293

PEERLESS

Introduction: Enjoy the Journey

Don't categorize Rouben Mamoulian. Don't even try. He won't come into focus that way.

The work of Armenia's greatest contribution to American classic film is still accessible, although the director himself, a loner who constructed a sturdy veneer of imperturbable sangfroid, is mostly hidden, occasionally revealing himself in bitter recollections of being pushed aside in Hollywood.

Mamoulian's work can be seen as its own genre. Few directors today imitate the lush rhythmic style that characterized *Love Me Tonight* (1932) and the original production of George Gershwin's only opera, *Porgy and Bess* (1935). His career mixed sixteen films (four are musicals) and seventeen Broadway productions, six of them musicals, including the hugely successful original stagings of *Oklahoma!* (1943) and *Carousel* (1945)—not because he was able to fully chart his own course but because he was taking what he could get or somehow falling into opportunities.

His journey eventually included the Gershwin opera, Richard Rodgers and Oscar Hammerstein's first two collaborations, and a Paris-set musical film audiences still find enchanting; this was, as Mamoulian put it, "a concatenation of unexpected circumstances, accidents, luck, destiny, whatever you choose to call it." In film, comparisons with other directors, including Ernst Lubitsch and René Clair on the basis of some notion of European sophistication, fall short. The closest parallel to Mamoulian in recent decades was Mike Nichols, who thrived on Broadway and returned there to great acclaim when film work was lean. But Nichols had far more consistent success.

One of Mamoulian's champions, film historian Arthur Knight, included Mamoulian with Lubitsch, Clair, King Vidor, and Lewis Milestone for having, in the early sound era, "the ingenuity and vitality to circumvent the experts and lift the new medium out of the rut of dully photographed plays and vaudeville routines into which it had fallen. They had no rules to go on, no precedents to quote."

Mamoulian's reputation rests on his first six films. These were all made before the Motion Picture Production Code cracked down, beginning in 1934, on nudity (fleeting in *Dr. Jekyll and Mr. Hyde*, 1931, and the pulpy "art" drama *The Song of Songs*, 1933), violence (stylish in the crime drama *City Streets*, 1931), and sly references to sex and sexuality (double entendre in *Love Me Tonight*, lesbian references in the historical drama *Queen Christina*, 1934, priapic burlesque audiences in the backstage soap opera *Applause*, 1929). After Paramount failed to renew his option in 1933, Mamoulian had to hustle for film work. His artistic visions seldom meshed with commerce. Only six of his films: *City Streets, Dr. Jekyll and Mr. Hyde, Love Me Tonight, Queen Christina, The Mark of Zorro* (1940), and *Blood and Sand* (1941), earned a profit on their initial release.

One of his inspirations was rooted in classic star power: believing that audiences didn't flock to Greta Garbo to hear her but rather just to gaze upon her, he framed the lingering close-up that famously ends *Queen Christina*. But his musicals *High, Wide and Handsome* (1937) and *Summer Holiday* (1948) were such colossal bombs, the former sent him on an extended European vacation and the latter sent him fleeing back to Broadway for whatever he could find.

Andrew Sarris dismissed him in *Film Culture* in 1963, writing, "Mamoulian's tragedy is that of the innovator who runs out of innovations." Sarris was being cruel, but not inaccurate. From 1930 to 1961, an escalating combination of Mamoulian's self-indulgences and badly timed decisions made him increasingly less useful in Hollywood.

Stage work ended in 1950 after Kurt Weill's death ended a musical production of *Huckleberry Finn*, and film offers withered after *Summer Holiday*. Mamoulian had one offer to direct at the Metropolitan Opera, but he didn't seriously pursue other theater work, attempt to relaunch himself as an instructor or even (notwithstanding his Armenian lilt) a TV personality like Alfred Hitchcock. After building a home in Beverly Hills, he chose to hold out for film work.

He landed his first film in nine years when MGM producer Arthur Freed needed an inexpensive director for a Fred Astaire musical, *Silk Stockings* (1957). That gave him enough momentum to pursue his long-held dream of directing the film version of *Porgy and Bess*, but in 1958, Sam Goldwyn, in a dispute over payment and publicity, abruptly dismissed him. More than two years later, *Cleopatra*, filming outdoors in a brutal London winter with millions of dollars down the drain, was adrift. Mamoulian resigned—perhaps a failed gambit to seize control, in the misplaced belief that the film's star, Elizabeth Taylor, was a friend who would stand up for him.

His legacy in the ephemeral medium of theater is more enduring. *Porgy and Bess*, *Oklahoma!*, and *Carousel* remain in the repertoire. His first Broadway production, *Porgy*, could have been just a footnote in the history of "Negro plays" dotting the landscape after World War I. But Mamoulian, with an interplay of chiaroscuro, stylized movement and thundering spirituals, turned it into a long-running hit and the foundation of his career.

Mamoulian's love of spectacle, which he said he learned from European opera, helped push movie art along in the early 1930s. His signatures in theater involved tightly choreographed mass movement (also favored by Austrian director Max Reinhardt), ensembles moving in time to offstage rhythms, and dances and music integrated into the story line. Not everyone was a fan. Reviewing *Carousel* for the New York *Daily News* in 1945, critic John Chapman complained, "His handling of spectacle is, as always, easy and colorful, although I think I would have the company lift its arms at the end of a number only once, instead of twice, during the evening." For *Oklahoma!* Mamoulian stripped away long-accepted tropes of musical comedy to pioneer the integrated musical, in which songs and choreography advance the plot. Broadway musicals were never the same after that. Neither was Mamoulian, who became hypersensitive about matters of who received credit.

Mamoulian's film milestones included multiple-track sound (*Applause*) and the first full-length Technicolor picture (*Becky Sharp*, 1935). On stage, he came up with a rhythmic sequence of street noises in *Porgy* repeated in *Love Me Tonight* and *Porgy and Bess*. The damage to his film career was partly self-inflicted—the result of ignoring budgets for moments that did nothing for the studio's profit margin. Mamoulian had a knack for misjudging the studio moguls, who had comfortable artistic notions of their own and ran their operations as medieval fiefdoms. This meant he risked the fate of Erich von Stroheim and Terry Gilliam, artists with a healthy disrespect for studio finances.

His personality didn't help, either. Producer Arthur Hornblow Jr. recalled, "In working with him, I find him impossible to achieve compromise with. He cannot work in harness." Mamoulian considered this to be a point of pride. "Professionally, I can't help being honest," he told an interviewer. "It has nothing to do with compromise. I am incapable of doing it any other way." Joseph Youngerman, who was Mamoulian's assistant director at Paramount and liked him, had another take: "He was a very brilliant man, but he was so brilliant that sometimes he thought he was right and nobody else knew a damn thing."

Mamoulian's ego sometimes propounded a view of himself as a mythological hero. In 1959, after blaming his agent, Irving Lazar, for the debacle that got him fired from the film of *Porgy and Bess*, he recorded that choreographer Agnes de Mille told him Lazar was a phoetus—an ugly armored creature, formed from the castration blood of Uranus, who attacked the Olympian gods. Well!

This kind of self-glorification frustrated film historian Scott Eyman in his pioneering 1997 book *The Speed of Sound*. In Mamoulian's later years, "the director's claims for his innovations grew ever more insistent and slightly frantic, as if he was claiming to be the Zeus from whose brow all talkie innovations sprung," he observed—quite correctly. But praising the lively camera work and use of sound on *Applause*, Eyman concluded, "The desperate ego needs of an old man should not obscure the very real style and audacity with which he adapted to a new technology while in his creative prime."

Mamoulian carries additional important historical significance. His direction of four Broadway productions with African American casts makes him a key player in the painful and often humiliating saga of how they were portrayed on stage with all creative decisions made only by white authors, directors, and producers. This began in 1927 with *Porgy*, an anthropological entertainment about a South Carolina fishing community that became the basis of *Porgy and Bess* eight years later. Mamoulian became the presumed go-to director for "Negro plays," from *St. Louis Woman* (1946), a crudely plotted musical about a jockey; the still vibrant *Lost in the Stars* (1949), based on Alan Paton's novel about racial injustice in South Africa; and *Arms and the Girl* (1950), a sprightly musical comedy based on colonial history in which Pearl Bailey played—yes, that really happened—a comedic runaway slave who offers sardonic romantic advice. Quite a few more pitched his way never saw productions.

A point needs to be made here about the racist language in which Mamoulian's working environment was sometimes saturated. Ignoring hateful words rooted in white supremacy, whether in stereotyped "folk operas," musical comedies or plays attended by paying audiences in Broadway theaters, or in casual show-business badinage, is not an option. These words had power then. Their power and offensiveness have since grown. They appear briefly here without intent to offend, but rather to be truthful about Mamoulian's complicated life and career as well as American entertainment history. Their use is not an endorsement.

Mamoulian's attitudes on race, locked in the ambivalence of his age, were aesthetic, not political. A graduate student asked him whether being an Armenian, a nationality persecuted by the Russians, had sensitized him to the position of African Americans in American life and culture. His answer—and it was the only time he was ever asked—fell short of a definitive answer:

> Are you saying to me that for any sensitive person, whether an artist or not, which may be questionable, that you have to undergo it personally in order to empathize with the suffering of the people?
>
> ... I've always loved Negroes. I think they're wonderful people. I think they're immensely talented people. But I would certainly never do a play only because it's a Negro play out of any humanistic impulse, because that's not my profession. My profession is to do something worth doing on the stage.

Born in 1897 in Tiflis (now Tbilisi), Georgia, then part of czarist Russia, Mamoulian said he grew up "in an atmosphere spiritually dominated by three major traits: a high sense of honor, a cavalier disdain of money, and the feeling that the world is half-reality, half-dream." Mamoulian was born to wealthy parents who lost their fortune as a result of political forces beyond their control. He was twice a refugee, first in 1906, when his family briefly moved to Paris, and again after the Russian Revolution of 1917, when his father lost his bank job; he helped his parents eke out an existence before moving them to America in 1929. The murder of his sister Svetlana in London in 1926 drew Mamoulian and his parents closer, although they kept their grief hidden from the world. Success on stage and screen restored the privileged life he had known in childhood.

Mamoulian moved easily among painters and sculptors, incorporating artworks in unexpected places in some films. Grant Wood's dour *American Gothic* couple appear in *Summer Holiday*, and El Greco images are in *Blood and Sand*. When he married at forty-seven, it was to Azadia Newman, a portraitist from Washington, DC, who had worked in the background of Hollywood. An alcoholic, she contributed to his personal and professional isolation.

Successful artists could disappoint Mamoulian, though. At a King Vidor dinner in 1940, he was thrilled to meet Walt Disney, who had just released *Fantasia*, the first feature-length combination of classical music and animation. Eager to discuss theories of color with a filmmaker of the first rank, he instead encountered a midwestern businessman: "Monsters in *Rite of Spring* because they had them in story." Why switch from green and blue to sudden reds? "Because we got tired of green and blue." Disney ended the conversation with, "Don't know about music."

Raised in the Armenian Apostolic faith, Mamoulian was comfortable with Christian themes and imagery, and once said, "I think personally I'm religious, though not in the conventional sense of churchgoing." He gave the matter of art considerable private reflection. He wrote skeptical margin notes in his 1949 copy of the Production Code, the document that decreed which images and plots were forbidden in motion pictures. In one passage, the Code stated, "Art can be morally evil in its effects." Mamoulian added, "Don't believe in this. This is not art. Art always involves man's soul."

Because Mamoulian changed the ending of *Porgy* to have the character embark on a long improbable odyssey, it is possible to believe that he identified with the character—even though he said nothing about it. Had Ali Hakim, the *Oklahoma!* peddler, remained an Armenian, which was

Hammerstein's original idea, we would see Mamoulian there as well. He must have also identified with Franz, the lovelorn Hessian soldier of *Arms and the Girl*, who sang, in a touching lyric by Dorothy Fields, about what he liked best about America: "There is no fear in this country anywhere," because "the right to be wrong over here is freedom."

And oh, the journey he was on.

CHAPTER 1

Tiflis to New York

Rouben Mamoulian's rootlessness and the sweeping real-life traumas he witnessed between Muslims and Christians, Bolsheviks and Cossacks, fed into a temperament that was already geared to stylization and artifice—containing reality and distilling it, immersing audiences in aesthetic sensations rather than naturalistic details.

He arrived in New York City in late August 1923 with an unbending faith in his own abilities and an unexpected serenity: "Strangely enough, the minute I stepped on this soil and took my first walk . . . I felt completely and utterly at home."

In May, while considering an offer to direct plays in Paris, he had received an astonishing cable from inventor George Eastman for a new opera venture at the Eastman School of Music in Rochester, New York. Eastman laid out generous terms for a post as dramatic instructor: a one-year contract at $120 a week—the steadiest income Mamoulian had ever seen—and two months of paid vacation. An adventure in a new country, offered by a man of stunning wealth to someone with slim professional credentials, was dumbfounding good fortune.

Vladimir Rosing made the connection. He was a charismatic tenor who had earlier talked his way into a post as artistic director of the English-language opera company planned as the school's touring showcase. Rosing, seven years older than Mamoulian, may have met him in 1915 in St. Petersburg. He influenced every career stride Mamoulian made through 1926. Rosing had been the impresario of a small opera company in London that debuted in New York in 1921, and he was a superb networker long before that term existed. During a transatlantic crossing in March 1923, en route to a Canadian recital tour, Rosing pitched his vision to George W. Todd, an office supplies magnate who was a tireless donor to the University of Rochester. Todd was a close friend of Eastman, who headquartered Eastman Kodak in the city along the banks of Lake Ontario.

To Todd and Eastman, the concept of small size coupled with big impact must have seemed like the right mix of European culture and American practicality. If there was gallus-snapping Babbittry at the heart of these tycoons' ambitions, they at least aspired to dignified taste. Eastman capitalized the venture with $250,000, under the naive proviso that the company, with thirty singers, would become self-supporting in three years. He expected that profits from the movie audiences at his theater could underwrite the Rochester Philharmonic—a projection based on robust attendance and the assumption that orchestral music during the films would instill a love of music among patrons.

In November 1922, Mamoulian had directed just one play professionally—*The Beating at the Door*—in London, and it had failed. In spring 1918, after briefly studying law at the University of Moscow, he had won a scholarship to study acting at the Moscow Art Theatre, not with the legendary Konstantin Stanislavski, whose teaching methods and naturalism altered the craft, but with his protégé, Yevgeny Vakhtangov, an Armenian. Vakhtangov advocated "fantastic realism," a synthesis of Stanislavski's realistic presentation with Vsevolod Meyerhold's emphasis on conveying emotion with movement. Mamoulian stalled Eastman for a little while to get in some cramming: "I went to the British Museum and read everything I could about the history of opera." He arrived in Rochester for the opening of the fall term.

It was a right-angle turn in his adventure. Born October 8, 1897, he had grown up the adored only son of Zachary Mamoulian, a bank president in Tiflis, and Virginie Kalantarian, a sometimes-actress from a family of wealthy landowners. Mamoulian once appended, in his lecture notes, "Not the wrong side of the tracks." His parents, he noted proudly, "and all of my ancestors so far as one can tell have been pure Armenians." Virginie, born in what is now Stepanakert in 1876, was one of five surviving children born of twelve. Like her mother, she was betrothed at age fifteen. She married Zachary, born in 1866, at age sixteen; they honeymooned in Paris. She later became a co-founder of the Armenian section of the Zoubalov Theatre of

Tiflis. Her father, Georgy Kalantarov, who owned a twenty-four-room dacha on the Terek River in Moukhrania, was a cousin of Mikhail Loris-Melkov, a famous Armenian general and statesman. Zachary "had a rather imposing library, which he turned over to me when I was still a schoolboy," Mamoulian wrote. "I was a hungry reader."

Raising two children (daughter Svetlana was born in 1899) never dampened Virginie's stage aspirations. "She wasn't allowed to act when she was a girl, by her parents, and when she got married, by my father," Mamoulian recalled. "Once or twice a year, she would perform for charity, and that was her outlet." She appears silently and expressively in *We Live Again* (1934) as a prisoner with Anna Sten. In Los Angeles in 1932, she founded the Mamoulian Dramatic Group, which performed Armenian plays.

Virginie once wrote of Rouben: "I live for him. He is my God, my joy and meaning in life." Paul Ignatius, whose parents were friends of Virginie and Zachary in the 1930s, saw that firsthand: "She was dramatic, and loved to be an important figure. She was very possessive about her son." The center of the family was Zachary's mother, Katherine, known as Kato Babo—Grandma Kate. Rouben loved her as a spinner of fables:

> People gathered in large groups in the evening to sit at the feet of my grandmother and to listen to one of her marvelous stories. These were always most exciting and interesting, and everybody enjoyed them hugely. But there was more to it than that. Each of her stories seemed to have a marvelous built-in idea which stayed with you for always. It was a kind of spiritual vitamin that Grandma Kate evolved her story about. Later, you found yourself pondering the point she made, and, like a seed, it seemed to grow within you and give you help, courage and a lift when you most needed it.

His own name, he wryly noted, had not been correctly pronounced—Rou-BEN Ma-mou-li-AN—since he was quite small. "Before I was six, I spoke three languages with equal fluency through necessity and circumstance. At home we spoke Russian, at one grandmother's Armenian, at the other grandmother's, Georgian." In his first year of school in Tiflis, he attended a Russian school, where his last name was Russianized to Ma-MOU-loff.

A painting of Mamoulian's grandmother Kato Bobo, a spinner of tales. Photograph courtesy of Zaghik Gourjian.

Mamoulian always elided the reason his family left Tiflis for Paris. His mother's account gave the year as 1906. They were escaping the Armenian-Tatar massacres, an outgrowth of the Russian Revolution of 1905. The guerrilla conflict between Armenian Christians and Muslim Azerbaijanis (Tatars) raged into 1907. Armed mobs on horseback brought terror in the night— a form of ethnic cleansing. Russian authorities did little to protect Armenian communities. Mamoulian never conceded that he'd been a refugee, possibly because an en masse flight from violence had not been his situation. Zachary and Virginie had the means to decamp to Paris, so they did. Virginie's father supported them, and Zachary took law classes there.

"We stayed [in Paris] for over three years," Mamoulian wrote. "The beginning of my school days was not much fun, as I knew not a word of French. However, new languages come so easily to a child that before long, French became *my* language. I could speak it as well as Russian and the others." The Lycée Montaigne, however, decided that his first name should be Robert.

The death of Virginie's father in 1909 ended the support, forcing the family to return to Tiflis. "For a while, all my relatives called me 'the little Frenchman' and teased me because it seems that my Russian, Armenian and Georgian had acquired an amusing French accent." The accent carried into adulthood. Guy Ramsey, writing in a British newspaper in 1937, noted, "if you listen to the slightly harsh voice issuing from the sallow lips and not to what he says, you will catch odd intonations, curious pronunciations that recall his many native tongues. He will say 'sewcessful' with the delicate French U; or, occasionally, "woik" with the authentic American diphthong."

Mamoulian wrote a children's story, "A Caucasian Tale," published in a Moscow magazine, *Young Russia*, in 1911. The fairy tale, probably first related by Kato Bobo, was about a peasant couple and a movable "star of hope" that leaps from animals to humans. Rouben took up the violin, and played well enough to perform for a visit to Tiflis by Czar Nicholas II. Mamoulian also acted in school plays, including Nikolai Gogol's *The Inspector General*.

Zachary believed that the performing arts were a perilous way for his son to make a living, so in 1915, Rouben enrolled at the University of Moscow to study criminal law in a four-year program. He took part in student plays there and briefly contributed reviews to a Moscow newspaper under

Mamoulian family portrait, 1915. Virginie, Svetlana, Zachary, Rouben. Photograph courtesy of Library of Congress.

a pen name. Political upheaval changed his plans. Moscow was the epicenter of Vladimir Lenin's Bolshevik Revolution that toppled the czar in November 1917. With the violence still months away, Mamoulian recalled the city as

> without blood and thunder. It came like a warmhearted holiday—the Russian Easter. The streets of Moscow were filled with crowds. People were walking not only on sidewalks but also in large masses right in the middle of streets. Strangers were shaking hands, kissing each other . . .
>
> For many days there were no police in town—the czarist police, having always proved themselves to be a notoriously corrupt and monarchist outfit, were now hiding, afraid that the freed populace might choose to square some of their accounts with them. Young students—always among the leaders of all liberal and revolutionary moments—were hurriedly organized into a kind of home militia . . .

> I remember the amusing sight: a young student with an enormous sword . . . was trying to pacify two citizens who had imbibed a little too much of the spirit of freedom as well as just plain spirit. Suddenly, they turned on him, forgetting their own quarrel. The student backed away in a panic and started yelling, "Help! Police! Police!"

For nearly a week, Muscovites experimented with their freedom of speech under the giant bronze statue of poet Alexander Pushkin in the center of Strastnaya Square. It was improvisational theater, and Mamoulian found he couldn't resist standing in line to try out his oratory before the throng. He learned about audiences, comparing one to

> a sea wave. When they like what you are saying, you can physically feel vibrations emanating from those thousands of people, coming toward you like a huge wave that lifts you up, higher and higher, and supports you there. When you somehow failed to interest them, that wave begins to recede as swiftly as it came, and you get the most awful sensation in the pit of your stomach. You feel yourself physically falling down.

Criminal law was not going to lead to a secure occupation when the government had ceased to exist and competing factions descended into violence. His time with Vakhtangov and the Moscow Art Theater must have seemed a refuge. Vakhtangov mounted a production of Maurice Maeterlinck's *The Miracle of St. Anthony*—a 1903 morality tale just right for the political climate of September 1918, when the communists decided it was an antibourgeois satire. It was, Mamoulian recalled, the first time he was aware of a director's power to shape images, or as he put it, "That was my first kind of a taste in the direction."

The brief calm turned to anarchy. Mamoulian's family had to stay on the move to avoid sectarian conflicts that erupted in the turmoil between competing Communist Party ideologies. In Virginie's account, they fled Tiflis when the Mensheviks arrived, heading north to a Bolshevik-controlled region in the north Caucasus. From there, they went to Kislovodsk to Pyatigorsk, and from there to Stavropol, where Svetlana came down with typhus. Mamoulian and Suren Khachaturian (an elder brother of future composer Aram), despite the turmoil, were planning their own studio theater in Tiflis.

He and Khachaturian, along with Virginie and Svetlana, were staying in the mineral springs resort of Essentuki. Zachary, a former officer in the czar's army, was keeping a low profile. In October 1918,

> Overnight, life became a nightmare. Bolsheviks and the troops of Cossacks under [Ataman Andrei] Shkuro [one of the most brutal White Army commanders] were at each other's throats. The city changed hands sometimes from day to day, and each time the conquerors, whichever side it happened to be, executed hundreds of their enemies. No quarter was given by either camp.
>
> Between them, the lot of the civilians was pathetic. If you wore a white collar and a necktie, your fate was sealed when Bolsheviks came in. If you didn't, you did when Cossacks took possession. By the time people knew better the danger of white collars—and everybody discarded them—the hands became fatal. If they were hardworking hands with calluses . . . you were shot by the Cossacks; if they were free of them, you were "bourgeois" and as such shot by the Bolsheviks. It came to a point where people stayed in their homes or hotels all the time.
>
> It was a thoroughly familiar sight to see a sailor of the Black Sea fleet [they had scuttled their ships and invaded the land] to take part in the free-for-all civil war, wearing a czarist general's overcoat thrown over his shoulder—smart gray with scarlet lining and golden epaulets—carrying two, sometimes three revolvers on his belt, with a sword hanging by his side, and several hand grenades pinned to his shirt like ornaments on a Christmas tree.

Bored by their isolation, Mamoulian and Khachaturian dared occasional walks. "The streets were completely deserted then. No civilian would venture out—shrapnel and stray bullets made open air dangerous." On one of these strolls, "a stray bullet whistled by and planted itself in a whitewashed wall just as we walked past, missing my head by hardly half an inch. We laughed at it—we thought it was funny."

In the midst of this, Mamoulian embarked on a romance with a family friend, Vardanoush "Vava" Sarian, who was two years older. Born in Turkey and educated in Russia, she was decades away from her own painting career and modeling for Henri Matisse. The pairing endured for a year, preserved in a tiny notebook they used to exchange messages. Mamoulian sometimes glowed with rapture: "I will be kissing the pillow that held your head, and

I will imagine you by my side." Most times, though, the relationship seemed to be stormy: "Why am I in love? My whole soul is bleeding." In fits and starts, the romance endured until Mamoulian left for London in 1920.

The family returned to Tiflis after the area was occupied by British troops sent to quell the conflicts. The studio theater opened by Mamoulian and Khachaturian in 1918 had about twenty members. His prospects for making a living with it were vanishing along with private wealth and his father's bank.

Svetlana left the household first. In August 1919, she married a Scotsman, Alexander McQuaker, a second lieutenant in the Royal Field Artillery that was occupying Tiflis. He was ten years older, and he quickly moved her to London. Rouben's account suggests that his father sent him to live with Svetlana and McQuaker as a way of pushing him out of the household before the Red Army invaded Tiflis in February 1921. In November 1920, before his voyage to England, his father gave him the equivalent of US$60, which was expected to last until he found work there.

After sailing to France, Mamoulian took a train to Calais and then a boat across the English Channel, where he arrived at Southampton on January 1, 1921, greeted by a "solid white wall of fog." His passport gave his occupation as "Student, Economics," and on that day, his name received its final pronunciation when a British passport official decided it was ROU-ben Ma-MOU-lian. He moved in briefly with his sister in Upper Tooting, in the south end of London. He was on his own just two months later when the McQuakers moved to Edinburgh after Alexander got a job as a bookbinder.

Mamoulian's first job was as an assistant to a wedding photographer who also took photos of handsomely attired couples on Sunday strolls in London's parks. His lack of job skills outside the theater left him scarce of food. "There is, I believe, quite a theory of long standing that hunger and want are good for one—they mold one's character, and they are especially beneficial to creative artists—look at the many masterpieces those starving geniuses have created. What drivel! Hunger and poverty are degrading and ignominious. Those artists created great beauty in spite of, not because of, their misery."

Opportunity appeared in the form of Grigori Makaroff, a former bass with the St. Petersburg Royal Opera. One evening in February 1922, Mamoulian looked up from his table at an Armenian restaurant to see Makaroff,

Mamoulian in Kew Gardens, London, 1922. Photograph courtesy of Library of Congress.

with whom he had a nodding acquaintance, huffing in his direction. He noticed that the singer sported a diamond stickpin in his cravat. The pin, Mamoulian wrote, often spent time with a pawnbroker depending on Makaroff's fortunes. On this evening, "he vaguely implied that somewhere in the background a rich and beautiful woman was hiding under a romantic veil of incognito."

Makaroff wanted to form a Russian theatrical troupe in the style of the *La Chauve-Souris*, a popular touring revue of the early 1900s that was making a comeback in the 1920s—"glorified variety," as Mamoulian described it. The company planned a tour in the English provinces.

> He said, "You know, I'm in a terrible dilemma. I have this wonderful bunch of people and set designers. I have everything, I don't have a director. I can't find a director." And he said, "Do you know anybody?" I was twenty-two then. I said, "Oh, yes, I know a very excellent director." And he said, "Who?" And I said, "Me." Well, you know, you can't afford the luxury of being humble, because when you're starting out, if you don't think much of yourself, who the hell else will?
>
> Well, anyway, after a long discussion, I said, "Look, what do you have to lose? Try me. Try me for a week or two, you don't have anyone, don't pay me anything, in the meantime look for a director." So he agreed to that: "Rouben, you are right; this must be fate! What a lucky man Makaroff is! Everything comes his way!"

The agreed-upon salary was thirty shillings a week. Makaroff ordered two brandies and raised his glass: "A toast! To Makaroff's luck!"

The production became a show for the King's College Russian Society. Makaroff sang, and Mamoulian wrote and directed a sketch, "The Unexpected Inspector," a burlesque of *The Inspector General*. Rehearsals were held at the abandoned Russian embassy where Makaroff had secured a ballroom. There were thirty members in the troupe, all of whom, Mamoulian wrote, negotiated for higher salaries until the top pay Makaroff was promising was a substantial £15 a week. He actually paid no more than ten shillings a week to anyone, including Mamoulian. Work was so scarce, no one was complaining. "By the time the show opened, Makaroff's debt to the company was so enormous it would have staggered a minor Balkan state, but not the old maestro—he wore the debt like a smile. It made him feel rich."

The rehearsals attracted visitors from London's Russian colony, including a special night with Czar Nicholas's sister, Grand Duchess Xenia Alexandrovna. That fall, "I remember for three consecutive nights, there were two very distinguished gentlemen sitting in the corner of the room watching the proceedings." With Rosing were producer Alexander Nethersole and American playwright Seymour Obermer, "a tall, slim, wiry man with steel gray hair and a sharp intelligent face." Because of rife anti-Semitism, Obermer was known professionally as Austin Page. Obermer's last play, produced in 1918, was a spy thriller, *By Pigeon Post*. He'd written a lavish new work, *The Beating at the Door*, about an aristocratic family surviving the travails of the Russian Revolution. Obermer thought he had a need for a Russian to co-direct.

Mamoulian took the script to his room in Soho, an address "with the glorious name of Diadem Court." (Years later, he impishly used this address for Ivy the prostitute in *Dr. Jekyll and Mr. Hyde*.) He spent three weeks discussing the play with Obermer, defining his own ideas. This led him into immediate conflict with the British director (whom Mamoulian never named), "a bald, conservative man of about fifty, casually but definitely conscious of his position in the theatre."

The director suggested that he would take the first act, Mamoulian the second act, and they would see how the play developed that way. After three days of rehearsals, Mamoulian realized the arrangement wouldn't work, so he conferred again with Obermer. "So you know, I started walking the room doing the play scene for scene . . . and I went on for two hours and [he] said, 'You know, I like it, but you realize there is nothing we can do about it, because the cast will never accept you as the director." Mamoulian returned his contract. But four days later, Obermer told him the other director had been paid off. Mamoulian was about to turn twenty-five, an age considered so young and likely to repel patrons that the publicity stated he was "about thirty," and was helming a high-profile West End production.

He had to win over the veteran actors. On his third day, Mamoulian confronted actor Franklin Dyall, who was playing the head of the Rosanova family.

So I started rehearsing him and he started to mumble. And I said "Mr. Dyall, please speak up." And he said, "Old chap, don't worry about it." He said, "You know, I've been in some performances before, and when we open I will try and do my best." And everybody went ho, ho, ho.

So now I got angry and said "Look, Mr. Dyall, you know I'm supposed to direct this play and getting paid for it. I'm going to direct and I'm going to direct my way, and my way you are going to act, so I will know what you are going to do. So do it." And he flushed red and got very angry, which is a good thing, probably because he was so angry he did the scene in a very lousy way, all wrong. He went through the whole scene and said, "Well?" and I said, "Well, it's all wrong."

Then there was this appalling silence. So he came up to me and I said, "Look," and I talked to him for 15 minutes about this scene. . . . He listened and then he said, "Mr. Mamoulian" for the first time—it was always "old chap"—"Mr. Mamoulian, let me try," and he worked, and I worked on him for two hours and he worked and he slaved and that broke the camel's back.

Mamoulian knew he was finally in charge after a day when he dropped his pipe and it broke in two. "And the next morning, four members of the cast brought me a new pipe as a present. So I knew I had them. From then on, it was very fine.

The warmer relationship with the performers didn't translate into success for *The Beating at the Door*, which critics labeled a French Revolution play—that is, it followed the formula of pampered aristocrats seized by revolutionaries and forced into prison and hard labor. After the audience enjoys seeing the wealthy get knocked around, it becomes clear that the revolutionaries are brutal murderers, and the aristocrats are rescued. The play opens on November 7, 1917, the first day of the revolution, and as it ends, the Rosanova family is making their way to England.

With a better understanding of English, Mamoulian might have fixed some third-act howlers before the opening on November 6, 1922. Wrote *The Observer*: "The first-night audience was unusually hilarious during the closing scene, when the aristocrats escape from the prison on their way to the frontier, and when one of them mentions that they are bound for England, 'where there is real freedom,' a shout of delighted laughter went up from the house." Even worse was the character of Prince Arnielief's hyperbolic final speech, after the jailer is thrown into a cell and begins to thump on the door: "The beating on the door, Russia crying out—poor ignorant devil—doing what he's told, not knowing why—caged—caged! There he beats, beats, beats, begging for liberty and light—we must work for him out there!" At this, the critic of the *Sunday Express* wrote, the audience roared. Obermer cut those lines after the first night, but the play limped along for just two more weeks, never to be staged again.

It was Mamoulian's last attempt at the realism of Stanislavski. "It was a totally realistic production. I even had them chop wood on the stage; real wood, real ax and all that. And then I saw it. And that's why I've always said you have to be an audience member to be a director. Well, I saw the final result, and I didn't like it. It just meant nothing to me. I suddenly realized that I had no penchant for the naturalistic manner of directing."

With the failure of *The Beating at the Door*, and hearing nothing more from Rosing on his travels, Mamoulian sought work in Paris. In July 1923, his search brought him to Jacques Hébertot, the flamboyant actor-director who headed the Théâtre des Champs-Élysées. Hébertot asked him to direct two or three plays during the season that would open that fall. Mamoulian was to work alongside Louis Jouvet (later the star of dozens of French films) and Theodore Komisarjevsky, who had directed operas for Rosing in London in 1921. But the day after that offer was extended, he received the cable from Eastman. So Rosing had been looking out for him after all—evidently making assurances that Mamoulian's English was competent and his knowledge of opera quite sufficient. Mamoulian extracted a promise from Hébertot that he could return to France in two months if the Eastman venture proved unsatisfactory.

The most prominent resident of Rochester dominated local arts and education with the noblesse oblige of Renaissance princes. George Eastman revolutionized photography in 1887 with the invention of the first practical roll film. The resulting explosion of snapshots the world over—Kodak sold both film and inexpensive cameras—produced untaxed Gilded Age wealth in many millions of dollars, and Eastman's near-monopoly on motion picture film in the early years of the twentieth century made him richer still. The unmarried inventor-philanthropist funded schools of medicine and dentistry at the University of Rochester and donated millions to the Rochester Institute of Technology and the second campus of the Massachusetts

Institute of Technology. He was a generous patron of the Rochester Philharmonic Orchestra.

In 1918, his munificence took another turn: $13 million for the Eastman School of Music, a conservatory for classical singers and musicians. Opening in 1921, it still graces the city with the Eastman Theatre—originally showing movies as well as hosting the Rochester Philharmonic. All this came from someone with little formal education and admittedly no knowledge of music other than "it helped him think." The grand visions originated with George W. Todd.

The European artists who dominated classical music at the time didn't have to understand Eastman's business methods—only that a wealthy patron was tossing money at their feet. A stampede ensued. From England, Eugene Goossens and Russian-born Albert Coates arrived as joint conductors of the Rochester Philharmonic, and Guy Fraser Harrison conducted the Eastman Theatre orchestra that accompanied silent films. From France, Abel Decaux taught organ. The Russian contingent, in addition to Rosing, included Nicolas Slonimsky, a composer hired as an accompanist. Eastman made personal use of the school. He had a chamber music quartet play for him on Sunday and Thursday afternoons, often with about a hundred people in attendance. Harold Gleason, a member of the music faculty, played Eastman's home pipe organ daily from six to eight a.m. over breakfast. Mamoulian eventually was invited to the twice-weekly concerts: "It was really a command performance—one had to be there."

Continental mannerisms intrigued and amused the locals, including the future novelist Paul Horgan, a nineteen-year-old student from New Mexico who signed up as a set designer. Mamoulian, he wrote, "had a distinctly European look, underlined by the beautiful London suits he wore. He was tall, slender, black-haired. What otherwise might have seemed a bearing of cold, remote superiority was saved and animated by the brilliance of his dark eyes, and by the sympathetic warmth of his smile, when he gave it." Wisconsin-born composer Otto Luening also noticed: "Like most nearsighted people, he had a glance that seemed both sexy and hypnotic."

Horgan recalled Mamoulian with spats, pince-nez spectacles, and a gold-topped walking stick. "Baritones and tenors from Altoona, Oberlin, Sacramento, Dallas began to wear spats, too, as if under sanction from the great artistic capitals of the old world. In the lapel of his lounge coat he habitually

Vladimir Rosing, left, and Mamoulian at the opening of the fall term of the Eastman School of Music, September 1923. Photograph courtesy of Library of Congress.

wore two or three dried and faded violets, a highly personal and individual touch, that (for all we knew and in much we said) hinted at a love affair left behind in Europe, a ballerina, a leading actress, a marchioness." (Or possibly just Vava).

Years later, a Rochester columnist put the description less sentimentally: "He was a dandified Armenian with a quick wit, a continental air and a desire to wear a bracelet on his left ankle" (he probably meant the slave bracelet Mamoulian wore on his left wrist into the 1930s). "Some people thought he had talent," the columnist sniffed. "Some thought he was a nut." Mamoulian lived in rented rooms on the second floor of an East Avenue mansion.

Rosing was not a promising impresario. This "vagrant" in rehearsals, Luening wrote, "muttered and mumbled about concentration and art and sometimes expounded on his long experience with the Moscow Art Theatre. But at heart he was a Gypsy. He arrived late and left late and wore people out." Luening recalled him bursting into an opera class, munching plums and tossing the pits carelessly across the floor, to teach an acting exercise from Stanislavski: "Haff discover new approach to opera . . . Iss interesting for opera make rhythmic movement from body to horchestra." He had the students spread out on their backs across the floor. Rosing's instructions: "Think of pink circle inside a skull, turning left to right. Now green circle other side, turning right to left. When I say hopp, change circles. Hopp, hop. Let's sing: *Ma, ma, man, man, ma, ma, ma, ma*; *mo, mo, mo, mo, mo, mo, mo*." The sound, Luening wrote, "was magnificent." Pleased, Rosing announced, "Method from Moscow Art Theatre!"

Mamoulian's style, as described by Horgan, was disciplined. Gathering his class around the walls of the rehearsal room and standing in the center, Mamoulian announced, "I will show you a scene, a commonplace from everyday life," then pantomimed both a barber shaving a customer and the customer's reaction. As he proceeded, "We knew every bulge of the recumbent figure and every protuberance of the heavy chair from the way the barber stepped—danced—around them, avoiding clumsy touches and contacts unwelcome to the customer. We knew the self-satisfaction, the self-respect and the social character of the barber himself . . . The astonishing performance took about fifteen minutes. It never faltered. There was not a false note, or a half-considered movement, or an incomplete gesture."

Mamoulian spent many evenings at the Corner Club, a refined version of a speakeasy set up by the Rochester arts crowd. Visiting concert artists were hosted there, and one evening in November 1923, it was pianist Josef Hofmann. Hofmann brought along a friend. "In walked . . . the great pianist, with a young guy, dark-haired fellow in a dark suit," Mamoulian recalled. It was George Gershwin. "And he was very much on the defensive. Rather insecure." Hofmann entertained his hosts with a classical selection, "and then he turned around to George and said, 'Why don't you play something?' Gershwin replied, 'I'll play something I'm working on now. It's not finished. But it's a little different from what I've been doing.' And he played parts of the 'Rhapsody in Blue'. And of course we all went insane—I thought it was terrific, you know." Gershwin premiered the work the following February at Aeolian Hall in New York, conducted by Paul Whiteman.

At the same time, Mamoulian was conducting a furtive romance with Goossens's wife Dorothy, known as Boonie. She and her husband divorced in 1928. Rochester was too small for faculty affairs to stay discreet, so Mamoulian and others took a train to Albany and from there, a boat down the Hudson River to New York City. The Albany night boat became notorious as a floating motel. "Just a note to tell you, dearest, that all through the day and night, in my dreams, too, you are with me," Boonie wrote on November 16. But a week later, the affair had wound down. "It helps me a lot when it is just tearing me to little bits leaving you," she wrote on November 23. "Oh, Roubenchik, you cannot know how hateful this is to me, my sweetheart. I just love you dearly—don't forget me. I read your letter every moment I can on the boat. Kiss me, darling."

Rochester's isolation forced the Eastman faculty into camaraderie. Slonimsky, who arrived there speaking no English, had a particular dependence on Mamoulian. He, Mamoulian, and Horgan founded "the Society of Unrecognized Geniuses," and formed "a cult of adoration for Lucile (Bigelow)," the principal harpist of the Rochester Philharmonic, with blond hair and "cerulean blue eyes," whom they dubbed "the Venus de Milo with arms." Horgan and Mamoulian, Slonimsky recalled, "had a great sense of histrionics. They would put on monocles, click their heels and spout torrents of ersatz German in public places."

Live entertainment preceding motion pictures was standard fare in the 1920s. In cities with Rochester's population of about 230,000, the acts typically consisted of a vaudeville comic supported by a singer or animal act. Eastman Theatre audiences instead got the grand opera repertoire directed by Mamoulian. A full performance of the Rochester American Opera Company wasn't staged until November 1924, with selections from Leoncavallo's *Pagliacci*, Gounod's *Faust*, Bizet's *Carmen*, and Mussorgsky's *Boris Godunov*; the first fully staged opera, *Carmen*, appeared in March 1925. Beginning in January 1924, Mamoulian staged excerpts from *Carmen*, Rossini's *The Barber of Seville*, a performance of "The Volga Boatmen's Song" and scenes from Wagner's *Tannhäuser*, and Gounod's *Romeo and Juliet*.

Mamoulian acknowledged that directing opera changed his directing style permanently. "I realized that it was utterly impossible and artistically absurd to do an opera realistically. You had to find a different idiom for it." That idiom was rhythm. "I found that rhythm was or should be everything. If you want action to really fit an opera, which doesn't happen in standard productions, it has to be rhythmic."

Rosing's erratic business acumen and his frequent absences for recital tours endangered the experiment. Slonimsky wrote that he "failed miserably as administrator of the American Opera Company . . . and ran through Eastman's money long before he could stage an opera that would possibly have brought in some return for the investment." Rosing and Mamoulian eventually had a falling out. In 1937, when Rosing's recital career had ended and a planned New Orleans opera venture fell through, he wrote to Mamoulian in Hollywood, begging for work: "Tell the film 'dictators' you have found a second Lon Chaney—I won't fail you." Although he may have laid it on a bit thick, he acknowledged the rift: "When I look back, I realize what a conceited guy I must have been—full of ideas and no knowledge—and I can now imagine how often I must have irritated you! . . . The first year there was the happiest year of my life, and I have never ceased to regret that my own stupid attitude over unimportant things estranged our relationship."

Survival was on Mamoulian's mind in spring 1925, when he set up an approximation of the Russian model of a studio theater where he would teach acting. Because Eastman didn't like theater, Mamoulian had to call it something else, and so was born the Eastman School of Dance and Dramatic Action. Mamoulian taught "dramatic action," and for dance instruction, he promptly attracted Martha Graham, lately of the Denishawn

Dancers, and Ester Gustafson as two of the principal teachers. The school opened in September with an enrollment of three hundred.

Mamoulian and Graham moved from opera repertoire to something with more flash: elaborate motion picture prologues of the type only seen in the giant movie palaces of New York and Los Angeles. When possible, these were tailored to the movie or musical performance that followed—for instance, "The Specter in Red," in which a soprano sang the Jewel Song from Gounod's *Faust*, preceded Lon Chaney in *The Phantom of the Opera*. Another, "A Pompeian Afternoon," with dances by Graham, preceded Wagner's *Rienzi* performed by the Eastman Theatre Orchestra. In November, Mamoulian was named director of all "deluxe programs" at the Eastman Theatre, a title that presumably gave him less outside interference.

In January 1926, a production of Maurice Maeterlinck's *Sister Beatrice*, with a new translation by Horgan in vernacular English and music by Luening became "really the occasion where I found my artistic self." Mamoulian promoted the play as a "new form of theatrical art." With a score "in the style of the 14th century, kind of a Gregorian chant effect," he noted, "it was like seeing dancers act or actors dance."

Sister Beatrice, written in 1900, was Maeterlinck's version of a medieval legend about a nun who runs away from her convent for the love of a prince. The romance is short-lived, and she returns to her convent twenty-five years later, after having turned to prostitution, wrecked in body and soul, to find that the statue of the Virgin Mary in the convent garden had come to life and fulfilled all of her duties during the ensuing years. The legend is durable Christian kitsch, from the Middle Ages in Belgium all the way to a Warner Bros. film, *The Miracle* (1959), starring Carroll Baker and Roger Moore. Playing Mary was Martha Atwell, later a famed director of radio dramas, whom Mamoulian often used as a teacher. This was the first time Mamoulian filmed actors, with the intent of critiquing their performances. Eastman Kodak was generous with its technology, and later Mamoulian made a short film of Graham's dance "The Flute of Krishna" using experimental color film.

Sister Beatrice was Mamoulian's bid for attention from the Theatre Guild—specifically, Lawrence Langner, one of its founders. Langner, a patent lawyer, met Mamoulian that year when the Guild sponsored performances by the opera company in New York City. When he visited clients in Rochester, he sometimes looked in on the Eastman School. Rosing made the introduction. Mamoulian's curtain speech primed the audience for a new theatrical form, although *Sister Beatrice* did not have the impact on critics he had hoped for. Luening recalled, "The final organist's score had very precise word cues and tempo marks that coordinated the music with the stage actions. Mamoulian molded the whole production with a psychic force that seemed to sculpt the performances."

The production was followed by personal tragedy two months later. Svetlana's marriage had taken a downward turn after the birth of her daughter Alexa in November 1922. In the fall of 1925, she wrote her father that she was miserable. Zachary took her and Alexa out of their furnished flat in Edinburgh, and shortly after that took them to London, allegedly telling Alexander's father in his halting English, "My daughter slave to your son. She do fire, wash dish, and I take her away." "Don't try to untie the knot, but just cut it," Rouben wrote his father. "They are completely different people in personalities and Alex is one of the most disgraceful persons I've met in my life, and he's completely hopeless."

On March 11, 1926, after writing her nearly every day and pleading for her return, Alexander got Svetlana to agree to meet him in London to discuss custody of Alexa. She refused to go back to him. Late that afternoon, he hailed a taxi at Hyde Park Corner and asked the driver to take them both to the Strand Palace Hotel. There was no conversation. The driver heard Svetlana shriek, then three pistol shots; Alexander shot her twice before putting the gun to his own head. A week later, a coroner's jury ruled, "Murder and suicide whilst of unsound mind."

The shock drove Mamoulian to a Buffalo hotel to deal with his emotions privately. "I can only imagine what you and Mother are feeling, but, my dears, do not lose courage," he wrote his father. "Apparently you cannot avoid destiny. After all, there's not much of good in this life." Later he lectured his mother: "If you give in to your grief, you will ruin me. Who is happier now—we or Svetlana? What is good in this world? What is happy and bright in this life? So little. Think of Svetlana with joy. She's happy, she's free there."

Newspaper accounts of the coroner's inquest disclose a grimmer portrait of the Mamoulian family's situation than either Virginie or Rouben would later acknowledge. It revealed that when Alexander first arrived in London with his new bride, "all she possessed was what she had on her body." The coroner, demonstrating a patronizing attitude toward immigrants, concluded that since Svetlana had married so young, she "probably didn't know her mind sufficiently well," and should have been happy to be living in the midst of England's freedom and tolerance toward foreigners.

After Svetlana and Alexander were buried in London, Alexa was taken in by Alexander's sister Margaret and husband, Frederick Arnold; Rouben provided financial support. Zachary and Virginie resettled in Paris until their son, with his newly acquired US citizenship in 1929, was able to sponsor their arrival in New York. Mamoulian participated in a family conspiracy of kindness. Alexa was told that her parents had both died in a taxi crash, and that's what she believed all her life, until her death in 2008. Perhaps with the pain of the murder renewed, Mamoulian, in *City Streets* (1931), cut a scene of Blackie (Stanley Fields), the bodyguard of mob leader Big Fellow Maskal (Paul Lukas) attempting to scrub blood off the back of a car seat.

However else his sister's death affected him, Mamoulian, determined to get his parents to America, quickly sought a new direction for his career. He started visiting commercial producers, who offered him no encouragement. Jed Harris and Winthrop Ames had no use for him, and George Abbott advised him to shorten his last name to Marmon. He visited Famous Players-Lasky at its Long Island studios; he had some notion he could be considered as an assistant to director Cecil B. DeMille. "About the middle of 1926 . . . I found myself, as it were, at the end of the street. There seemed to be nothing further I could do there," Mamoulian recalled. Atwell remembered him "walking up and down that two-by-four office . . . saying, 'Martha, I'm twenty-eight and I've accomplished nothing!'"

Eastman finally cut the opera venture loose, although it survived as a touring company with Rosing for three years until the Great Depression demolished its prospects. Even though Mamoulian's acting school had broken even, there was no interest in continuing it, and the dance instruction was absorbed into the Eastman School. Mamoulian resigned in June after appealing to Langner, who tossed him a lifeline: teaching at the Guild's new acting school in Scarsdale. It was a pay cut at $75 a week. Langner included a vague promise that Mamoulian's work at the school might lead to full-time directing.

Hugh Rennie, Arline Kanzanjian (later Arlene Francis), and Mamoulian at the Theatre Guild acting school in Scarsdale, New York, spring 1927. Photograph courtesy of Library of Congress.

In 1926, the school was in its second and ultimately final year. Its goal was to provide the Guild with a continuous crop of performers for its repertory company, although it never worked out that way. The first year's class had Sylvia Sidney, who quickly went into motion pictures. Mamoulian's class included Hugh Rennie, whom he would cast as a policeman in *Porgy* in 1927, and a nineteen-year-old Armenian American girl from Manhattan, Arline Kazanjian, who found later success on Broadway, radio, and TV when she changed her name to Arlene Francis. Mamoulian expected the student productions to be his own showcase as much as the students', but the Theatre Guild board ignored his production of Leonid Andreyev's *He Who Gets Slapped*.

Mamoulian felt it was time to call them to account at a Guild dinner at the Plaza Hotel in March 1927: "You've got me here under false pretenses. The whole idea was, I told you the only reason I would join this school would be as a step for directing for the Guild." He remembered, "They were kind of ashamed and they said, 'Well, the difficulty is, we're doing mostly American plays. It's not really for you. Now if we had a Russian play, or a French play, we'd give it to you.' So they finally said, 'Why don't you take a play and we'll give you special matinees at the Garrick Theatre.'

"So I took [George M. Cohan's comedy] *Seven Keys to Baldpate*, which God knows is American. But I stylized it thoroughly." It went on the first week of May. At the first matinee, the Guild board told him they could only stay for ten minutes, because of a meeting coming up. "Well, they walked in and of course, they stayed through the whole performance." Mamoulian finished up his run at the acting school that summer with stagings of Gilda Varesi's *Enter Madame* and Booth Tarkington's *Clarence*.

The Guild's eventual offer came as a surprise. *Porgy*, adapted from DuBose Heyward's best-selling novella of 1925, was about African Americans in a fishing ghetto in Charleston, South Carolina. "We were very enthusiastic about it, but no one was keen to direct it, mostly on account of lack of knowledge of dealing with colored actors," Langner wrote.

"It's very interesting," Mamoulian wrote his parents. "It's about the life of American Negroes."

CHAPTER 2

Catfish Row

It is a historical quirk that a single "Negro play" of the 1920s, later enhanced by George Gershwin's score in 1935, did not become a museum piece but is instead performed and widely enjoyed nearly a century after it debuted on Broadway. Complaints about racist stereotypes, particularly the craps game that opens the production, have receded. As an opera with an insular setting, no one still thinks *Porgy and Bess* shows what African Americans in South Carolina are "really like."

DuBose Heyward and his playwright wife, Dorothy, regarded themselves as ethnologists and cultural preservationists, even if they didn't portray African Americans as having internal lives and ambitions. *Porgy* had 367 performances on Broadway, two national tours, and a three-month run in London—a stunning success. Mamoulian's script changes gave *Porgy* energy and warmth. His professional opinion was that the piece was underwritten, so he contributed what he called a "kind of Don Quixotean" ending: Porgy leaves for New York in his goat cart in search of the unfaithful Bess, instead of "Porgy and the goat alone in an irony of morning sunlight."

The play, which opened October 10, 1927, is a vital historical document. *Porgy* is not about "us" and a common humanity. It is about "them" and "their" vices and animalistic urges from the perspective of a white author. Interest in this tale of poverty and death preceded the Amos 'n' Andy craze of 1929–31, when two African American characters voiced by white men on radio migrated (like many thousands of others) from the rural South to industrial Chicago. In Jerome Kern and Oscar Hammerstein's *Show Boat*, which opened on Broadway in December 1927, miscegenation remains a key plot point.

Porgy shows injustice in the form of two bullying policemen who arrest an elderly man to instill fear in Catfish Row so they'll get a confession to a murder. There are no subsequent comments about or calls for racial justice. The audience was supposed to identify with Archdale, a white lawyer who lectures Frazier, a Black predatory shyster, about selling phony "divorces" to the illiterate poor. Catfish Row also is marked by ancient superstitions about death.

In the novella, Porgy is the prototypical "good Negro," with "an atavistic calm" and "the almost purple blackness of unadulterated Congo blood," not far removed from Harriet Beecher Stowe's Uncle Tom; pimp and drug dealer Sporting Life, an octoroon, is the "bad Negro"; and Crown's murder of Robbins after a dice game is called an "atavistic ritual." Bess is described in the draft script as "very black, wide nostrils and large, but well-formed mouth. She flaunts a typical, but debased, Negro beauty."

The Heywards were hardly unique in their stereotyping. Tennessee-born Roark Bradford, who wrote *Ol' Man Adam an' His Chillun* in 1928, which became the hit musical *The Green Pastures* (adapted by Marc Connelly) in 1930, stated his crudely in his introduction, describing "three types of Negroes: the nigger, the 'colored person' and the Negro—upper case N." The Negro he considered the race leader, while the "colored" of mixed blood was the troublemaker, and the third category was a shiftless layabout.

Porgy was the Theatre Guild's first "Negro play." The genre had grown in the 1920s, with the works nearly always originating with white playwrights, and with white actors in dark makeup. Notable plays of the time, all of which faded into obscurity, included Eugene O'Neill's *All God's Chillun Got Wings* (1924; Paul Robeson in an interracial marriage); Edward Sheldon and Charles MacArthur's *Lulu Belle* (1926; Lenore Ulric in blackface as a prostitute tallied 462 performances); and Nan Bagby Stephens's *Roseanne* (1923; Chrystal Herne in blackface as a washerwoman fending off a predatory preacher). But the principal influence on the prestige-conscious Guild likely was *In Abraham's Bosom*, a 1926 drama by Paul Green with a Black cast, about an attempt to build a school during Reconstruction. It won the Pulitzer Prize for Drama in 1927.

In December 1926, the Heywards asked Langner whether he thought it possible that the Theatre Guild might add *Porgy* late in its current season.

Langner told them to deliver it to Philip Moeller. Moeller either didn't want to direct it or didn't think himself capable. In any case, the play was put on the 1927 fall schedule without a director named, more than a month before Mamoulian passed his directing "audition" with *Seven Keys to Baldpate*.

Few other producing organizations at the time could have made Mamoulian a home—and, as he assured his parents, "it will give me a good name." Beginning in 1914 as the Washington Square Players and regrouping in 1919, the Theatre Guild prided itself as a beacon of America's serious art theater in the era dominated by vaudeville and burlesque. Often dilettantish and never offering star salaries, by its third season, the Guild staged George Bernard Shaw's *Heartbreak House* and thereafter negotiated an agreement to be the exclusive presenter of Shaw's works in New York.

Its budding stars included Alfred Lunt and Lynn Fontanne. By 1925, the Guild had its own theater on Fifty-Second Street. The group staged works by Ferenc Molnár (*Liliom, The Guardsman*), Luigi Pirandello (*Right You Are if You Think You Are*), and Sidney Howard (*The Silver Cord*) but never musical productions except for a 1923 revue from Richard Rodgers and Lorenz Hart, *The Garrick Gaieties*. The Guild built its audiences through subscriptions and by the late 1920s had nearly 30,000 subscribers in five cities for its touring productions. In 1927, its board had six members, including Langner, who sometimes penned domestic comedies. His wife, actress Armina Marshall, joined years later. Executive director Theresa Helburn, a graduate of Radcliffe College, had been both a playwright and critic, and was considered the Guild's artistic conscience. In addition to Moeller, rounding out the board in 1927 were Lee Simonson, scenic and lighting designer; actress Helen Westley; and banker Maurice Wertheim.

DuBose Heyward was familiar with the milieu he had captured in his novella because he had grown up in Charleston near a decrepit neighborhood called Cabbage Row; this became the fictional Catfish Row. Heyward knew the Gullah culture with its mix of West African expressions and English because he had sold burial insurance in those neighborhoods. Before that, as a cotton checker for a steamboat line, he had seen the prototypes of the muscular Crown with his hook for grabbing cotton bales. The character of Porgy came from a local beggar, Samuel Smalls, who did indeed use a goat cart; this came to Heyward's attention from a newspaper item when Smalls was charged with assaulting his wife.

Like Porgy, Heyward was physically frail, with a withered arm from polio at age eighteen. Like his mother, Jane, who gave lectures based on Gullah poems and stories, he considered himself an authority on local folkways. He had written one successful book of poetry and started writing plays in his spare time in 1913. He didn't become a full-time writer until 1924, after he married playwright Dorothy Kuhns two years before.

Dorothy later generously claimed that both *Porgy* and their later play *Mamba's Daughters* "were nine-tenths DuBose's." If so, her one-tenth of *Porgy* is far more noticeable. The script introduces characters through the audience-focusing activity of a craps game and pares away distracting secondary characters from the nearly plotless novella and shows a firm hand that undoubtedly was hers alone. In the novella, for instance, Bess does not appear until after Robbins's funeral. Dorothy brought her, somewhat drunk, stumbling into the craps game.

There were parts for twenty-five men and women, and eventually, seven children—the eleven-member orphans' band from Charleston leading the picnic to Kittiwah Island was a late addition. Published accounts of the casting fostered a comic image of Mamoulian as a foreigner working frantically out of his element: "When he saw a Negro on the street who looked right, he would simply walk up and say, 'Do you want a good job?'" The diary Mamoulian kept at the time, however, indicates only a completely professional approach.

From a performance of *In Abraham's Bosom*, Mamoulian cast two leads. Frank Wilson, who was trying to make acting his full-time job and in the meantime held onto his mail route on 135th Street in Harlem, became Porgy. Rose McClendon was cast as Serena, the devoutly Christian widow of the murdered Robbins (Lloyd Gray). Other actors came out of the Lafayette Players in Harlem, including Evelyn Ellis as Bess. Crown was Jack Carter, "a tall octoroon with blue eyes and a terrific temperament, beautifully built—the ideal Crown," Mamoulian said. As he had done in other plays, Carter wore dark makeup, like a minstrel performer. Percy Verwayne, who played Sporting Life, was as light-complexioned as the character was supposed to be. Georgette Harvey, who played Maria, owner of the Catfish Row cookshop and the neighborhood's stout moral force, knew how to converse in Russian from her international touring days, leading to a long friendship with Mamoulian.

After nine days of auditioning principals, and with his last two student productions to complete in July, Mamoulian, having proven that *Porgy* could be put on the boards, signed his contract: $1,000 for seven weeks of rehearsal, plus 1 percent of the weekly gross above $8,000. He would cast the background parts when rehearsals began in September 1927. He and set designer Cleon Throckmorton sailed to Charleston in mid-August for a week of research.

His host, writer John Bennett, a close friend of the Heywards, showed him the sights. "[He] was taken to Folly Beach to see the full moon rise—fiddler crabs scuttled across the beach, and Mamoulian . . . had never seen anything like it," recalled Bennett's daughter, Martha Stiles. "He got the moon into the play, but not the crabs." Mamoulian was more focused on sounds. His notes from the trip mention street cries of shrimp and watermelon peddlers (the Strawberry Woman and Crab Man went into the script as a result). Interviewed by the local newspaper, he hinted at his ideas about noise: "A Negro handles a hammer rhythmically—this rhythm I wish to transfer, if possible, to the stage." He added, "The essence of the play will, I think, be found in the group work, the mass scenes." He decided on the spot to include the Jenkins Orphanage Band as an authentic element.

Near the end of the trip, Mamoulian wrote his parents. He had met an architect who took him to his plantation house, where he saw "Negro dances." Half of Charleston's population, he noted, were descendants of former enslaved people, and he found them all to be colorfully dressed. "Today is Sunday and very hot. I would like to try to visit a Negro church where they sing their wonderful songs—'spirituals.' The problem is that whenever a white person walks into their church, they freeze and continue the service in a more formal way." The solution to that matter of etiquette was to stand with Bennett outside the small house of worship (which he never named). The spiritual he heard was "I'm on My Way." Although its pleasant, swaying rhythm remained with him, in the press of work, he eventually forgot the words.

During the first two weeks of rehearsals, "it all seemed utterly hopeless to me," Mamoulian recalled. "Practically everyone in the cast was trying to copy what they thought was 'legitimate' acting. The result was rank artificiality—nothing came through emotionally. Also, they were most self-conscious, even unwilling, about singing the spirituals the passionate, religious way in which they should be sung. They were inclined to do it in the manner of a cold, formal concert." He was speaking of his difficulty in getting Harlem actors to speak in what was known as "conventional Negro dialect," as the script mentioned. Never mind that the dialect, with its molasses-like vowels and dropped consonants, was an exaggeration invented by whites on nineteenth-century minstrel stages.

The cast noticed the cultural disconnect. One of the older actors, Leigh Whipper, who played the Crab Man (Whipper is best remembered as originating the role of Crooks in Lewis Milestone's *Of Mice and Men*, 1939) decided to take initiative. "I found out very quickly that Mamoulian didn't understand the type of Negro with which he was dealing," adding that he told the director, "You don't know these people. . . . I said, 'I see you trying to do the church scene, the wake for Robbins. Do you want to see the scene unrehearsed?" So he escorted the director around Harlem.

At the Harlem Association of Trade and Commerce, he introduced Mamoulian to two lawyers "and a couple of doctors who were in there playing bridge, and he didn't say anything, but I could see his reaction to what he was going through."

The tour ended at a storefront church on 136th Street.

By the time we got to within a hundred feet of the church you could hear clapping, and so we went in . . . and we heard the singing and the shouting, the amens and all, you know, and we stayed there. There were some testimonies given and then they looked for a collection and we put in ours . . . and came out. Mamoulian says, "I see what you mean." I says, "Yes, you don't know these people . . . Now you let them be themselves, and not take up that tragic way you have of trying to put fright into Evelyn Ellis. Let her put her fright into it and you'll see."

Whipper recalled that the play was never quite "set" and allowed some room for improvisation. He was thinking of his own part and probably had in mind Annie, played by Ella Madison. The publicity story about Madison, who in her early seventies was the oldest cast member, was that she had never been on the stage before. In fact, she had begun performing professionally in 1878, playing Topsy in a pageant-like production of *Uncle Tom's Cabin* that played in New York and toured Europe. At the Kittiwah Island arrival in the second act, she performed a minstrel tune about an encounter with Satan called "All De Gold in De Mountains," then improvised some dialogue with Wesley Hill as Jake. In *Porgy and Bess*, this was replaced with the blasphemous Sporting Life singing "It Ain't Necessarily So."

The only Gullah term that remained in the script was "buckra," meaning "white man," Its two hard consonants made it easily understandable from the stage. There was never a question about the hard consonants in a racial slur. In the 1920s, even New York sophisticates and artists could casually drop it. This context explains George Gershwin's often-quoted 1925 remark about his future opera: "I shall write it for niggers. They are always singing. They have it in their blood. I have no doubt that they will be able to do full justice to a jazz opera." Many Gershwin biographers have observed that this is the only time he was known to use the word, assuming that his Canadian interviewer didn't twist "Negro" himself.

The word was deleted from *Porgy and Bess* for its 1942 Broadway revival, never to return. It appears fifty-nine times in the novella and forty-four times in *Porgy*—cut down by Mamoulian from sixty-six uses in the draft script. Racial sensitivity would have had nothing to do with his cuts; with that many casual uses, any effect was diluted. It's used in the first complete sentence the audience is supposed to comprehend out of the stream of Gullah dialect that opens the craps game: Mingo complains, "Y'all is all too talky 'round hyuh. A nigger can't get time tuh read de bones atter he done t'row um." Mamoulian cut the lyrics to be sung as the brass band plays Catfish Row off to the island picnic—a lively ditty called "Ain't It Hahd to Be a Nigger" that would blur the serious tone created by all the spirituals. The rest of the uses aren't boldface exclamation points, except perhaps for Crown as he bursts into Serena's room during the hurricane and announces, "Yo' is a nice pa'cel of niggers!" (For the 1959 film, the line became "You're a fine bunch of Christians!")

The Heywards wrote four acts; Mamoulian compressed them to three, with a violent death in each, two of them on stage. Cocaine use by Crown and Bess was made clear in this addition to the opening scene:

> CROWN: I ain't drunk enough to read 'em, dats de trouble. Likker ain't strong 'nough. Gimme a pinch ob happy dus,' Sportin' Life. Give um a dollar, Bess.

BESS: Don't give him that stuff, Sportin' Life. He's ugly drunk already.

CROWN: You's a good one to talk—Pay um and shut up!

The combination of liquor and cocaine explains (but doesn't justify) Crown's violent rage when he accuses Porgy of cheating at dice, then fights Robbins when Robbins comes to Porgy's defense. The novella describes the fight in animalistic terms, referring to a "heady, bestial stench" and describing Crown's cotton hook as "a prehensile claw."

The theater audience was going to see a fatal fight by two mismatched opponents; Mamoulian's script notations read: "Shutters bang open—shafts of light from them flash across the court. At end of fight, Crown swings Robbins into a shaft of light from one of the open windows. Crown is facing the audience and is holding Robbins by the throat at arm's length.

Jack Carter as Crown taunts the residents of Catfish Row during the hurricane scene in *Porgy*. Left to right: Frank Wilson as Porgy, Evelyn Ellis as Bess, Rose McClendon as Serena. Photograph courtesy of Library of Congress.

Robbins drops back toward the audience into darkness, and Crown stands in high light. With a triumphant snarl, he swings the hook downward."

Mamoulian emphasized raw horror through stylized movement. When Bess warned Crown the police would be arriving, he noted, "the crowd, which is backing slowly from the body, turns upstage and one by one move silently but swiftly to their rooms." Bess goes from door to door in Catfish Row after Crown runs off. Bess gets more excited with each failure and begins to sob and cry. She reaches Porgy's door, puts her hand on the handle, then slowly opens it, enters, and closes it behind her.

The impact of Robbins's "saucer funeral," in which his corpse was laid out in Serena's room with a saucer on his chest for burial donations, was the result of Mamoulian's choreography and a lighting effect that all agreed was serendipitous. "Mamoulian asked to have a lamp placed in front of the group of mourners. By accident, the main lights were brought down, and suddenly we saw the gigantic shadows of the mourners outlined against the back of the room. Everyone gasped at the effect, and of course Mamoulian kept it," Cheryl Crawford, then the stage manager, recalled. The effect was eventually achieved by a single amber spotlight in the center of the footlights.

The funeral begins with the mournful "Death, Ain't Yuh Got No Shame" and a call and response led by Porgy, who, although an outsider because of his disability, is still part of the larger spiritual community, even with Bess at his side. The mourners produce only $15 of the $25 needed for a proper burial; the undertaker assures Serena, "I'll see you through." The service is interrupted by the arrival of a white policeman who arrests the elderly Uncle Peter in a show of force intended to scare the truth out of Catfish Row.

After the arrest, the grief picks up intensity. The mourners begin to sway and Mamoulian noted, "Crowd takes up moan and raises it like an organ, *vox humana*, until it vibrates." They segue to "What de Mattuh, Children" and the scene charges to its bravura climax, with Serena at the center creating the tallest shadow. At the first line of the spiritual "Promis' Land," Mamoulian noted: "Dim starts. Lamp on mantel flickers and goes out and spot in foots comes up. First rows on each side start double swaying, the rest single. They take up the double successively by rows until by last verse everyone is double-swaying." Three counts after Serena rose and spread her hands over her head, the curtain fell. Mamoulian had never actually seen the real thing in Charleston, he had merely heard it from outside a church window there, and he never credited his visit to the Harlem storefront.

In the *New York Times*, Brooks Atkinson called Mamoulian's staging "splendid theatrical generalship." In the *Evening Sun*, Gilbert Gabriel noted, the mourners "turn for a moment or two into something monstrously beautiful." In the New York *World*, the city's best-known critic, Alexander Woollcott, swooned, "It is in this bare, stained, cheerless room that they lay the body of the 'saucer-buried' darkey and when the huddle of lamentation finds a ghostly accompaniment in the ballet of the mourners' shadows upon the wall *Porgy* reaches one of the most exciting climaxes I have ever seen in the theatre."

Mamoulian built the atmosphere in the next two acts. After Porgy buys a cheap "divorce" from Frazier for Bess, and after the brass band leads the "Sons and Daughters of Repent Ye, Saith the Lord" to the Kittiwah picnic, it's time for Crown to reappear—he's been hiding out on the island—and reclaim his hold on Bess. The Heywards, in their draft script, thought Crown could be detected merely by the sight of his eyes glowing from the cover of palmetto leaves. Mamoulian knew better and had Crown whistle from the thicket. Bess's attraction to Crown is savage. As in the novella, she "threw back her head, and sent a wild laugh out against the walls of the clearing."

Hysterical and moaning after the return from the island, Bess recovers as a hurricane bears down as strong winds begin to blow. Maria explains that fifteen rings of the offstage bell means a hurricane. The ambitious Jake has left Clara and their newborn son to take his fishing boat out to the Blackfish Banks. Clara shrieks in terror at the thirteenth ring: "Fifteen! Jake! Jake! Oh, Lord!" The second act closes with more of Mamoulian's noises, with Catfish Row denizens huddled in Serena's dimly lit room, waiting out the sky's fury. At the hurricane's peak, Crown, who has somehow made his way off the island, arrives to mock the religious utterances:

> CROWN (his voice rising above the wind): Don' yo' hear Gawd A-Mighty, laughing up dere? (CRASH, all effects)
> Dat's right, ole frien'. Gawd laugh, and Crown laugh back!

Clara, in a panic, leaves her infant behind to run out in search of Jake, and Crown runs out to get her back inside. His effort is futile. With Crown still a menace and trying to get Bess back as the third act begins, it's clear he must die. His death, in both novella and the script draft, was not shown—there was only "a muffled thud from Porgy's room." Mamoulian understood that the audience would be disappointed by that. So he choreographed the only way Porgy could overcome Crown's strength: Porgy leans from his window as Crown approaches, with Bess and Clara's baby asleep inside the room. He stabs Crown in the back, then chokes him and addresses the unseen Bess: "Dat all right, honey. Don' you be worryin'! You gots Porgy now, and he look atter he woman. Ain' I don't tell yo'! You gots a *man* now!"

Crown's body is at the morgue when a detective arrives at Catfish Row. Faced with a wall of silence, they tell Porgy they want to take him to the police station to identify the body, and he won't be allowed to leave until he does. Regressing to superstition, Porgy believes that in the presence of his killer, Crown's body will begin to bleed, indicting him. The police haul him away over his protests.

Mamoulian wrapped up the play with two distinctive flourishes. The first was in sound: *Clank! Zzzzz! Clank!* Swish! *Snap!* Porgy, loaded with jailhouse craps winnings, was returning from lockup. First, to mimic a street repair crew, the offstage clank of a hammer on iron, followed by a silent beat and the swish of a broom. Added to the mix was a man snoring on a stoop, followed by the clank of a bottle, the snap of a towel in an upstairs window, and the sound of wood being sawed, achieved by rubbing two sandpaper-covered boards. Over two minutes, the collection of noises went from 4:4 time to 2:4 and then into syncopation before the bell of the police paddy wagon announced Porgy's arrival.

Mamoulian called it the "Symphony of Noise." Its use as a dramatic device suggests inspiration from Vakhtangov. Its application here is purely Mamoulian. "I didn't want noise to be uncontrolled on the stage. It is in life, but I didn't see why noise on the stage couldn't be made as rhythmic and architectural as music. Rhythm and composition still can be applied to noise. This again was an elevation of life, but basically very true to the spirit, and manner of living, of colored people."

Mamoulian reprised the noises when Paris comes to life in *Love Me Tonight*, cut some of Gershwin's music to repeat them in *Porgy and Bess*, and considered another version involving barnyard sounds while rehearsing the opening scene of *Oklahoma!* Prerecorded by Mamoulian, the sounds appear again in the woebegone 1959 film of *Porgy and Bess* directed by Otto Preminger. The sounds received no critical or popular attention in 1927. The critics from the morning newspapers, to make their deadlines, all left after the second act (in the years before press previews, critics seldom saw opening-night finales) and even the afternoon daily and magazine critics didn't mention it.

The novella and the Heywards' draft contained no big temptation scene for Sporting Life to work his wiles on Bess. When Porgy returns from jail, Maria simply tells him the pimp got Bess hooked on "happy dust." Mamoulian had the Heywards write a scene, before Porgy's return, in which Sporting Life details the life he and Bess could have if they ran away, including the money they could make putting her into prostitution. This became, in *Porgy and Bess*, "There's a Boat Leaving Soon for New York."

The second flourish was Porgy's decision to go after Bess. Stephen Sondheim wrote that "one of the most moving moments" in the history of musical theater is Porgy's demand, in *Porgy and Bess*, "Bring my goat!" Mamoulian was mostly thinking about how to get the animal on and off the stage.

Dorothy Heyward, with a limited knowledge of goats, had given the animal five appearances, including in Serena's room during the hurricane, and a comedic moment in the first scene of act 2 when the goat was supposed to querously poke its head out of Porgy's window. Cranky by nature, goats can't be trained like dogs or horses, so none of that worked. Mamoulian still had to handle Porgy's return, in which he was supposed to steer his cart in and out of the gate. That worked fine early on, but no one had considered how the goat would react to applause from the dress-rehearsal audience. The resulting mishap postponed the premiere for a week.

"That goat doesn't know 'whoa' from 'back,'" Mamoulian quipped in a newspaper interview. "Maria's lines here are, 'Porgy, what you going' to do? Where on earth you drivin' to? And one night when she said this the goat began to back, and he ran round and round the stage and up the side of the wall. That goat never will get another chance. He has no ambition. So now someone leads him on and off and the rest of the time he eats."

Under the terrific stress of his first Broadway production, Mamoulian's memory of the Sunday underneath the church window returned:

The end of *Porgy* was in dialogue. And I felt it needed the lift of a song. . . . [And I thought] of "I'm on My Way" because Porgy's going to New York, and I couldn't remember the tune. So I got the whole cast . . . and said "Look, 'I'm on My Way to a Heavenly Land,' have you heard that?" No one ever heard it. A typical Charleston spiritual. And for weeks, it just ruined my life. And once, I was going to the rehearsal, I was crossing Seventh Avenue with the traffic going both ways, and in the middle of that traffic, suddenly that melody came back. . . . So I kept humming it to myself. . . . And then I went upstairs to the rehearsal room and I kept humming, and I hummed it for them. . . . And they picked it up, and that's what George Gershwin used. . . . He changed the rhythm some.

Porgy is still a tragic figure as he heads to New York—a thousand-mile journey, if he makes it. But now he's also sanctified. Mamoulian wrote the recalled lyrics on a back page of his script. A month after the opening, Gershwin purchased the rights to turn the play into an opera, although he didn't begin to work on it seriously for six more years.

CHAPTER 3

From Eugene O'Neill to Burlesque

The success of *Porgy* gave Mamoulian a type of celebrity he might not have expected. "Who is this Rouben Mamoulian?" gushed columnist Harriette Underhill in the *New York Herald Tribune*. "He is tall and handsome and greatly resembles Prince Serge Mdivani, the one who recently married Pola Negri." To earn that comparison, Mamoulian may have dropped a lot of hints about his distant link to Armenian nobility. For a brief time, Alexander Woollcott, a champion of new discoveries, asked Mamoulian to accompany him on his nightly social rounds, although those didn't seem to extend to the sharp-tongued coterie of the Algonquin Round Table or the hard-drinking Long Island party set that inspired *The Great Gatsby*.

Porgy launched Mamoulian on a two-year sprint of directing assignments. The Theatre Guild offered him a contract for two more plays, but within six months, he was testing the waters with other producers and had received his first overture from a motion picture studio. Any ideas he may have had about his career being one quality art production after another quickly dissipated. The Guild offered him one of two Eugene O'Neill plays on its slate. But it came with a price: Langner wanted to stage a play of his own, a forgettable lightweight comedy about an extramarital affair called *These Modern Women*.

O'Neill's reputation as the American Ibsen rests largely on his straightforward masterpieces, *Mourning Becomes Electra*, *The Iceman Cometh*, and *Long Day's Journey into Night*, and this obscures his work of the mid-1920s, when he was experimenting with large casts and lengthy plots. In 1925, *Lazarus Laughed*, O'Neill's version of a medieval mystery play about Lazarus of Bethany, raised from the dead by Jesus, used more than 150 actors in its four acts. He had envisioned *Marco Millions*, which turns the story of thirteenth-century explorer Marco Polo into a satiric allegory of American materialism, as a two-night epic (much longer than *Strange Interlude*) with music and dance and a cast of roughly 100.

O'Neill, who won the first of his four Pulitzer Prizes in 1920 for *Anna Christie*, had taken *Marco* to three other producers before the Guild took it on. When Langner visited O'Neill in Bermuda in early 1927, the playwright let him read part of *Strange Interlude*—a nine-act, five-hour drama involving a series of love affairs, mental illness, an abortion, and an out-of-wedlock pregnancy. The principals express their troubled inner thoughts as soliloquies. Langner handed that play to Moeller, and *Strange Interlude* went on to win O'Neill's second Pulitzer Prize. Opening on January 30, 1928, it ran for 270 performances, in part because its tawdry subject matter gave it cachet. The curtain went up at 5:30, audiences were sent on a dinner break at 7:30 and returned at 8:30, sometimes changing into evening dress. The play was made into an MGM film in 1932 and sank from sight for decades after that, best remembered for Groucho Marx's spoof of the soliloquies in *Animal Crackers*. *Marco Millions*, starring Alfred Lunt, had just ninety-two performances. It has been revived in regional theater in recent decades—always in stripped-down versions—because its satire of chest-thumping American bluster and yearning for wealth renews itself with each generation as Marco Polo, his father, and brother, like bigoted, provincial traveling salesmen, mock other races and cultures.

Mamoulian's story seems to indicate that Langner was willing to have fun at his expense. Either that or O'Neill, who had seen *Porgy* on its opening night, was not prepared for Mamoulian's eagerness to slash dialogue:

> So I did read the script and looked at the sketches and came back to the Guild and told them that the script could be greatly improved by some cutting. They all laughed. I said, "What's so funny?" They said, "Mr. O'Neill doesn't cut. You have to do it exactly as it is." I said, "Why don't you people talk to him about this?"
>
> And they replied, "Do you want to talk to him about it, because we don't want to." I said, "I don't mind. Why not? I can show him the reasons." . . .
>
> I went down to this Wentworth Hotel. The door opened and there was this magnificent man with those smoldering eyes. He had a tiny room . . . with just room for a bed and an armoire, a chair and a little table. . . .

So finally I said, "Well, Mr. O'Neill, look. I'm speaking as a director. I feel that this play, in terms of a stage production, could be improved in its effect if you made some cuts." He said, "Cuts?" He went red in the face with anger.

I said, "Mr. O'Neill, it's your play. Let me tell you about it. If you don't agree, fine. I'll be happy to do it as it stands." He repeated the word. "Cuts. All right, sit down."

So I sat next to him on the bed and I opened the book. I said, "Take this, for example," about many different moments in the play, and I kept on explaining my position from a stage point of view.

He grabbed a thick blue pencil and said, "From here to here?" Yes. "Next?" Fine.

I said. "No, no, that one's too much. You stop at such and such a line."

He said, "Fine. All right." Every cut he approved.

Mamoulian said a single powerful lighting effect contributed to the success of *Marco Millions*. "It was the court of Kublai Kahn. People were grouped, not symmetrically, but in balanced masses of costume and color. Then we hit it with all the lights, hard, suddenly. It was terrific . . . they're delighted with the spectacle and they're with you. You don't lose them. The point is, you shouldn't lose them."

There were some stumbles after this. *These Modern Women* was an inexpensive production with just twenty-seven performances after opening February 13 at the Eltinge Theatre. Mamoulian's reputation for spectacle meant he often had offers from producers hoping to lure audiences with exotic fare. Bandleaders Ben Bernie and Phil Baker were producing *Café Tomaza*, an adaptation by William DuBois, then a reporter for the *New York Times*, of *La Maison des Danses*, a long-running drama from Europe by Fernand Nozière, Paul Reboux, and Charles Müller. The show featured specialty dancing acts; the star was doughty character actress Alison Skipworth. The plan was for a long run in Chicago. Instead, Mamoulian's production expired after brief tryouts in Queens and the Bronx.

His next venture was unexpectedly generous. Sam Harris, the former partner of George M. Cohan, wanted to produce the comeback of the tempestuous Jeanne Eagels and also had a script in mind for Helen Menken. Eagels was an alcoholic and missed performances of *Her Cardboard Lover* in Milwaukee and St. Louis in 1928, which resulted in an eighteen-month suspension from the stage by Actors Equity. The play for Eagels (the author's name is not known) was to have been her Broadway return. In 1922, she was a sensation in Somerset Maugham's *Rain*, in which she played his hardbitten prostitute, Sadie Thompson; in her only talking picture, *The Letter*, also from a Maugham story, she played the jealous wife Leslie Crosbie. Harris's project ended with Eagels's unexpected death at age thirty-nine in October 1929. The producer also gave Mamoulian a murder mystery by Edward and Edith Ellis, *Women*, which starred John Halliday; it closed in late October 1928 during its Philadelphia tryouts.

Congai, a drama by Harry Hervey and Carleton Hildreth based on Hervey's novel of the same name, debuted November 27, 1928, at the Sam Harris Theatre, running for 137 performances and laden with special effects and Throckmorton's elaborate sets. *Congai* was the saga of Thi-Linh, a "halfcaste" (Annamite and French) woman in love with Kim Khouan, a native boy with whom she has a child. Because his family won't permit marriage, she becomes a concubine (somewhat like a Japanese geisha) for a series of French officers, part of the occupying force of French Indochina. There was no attempt to cast Asian performers. Helen Menken played Thi-Linh. Ted Hecht was Kim Khouan, and their son, Qu-yan, was played by Alan Campbell, later a screenwriter best known for having been married to Dorothy Parker.

Mamoulian dressed up the production with incense pots, Menken in a body suit to simulate nudity in the first scene, an offstage tom-tom, and a marching "army" seen through a window, consisting of shadows of stagehands and extras marching in a circle before a floor light. The second act ended with Thi-Linh angrily applying lip color in time to an offstage gong from a nearby temple.

Mamoulian closed out 1928 with the Guild's contemporary antiwar drama *Wings over Europe* by Robert Nichols and Maurice Brown, opening December 10 at the Martin Beck Theatre and running just thirty-three performances. The earliest play written about atomic weaponry was in the style of what later audiences would associate with Reginald Rose's juryroom drama *Twelve Angry Men*. It had a single set at the British prime minister's office; sixteen men argued around a conference table. Scientist Francis Lightfoot (Alexander Kirkland) has invented an atomic bomb. He promises the British prime minister and his cabinet that he'll abandon it provided that it's given to the League of Nations, so no country can begin a war. He gives the cabinet, which wants to keep the bomb for Britain, a day to decide.

Stylized action, Mamoulian insisted, was the only way to keep audiences interested in any play. The table was tilted slightly so it was three inches taller upstage; that way the audience would see all the actors. In the original script, Lightfoot was killed offstage, hit by a truck. Mamoulian dispensed with that, and instead focused on the impact of a single noise:

> Lightfoot leaves the room and all the cabinet ministers are holding their positions. Some are standing, others are sitting. No one moves. It's like a wax museum. On the mantelpiece, there was a clock.
>
> A metronome held by the stage manager moved closer to the set. Now, as the ticking grew really loud, I had one man pace in counterpoint. I had the foreign minister (Frank Conroy) take out his cigarette case. No one else is moving, you see, just him. . . . He clicks the case shut. You know, a small click? Well that click brought a loud gasp from the audience. The most incredible thing. An absolute gasp!

Nichols, Mamoulian said, objected violently until he sat through a rehearsal and sent Brown a telegram proclaiming the director's genius. On opening night, Nichols insisted that Mamoulian take his curtain call with him: "He dragged me out and made a speech that would have embarrassed Jesus Christ.

～

Mamoulian's theatrical success led the far more lucrative motion picture industry to come calling only two days after *Porgy* opened in 1927. Walter Wanger, the general manager of Paramount's Astoria studio (and later the studio's chief of production) was a perfect fit for Mamoulian. The Dartmouth College graduate, cultured and multilingual, was a sharp contrast to other movie executives Mamoulian met at the time, whose typical backgrounds were in vaudeville, nickelodeons, or amusement arcades.

Paramount shuttered its Astoria studio in 1927 to consolidate production in Hollywood. The advent of talking pictures and the proximity of Broadway talent—actors who could speak distinctly enough to make their voices

Mamoulian, Joan Peers, and Helen Morgan on the set of *Applause*, filmed in June 1929 at Paramount's Astoria Studios on Long Island.

clear through primitive technology—brought it back into operation just a year later. The industry was hungry for stage-trained actors and directors who understood dialogue, not just pantomime skills. Wanger had already recruited George Cukor.

Wanger's first offer to Mamoulian in February 1928 was a job as dialogue director for part-talkie films, with contract options increasing the pay to $1,500 a week after two years. Mamoulian rejected it; "I will not give you the right to tell me no," is how he put his refusal. Mamoulian, Wanger, and Paramount chief Adolph Zukor finally came to terms early in 1929. Part-talkies had faded out, full sound was in, and the movies' demand for theater directors was at its peak. Sound films, Mamoulian assured his parents, "will have a big future!"

Mamoulian had an unpleasant brush with the seedy elements of show business in March 1929, when he worked on some sketches for the long-running revue *Americana* (which later produced the enduring "Brother, Can You Spare a Dime?") for producer J. P. McEvoy. Mamoulian was stunned when McEvoy's idea of compensation was a brace of pipes. "When I mentioned to you some days ago the fact that have not received any compensation for my work in *Americana*, I spoke of a *cheque* and not of pipes, though they be Dunhill's," Mamoulian wrote. "I like the word 'sucker' but I do not like either to be one or be considered one."

Mamoulian already knew that theater audiences could be fickle and cruel. The first time he showed an audience on screen, he went to an extreme: leering men, humiliating a daughter aghast at her mother's show business descent. But he wasn't expanding the source material as he had done with *Porgy*. He was faithfully translating *Applause*, a novel of sacrificial mother love written by former chorus girl Beth Brown (adapted by Garrett Fort) while attempting to push then-primitive sound technology to its limits. Filmed during the summer of 1929 and released in January 1930, it's appreciated for its cinéma vérité glimpses of New York City landmarks, such as Pennsylvania Station, as well as Mamoulian's success at keeping his camera, encased in a giant box to muffle its noise, in motion. *Applause* reveals small-time show business in its threadbare state of bawdy humor, chorus girls who have seen better days, and flashes of bare skin.

He found his research discouraging:

> I had to visit all the burlesque houses up on 125th Street. I thought the whole thing was so shabby and degrading, both on the stage and in their reading, that I thought, "The hell with it. I don't want to have anything to do with it." And then I thought, "For heaven's sake, why not? Why don't I show it for what it is?" I could show it as I thought it was, and then play against that the purity of the young people in love and their capacity to overcome their environment.

Mamoulian's only education in film technique other than what he had picked up at the Eastman School came during February and March 1929 when "[they] allowed me to walk around the studio and ask silly questions" (Orson Welles told a similar story about wandering around RKO before he made *Citizen Kane*).

> So there were two directors shooting and I would ask the cameraman, you know, what does this lens do, et cetera. I went to the cutting room and the

projection room, and I watched some shooting and again, I guess I was just born contrary, whatever was done I thought I would do things opposite. So after five weeks I felt, well, that's it. Actually you don't need longer than that to learn the mechanics of making motion pictures. That's all you need. The important thing is whether you have a cinema eye or not.

The two directors he mentioned were both French: Jean De Limur, then filming Jeanne Eagels in *Jealousy*, and Robert Florey, assigned to guide the Marx Brothers (Groucho, Harpo, Chico, and Zeppo) through the film of their musical comedy *The Cocoanuts* during the day while they were still performing in *Animal Crackers* on Broadway. Mamoulian used Florey's cinematographer, George Folsey, for *Applause*. Mamoulian and the Marxes shared a Sam Harris connection, since Harris was producing *Animal Crackers*. One day at lunch in the studio commissary, the brothers startled him by singing, "We'd walk ma-million miles for one of your smiles, Ma-mooooooo-lian!" The Marxes invited Mamoulian to an intermission visit in their dressing room at the theater. "Sam Harris was there, and the Marx Brothers started doing a show for us, ad-libbing. They were very funny, and when people came into the dressing room to tell them to go onstage, they made those people part of the act, and then they put the people out and continued doing the show just for us."

Helen Morgan was a Broadway sensation as the doomed Julie in *Show Boat* two years earlier and famous for her cabaret act performing winsome love ballads while perched atop a piano. She was just twenty-six; the part of Kitty Darling in *Applause*, a faded star, required her to play the mother of a seventeen-year-old daughter, put on twenty-five pounds, and don a frizzy blond wig and gaudy, unflattering costumes. As an alcoholic, Morgan was a production risk. Mamoulian dealt with the matter directly, extracting a promise when she asked, "'Can I have a glass of beer after shooting?' I said yes. And she kept her word." Joan Peers, playing April Darling, was the daughter of the manager of the Adelphi Theatre in Chicago. Henry Wadsworth, an experienced young man in stage roles, was cast as Tony, April's love interest. Fuller Mellish Jr., who played the villain, Hitch Nelson, also had lengthy stage credits.

For auditions for the chorus girls, Mamoulian held three casting calls. The attractive younger women undoubtedly found it puzzling that the director had his eye only on the saggy and the plain as he chose prospects, winnowing the list further after screen tests. The term "beef trust" is usually applied to a chorus consisting entirely of larger women; they still had to be good dancers performing dainty moves identical to those of slim terpsichoreans. Impresario Billy Watson specialized in producing these routines, and Walt Disney memorialized them with his balletic hippos in *Fantasia* (1940). Mamoulian's dancers are lackluster; the script calls them "a tired, haggard lot, smiling with their lips alone."

Seldom has show business been portrayed as more full of parasites, lechery, and squalor as in *Applause*. Brown's novel is even coarser. *The Dance of Life*, produced at Paramount the same year and based on the stage hit *Burlesque*, with an alcoholic comedian as its protagonist, is redeemed by glamor and lavish production numbers. *The Jazz Singer* (1927), also from a stage play, presents Al Jolson's jazz performances as being as respectable an enterprise as his father's singing as a cantor. The closest approximation to *Applause* in other films might be Federico Fellini's 1950 debut, *Variety Lights*, about touring second-rate performers.

Mamoulian opens with a shot of a wrinkled poster of "Kitty Darling, Queen of Hearts" on a dirt street in a vaguely Midwestern city (it's supposed to be Oil City, Oklahoma). A small dog runs to the poster before a young girl picks up the animal, on her way to the parade as Kitty's troupe marches down the main street. Kitty is in a horse-drawn carriage and deludes herself as being bound for the New York stage, although she's only a star in rustic locales. When the show begins, the pit orchestra happily quaffs pre-Prohibition beers while thumping out "Oceana Roll," establishing that the year is circa 1912. Although Kitty's show is down-at-the-heels, clearly performers and audience are having a good time.

Melodrama clatters in swiftly. First, there's a telegram from Kitty's imprisoned husband: "Governor refused pardon. Death sentence. Forgive and forget—Eddie" (The explanation, that Eddie had murdered a Tammany Hall politician who had put moves on Kitty, goes by quickly.) The resulting shock sends the pregnant Kitty into labor, leading the comic Joe King (Jack Cameron) to run on stage to implore, "Is there a doctor in the house?" That was an ancient wheeze even then, producing raucous laughter until he pleads, "No foolin' boys, is there a doctor in the house?" A shamefaced physician extracts himself, and the announcement of the birth of Kitty's daughter is passed down the chorus line during the performance. Mamoulian next shows a circle of chorus girls from above and below, surrounding the tear-stained Kitty and her newborn daughter.

Unfortunately cut was this snappy dialogue:

FIRST CHORUS GIRL: April! Can you beat that for a name to wish on a kid!
SECOND CHORUS GIRL: That's when she was born—April.
FIRST CHORUS GIRL: Thank God my fambly got some sense, then. I was born on Yom Kippur.

Mamoulian used dissolves and montages to squeeze out every bit of melodrama. He dissolves to Kitty, five years later, teaching April to tap dance to a phonograph record of "Pretty Baby." Kitty has refused Joe's offer of marriage. All the same, he advises her to put April into a convent school in Wisconsin, since she's been picking up bawdy jokes. The next dissolve transforms April's gaudy necklace into a rosary and Kitty's hands into those of a nun at April's school. Without an intertitle, Mamoulian leaps forward twelve years to Kitty in a dingy New York City hotel room sorting through letters and souvenirs and crooning "What Wouldn't I Do for That Man" to a photograph of her new lover, comic Hitch Nelson. Hitch is unfaithful, later seen kissing a chorus girl.

Back in Wisconsin, the nuns are singing Schubert's "Ave Maria," and as April takes a final look at her place of sanctuary, Mamoulian dissolves the chapel ceiling into the cathedral-like ceiling of Pennsylvania Station, where she disembarks. When April finally sees her mother's performance, it's clear that the good-hearted Kitty has made no ascent in the business as she and the other girls trot onto the ramp to flirt with the customers during "Give Your Little Baby Lots of Lovin'." One man sneers, "They ought to pension off that faded old blonde!"

The chorus girls in slapped-on makeup, seen one by one, are as homely as the audience. The script describes "Men's faces—boys' faces—grinning, leering, bestial, amused, fascinated, disgusted." A girl with a single gold tooth is twinned with a grotesque fellow with a mouthful of gold caps. Mortified, April flees backstage. Preparing for bed that night, she cries, "Everything is so different from what I thought it would be!" Kitty calmly responds, "It ain't what you do—it's what you are." Her next line was sensitive: "Why there are a couple of dames in this troupe who are as good a Catholic as you'd ever expect to see, even if they do make their living shakin'." To avoid the ire of the Catholic press and state censor boards, Paramount advised exhibitors to quash the sound on "Catholic." Later on, the studio snipped the word from the soundtrack, so the line became, "as good as . . . you'd ever expect to see."

Kitty reprises "Pretty Baby" as a lullaby while April prays the rosary. Filmed on the third day of shooting, the scene looks unremarkable today. It then required the challenge of two-track sound recording and was, in Mamoulian's recollection, the culmination of all his early frustration with the crew. His version of events amounts to an unconditional victory:

> Nobody would do anything I told them because [George] Folsey would say, "You can't do that." I wanted to move the camera. They said, "We can't do that. We have three cameras, two close-up and one medium shot and they intercut and that's the picture. Also, you can't have shadows because Mr. Zukor and Mr. Lasky want to see everything on the screen." . . . I wanted the girl just out of the convent to take her rosary and recite, whisper her prayer. Well, the sound man [Ernest Zatorsky] said, "You can't do that." . . .
>
> Naturally, if Helen Morgan is singing, you can't hear the whisper. You couldn't hear it in life, you couldn't hear it on stage. I said, "That's why the sound is magic like a camera. I would like to hear both, the whisper and the sound. The way to do it is, let's have one microphone for Helen and another one under the pillow for the little girl, and we recorded it on two separate channels and put it together." "It has never been done. It is going to be a mess," they said.
>
> Now, then, the straw that broke the camel's back. Helen came down in beautiful pajamas. I said, "What is this?" I told the head of the costume department that she was a slovenly aging burlesque queen. She should look sloppy."
>
> [He responded], "She is a star. She must look glamorous."
>
> I got so angry. I threw down my megaphone on the floor, I dashed up the stairs, and luckily, everyone was there having a very important meeting—Zukor, Walter . . . So up came Folsey and the sound man and the wardrobe man. George said, "Now, I have the greatest respect for Mr. Mamoulian as a stage director, but I have been in films all my life. What he asks is impossible,

and I don't want the studio to waste money, and that is a very strong argument." The sound man says, "He wants two channels. It has never been done . . ." I said, "Now you tell them to do what I ask for and the responsibility is mine. So that if it doesn't work out, you can fire me. You don't fire Folsey, you don't fire them."

George says, "Well, you just give me the word and I will do anything he says." . . .

I had to light it. I had to get eleven men to move this house, and I finally got two takes. I couldn't sleep that night at all and I said, "This is my last day in movies because it is going to be a mess. Maybe it can't be done."

It could be done. As film historian Richard Koszarski notes, the problem wasn't the technological difficulty of two-channel sound. It's that Mamoulian was being a channel hog: "There already were two microphones on the set; what Mamoulian wanted was for the output of each microphone to be recorded separately, a demand which required the use of two separate recording channels. . . . The problem with this idea was that the studio still only had three or four channels available for direct recording, and if Mamoulian was using two channels, someone else in the studio would not be able to use any."

Mamoulian relished the outcome:

So I walked through the front door and there was Earl Redding. . . . He said, "I want to talk to you before you go on the set . . . You know, this was going to be your last day in the movies. The big fellows ordered the laboratory"—you never got rushes until the evening of the second day—"they told the laboratory to keep working all night and get this scene, and everybody was here at 7:30 in the morning, including Zukor, Lasky, and they ran the scene in the projection room and if that didn't work out, that was going to be it for you. . . . They are sending it to Kansas City to the convention of Paramount salesmen as an example of the forthcoming product . . . In the meantime, the order to everybody is, give Mamoulian anything he asks for."

Kitty is launching a new show, *Parisian Flirts*, and Hitch, teaching April dance steps, aggressively kisses her, assuring the ever-trusting Kitty that it's part of the new routine. Kitty has to serve as a hostess at a stag smoker, so

April breaks away and walks outside. She bumps into Tony, a sailor from Wisconsin. He takes her to the top of the top of the AT&T Building, where Mamoulian's camera takes in views of the New York harbor, elevated trains, and a monoplane. Tony eventually proposes marriage, telling April they'll go back to his farm and grow wheat. Nothing's coming up roses for Kitty, though. In the next scene, the abusive Hitch tells her the producer wants a younger performer in their act, adding, "Can't you tell you're all washed up?" Refusing to believe him, she calls agent Gus Feinbaum (William S. Stephens, a real agent who helped cast the film). He confirms Hitch's bad news. Distraught, Kitty heads to the medicine cabinet, Mamoulian's camera following every step, to take a fatal overdose of sleeping pills.

Dying from her overdose, Kitty stumbles to the theater and collapses on a divan. April offers to go on for her, declaring, "I'll give them what they want!" Her scantily clad appearance in another performance of "Give Your Little Baby Lots of Lovin'"—"a mad, abandoned bacchanate" in the script—is in the manner of a sacrificial virgin. The men roar appreciatively as the sight of dewy young flesh. April hates every second of it, and runs offstage into Tony's arms: "Take me away from this terrible place!" They embrace in front of a poster of Kitty, where her arms are raised in triumph. Her devotion has been rewarded.

Executive suite enthusiasm, Mamoulian recalled, ran high before the picture opened. Zukor and Lasky promised him a new contract in two weeks. "I was overwhelmed, you know.... I went home saying, 'God, what wonderful people. This is something.' Well, the picture opened, and they, of course, had sensational reviews, critically, but the box office wasn't doing so well. Two weeks went by, three weeks, a month, two months, three months. I never heard from them."

It was more than a year before Mamoulian directed his next film, this time in Hollywood and accompanied by a new romance.

CHAPTER 4

Finding Elissa

Undoubtedly only Mamoulian could lay claim to meeting with modernist composer Arnold Schoenberg to discuss a dancing bat in the same week he was meeting with Walter Wanger to determine the chances of getting a new Paramount contract. His next stretch of stage work—three plays for the Theatre Guild, two for other producers, and an avant-garde Schoenberg ballet—usually had him overlapping on two productions at once.

This work also involved three young actresses on their way to movie stardom. That happened quickly for Bette Davis and Elissa Landi, who had starring parts in their plays and got movie contracts immediately. Katharine Hepburn, with a smaller part, had to wait a little longer before reaching stardom. Davis played the first of her string of Southern belles in Lawton Campbell's comedy *Solid South*. Landi, whom Mamoulian found in London, got a Fox contract following her brief run in an adaptation of Ernest Hemingway's *A Farewell to Arms*, and Hepburn played a maid in the US premiere of Ivan Turgenev's comedy *A Month in the Country*.

The Game of Love and Death, a French Revolution drama by Romain Rolland produced by the Theatre Guild in November 1929, brought negative reviews for star Alice Brady under Mamoulian's direction but "made an outstanding fellow out of Mr. Claude Rains," he recalled. (Lionel Stander and Henry Fonda were background players.) Mamoulian assembled the Guild's touring revival of Karel Čapek's *R.U.R.* (Rosson's Universal Robots, the play that introduced the word "robot" to the lexicon) in February 1930 and *A Month in the Country* in March. In April, he worked on his first full-scale classical work: a ballet for the Metropolitan Opera, *The Hand of Fate*, (with a dancer in a bat costume waving his wings) with music by Schoenberg, conducted by Leopold Stokowski.

Mamoulian made his own translation of *A Month in the Country*, a play famed for Stanlislavski's Moscow Art Theatre production of 1909, and reproduced the original sets and costumes. The sexual frankness and complicated romances led czarist authorities to ban the play for decades after Turgenev wrote it in 1848. Mamoulian's version opened in March 1930 after a tryout in Washington, DC; the play ran for just seventy-two performances. One of Hepburn's biographers reported that Mamoulian told the twenty-one-year-old he didn't think she was ready for a large part, so she understudied the ingénue at $30 a week. Five weeks later, shortly before the opening, Hepburn replaced Hortense Alden as Katia, the maid.

Mamoulian didn't get his new contract until June 1930; he jumped into *Die Glückliche Hand* in late March. Schoenberg wrote it in 1913 as the curtain-raising ballet for Igor Stravinsky's *Les Noces*, and as directed by Mamoulian, it was the second half of a double bill with Stravinsky's *Le Sacre du Printemps*. It had a Philadelphia tryout, then ran at the Met for two nights in April.

Lawton Campbell, author of *Solid South*, was a former advertising copywriter from Montgomery, Alabama. He was a Princeton classmate of F. Scott Fitzgerald and had also been acquainted with Fitzgerald's Montgomery-born wife, Zelda. *Solid South* was his third Broadway production after *Madam Malissa* (1924) and a mix of history and contemporary sexiness, *Immoral Isabella?* (1927), about the queen of Spain who sent Christopher Columbus to America. *Solid South*, directed by Mamoulian for producer Alexander McKaig, concerned an aristocratic but impecunious Southern family headed by Major Bruce Follonsby (Richard Bennett); his sister, Geneva (Elizabeth Patterson); and her widowed daughter, Leila Mae (Jessie Royce Landis), mother of Bam (Mary Thayer, then Bette Davis). Rex (Owen Davis Jr.) romances Bam (short for Alabama) when he visits with the intent of buying the plantation and turning the property into a factory.

Mamoulian replaced Thayer with Davis shortly before *Solid South* opened in Chicago in May. It was the twenty-two-year-old's second Broadway assignment after *Broken Dishes* the year before. Bennett's performances were unpredictable, Davis wrote: "When one of the major's windy stories failed to elicit so much as a chuckle from the audience, Bennett stopped dead, walked to the footlights and said, 'I guess I'll have to tell this audience a dirty story to get them to laugh,' then turned and left, leaving me and Elizabeth Patterson alone on the stage."

Solid South is notable mainly for what was considered a comedy scene in 1930. Unreconstructed Confederate gasbags had long been stock figures, but Major Follonsby's murderous racism may make him unique. Mamoulian kept a rambling exchange that sounds as if it might be the kind of racist story told in the back room of a men's lodge in Alabama.

Major Follonsby discusses the number of times he has killed Black Americans, using the familiar slur. The bit ends with the major saying he had a friend who killed eleven, and when the judge told him that if he killed one more, he'd have to stand trial or move to another county, he "killed one mo' and moved!" Mamoulian never directed anything as breathtakingly repulsive again. *Solid South* had only thirty-one performances after opening October 14 at the Lyceum Theatre, after which Davis was signed by a talent scout for Universal Studios.

Mamoulian's glimpse of the Fitzgeralds probably was the opening night party:

> I met Scott Fitzgerald and his wife [Zelda] once . . . I was at a party in New York, a lot of people were there, and the entrance led right into the drawing room. The doorbell rang, and the maid opened the door and I looked to see who was coming in, and there was no one there. I thought, "How strange." Then my eyes went down, and there was this handsome blond man and beautiful woman on all fours in front of the door, and the two of them walked in on all fours. And the hostess began the introductions: Mr. and Mrs. Scott Fitzgerald. They were both drunk.

In June, Mamoulian broke with the Theatre Guild in a dispute over the direction of Sergei Tretyakov's *Roar, China!* He had wanted to direct this epic attack on Western imperialism possibly because he had known Tretyakov, who had been a law student at Moscow University while Mamoulian was there. The Guild board signed Herbert Biberman instead. Mamoulian quickly signed with producer Al Woods, who was planning the stage version of *A Farewell to Arms*. Woods sent Mamoulian to London to scout actors. Just before that, Mamoulian signed the only long-term contract he would get in motion pictures, with Paramount Pictures, for what became his most intensely productive years, encompassing *City Streets, Dr. Jekyll and Mr. Hyde, Love Me Tonight,* and *The Song of Songs* before a loan-out to MGM for *Queen Christina.*

Elissa Landi, congratulating Mamoulian for *Carousel* in 1945, was in a reflective mood. After a career that included Broadway, motion pictures, writing, lecture tours, and a personal life that now included a stable second marriage and a daughter, she wrote, "One very simple thing runs through my mind at this moment: A desire to express the fact that I am conscious of all that has happened to me because one summer day I read a part for you."

The part was Catherine Barkley, the nurse heroine of *A Farewell to Arms*. Mamoulian spent the first two weeks of July 1930 auditioning actors in London, although Woods wanted him to sign Herbert Marshall and Edna Best for the leading roles. Marshall, a World War I veteran who had lost part of his right leg, could have brought realism to the character of Lt. Frederic Henry, who sustains a leg injury during fighting in Italy. Woods likely wanted them because they were an established star team in London but would be fresh faces on Broadway. Seymour Obermer instead suggested Landi, a twenty-five-year-old red-haired, green-eyed stunner who had already published two novels and was estranged from her barrister husband. She had a dubious Austrian heritage—in 1915, her mother Karoline published a book in which she claimed to be the youngest granddaughter of Austrian emperor Franz Josef—a childhood in Vancouver, and a stepfather who was an Italian count. "She was really complicated, and at the bottom of it all, she led with her heart and lost out most of the time because of it," says her daughter, Caroline Thomas. "But then, that was what was so great about her, too."

The Hapsburg connection, she says, was not true, but was easy for her grandmother to invent because of the complicated love lives of Austrian royalty. "That's where a lot of conjecture happens. There were two possible candidates, one a lot less likely than the other. And Empress Elizabeth was not the type to sleep around, but 'sleep' she did, or there wouldn't have been so many legitimate children."

Landi's combination of beauty, intelligence and distant claim to nobility captured Mamoulian instantly. He cabled Woods: "Don't dismiss Elissa

Landi lightly unless you have a real star. We should grab her. She's well known in London. Pretty, has great SA and charm, very clever. Read Catherine beautifully." Marshall and Best were committed to a production of Ferenc Molnár's *The Swan*, so Woods decided to find a leading man in New York and accept Mamoulian's endorsement. Laurence Stallings adapted the novel for the stage.

As Hemingway's first bestseller when it was published in 1929, and the first of his works to be dramatized, *A Farewell to Arms* generated high expectations. Catherine Barkley combines traits of Agnes von Kirowsky, a nurse Hemingway, an ambulance driver, fell in love with after he was wounded in Italy in 1918 (she rejected his marriage proposal), and his first wife, Katherine. Lt. Henry is an idealized version of the author. Disillusioned reflections on the human cost of World War I combat began on stage with Maxwell Anderson's and Stallings's *What Price Glory?* (1924) and continued with *All Quiet on the Western Front* (1930). Still, that didn't make *Farewell* easy to adapt. "As you know," Mamoulian wrote Obermer, "any attempt at putting a novel on the stage is at best a most difficult and rather ungrateful task."

Stallings's adaptation limited the warfare to offstage explosions. He focused on the Barkley–Henry relationship and Hemingway's language. The novel used a demure blank underscore to stand in for "shit," "fuck," "balls" and "cocksucker." Stallings couldn't use those. He kept another famous line from the novel, when Henry asks an officious nurse, "Miss Van Campen, did you ever know a man who tried to disable himself by kicking himself in the scrotum?" He then explains, "It's the nearest sensation to jaundice," which he has and has extended through his heavy drinking. As in the novel, Catherine's baby is stillborn, and she dies from hemorrhaging. The play opened September 22, 1930, running for just twenty-four performances.

Stirling Bowen, in the *Wall Street Journal*, complained of a Mamoulian extravagance:

> There are many people who do not object to the banging of blank cartridges, in an ordinary thriller, who will find the excessive caliber of Mr. Mamoulian's pistols, to say nothing of heavy artillery, unpleasantly distracting. When Lt. Frederic Henry is to be injured in the first act, in the street just outside

the door of Medical Staff headquarters on the Italian front, Mr. Mamoulian touches off a shell that shakes the sturdy walls of the National Theatre. If it were customary for first night audiences to come armed, Mr. Mamoulian's fire doubtless would have been returned, as constituting a general attack on everyone present.

Glenn Anders, who played Henry, was a Guild regular who had portrayed Worthington Smythe in *Strange Interlude*. Mamoulian's intense focus on Landi may have kept him from noticing that Anders in military uniform didn't come off quite as ruggedly masculine as Hemingway had intended. Arthur Pollock, the critic of the *Brooklyn Eagle*, zeroed in: "To put into the role of the young soldier-hero Hemingway created the thumbsucking, infantile Glenn Anders would be amusing if he were not so offensive to the recollection of the novel." That was a cruel way of outing Anders, later known as a gay icon for his role as the sexually ambiguous villain George Grisby in Orson Welles's 1948 film *The Lady from Shanghai*.

Hemingway noticed the conundrum, too. After the play closed, he wrote Archibald MacLeish, "I've finally solved the mystery of why there were fifteen curtain calls the night *Farewell to Arms* opened, and yet it only ran three weeks. They must have all been by people who wanted to sleep with either Mr. Anders or Miss Landi."

CHAPTER 5

Those Darn Cats

Elissa Landi signed a contract with Fox in late October 1930 and immediately left for California. She found herself missing Mamoulian quickly:

> Since I have met you it is very hard to know what is right. There is what you want and she is battling with what I am. I am lonely. To write you that is perhaps selfish, not to write it is probably British. To tell you I want you here and that sunny California is gloomy because it does not contain you is (from a certain angle) selfish—and self-centered in that it describes *my* needs.

Mamoulian arrived in November. In Chicago, he found himself a traveling companion of Paramount production chief B. P. Schulberg. He told variations of this freewheeling anecdote many times, always beginning with Schulberg barking,

> "Do you play poker?"
> "Well, I know a little bit about it."
> "Good! Come on over!"
> A game started. All I can tell you is, that on this, my first trip to California, I never saw a single inch of scenery. They kept the shade down and the poker game was continuous—lunches and dinners were brought into the compartment.
> Finally, when the train got to the state of California, Mrs. Schulberg came into the compartment and asked reproachfully, "Rouben, don't you want to see the orange groves?"
> I said, "Of course I do!"

So Schulberg flipped the shade up and said, "Take a look." I saw neat rows of beautiful dark green trees spotted with oranges passing by the window.

I had just gotten a short glimpse of them when Schulberg pulled the shade down and said, "Your deal!"

In California with a studio contract, Mamoulian found an apartment in the Hollywood Hills. The following year, he moved his parents in with him. He and Landi gave all outward impressions of functioning as a couple during his first three years in California. He took up horseback riding under her encouragement. One of Landi's letters from a year later portrays that life:

Yes I have a "pose," I must admit. It's the "pose" of "leave me alone," I want to be alone, please! Of course I have friends, mainly RM and the Massie [Margel] Glucks and John van Druten and Auriol Lee. . . . My publicity is, "Landi doesn't care about her appearance. But she wears severe clothes with an air and doesn't look crazy in flat-heeled shoes." RM scolds me for not dressing up enough in "pretty" things; he's still got the lesbian scare in his mind.

But when I see all the script girls suddenly appearing in sweaters and berets and tweeds, with the sweaters tucked inside their skirts and dead severe clothes, I don't feel I'm so silly! I have the "pose" of no makeup, too. And the consequence is I look 18 among all those faded sophisticates.

By December 1930, Paramount sent Mamoulian Dashiell Hammett's synopsis "After School," which told the story of a sixteen-year-old girl whose stepfather, Cooley, is a bootlegger. She abets him in the murder of Blackie, a rival mobster, by disposing of his pistol and is sent to a reform school. Cooley later pulls her boyfriend Slim into the bootlegging trade, where he becomes known as the Roscoe Kid. Out of reform school, the girl helps the Kid escape from a murder trap set by another gangster. Adapted by Max Marcin with a screenplay by Oliver H. P. Garrett, that treatment became *City Streets*, starring Gary Cooper and Sylvia Sidney.

"I liked it very much, because I thought I'd do a gangster film that would be different, would have style," Mamoulian said years later. At the time, he thought quite little of it. "The story is trash, but you may enjoy the treatment," he wrote Paul Horgan; to Robert Sisk, a Guild publicist, he mentioned, "The story was planned originally for Clara Bow, and when

[she] dropped out, I did not want to go on with it. I did it, finally, after three days' coaching by the Paramount executives, and did it as a favor to the corporation. It was a very hard job to make the story appear either fresh or plausible."

Three days of arm-twisting by studio executives reminding him of his contract probably was closer to the truth, although he was certainly disappointed that Bow wasn't to be the lead. Bow had been the studio's biggest female star of the 1920s, but her penchant for scandals involving men and money began to hurt her at the box office. Schulberg planned this film as Bow's final chance at a comeback, co-starring with Cooper, one of her former lovers (Sidney became Schulberg's mistress when filming ended). To Sisk, Mamoulian made no apologies for his sound tricks or the clumsy appearance of two china cats while a murder was planned: "There isn't a slight doubt in my mind that if the story of *City Streets* had been told in a straightforward manner, it would have been a deadly bore and even a lousier picture than it is now."

Cooper as the Kid, Mamoulian acknowledged, "was mostly personality. He had great charm and great charisma." Sidney is best known for a string of gritty 1930s classics, including Fritz Lang's *Fury* (1936) and William Wyler's *Dead End* (1937). Guy Kibbee, a comic actor, was cast as Pop Cooley.

Gangster pictures had been a staple since *Underworld* in 1927, and their clichés perfected in 1932 in *Scarface*, with Paul Muni as a character based on Al Capone. Although *City Streets* has four murders, none are shown explicitly. It was a way of keeping a high violence quotient without raising the ire of state censor boards, who had the power to snip films into feeble reels of celluloid. The film is also notable for having a woman as the central character and for eschewing machine guns.

Mamoulian depicts the deadly practices of the Prohibition-era beer racket in the opening montage, when Pop's gang muscles another bootlegger out of the business. He indicates his death with a monogrammed derby (RZ, as in Rouben Zachary) floating in a river. Pop lights his cigar and winks at Nan, who is sitting at a soda counter. The next scene opens with Nan squinting as she aims a pistol at the amusement park shooting gallery where her boyfriend, the Kid, works. She tries to persuade him to join Pop's enterprise: "It isn't work. You just go around an' collect from the saps who do."

Mamoulian, Sylvia Sidney, and Gary Cooper filming a scene from *City Streets*, February 1931.

Blackie is the next to die, since he's been hitting Agnes (Wynne Gibson), a woman Big Fellow Maskal (Paul Lukas) fancies. Pop's real incentive, though, is that Big Fellow has offered him Blackie's bootlegging territory, since Pop has a better disposition.

Pop enlists Agnes for his alibi. He mentions how difficult it is to get a long ash on his cigar, and she knows exactly what she has to do when he walks out. Before that, he quickly and indirectly gets her assent. Mamoulian's playful cross-cutting with close-ups of the cat statues is the film's best-known segment:

> POP (with an ironic smile): Anything wrong, sweetheart?
> AGNES (venomously): He better stop slappin' me around or he'll get his someday.
> CU WHITE CAT (Pop's voice, sweetly): Suppose he don't live that long?
> CU OF BLACK CAT (Aggie's voice): Hm?
> CU OF WHITE CAT (Pop's voice): It'd be all right by you, wouldn't it?
> LARGER CU BLACK CAT (Silent)
> LARGE CU WHITE CAT (Pop's voice): I don't hear you sayin' no.

Richard Watts Jr., in the New York *Herald Tribune*, ridiculed *City Streets* for being "all decked out in camera angles and symbolism." As for the statues, he wrote, "In addition, there are moments in which that constant use of pictorial symbols, of surf or statuary or anything else available for the camera, with the hint that they possess some profound import, results in unintentional amusement rather than impressiveness."

Sisk wrote Mamoulian, "I didn't like the symbolism of the crackleware cats . . . Forgive me for saying it, but I think this was too obvious for intelligent audiences and meaningless to the mug element." Alexander McKaig was moved to write, "I felt it was open to the charge of cheap and easy symbolism simply lugged in." Another friend "said he agreed with me and said also that it was the very natural reaction of an imaginative mind, intoxicated by its first contact with new and unlimited possibilities and means of making points. He said, in fact, it was almost the inevitable reaction."

For Blackie's murder, Mamoulian showed Pop's shadow, enhanced by a powerful spotlight, creeping behind him. He didn't invent that effect—

Lewis Milestone used it in *New York Nights* (1929), in which a shadow figure is shown pulling the trigger. Nan is standing under a lamppost, with a silk scarf made into a sling, since Pop had told her, "If you have to break an arm to get there." Three revolver shots sound, and Pop hands his pistol to Nan with the instructions, "In the river." The long cigar ash, the result of Agnes's cautious puffing, clears Pop with the police. Thinking she'll be acquitted, Nan takes the rap, but is sent to prison for a year. When the Kid, now in Pop's mob, visits, Mamoulian worked out improvised dialogue, ending with Nan remarking of the Kid's fancy new wardrobe, "Has the circus come to town?" as they talk through a wire mesh screen. After the Kid tells her he's joined Pop in the illicit beer business, Mamoulian's script dwells on audio effects, specifying that the bell rings "as if piercing through Nan's heart."

Back in her cell, Nan mentally replays their conversation as well as things Pop has told her. Voice-overs were not common in films at the time. Mamoulian accomplished the effect by shooting the scene with all the voices on a single channel: "Today we would dub it," he recalled. "So while we were photographing a silent shot of Sylvia Sidney, all around her were the other actors speaking the lines allotted to them, as well as property men making the necessary noises, ringing the bell, shutting the gate."

For the finale, Big Fellow—who, as Lukas portrays him, has a European accent that's difficult to place—calls a cohort, McCoy (William Boyd) to tell him not to kill the Kid, but all McCoy hears over the phone is the sound of a pistol shot. Big Fellow is sprawled on the floor; Agnes tosses her pistol into the room to implicate Nan. Both the Kid and McCoy vie to take over the gang; close-ups of the gangster's suspicious faces as the Kid is talking indicate whose side they're on. The Kid has an entirely different plan. He calls Nan: "Meet me outside Pop's in five minutes." Three thugs get in the back seat of the Kid's Chrysler. He barrels between a speeding train and a cliff, telling them they can't shoot him, since he's driving, and if they shoot Nan, "you'll get the cliff." The mobsters toss their guns out the windows.

Originally, the picture was supposed to end with a long shot of the highway as the car sped away. Mamoulian dipped into symbolism with "a flock of birds, wings lit by the rising sun" circling in the sky. The Kid turns on the car radio and the overture to Wagner's *Die Meistersinger* plays.

Again, a story about victory over the studio: "That's what it calls for. When the head of the Paramount music department [Roy Finston] said, 'You can't do that because it's over the head of the audience, but I have a couple of young boys who will write you better music than Wagner,' then I just took my script and said goodbye. Then he stopped me and got all red in the face and said, 'Forgive me, forgive me.'" That's not the reason *Meistersinger* plays, though. It's a shout-out to Rochester and the Eastman School. The Kid has tuned in the Sunday afternoon broadcast of the *Stromberg Carlson Hour*; the *Meistersinger* overture was the theme tune of the Rochester Philharmonic and Lucile Bigelow, now married to Guy Fraser Harrison, was the orchestra's harpist. "Lucile and I nearly fell off our seats when we heard it!" Harrison wrote.

Landi was tiring of Mamoulian's temperament. She began to refer to him to her mother as the Prehistoric Animal, or the PA:

> The PA is deliberately in love; he is grown-up. Yet he doesn't give himself any more than I do. So with me to myself, he comes first—to himself. Because he has no illusions, he doesn't have to defend himself by finding fault. . . . He is plainly good for me. For the first time in my years, I feel a pupil. I do not hold the floor. On the other hand, he says, frankly, "What you have taught me is amazing. What *would* I do without you? He was on his way to becoming a softy . . . I jeered it out of him, yes *jeered* it. Now he swims every morning and rides with me on Sundays and drives his car with a dash, and takes sun-baths and has a tan. . . .
>
> I've taught him all the bits and pieces I know, of music, glands, intestines, insides of cars, cooking, food values, English poetry, furniture, painting, literary style, German mythology and the care of babies—and cats. I've shown him he was an autocrat, an achievement-snob, prejudiced, spoilt by women and intolerant. He went for me because he said I forgot to powder my nose and manicure my nails; I returned the compliment by saying he was physically unattractive to me anyway because, for all his six-feet of height and broad shoulders, his skin was bad and he looked like a champignon . . .
>
> The PA flattered me by coming to me with all his problems, both mental and physical, until I feel *City Streets* is my godchild and his own present state of health my personal achievement.

Mamoulian took her to the Los Angeles premiere on April 18:

> At 6:30 Mrs. Massie and Margel appear—then the PA then Mr. and Mrs. Dudley Nichols. This is my first Hollywood party (!!) I give them a "help yourself" buffet dinner: Bouillon, hot roast turkey, green peas, salad . . . strawberries and cream, chocolate cake and various cookies and coffee. At 9, we sally forth to see the PA's *City Streets* . . . Altogether the evening is an unqualified success. *City Streets* properly cut and edited is a grand picture. I really love it, and honestly think you will. This time, he has something "new" in treatment.

By early May 1931, Mamoulian was preparing the first draft for *The Story of San Michele*, based on Swedish doctor Axel Munthe's rambling memoir of his time in a villa on the island of Capri. Two weeks later, that project screeched to a halt. "We suddenly discovered at this late date . . . that we do not own the book," he wrote McKaig. "All that Paramount has had in regard to it were verbal promises, but nothing on paper. So when Dr. Munthe suddenly came forth with a demand of $200,000 for his book, an obviously impossible figure—the deal was called off. So now I am stranded and have to find another story to do." It didn't take long. On June 11, he wrote Harrison that he'd decided to direct a new version of Robert Louis Stevenson's *Dr. Jekyll and Mr. Hyde*: "I am rather excited about this tale and I think it will be good fun making it."

The preproduction of *Jekyll* would be the last time Mamoulian was eager to jump between Broadway and Hollywood; after that, his returns to the stage were the result of film work drying up. He negotiated with the Theatre Guild to direct a new comedy scheduled for that fall, *Reunion in Vienna*, by Robert Sherwood for Alfred Lunt and Lynn Fontanne. When that foundered over Mamoulian's demand for at least $1,000 a week during rehearsals, he made overtures to direct Martin Flavin's *Achilles Had a Heel*, starring Paul Robeson, for Alexander McKaig, and S. N. Behrman's *Love Story*, produced by Kenneth Macgowan. *Achilles* fell apart when Robeson withdrew, and the *Jekyll* shooting schedule precluded *Love Story*.

Visceral and sensual, with occasional forays into unwieldy symbolism, Mamoulian's *Dr. Jekyll and Mr. Hyde* hardly resembles a fallback project.

Fredric March as Mr. Hyde, Miriam Hopkins as Ivy in *Dr. Jekyll and Mr. Hyde*, 1932.

Fredric March won an Academy Award for Best Actor in a Leading Role—a rare win in the horror genre—and was the breakthrough film for Miriam Hopkins, the Georgia-born former chorus girl who played prostitute and singer Ivy Pearson, the victim of Mr. Hyde's lust and violence. Hopkins's fluttery vulnerability has proven as durable as March's sneering grotesquerie. Mamoulian considered the film to be a triumph of technology and his own on-the-fly decisions, although the craftsmen behind the special effects never credited the director in return.

Scripted by Samuel Hoffenstein and Percy Heath, the pre-Code nudity and coarse Hyde have long made horror fans prefer Mamoulian's version to the 1941 film directed by Victor Fleming at MGM. In the procession of *Jekyll/Hyde* film adaptations going back to 1909, Mamoulian's comes after the 1920 silent version that starred John Barrymore, but the story is permanently yoked to MGM's remake starring Spencer Tracy.

MGM bought the rights to both the 1931 film and its underlying 1912 stage play, so no two films of Robert Louis Stevenson's story are as similar. Both have laboratories strewn with bubbling concoctions, a contrast between Jekyll's virtuous fiancée (Rose Hobart/Lana Turner) and Ivy Pearson (Hopkins/Ingrid Bergman), long discussions about man's dual nature, a dusting of theology, a descent into the London demimonde of the 1880s, and a Mr. Hyde who bounds about like a gymnast when he's not hurtling down foggy streets. Mamoulian thought little of Fleming's version: "Strengthens my faith in myself. Bad and stupid copy."

Mamoulian made his at a high tide of studio horror that included *Dracula* (1931) starring Bela Lugosi and *Frankenstein* (1931) with Boris Karloff as the monster. Mamoulian has Hyde in a simian wig and makeup with jutting teeth. But Fleming's version was the beginning of a Mr. Hyde not grotesque in appearance but as the ribald half of a split personality. He's stayed that way ever since. In a 1968 TV version, Jack Palance's makeup merely extends his forehead a little and gives him a unibrow. Audiences expect at least a little makeup on the character. A freewheeling 1990 TV adaptation with Michael Caine has a pasty, bald Hyde. In Stephen Frears's *Mary Reilly* (1996), John Malkovich doesn't outwardly change as Mr. Hyde, although during his transformation, special effects add what appears to be a humanoid attempting to escape from his torso.

With shots of a fireplace early on and a bubbling cauldron throughout the picture, Mamoulian signals that Jekyll is headed straight to the flames of hell for daring to tamper with the cosmic order. The coolly intelligent Hobart was not impressed: "The only thing that really bothered me about the way he directed was that I thought he really dotted his i's and crossed his t's, because when he finished a scene he would always have something symbolic of the scene to finish up with. That was really overdoing it." Hobart had just played Julie in Frank Borzage's film of *Liliom*, and wrote of her character, "the fiancée is probably one of the dullest ingénue parts ever written."

In Mamoulian's version of events, Schulberg had Irving Pichel, a middle-aged character actor (later a director) in mind for Jekyll. That's in keeping with Stevenson's novella, in which the character is a respectable Victorian gent of about fifty, "with something of a stylish cast perhaps, but every mark of capacity and kindness." Mamoulian claimed it was his idea to cast March, who was thirty-three. "I had never met March but I had seen his film called *Laughter* (1930). So [Schulberg] said, 'Are you crazy? He is a light comedian.' I said, 'So far he is, but he will be perfect for this. Perfect for Jekyll and I will be responsible for Hyde.'"

Hopkins, at twenty-eight, was just a few months out of her latest Broadway play and had worked in films at Paramount's Astoria studio (including Ernst Lubitsch's *The Smiling Lieutenant*) for just a year when she met Mamoulian. Penciled in as Ivy, she didn't think the part up to her standard, going by his recollection:

> She said, "I don't want to play it. I want to be the other girl, the good girl." I said, "Are you crazy? Look, Miriam, the other girl is nothing. This girl will be a hit. You play this and you will be a hit. I guarantee it." She said, "No, no." So after arguing for a while, I said, "All right. You make it very easy for me because any actress would give her right arm to play Ivy. You have the other girl, it is yours." She starts walking out and says, "Now, wait a minute. . . . You really think I should play Ivy?" Anyway, she took it, and of course it made her a star.

The subjective camera that begins with Jekyll at the keys of his pipe organ, and the organ, were not in the first script Mamoulian read in June 1931; they are in the next draft of early August—an effective audio touch. Given

Mamoulian's penchant for Rochester shout-outs, the pipe organ is likely a reference to the one in George Eastman's home.

Mamoulian has his camera look into a "mirror" while March appears on the other side of the glass to straighten his wardrobe before heading to his lecture. He leaves no doubt that Jekyll is saintly. He takes on an operation in a charity ward that delays his dinner appointment with fiancée Muriel; he also appears Christ-like as he encourages a crippled girl on crutches to walk. Before that, he delivers a lecture on the nature of man: "Man is not truly one, but two!" He advocates better living through chemistry—by taking certain substances, the evil side, once it escapes, will no longer be a burden to mankind.

Jekyll also has a more urgent suppression: marriage to Muriel. "Marry me now! . . . I can't wait any longer. We shall go to Devon for our honeymoon and live on love and strawberries and the sight of the sea." As they kiss, Mamoulian's camera pans down to a fountain, where two water lilies appear to be embracing (Hobart wasn't kidding about "overdoing it"). Muriel must hold off, since her father, Brigadier Gen. Sir Danvers Carew (Halliwell Hobbes), wants the nuptials to take place eight months later on his own wedding anniversary.

With the sexual tension established, it's time to meet Ivy. Jekyll sees her on his walk home with a colleague, Dr. John Lanyon (Holmes Herbert), when a large man is slugging her. The draft script had a passing Cockney identifying the man as "one of Ivy's customers trying to swindle her." Jekyll takes her to her room in the boardinghouse on Diadem Court. Ivy has a bruise on her leg, so after telling her that she mustn't wear so tight a garter, he advises her to rest. That sets off her playful striptease that has them both giggling.

The sequence likely has not been seen in full since the film's original release on December 31, 1931. Judicious snips by state censor boards and cuts mandated by the Production Code for the 1936 rerelease linger today. In 1941, MGM suppressed the film to the point of extinction when it bought up all available prints when its version was released. The full sequence may now exist only in Mamoulian's handwriting.

Ivy is getting into bed. Here's the shot list from Mamoulian's script:

She takes off a garter with a chuckle, and throws it at Jekyll.
Close-up of Jekyll's face as the garter falls at his feet.

Ivy takes off the other garter—throws it.
Close-up of Jekyll's feet as the garter lands—his cane sends it back.
Ivy catches it, puts it back on a bare leg.
Takes off other stocking.
   The cut parts:
Stands up—takes off blouse.
Lets shirt fall down.
Turns her back to Jekyll—throws it at him.
Gets under cover of bed—uses it as screen (silhouette)
   Back to the restored parts:
Slips off her petticoat—gets in bed—pulls cover up to her neck—smiles.
JEKYLL: How's the pain now?

"It is not a nude scene," Mamoulian insisted. "You never see an inch of her, except for the leg at the end, and that's what made the scene so attractively erotic." Hopkins clutches a blanket, her right leg swinging like a metronome arm over the side of the bed, whispering "Come back soon, won't ya? Sooon!"

Lanyon lectures Jekyll, reminding him that he's engaged. The doctor responds, "Can a man dying of thirst forget water? And do you know what would happen to that thirst if it were denied water?" After this struggle between conscience and primal instincts, Jekyll spends the next three days and nights in his laboratory to see whether he can "separate the two natures." He mixes up a clear potion. After a quick glimpse of a skeleton to remind himself of his mortality and a dashed-off farewell note to Muriel in case he dies in the attempt, he quaffs his formula in a single gulp. This sets off the first of the film's seven transformation scenes—five from Jekyll to Hyde, and two from Hyde to Jekyll.

March grimaces as streaks and shadows cross his face while his hands and forearms darken. This was the work of cinematographer Karl Struss, who invented the technique for the 1925 MGM production of *Ben-Hur* in the scenes where Christ healed lepers. It was straightforward in execution, involving makeup changes and colored filters. Struss recalled that Mamoulian didn't have any input:

> It was done by using a red filter on strong red makeup so that when you photographed red with a red filter, the object was white. In front of the lens

you put a two-inch-square red "A" filter that had the same speed as a green "B" filter so that when you went from one exposure to the others, the density remained the same. The filters were little gelatins hooked together in a little holder with the red on top and the green below. They were done as close to the two-inch focal length as you could get then.

When the transition started, it would slowly change and with the green filter you could see the image, the face, become quite dark, with lines and so forth, depending on how much makeup we had put on in the first place. I controlled the makeup with the makeup man.

But Mamoulian insisted that the rest of the effects, including the spinning camera, were his ideas alone:

To capture the feeling of Jekyll's vertigo I had the camera revolve around on its axis 360 degrees. One cameraman had to sit on the floor, and the man handling the focus—luckily a very small guy who looked like a jockey—was tied with ropes on top of the camera box, so that he could control it from the top. Because the camera revolved, the whole set had to be lighted, which was a real tough job.

[For the sounds of the transformation] I said, "Let's photograph light. Light of a candle," in various frequencies of intensity directly transforming light into sound.

Then I said, "Let's record the impact of a gong, cut off the impact, run it backwards." But—it all lacked rhythm. [He had drums brought in, but] finally, in exasperation, I got this wonderful idea. I ran up and down the stairway for a few minutes, and then I put a microphone to my heart and said, "Record it."

And that's what's used as the basic rhythm in the scene—the thumping noise which is like no drum on earth because it's the heartbeat, my own heartbeat.

Studio publicity claimed instead that the heartbeat was March's. As the room spins, Jekyll also sees images of himself begging Muriel to marry him quickly and Ivy's coo: "Come back! Come back!" It's back to a real mirror, where Hyde sees himself for the first time. Mamoulian always said that for Hyde's prototype,

I didn't take a monster but our common ancestor, the Neanderthal man. Mr. Hyde is a replica of the Neanderthal man. He is not a monster or animal of another species, but primeval man—closest to the earth. I explained to Freddie that Hyde is not evil to start with, that he is primitive like an animal. To an animal there is no evil. A tiger attacks to eat and sheds blood, but we don't call that evil . . . But just as Jekyll gets gradually corrupted as he carries on this experiment, so does Hyde. To me the most attractive person in the story is the first Mr. Hyde, full of exuberance and joy and freedom.

This puts Mamoulian's version at odds with Stevenson's story, which is simply about the vanity of separating good and evil. Mamoulian's interpretation puts a post-Freudian spin on a pre-Freudian fantasy. Exuberant, Hyde addresses his reflection: "Free! Free at last! Free to dare and to do! Mad, twaddle, eh, Lanyon? Eh, Carew? Hypocrites! Deniers of life!" After that, to show the destruction of his soul, Hyde's face begins to melt in each successive transformation. This was the makeup Hobart recalled: "So they just put liquid rubber on his face. . . . And when they took it off, his face came with it. He was in the hospital for two or three weeks; he was lucky he wasn't ruined for life."

Jekyll returns to Muriel to beg her to marry him. She's headed off on a month-long trip to Bath with her father. Poole suggests that Jekyll take in some London nightlife, but Victorian propriety keeps Jekyll from acceding. Another chug of the magic brew, though, and Hyde is happily out in the rain—a favorite scene of Mamoulian's. "I had it raining very hard. The average Englishman would have opened an umbrella, but Hyde not only enjoys the rain, he takes his hat off and luxuriates in the rain falling on his face—like a young, innocent animal."

Eager for sex, Hyde heads to Ivy's boardinghouse. Her landlady, Mrs. Hawkins (Tempe Pigott) directs him to the Variety Music Hall, where Ivy is performing. Hyde's sadism isn't quickly limned in detail in the finished film. Mamoulian, lover of cats, had a scene in which Hyde dropped a kitten into a river. In another unused scene, Hyde stole the cane of a blind beggar, leaving him in the middle of a street. In the finished film, he merely trips a waiter at the music hall.

Hyde orders the waiter to summon "that wench in black," and Ivy joins him at his table. She is startled at his appearance, conceding, "Ya ain't no beauty," and is repelled by his touch. Ivy may be fearful, but Hopkins was not. Even in a two-shot with a garishly made-up March, the five-foot-two Hopkins moved in on his camera angle with a linebacker's aplomb. Hobart recalled: "I used to . . . go on the set and hear about her endlessly from Fredric March. She was upstaging everyone, all of the time. I don't even think she thought about it anymore because she was so used to doing it."

Mamoulian's solution was to rig a dummy camera for the scene at the music-hall table. "Mamoulian had set up a camera out on the floor," Hobart said. "They were facing each other and as the scene started, Miriam managed to edge up so that she was facing the camera and Freddie almost had his back to it. When the scene was finished, the word 'Cut' came from behind the curtain at the back of the box and Miriam whirled around and said, 'Is this where the camera was?' and Mamoulian answered, 'Yes, that's where the camera was.'"

Ivy succumbing to Hyde's brutality are Hopkins's finest scenes, especially when he demands she sing her "Champagne Ivy" song. In the space of a very few minutes, Ivy had to show attraction, repulsion, and tremulous fear and be entirely sympathetic. She's more realistic being fearful than she is in the music hall with a Cockney accent. Mamoulian returns to diagonal wipes to contrast Ivy, receiving unexpected money from a remorseful Jekyll, with Jekyll's explaining to Muriel that he's been ill. He finally gets Carew's approval for an earlier wedding, although his future father-in-law still thinks Jekyll "too flighty, too impatient."

The concession sends Jekyll into a paroxysm of joy. This would seem to bury Hyde forever. Fat chance—Ivy turns up to thank Jekyll for the money. She tries to return it when he tells her someone told him she needed it. Thinking it probably was Hyde, she shows him the whip marks on her back. He promises her that he'll see to it that Hyde never returns. Ivy grows increasingly hysterical; the scene was Hopkins's favorite. She recalled saying, "Well, I don't know. Forgive me for saying this, but this is . . . I want it to play itself because it's a terribly emotional thing, into deep hysterics at the end but starting with quiet pleading."

On the first take, Hopkins faltered after her first six lines. Mamoulian quickly gave her a second take:

And I was just sobbing like this and a wreck on the floor holding onto [March's] shoes at the end, and that was the scene printed. And it was done in one take. . . . So it was worth his time to have it done that way, and that's why [Mamoulian's] great, because if it hadn't been good in four, five takes or something, then he would have said, 'Wait a minute.' But he wanted to see first what I wanted to bring to him, without having his ego so great by saying, 'Just a minute, what's she trying to do?'"

By this point, Jekyll can't control his transformations. On a park bench at night, after an act of nature's cruelty—a black cat attacks a nightingale—he becomes a decrepit, gray-haired Hyde. He runs off to Ivy's flat to murder her, then takes a potion in front of Lanyon to prove what he's done and confess his crime. Mamoulian put three-inch lifts under Herbert's chair: "Jekyll is always photographed from above, looking up into the camera—an abject supplicant. Lanyon is always photographed from below, looking down at the camera—a stern and uncompromising judge."

After Lanyon's judgment of blasphemy, a contrite Jekyll confesses to God: "this I did not intend. I saw a light—I did not see where it was leading. I have trespassed on your domain. I have gone farther than man should go. Forgive me! Help me!"

He stops by the Carew mansion to ask Muriel's forgiveness and bid farewell. "I dare not ever touch you—in this world or the next. I must give you up." He is barely out of the house before he becomes a decaying Hyde who bursts through the French doors and tries to strangle Muriel before sprinting back to his lab for a fatal confrontation with police. Mamoulian's camera, lingering on a boiling cauldron over flames, leaves no doubt of Jekyll's destination.

By this time, Mamoulian had turned his back on Broadway, going by a letter to McKaig: "My greatest personal achievements since my arrival in California are swimming and driving a car. I have a very comely-looking Ford roadster which I can steer down Hollywood Boulevard without running over dogs, cats or even just pedestrians. I also own a dark blue bathing suit and can dive into a pool without swallowing chlorinized water." The success of the horror film set in London allowed him full rein for his next project, a musical fantasy set in France.

CHAPTER 6

Isn't it Romantic?

"The story is very slight and fluffy," Mamoulian wrote Lawrence Langner before heading into preproduction on *Love Me Tonight*, "but I have a few crazy ideas about music and the treatment of sound which may prove effective."

They were very effective, aided by a collaboration with Richard Rodgers and Lorenz Hart, some elements from *Porgy*, "smart" Broadway patter, and sight gags still in use from silent movie days. In Rodgers's recollection, *Love Me Tonight* was one of his happiest movie experiences. "We got along wonderfully with him. We had ideas we thought were progressive, and we loved his ideas." Mamoulian "was the fairhaired boy and they were perfectly willing to let him spend whatever he wanted to. And they were right."

In his pioneering study of romantic comedies, James Harvey wrote, "The [Ernst] Lubitsch films preceding it, even *The Love Parade* (1929), are chamber films, essentially small-scale and intimate. *Love Me Tonight* is a kind of bravura effusion. That bravura element ran through all of Mamoulian's films . . . Mamoulian is a spectacularist; Lubitsch, the erstwhile 'Griffith of Europe,' is not."

Director and scholar Mark Cousins sees the influence of René Clair on *Love Me Tonight*—specifically, from Clair's 1931 film *Le Million*, in which everyone except the winner of a million-franc lottery bursts into song, and *À Nous la Liberté*, in which a close-up "of a quivering bell-shaped flower is combined with the sound of a singing voice, as if the flower is literally in song. Such metaphorical use of sound freed directors from sonic literalness and clearly led to Mamoulian's yapping dogs" (with the three spell-casting aunts).

Mamoulian only ever credited himself as an influence. *Love Me Tonight* has none of Clair's cynicism in *À Nous la Liberté*, which shows two ex-convicts faking their way into respectable society. One of the special moments in *Love Me Tonight* consists of a vase that makes an exploding sound as it shatters on the floor, signifying the fall of the old social order to set up "The Son-of-a-Gun Is Nothing But a Tailor." "I can't remember anyone using sound stylistically to express not the reality of sound but the psychological meaning of it," Mamoulian recalled. "Well, the audience delights in it because they know what it means—it's the effect."

Critic Tom Milne, comparing *Love Me Tonight* to two Lubitsch musicals, *The Love Parade* (1929) and *Monte Carlo* (1930), praised Mamoulian's skill as "a deft, airy legerdemain which makes the famed Lubitsch touch fall like a dull thud." That's not quite accurate; Lubitsch lurks in the background. He'd also had a duet sung in separate locations, as Mamoulian does with "Love Me Tonight." When Jeanette MacDonald takes off after Maurice Chevalier's train on horseback, it's a riff on the ending of *Monte Carlo*.

Mamoulian had two versions of how he came to direct this film. In one, "Zukor said Paramount was on the verge of bankruptcy" (it was, briefly going into receivership the following year), "and would I do it as a favor to the company. And then he started crying. I mean, crying. Well, you know, I'm just a man, especially then I was too young to realize, although I had a hunch, he was putting it on. But still it moves you when an old man like this starts crying. So I said, 'You make it impossible for me to say no,' so I was in."

In another version, he put his involvement in more businesslike terms: Zukor "said they had Chevalier and MacDonald under contract and they'd been paying them $5,000 a week for ten weeks already. They had no property, and would I do a musical with them." Playwrights Paul Armont and Léopold Marchand had an unproduced play they were trying to sell the studio. Mamoulian met Marchand the following night. "I told him I'm supposed to do this and I can't find a story. He said, 'Well, I had a draft of a play once. You could make a musical. However, I don't think the studio would like that—it's sort of a fairy tale.'" Marchand was a stunning character. Mamoulian recalled:

> A fat man, a bon vivant, a terrific gastronome and gourmet, and the greatest authority on wines I have ever known. He said, "I have an idea," and he

wrote it down on a long sheet of yellow paper: a tailor falls in love with a princess who lives in a chateau in the south of France; he arrives to collect a debt, pretending to be an aristocrat; she falls in love with him, then discovers he's a tailor, and they get together. I liked it, and started planning.

The idea of a song traveling from Paris through various people down to the south of France came from a story my grandmother told me, about a prince who finds a piece of embroidery blown by the wind over seven seas and seven lands, and says that whoever made it must be his wife. Finally he discovers her, and she's a princess. Instead of using the embroidery, we used the song.

Rodgers and Hart wrote a string of successful Broadway shows in the 1920s; with the cold hand of the Depression ending that era of carefree gaiety, they began testing the Hollywood waters. They contributed songs to an unsuccessful film at First National, *The Hot Heiress*, in 1931; its star, Ben Lyon, was no singer. Mamoulian first met Rodgers—the businessman of the two men—for dinner in late December 1931. He asked for a full score, including the incidental music. Rodgers was delighted: "This was—and still is—highly unusual, since film scoring has generally been left to composers specializing in the field." That's why Charles Ruggles and Chevalier walk-dance as they step to the prerecorded score. Ruggles arrives at the chateau at a brassy *presto* stride. Each step is a musical beat, and he executes a quick Chaplinesque side step to inspect a dozing footman. Chevalier later gets a walk-dance after arriving at the chateau, sprinting up staircases to the "How Are You?" motif.

Mamoulian recalled Chevalier's demeanor as consistently miserable. On the first day of filming in March 1932, the actor "walked in . . . as if he was carrying the whole weight of the world on his shoulders" and sat in a corner "like an orphan." Mamoulian feared disaster. However,

> as I said, "Action!" a miracle happened. Suddenly Chevalier became what he is—you know, full of vim and energy and joie de vivre, brightening the whole stage, and then I said "Cut," and he collapsed. And he shuffled off. And that's the way he was practically through the film. In those days, he was very insecure. You see, he came from a very poor background, and somehow he was always afraid that he's going to wind up again without fame, without money. So he was in life, very, very unhappy. Very frustrated. And also—he had a child in him—he was in great need of friendship.

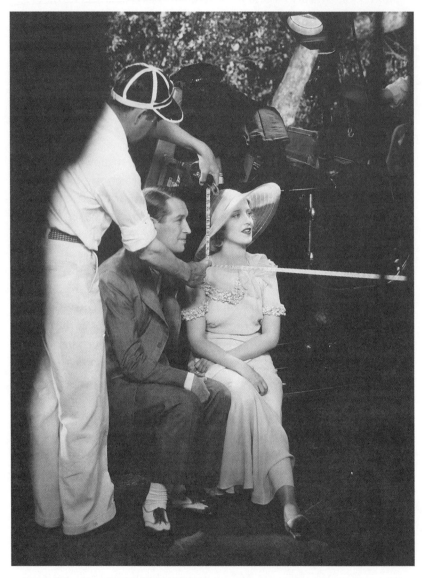

Maurice Chevalier and Jeanette MacDonald sit still for the focus puller during filming of *Love Me Tonight*, April 1932. Photograph courtesy of Library of Congress.

MacDonald could be quite stubborn when it came to her wardrobe. "My assistant came to me and said, 'Miss MacDonald doesn't like her costume in the first scene and she said she is the one to pick her clothes.'" He ended up telling her, "We are shooting this scene tomorrow, so you go ahead, pick your wardrobe and if it is suitable and makes you happy, that is all right with me." The result sent him into peals of laughter. "You never saw anything like this in your life. Looking dowdy. . . . The worst combination of irrelevant things you could put on—ostrich feathers. She was a wonderful girl. I loved her, but she never dressed well in life, either. So I realized this girl is serious." Mamoulian told her he was returning to his office and it would be up to her to inform the studio why they weren't filming. After an hour, "My assistant called and said, 'Okay, she is ready,' and here she is, hating my guts. At the end of the day, that was it. From then on it was a love affair between all of us."

What makes the film completely Mamoulian's is its sustained inventive spirit and rhythmic action set to music. What keeps it fresh is the elegantly playful score. There are no wasted moments. It opens with a version of the "Symphony of Noise" as a contemporary yet fairy-tale Paris comes to life in the morning.

Thump! A street repairman wields a pickax. Snore! A man dozes by a barrel. Sweep! A woman takes a broom to her doorway. These combine in rhythm with three puffing chimneys. Prop man Joe Youngerman, later an assistant director, accomplished the effect, timed to a metronome Mamoulian brought to the set. As the noises increase to resemble a heartbeat, an infant cries as a woman opens a window, there are additional sounds of sawing wood, a large knife sharpener, the flap of clothes being hung out to dry, two cobblers nailing heels, a woman beating a rug, and a taxi horn. Finally, another woman turns on a Victrola to add a musical background.

As the noises end, Mamoulian's camera dollies though the window of an apartment. A straw hat—Chevalier's trademark accessory—hanging on a peg announces him to the audience. Chevalier, as tailor Maurice Cortelin, pulls on a turtleneck sweater, looks out his window, and concludes, "Song of Paree, you are much too loud for me!" He lists the charms of his city ("There are taxi horns and klaxons / to scare the Anglo-Saxons / That's the song of Paree!") then heads to his tailor shop with "How Are You?" rhyming dialogue among passersby.

The first customer of the morning is stocky Emile (Bert Roach), for whom Maurice has made a wedding suit. While he's trying it on, the feckless Vicomte Gilbert de Varèze (Ruggles) arrives, in the midst of a cross-city race, in his top hat and underwear, having been chased from his lover's nest by an angry husband. He asks Maurice for one of the fifteen suits he's had made, and since he doesn't have his wallet, also borrows the 2,000 francs Emile has just paid. He's quickly out the door, while Emile proudly models his new suit. This introduces *Love Me Tonight*'s celebrated set piece. "Isn't It Romantic?" at first mentions only Emile's plebeian dreams as a new husband: "Isn't it romantic? Soon I will have found a girl that I adore! Isn't it romantic? While I sit around my girl can scrub the floor!") He eventually sings of the joys of parenthood and Bert, who finds it "a very catchy strain" picks it up, although he can only remember "Isn't it romantic?" If it was Mamoulian's idea to have the tune waft from one actor to another, it probably was a Rodgers and Hart notion, acquired from their years of composing, that most people can only recall tunes and usually bungle lyrics.

As he sings on the street, a taxi driver (Rolf Sedan), and the driver's customer, who just happens to be a composer (Tyler Brooke) also pick it up. While the composer adds lyrics on a train, a group of soldiers pick up the tune in full chorus. They're next seen marching over the horizon with their own version of the lyrics when a passing Gypsy violinist picks it up and plays it at his encampment at night. From there, it wafts to a moonlit balcony at a chateau—the castle of Sleeping Beauty, as the plot will reveal. MacDonald as the lovelorn Princess Jeanette, sings, "Isn't it romantic? That a hero might appear and say the word!"

As she finishes, a ladder clunks on her balcony, and the dialogue shifts to what was considered "smart" double-entendre. The likely author: George Marion Jr., who adapted *The Gay Divorcee* in 1933. Appearing atop the ladder is no "hero"; it's fluttery Count de Savignac (Charles Butterworth), a rose clenched in his teeth as he pitches an unusual brand of woo, carrying his flute, "hoping to entertain."

"I was just going to bed," Jeanette tells him.

He replies, "I just came up to join you."

"Join me?"

"Join you in a little chat—before dinner."

"Not tonight. I've had another fainting spell and my uncle the duke thought bed was the best place for me."

"I trust you do not find my wooing too ardent?" he asks, and as he bids farewell, falls backward off the ladder.

"Oh, I'll never be able to use it again!"

"Oh, Count, did you break your leg?"

"No, I fell flat on my flute!"

Mamoulian's still setting up the story, and to a *misterioso* with flute and harps, his camera moves to a window of a tower room where three elderly aunts (Ethel Griffies, Elizabeth Patterson, and Blanche Frederici), like jolly versions of Macbeth's witches, concoct a spell for the end of the princess's fainting episodes. As it ends, Patterson stands, extend her arms and casts— Yes, there it is—Serena's *Porgy* shadow. Next to the ground floor, where the Duke d'Artelines (C. Aubrey Smith) is arguing with his man-hungry niece Countess Valentine (Myrna Loy), who wants 20,000 francs from her inheritance. He tells her she'll only waste the money in Paris. His chateau goes beyond dull to soporific.

The ne'er-do-well Gilbert hopes to extract more funds from his uncle— "I'll tell him I need the money for charity—to find good homes for bad stenographers!" Valentine and Gilbert are trapped just like Jeanette, who's widowed and cannot marry beneath her station. Back in Paris, the credit manager of the retail merchants association (Gordon Westcott) arrives at the tailor shop to warn Maurice, the shirtmaker (Clarence Wilson), the hatmaker (Tony Merlo), and the bootmaker (William H. Turner) that the viscount never pays his bills. Maurice is dispatched to collect, taking off in a chauffeur-driven car that breaks down along the way. What better way to "meet cute" with Jeanette, who runs her horse-drawn buggy into a ditch while singing "Lover." This being a fairy tale, Maurice partly wins her over by singing "Mimi," which ends with his suggestion that he would like "to have a little son of a Mimi by and by." She speeds off in her cart, returns to the chateau, and promptly faints. A doctor (Joseph Cawthorn) is brought in, insisting that he get a good look at the princess—at that point in her career, MacDonald and lingerie were as synonymous as Chevalier and his straw boater.

After seeing the photo of her grim-faced husband, who died three years ago at age seventy-five, the doctor concludes that Jeanette is in need of a virile man. His patter prescription, with some of Hart's most creatively ribald imagery, was considered too risqué for Paramount and was snipped before the film's release.

> Let me tell you this, my dear
> A doorbell needs tinkling
> A flower needs sprinkling
> And a woman needs something like that
> A car needs ignition
> To keep in condition
> And a woman needs something like that!
> All inventions of Edison
> And medicine would leave you flat
> A peach must be eaten
> A drum must be beaten
> And a woman needs something like that!

Only his conclusion survives: "You're not wasted away—you're just wasted!" Maurice arrives at this opportune moment, and after Gilbert introduces the reluctant tailor as Baron Courtelin, all is temporarily well, since Maurice's "title" makes him a suitable mate for Jeanette. At the next day's stag hunt, Maurice is assigned a wild horse named Solitude—"because he always comes home alone." The horse, with him on its back, takes off at high speed as the hunt begins. The stag, chased by baying hounds, gets a pleasant trilling theme contrasting with the martial brass of the dogs. "Mamoulian staged the entire sequence as if it were a zoological ballet," Rodgers wrote. After parting ways with Solitude, Maurice rescues the stag, as Jeanette sees when she arrives at a distant cabin. He thinks the hunters should return, and the duke orders them, "Go back, quickly and quietly. On tiptoe." This they do—in silent slow motion.

Eventually, it's time for the jig to be up. Maurice earlier criticized Jeanette's riding habit as unflattering. He insults her seamstress's work, the seamstress storms off, the duke and the rest burst into Jeanette's room to see what the fuss is about, and Maurice and Jeanette stop kissing long enough for him to start taking her measurements. He shoots the princess an amused glance when he finds she has a thirty-four bust. The riding habit is perfect.

So perfect, she asks, "How are you able to make it in two hours? How are you able to make it at all?" He tells her the truth that he is a tailor, not a noble. Distraught, she runs out, and the aunts conveniently rush in. He tells them as well, and they run off to tell the others. Exhausted by their run, Patterson topples a vase with an outstretched arm, wailing, "The son of a gun is nothing but a tailor!"

From the duke on down to a laundress, the staff chant their outrage, and a dejected Maurice departs after collecting his bill. Romance naturally means second chances, and Jeanette decides she loves him so much, she races after his train on horseback. She eventually overtakes it—we've already seen how speedy Solitude is—and stands astride the tracks to stop it. The princess gets her man, and love conquers social status.

Released in August 1932, *Love Me Tonight* produced reviews that were downright giddy although only modest box office returns, profiting a little more than $780,000. In *The Hollywood Reporter*: "It is our humble opinion . . . that every other feature of this picture is secondary in importance to Mamoulian's marvelous handling of every moment, and the extra grand music, lyrics underscoring and addition of dialogue contributed by Richard Rodgers and Lorenz Hart." Mordaunt Hall wrote of Mamoulian in the *New York Times*, "although he may not reveal Ernst Lubitsch's satire and keen wit or René Clair's clever irony, he, in a somewhat precise and often theatric fashion, gives to his scenes a charming poetic suggestion." In London, where the picture opened in November, the reviewer for the *Times* wrote of the director: "He has the artist's gift of discovering formal relations in any material, and by so doing, by some mysterious and recondite process, he lifts the squalid yearnings and base humor which the musical comedy is intended to express into another and far more delicate world."

In the fall, Mamoulian took a European vacation that included Baden-Baden (where he had an emergency appendectomy) and Paris. His personal life had taken a turn for the worse in June. Landi's film career was not going the way she had hoped. She wrote:

> This morning's *Examiner* confirms the fact that Helen Hayes is to play Catherine Barkley. The other Sunday, you yourself told me that Mr. [Sam] Katz had implored you to direct *A Farewell to Arms* and that he would *do anything* if you would do so. The full purport of this did not enter my bright

skull until to-day. I know Fox definitely offered me to Paramount for the role . . .

I think that had you seriously recommended me, I might have played it. I feel sure that had you consented to direct the picture you could have asked for me and have had me for it. I know how you can get almost anything you really want at Paramount. . .

On the other hand I feel rather a fool! The actual *proofs* of your friendship have always been a trifle vague but I believed the things you *said*.

Their relationship ended the following year after her ill-chosen words in a newspaper interview applied a flamethrower to her professional bridges. Shortly after her arrival in Hollywood, Landi had written her mother, "Here I am living in the most gossipy place in the whole universe, seeing the PA almost daily—and no talk in consequence." In 1933 in the *Los Angeles Times*, she was doing the talking, and there were consequences.

She started by calling herself "the miraculous survivor of seven bad pictures." Then it got worse: "My directors to date have been incompetent. Each one, noticing some mannerism or characteristic of mine, duly complained about it—and, of course, out it came. A great director, Rouben Mamoulian, for whom I worked on the stage in New York, had other ideas." One of the "incompetent" directors she blasted was Cecil B. DeMille, who had directed Landi and Fredric March in *The Sign of the Cross* (1932). Mamoulian's only option for self-preservation after this article came out would have been to put considerable distance between himself and Landi. She continued to appear in films at Fox until the studio canceled her contract in 1936, and she appeared in only two films after that before leaving acting to write and lecture.

CHAPTER 7

Dietrich and Garbo

Song of Songs and *Queen Christina* marked Mamoulian's creative peak in Hollywood. Stylization and rhythm could only take him so far with audiences. *Song of Songs* with Marlene Dietrich at Paramount nearly derailed him. He committed the cardinal sin of blithely ignoring the studio-approved shot list and filming to his heart's content. He indulged in that for *Queen Christina* at MGM for a bit as well, and for that, studio chief Louis B. Mayer confronted him.

Dietrich and her husband Rudolf Sieber, sometime after the birth of their only child, Maria, in 1924, declared their sexual independence from each other, although they never divorced. They each went on to have a series of lovers, with hers including Josef von Sternberg, Gary Cooper, the Spanish American poet Mercedes de Acosta (who was more famously Garbo's lover) and John Wayne.

Dietrich's American career had been the creation of von Sternberg, who cherished his Svengali image: "Miss Dietrich is *me*—*I* am Miss Dietrich," he told Peter Bogdanovich. In *The Blue Angel* in 1930, her performance as temptress Lola Lola and her singing of "Falling in Love Again" made her an international sensation. That was quickly followed by *Morocco* (1930), *Dishonored* (1931) *Shanghai Express* (1932), and *Blonde Venus* (1932). After *Song of Songs*, they made *The Scarlet Empress* (1934) and *The Devil Is a Woman* (1935). Von Sternberg's professional insecurity gave Mamoulian an opportunity. *Blonde Venus* did poorly at the box office, and in early 1933, von Sternberg seized an opportunity to work at the UFA studios in Berlin, with plans to build careers for himself and Dietrich there, leaving her temporarily at Paramount's full disposal. (As a Vienna-born Jew, he fled back to

America in May 1933 after the burning of the Reichstag spurred the Nazi regime to revoke citizenship of Jewish authors, artists, and filmmakers.)

Paramount demanded that Dietrich star in the first sound version of German author Hermann Sudermann's 1908 novel *Das Hohe Lied*, previously filmed in 1918 with Elsie Ferguson as *The Song of Songs* and in 1924 with Pola Negri called *Lily of the Dust*. In Sudermann's novel, "The Song of Songs" is a cherished oratorio based on the Song of Solomon. A copy belonged to Lily Czepenak's late father, she occasionally sings parts of it and carries it around until it's practically in shreds. After concluding that she's "a poor exploited and plundered human creature who must drag on through life as best she could," and with the oratorio now symbolizing that pain, she finally tosses it into a river before going to Italy to be married.

Sudermann drew harsh sketches of squalid artistic lives, especially August Kellermann, the Berlin painter and bronze artist to whom Lily is apprenticed and for whom she finally poses nude after he chastises her for being a "chained Venus." Other characters discuss Nietzschean philosophy. Film versions ditched the Nietzsche for the erotic *frisson* of a young girl's nudity and moral descent. Paramount dusted off the property for Dietrich to get one more picture out of her before her contract expired.

Dietrich balked. She had never made an American film without von Sternberg. Besides that, the story of the virginal German girl was a badly dated melodrama. Dietrich played prostitutes in her first four films and surely thought that the public wouldn't accept her as an unspoiled country lass in braids. Paramount took Dietrich to court. The studio suspended her salary when she refused to meet with Mamoulian for a preproduction conference in December 1932. A month later, the studio sued her for the full cost of preparing the picture and received a temporary injunction prohibiting her from working elsewhere. She announced her return, although she still found her role "unsuitable," and the day after that, Dietrich and Mamoulian were lunching. Having directed one striptease for Miriam Hopkins, he discussed another with Dietrich. Filming began on February 6, 1933.

Brian Aherne, who played Waldow the sculptor and began an affair with Dietrich during production, called it "rubbish, but perhaps not as bad as I feared." Mamoulian, who had the most to lose, had to take every detail seriously. "It was all right, but there was nothing new in it," he concluded. "I couldn't open any doors in it, creatively." Already he was repeating what he had done in *Dr. Jekyll and Mr. Hyde* and *City Streets*. Dietrich's nudity is implied as Lily disrobes to pose for Waldow for the first time. As she removes her stockings, Mamoulian intercuts a nude statue with legs crossed. As she works on her camisole, Aherne happily whips a tarp off another female nude. Not quite an elegant striptease style, but as a cinematic fête of nudity, quite effective.

Mamoulian said Dietrich's makeup was the key to breaking her out of von Sternberg's mold:

> They worked out this makeup where her eyes started at the bridge of the nose and ended at the temple. And that's the way she came on the set the first day. And I said, "My god, what are you playing? You're from some small village in Bavaria coming to the big city. You must have natural eyebrows." She said, "Oh, no." So she got them down a little, and I said, "No, down to here." Then we shot her that way. The next day she came on the set, and they were a fraction of an inch higher. Well, I thought, that doesn't make any difference. The third day, they were higher, so I said, "Back you go. Bring them down."

Aherne was unhappy with Mamoulian's insistence that he play the part of the sculptor as a "straight romantic lead," and he told the director it was a "thankless, detestable part" that demanded "an off-beat characterization." Mamoulian replied, "Somebody has to be the captain of this ship, and it is going to be me. You will do what I say and I will take full responsibility."

As Samuel Hoffenstein revised a script by Leo Birinski, the story became simpler. After the death of her father, Lily goes to live with her harridan Aunt Rasmussen (Alison Skipworth), who operates a lending library in Berlin. Lily is modest—wearing so many petticoats that her aunt exclaims, "I've never seen a girl unpeel herself like an onion before!" Lily tells her that she used to read from the Song of Solomon to her father every night, to which Aunt Rasmussen retorts, "Knowing your father, I imagine there was something dirty in it!"

Waldow, the sculptor who lives across the street, comes in to browse because he's been stuck for inspiration. One glimpse of Lily's leg as she stands on a ladder solves his dilemma: "I've got to sculpt you!" He persuades her to come to his atelier that night to pose. She is surprised to find he's already made a preliminary sketch. She's thrilled: "How did you know I was like that? It's the way I want to be! It's the way I dream to be! It's the girl in the Song of Songs! It is the voice of my beloved—that's what I am!"

When he sees her standing nearly on tiptoe with her shoulders thrust back: "That's what I've been looking for! We'll call it the Song of Songs! Take your clothes off!" After her disrobing is intermingled with nude statues, Lily hesitates a bit before announcing, "I said I'd do it—and I *will* do it." Down comes her coat, the audience sees only her bare ankles and feet, and Waldow quickly starts making another sketch.

As he finishes, up the steps comes Baron von Merzbach (Lionel Atwill), who buys Waldow's art and has commissioned a statue, although he doesn't yet know what it will be. Hearing the steps, Lily runs to the back room. Applying his monocle, the baron leers at the full-frontal sketch: "She's a little bee-yoo-tay!" He is even more aroused when he asks about Waldow's model: "Not overdone? As good as this? Really?" His "Ah-*hmmmmm*!" is redolent of Mr. Hyde.

The question has lingered: was Dietrich's nude form "as good as this?"

Well, no. But also yes, sort of. Mamoulian went the gallant route: "[Dietrich posed] fully clothed. The sculptor [Salvatore Scarpitta] was very anxious to see her—you know, 'I have to get the proportions right.' We were at this studio, and Dietrich was looking at me, smiling, and I was looking at her, and I said, 'Well now, Signor Scarpitta, you can just get the measurements, and then I suggest you use your imagination.'" Dietrich's daughter, Maria Riva, agreed: "She did *not* pose for the statue, although often [said she] she wished to have those perky breasts."

Scarpitta's granddaughter Lola Scarpitta tells the story passed down in her family: "Marlene *did* pose nude and I heard that story straight out of my very jealous and smart grandmother Nadia, who knocked on the studio door every twenty minutes with refreshments. Marlene . . . had enormous feet and my grandfather used my grandmother's feet in place of hers." As for the breasts, Nadia's words as well: "Marlene's breasts sagged a bit. My Aunt Carmen heard from my grandmother that even fudging to model them better in front of Marlene, they were not good enough. My grandfather had my grandmother model the breasts to achieve a better look."

As filmed, the statue is a cross between the *maschinenmensch* android in Fritz Lang's *Metropolis* (1926) and the "Spirit of Ecstasy" hood ornament on a Rolls-Royce. Mamoulian hired Scarpitta after the studio refused to pay his friend from Paris, Boris Lovet-Lorski, $5,000 for plaster copies of one of Lorski's bronze nudes. Scarpitta was paid $1,000. The hands seen molding Dietrich in clay are Scarpitta's own hands.

The Hays Office, the precursor to the Production Code Administration, didn't express concerns about simply having nude statuary: "The action seemed to be treated in good taste in the script and we have gone over it in some detail with the studio . . . We trust that the fact that Mamoulian is directing would be a further guarantee that it will be handled properly." It didn't foresee a mischievous touch: Mamoulian saw to it that Scarpitta included erect nipples.

Waldow finds himself besotted while completing Lily in clay, even though he earlier assured the baron that she meant nothing to him. The Hays Office got involved on this point: "Care must be taken with this scene of Waldow working on the statue, that undue prominence be not given to his handling of the breasts to the point where it might become censorable." Waldow doesn't do that; instead, he begins to massage the clay shoulders until, overcome, he kisses Lily and the film moves to happy montages of the two of them in a rowboat and underneath blossoming trees.

Baron von Merzbach's wealth gets his way. He tells Waldow, "I'm getting old. It would amuse me to devote the rest of my days to her . . . to make her my *masterpiece!*" He demands, without a hint of eye-rolling irony, as they flank the statue: "Tell me again if what I'm asking is obscene!"

Still hoping for a respectable advance in polite society, Lily does so well learning horseback riding that groundskeeper Walter Von Prell (Hardie Albright) makes a crude advance and tells her he loves her. The baron invites Waldow to dinner to show off his Pygmalion-like success, and while the baron is passed out drunk, Lily insists to Waldow that she and Von Prell are lovers. She marches to the lodge for her seduction. As Von Prell carries her into the bedroom, he knocks over a kerosene lamp that sets the place ablaze. As they escape, the baron realizes Lily will never be faithful to him, and Miss von Schwertfeger, eager to resume her former romance with the baron, tells Lily to run away and the baron not to chase after her, since it will only make him look foolish. Waldow looks all over for Lily. "Have you tried the gutter?" Aunt Rasmussen snarls.

It's a plush gutter. Mamoulian cuts to a Berlin cabaret, where Lily is introduced with a smile and a puff of smoke that recalls von Merzbach and his

Marlene Dietrich as Lily with her statue in *The Song of Songs*, 1933. The head and body are hers, but the breasts and feet are those of the wife of the sculptor, Salvatore Scarpitta.

cigarettes. As she sings "Jonny," she is revealed to be something of a chanteuse. Mamoulian wanted it that way. His memo to costume designer Travis Banton specified, "A decent looking evening dress—smart—the sort of thing that doesn't stamp her immediately as a tart."

Waldow and Lily return to his atelier, where she gazes upon the statue symbolizing her lost innocence, while he assures her that he's loved her all along. Lily reflects: "What is she waiting for? What is she listening for? What a fool I was. Remember how ashamed I was to take my clothes off?" She is enraged after Waldow recalls, "It is the voice of my beloved."

"I'm dead, do you hear, dead! I'm dead! What right has *she* to live?" Lily screams. She takes a sledgehammer to the statue. The head goes flying first, and the nipples in opposite directions.

It was the last sequence filmed; Aherne recalled that Hoffenstein had not provided lines to end the picture. The front office rejected dialogue Aherne wrote, so Mamoulian wrote the ending instead, as Waldow consoles Lily: "Do you remember the hill we used to climb? Let us begin again, and we'll find the sky, perhaps."

Mamoulian was just about to be shown the studio gate, as Paramount executive Albert Kaufman warned on March 4:

> To date you have lost twelve days on a 42 days schedule, and based on the speed you are going, it means that the picture will take 12 weeks to photograph and will cost over $1,000,000 and we cannot sit back, in times such as we are at the present, and see this go on without making every kind of possible plea to you to help us hit a normal gait. . . .
>
> *Jekyll and Hyde*, a subject at least as difficult to handle as *Song of Songs*, took 54 days, a most liberal schedule for any director. *The Sign of the Cross*, a subject with double the canvas of *Song of Songs* and a far more difficult picture to make, was photographed in 43 days.
>
> I see your daily takes, as well as those of the companies in work, and really, Rouben, you are wasting an awful lot of time in taking as many unnecessary angles that we know in advance never will be used, with the result that to date you have shot 75,000 feet of negative—an almost unheard-of amount.

Mamoulian replied that the extra footage was needed because of the nudity involved, but that wasn't a persuasive argument. He completed filming on

May 6. On June 13, he wired Dietrich, who was vacationing in Paris: "Had two secret previews. Audience reaction marvelous. Everybody says you are too too divine." The film opened July 19, 1933. Mamoulian left Paramount a month before that, and at MGM as a loan-out director, he started shooting *Queen Christina* on August 10.

~

The lesbian interpretation long applied to *Queen Christina* relies on the title character wearing male attire, kissing her young countess friend on the lips, and announcing, after she's warned that she'll die an old maid, "I shall die a bachelor!" The screenplay by S. N. Behrman, based on a story from Greta Garbo's friend Salka Viertel and Harold M. Harwood with story contributions from Viertel, isn't about sexual identity, though. It's about playful gender-bending by a Swedish queen who is just looking to settle down with the right man. She's a wise and temperate ruler who doesn't like the details of governing.

There's a gossamer veneer of historical drama about seventeenth-century Sweden and the Thirty Years' War, conveniently not mentioning that the war largely involved Protestants fighting Catholics. Forget about accuracy. The real Christina abdicated and went to Italy to become Catholic, not for the love of a Spanish ambassador. Mamoulian understood the approach:

> She was an immensely educated, erudite woman; she was interested in the arts; she did reign; she was the daughter instead of the son the king wanted, so that's why she wore men's clothes. And then she resigned her throne and went to Italy. But from there on you forget history, and you dress her in these beautiful things Adrian designed. They carried the feeling of the period, but certainly were not precisely correct.

Christina has many lovers. Early on, after we see her beneath her hat, she's kissing her latest one, Magnus (Ian Keith) and mentioning that they had spent the previous night together. When she greets Countess Ebba (Elizabeth Young) with a quick kiss on the lips, it's meant to convey no deeper meaning about either Christina or Garbo's own liaisons, because it's seventeenth-century Europe—long ago, far away—and it's established that she has sex with men. She likes them so much, she later cheerfully settles a tavern argument over the number of the queen's lovers by announcing that she's had not six, not nine, but twelve in the past year ("Any lie will find believers as long as you tell it with force," she remarks).

At MGM, Mayer didn't bother with memos about overshooting. Reginald Owen, who played Christina's distant cousin Charles, recalled that the studio chief preferred a personal approach: "I remember on one occasion, L. B. Mayer—who never interfered, or never did interfere with any director's work—saw that twenty takes had been taken of a scene. So he had them all printed. And then he asked Rouben Mamoulian to explain the differences between the takes. And Mamoulian couldn't. They were all equally good."

Mamoulian said he talked Garbo out of her insistence that she was only good on the first take:

She said, "You tell me what you want me to do, where to stand, where to go, and then we make a take." And she says, "Usually, the first take is my best. And I said, "Well, look, if this is true and it works that way, it's marvelous because it saves me an awful lot of time and we can get it all in one take, but I said I'd like to do it this way provided that if it is not satisfactory, you'll have to do it my way." . . .

So I rehearsed [Garbo and Lewis Stone] and I told her what she would be doing, and I said all right, now are you ready? She said yes. So we made a take—she went through the thing. And then she is coming towards me, I was sitting in a chair, and I said, "Well, how do you feel about it?" And she said, "Fine." I didn't say anything. And she said "Well, what about you? Don't you like it?" I said, "No, I don't like it." So her face fell . . .

So I started rehearsing—we rehearsed for two hours. And she said, "Well, you know, I'm completely gone; this is going to be terrible. So I made a second take, third take, fourth take—by now she says it's getting worse and worse. Eighth take—that's it. I said, "Miss Garbo, I'm going to print take one, your take, and then I'm going to print take eight, after all the rehearsals and seven other takes, and you are going to come to the projection room in the morning at 8 o'clock, I won't even be there, you sit there, run the two scenes, then you tell me which you would like to be in the film. And I promise you I'll take your judgment. So she leaned over and she whispered, "Please don't print take one." And that was it.

Greta Garbo, John Gilbert, and Mamoulian on the set of *Queen Christina* (1934).

"Life is so gloriously improbable!" Antonio, John Gilbert's Spanish ambassador, proclaims when he realizes that Garbo's "count" is a girl and they'll be sleeping together. He could also have been speaking about his casting. Mamoulian was vague on how Gilbert, Garbo's former costar (*Flesh and the Devil*, 1926; *Love*, 1927; *A Woman of Affairs*, 1928) and lover came to be cast. Gilbert's tenor speaking voice made him a victim of early sound technology when his voice didn't match public expectations: "I had to . . . watch him to use the lower span of his vocal range. He had a tendency to go up high and then the sound man did a great deal by giving preferential treatment to lower frequencies, which you can do when you're recording sound—you can change the voice. So that was a great help."

The vocal track wasn't the only problem: "And he was subjected to a great deal of harassment and indignities—he had to report without working, and they did all these awful things to the man. So in a way, coming into *Christina* was almost like a kind of redeeming the soul, saving the guy a complete rebuff. . . . You had to nurse him, because with all these experiences, he was very insecure, nervous and afraid and touchy." Behrman wrote, "The film was rolling when Gilbert would disappear for a day or two—he drank. This stopped everything. The delays were tremendously costly."

To a soft musical accompaniment, Garbo "memorizes" the bedroom in which she's found love with Gilbert after three snowbound days and nights. She strokes a table, mirror, wall, spinning wheel, Gilbert's pillow, a painting, and finally, in a phallic moment, a bedpost. "What are you doing?" Gilbert asks. She replies, "I have been memorizing the room. In the future, in my memory, I shall live a great deal in this room."

"To my mind it's a sonnet," Mamoulian said. "It was done to a metronome. I explained to her, 'This has to be sheer poetry and feeling. The movement must be like a dance.'" Gilbert's question "is almost necessary to explain to some people in the audience what in hell is going on." She's touching objects "because I like to do that," Mamoulian explained. "Anything I see, I like to touch."

The Garbo close-up that ends *Queen Christina*. "Just be a mask, just be a face," Mamoulian told her.

The ending in the script had Gilbert's death in a duel and Christina leaving Sweden; there was just to be the ship sailing into the horizon. The lingering close-up of the impassive Garbo was a Mamoulian inspiration. Garbo had had long close-ups in silent films, although usually they were interrupted by intertitles. Mamoulian gambled that audiences would fill in the thoughts crossing that enigmatic face. "She has just abdicated her throne for the love of the Spanish ambassador and she is leaving for Spain, some island, and he's dead. So the captain says, what shall we do? Shall we sail? The wind is with us. And she says yes, we'll sail. Then I had her walk toward the bow of the boat and stand there, and I was going to make a large close-up of her and hold it for 100 feet."

In Mamoulian's telling, the scene was a three-part triumph. He said an inspiration from his childhood resulted in new technology—a strip of glass that changed the light diffusion four times. The closer the camera gets, the greater the diffusion, but the face still appears soft and evenly toned. Without that, a close-up would become a clinical examination under very bright light. First, he had to overcome cameraman William Daniels's skepticism:

> Suddenly I remembered that when I was a boy, my parents gave me a magic lantern—it was a little red lantern, a little kerosene lamp. And it had panes of glass with four pictures on it in color, and you'd put one in front, you projected it on a sheet on the wall, and then you'd push the next one in. . . . Now I suddenly said to myself, well, why don't we make a pane of glass this long with an intensified diffusion? It becomes stronger and stronger, thicker and thicker, as we come closer and closer. We might do it with a 40mm lens. . . .
>
> So we got the laboratory men in and they went to work and we sat there waiting until 5 o'clock. And finally this thing came back and they'd made a little frame in front of the camera and Bill Daniels . . . said it would never work . . . if his hand shakes, or if he pushes it too late. So I said we had to do it.
>
> So I asked Miss Garbo to stay later; she usually quits at 5:30. So we finished at 7:30 and we made two takes of this, and the first one was absolutely impossible, no good. The second one is in the film, so it worked.

Second, he talked Garbo into the scene:

So naturally, she says, "What do I act?" And I said, "This is a very ticklish spot." I said, "You see, I believe that if the audience is involved in the film . . . they will supply a great deal of emotion that isn't there." In other words, I said the famous queen was a *tabula rasa*, a blank sheet of paper. I said "I'd like you to just be completely passive, don't think about anything, express nothing, and preferably don't even blink your eyes, just be a mask, just be a face. Then the audience will write in whatever emotion they felt should be portrayed here."

Finally, a less plausible anecdote, although essential in Mamoulian's framing of history, about overcoming Mayer, who he claimed told him, "the audience would be very depressed, and you don't want to depress the audience, do you?"

I said, "Mr. Mayer, you know Greek tragedy? "Oh," he says, "yes, I know Greek tragedy." Well, I said usually it has an unhappy ending, but it never depresses the audience, it exhilarates them. He said, "This can't—they're not going to like this. So I said to him, "Look, you always have six to eight weeks' retakes on every picture and I've never had retakes on my films because I think them over thoroughly." So I said I would like to shoot it just the way it is, and then we can show the film and if it depresses the audience, if they walk away miserable, unhappy, then I'll do something about it.
. . . We had this run for the executives before any preview, and [MGM board chairman] Nicholas Schenck came from New York, [Irving] Thalberg was there, everybody was there, and Mayer. . . . And they all walked out, you know, on cloud number nine, not a word was spoken—they didn't even wait for a preview. So it shows you that you have to actually see it.

The film's historical inaccuracies annoyed Garbo. "I am so ashamed of *Christina*," she wrote to a friend the following January.

I often wake up and think with horror about the film coming to Sweden. It's really bad in every respect, but the worst thing is they'll think I don't know any better—just imagine Christina abdicating for the sake of a little Spaniard. I managed to believe for ages that it would look as though she did it because she was weary of it all and from a boundless desire to be free.

But I'm not strong enough to get anything done so I end up being a poor prophet.

~

"Just a little vacation trip. There seems to have been quite a stir, doesn't there?" That was all Mamoulian had to say about his post-*Christina* jaunt with Garbo to Arizona in early January 1934. He recorded nothing of it in his diary and never spoke of it afterward. It gave him brief national fame of the gently mocking variety. Newspaper reporters were having a little

Garbo photographed by Mamoulian in Taos, New Mexico, January 1934. Photograph courtesy of Library of Congress.

fun, just like they did years later when Garbo vacationed in Europe with Leopold Stokowski.

Perhaps Garbo felt the need to get away from Mercedes De Costa's possessive clutches for a while, and MGM publicists felt that a quick road trip with her director might reassure the public of her robust heterosexuality. But it's also quite possible that Garbo and Mamoulian simply wanted to take in the Grand Canyon. If so, it was the height of naiveté, particularly for Garbo, not to know that any time two celebrities were spotted together in Arizona, it was believed they had gone there to get married. Arizona didn't require a waiting period for marriage licenses, so Yuma, just across the border from California, had a brisk trade in celebrity nuptials.

It's also a stretch to imagine that Garbo thought she and Mamoulian could travel incognito in her chauffeur-driven car. They certainly gave it a try, signing in as Mary Jones and Robert Brown for a three-room suite (the two-bedrooms-with-parlor layout might be a clue as to whether their relationship was sexual, but that would be an exceptionally soaring height of naiveté) at the Holbrook Hotel. At the El Tovar Hotel, on the south rim of the Grand Canyon, they signed in as Mary Jones and Robert Bonji. Reporters relied on Joe Gerwitz, proprietor of the Holbrook, who had extracted their real identities. They fled the canyon when a park ranger attempted to talk to them. Afterwards, Mamoulian sputtered to a reporter, "Do people who work in entertainment always have to be in the public eye?" That, of course, depends on whether that person is Garbo, who, decades after making her last film, was hounded by paparazzi until her death in New York City in 1990.

Mamoulian brought a camera along. But he never photographed the Grand Canyon. There was more to their jaunt than reporters knew about. He took snapshots of Garbo not in Arizona but at their first stops—resorts in La Quinta, California, and Taos, New Mexico. Garbo on vacation—as enigmatic as ever.

CHAPTER 8

In Which Anna and Miriam Star

Paramount's meltdown in late 1933 kept Mamoulian and his friend Jesse Lasky from returning there. Lasky was ousted after the studio went into receivership; the year before, Zukor fired producer B. P. Schulberg and replaced him with Manny Cohen, who had been Lasky's assistant. Mamoulian was without any studio patrons. Paramount did not pick up his option for the remaining time on his contract.

He found a safe landing. After completing the editing of *Queen Christina*, Mamoulian checked out of the MGM lot on December 26; on January 4, 1934, thanks to agent Charles Feldman, he was lunching with Samuel Goldwyn just before heading off on his road trip with Garbo. That trip's aftermath was likely deliberate on Mamoulian's part: Columnists started linking him alternately with Argentine actress Mona Maris, who had been engaged to MGM director Clarence Brown, and Gertrude Michael. The Alabama-born Michael, best known for singing "Sweet Marihuana" in *Murder at the Vanities* (1934), was the longest-lasting relationship; in 1937, columnist Sheilah Graham noted Mamoulian's "resist-proof way with women."

Goldwyn's dramas such as *Wuthering Heights* (1939) and *The Best Years of Our Lives* (1946) were still to come. In the early 1930s, the mogul, famous for his malapropisms, operated the way a small boutique studio does today, relying on elegance from Ronald Colman and Walter Huston (*Raffles*, 1930; *Dodsworth*, 1936) and comedies from Eddie Cantor (*Roman Scandals*, 1933; *Strike Me Pink*, 1936). He also was a faithful believer in importing European talent. Ever since Louis B. Mayer hit a jackpot when he brought Greta Garbo to Hollywood, other studio chiefs hoped to duplicate his success. Goldwyn had a spotty record with it; on-screen charisma slammed into the

American tendency to resist accents other than British in actors in leading parts. Accents were for supporting roles in dramas or Garbo and Dietrich. That's how Lupe Vélez, a romantic lead in silent films, became the comic "Mexican Spitfire." Maurice Chevalier's day in film, for the time being, had come and gone.

Now Goldwyn was launching Anna Sten, a twenty-five-year-old from Ukraine. *Nana*, her first Goldwyn film, was a big-budget costume drama set in Paris with a Rodgers and Hart song, "That's Love." Under the direction of George Fitzmaurice (replaced during production by Dorothy Arzner), Sten performed it like a Dietrich manqué, right down to the cigarette. Its release was a month away when Goldwyn and Mamoulian met. When Sten arrived from Europe, "I was given a teacher because I didn't speak any English at that time at all, and she was a German," she recalled. "I don't know how I ever got out of it without a German accent."

Goldwyn planned a major remounting of Leo Tolstoy's 1899 novel *Resurrection*, a morality tale so sturdy it was adapted seven times in the silent era. Watching *The Song of Songs*, *Nana*, and *We Live Again* (1934) in sequence is to see Goldwyn's reasoning at work. If Mamoulian could make Dietrich a convincingly naïve virgin peasant girl, surely he could turn Sten into Tolstoy's martyred country maid. Lectures at Paramount and MGM about his excesses may have had their effect: *We Live Again* clicked along in thirty-nine shooting days between June 12 and August 3, 1934.

Returning in mid-March from New York, Mamoulian brought his own scenic designer, Sergei Soudeikine, who was then working for the Metropolitan Opera. Soudeikine shared art director credit on *We Live Again* with Richard Day; the icons in the Russian Orthodox Church used in the Easter service are his.

Tolstoy's novel criticizes the use of organized religion as a respectable veneer for a corrupt judicial system. Katerina Maslova, known as Katusha, is imprisoned and explains how she got to that point. She was first seduced by Prince Dmitri Ivanovitch Nekhludov, for whom she worked; after she was forced off his estate for bearing his illegitimate child, she worked for a corrupt couple who arranged a murder in which she was implicated. Although not guilty of any crime, she was convicted, imprisoned, and exiled. Dmitri has a change of heart and begins to give his lands to the peasants. The novel ends with him reading from the Gospel of Matthew. *He* lives again, but Katusha does not—she sacrifices herself by accepting her flawed punishment in Siberia, and she rejects Dmitri's offer to join her. True goodness, Tolstoy tells us, resides in the people serving God through good works.

Japanese director Kenji Mizoguchi is credited with saying, "All melodrama is based on Tolstoy's *Resurrection*." (It inspired his 1937 film *The Straits of Love and Hate*). Theological discussions and unhappy endings make difficult pictures, however, and Tolstoy described Katusha as having "unfathomable, squinting eyes," so film adaptations like Mamoulian's strip it down to the attractive poor girl done wrong by the rich boy and give them a final chance at love. Preston Sturges was hired to punch up the script. Like a hero in a Sturges comedy, Fredric March's Dmitri breezily reflects, "Russia is in pretty rotten condition. We're going to have a revolution if we don't look out."

Sturges rewrote an adaptation turned in by playwright Maxwell Anderson. He was followed by Leonard Praskins (*Bird of Paradise*, 1932), who shared screen credit with Sturges and Anderson.

Uncredited contributions came from Thornton Wilder, whose reputation at the time rested on his 1927 Pulitzer Prize–winning novel, *The Bridge of San Luis Rey*, and Paul Green (*The Cabin in the Cotton*, 1932). Sturges found the work frustrating: "Mr. Goldwyn also loathed me and . . . he used to go every morning to the director . . . and say eagerly, 'When can we get rid of this fellow Sturgeon?'"

Mamoulian "solved" Sten's accent with timing—she has very little to say for the first two reels of the film. Most of the dialogue comes from the fast-talking March. Despite his privileged life, Dmitri's an idealist, presenting Katusha with his copy of *Land and Freedom*, a book urging the redistribution of wealth and the end of the class system. A studio memo requested that the serfs congregating outside the Kasanova mansion be "Good Boyle Heights types, real beards and wrinkles."

Dmitri is a high-art example of the good-bad guy. Heading to military service, promising to return to Katusha every summer, he is corrupted by the other officers, who tell him that the quickest way to advancement is by seducing wives of the generals. Mamoulian reveals that Dmitri has abandoned his youthful enthusiasm for wealth redistribution when he casually uses a page of *Land and Freedom* to light his cigarette.

The Easter service to which he returns is the film's moral center. As the service in the tiny but spectacularly painted church moves along, the script notes, "During the Mass, we see the looks exchanged between Dmitri and Katusha—we perceive that they are more interested in each other than in the worship, although Katusha remembers her devoutness now and then, and tries sedulously to avoid Dmitri's glance."

Dmitri seduces her that night in the greenhouse, as rain beats down on the glass and the wind nearly extinguishes the altar candles at the church. He runs out the next morning after leaving her a hundred rubles. Katusha's pregnancy means her banishment from the household, even though the aunts suspect Dmitri is the father. When Mamoulian next shows her, she is holding a baby's coffin and burying it without a service. She wouldn't tell a priest the name of the father, so the boy died unbaptized.

Seven years later, Dmitri is in Moscow, stuck with jury duty since it's considered good practice for the judgeship to which he aspires. It's a case of two peasants and a prostitute—Katusha—accused of murder by poisoning a merchant. The peasants, Simon Kartinkin (Leonid Kinsky) and Eugenia Botchkova (Dale Fuller) are clearly guilty. In the jury room, Dmitri argues for Katusha's innocence, since she administered the poison thinking it was a sleeping powder and had no intent to murder. As in the novel, the jury's written verdict gets boggled in a technicality, and they report to the judge that she is guilty only of administering the powder without intent to rob. Prince Kortchagin, the judge (C. Aubrey Smith), recognizes the blunder and calls the jury "those idiots" since the verdict gives him no choice except to sentence Katusha to five years' hard labor in Siberia.

Life has been cruel to everyone; before her arrival in Siberia, Katusha is tossed into a jail that includes Gregory Simonson (Sam Jaffe), the author of *Land and Freedom*, who is beaten up by the guards. Also there: Virginie Mamoulian, making her only appearance in a Hollywood film. She has no lines. She lingers near Sten, her eyes seeming to question every complaint.

Dimitri is unable to persuade Prince Kortchagin to alter the verdict. His crisis of conscience culminates in prayer: "Dear Heavenly Father, give me courage. . . . Help me, dear God, to live—again!" The rousing music of the Easter service as he gazes on an icon is affirmation from the Almighty. Dmitri quickly sets about divvying up his property to peasant farmers so they can have the pride of ownership. He catches up with Katusha just as

Virginie Mamoulian played a mute prisoner in *We Live Again*, 1934. Photograph courtesy of Library of Congress.

she and other prisoners are about to pass through the massive gate that marks the border with Siberia. The rest of the plot departs from Tolstoy for an upbeat ending: Dmitri tells Katusha he wants to join her in Siberia.

Here is where Wilder and Green were brought in. Goldwyn was dissatisfied with March's final speech, which ended with, "There are too many chains in Russia—in the entire world. We must work to unlock them." In Wilder's rollicking letter to his family, the producer announced:

> "Gentlemen, I throw myself on your mercy. I want you each [including Praskins] to write a big closing scene. We have only one day to shoot it—Friday, because Fredric March is going to Tahiti and can give us only one day's work."
>
> Well, we all went off into different corners and wrote the scene. I appeared with mine on 3:00 on Thursday. The plan was to pool the best points of all three scenes, but the final scene was almost entirely mine. But it took from three to half past eleven to cut it and shape it in endless long conferences.
>
> [When done] then one of the under-executives entered with the expression of greatest gloom: "Miss Sten has just telephoned that she has a pimple on her nose." It wasn't funny; it was tragic.
>
> The shooting took place the next day. The pimple was indubitably there, right on the end of her nose. Her close-ups could be taken after March's absence, but the shot with them both couldn't be closer than eight feet, which greatly damaged the intimacy and intensity of the scene.
>
> As usual, they took the scene twenty–thirty times. March had to memorize my lines at 8 o'clock and play them at 10 and kept forgetting them.

Wilder's lines for Dmitri are at least Tolstoyesque, including, "All those who have been crushed in life are holy," and his plea to Katusha: "All I ask is to live again with your forgiveness and your help—and your love." When the picture failed at the box office, a Goldwyn quip allegedly spoken to George Cukor made the rounds: "The public stayed away in droves."

Mamoulian hoped to keep working with Goldwyn on a remake of *The Dark Angel*. Samuel Hoffenstein was adapting Guy Bolton's play to star Dietrich opposite March. But discussions broke down, and the film was eventually made in 1935 with director Sidney Franklin and the debut of Merle Oberon. That sent Mamoulian to quick meetings with Joseph Schenck at Fox, Thalberg again at MGM, and Harry Cohn at Columbia. Only Thalberg held out a possibility—a film of Franz Werfel's *The Forty Days of Musa Dagh*. It would have been Mamoulian's only politically charged work. The story about six villages' resistance to forced deportation by Ottoman Turks in 1915 is one of the best-known episodes of the Armenian Genocide. More than 4,000 Armenians were eventually rescued by French warships and moved to sanctuary in Egypt until the end of World War I. Thalberg's need to placate international distribution took precedence, according to Mamoulian.

In early February 1935, "We started working on it, and then suddenly he called me back and he said Turkey is raising Cain about it, they don't want to the film made. So he said, 'We had a big meeting and decided, well, let them kick up their fuss—so they won't allow the film in Turkey, we don't care about that.' A few weeks later he said, 'It's worse now. France is an ally of Turkey and France said don't make the picture. If you make the picture, we won't show it.'"

For the first time since Mamoulian's arrival in Hollywood, he had no motion pictures looming. He had known for a year that George Gershwin was writing his opera based on *Porgy*, but not until early December did he express any interest in directing it. A telegram or phone call from Theresa Helburn preceded his December 10, 1934, letter: "I am interested in doing *Porgy* and I think I can arrange it so as to be free next September . . . It would be great fun working with Gershwin as I have great admiration for him."

~

An unexpected death gave Mamoulian his next movie job. The strong light levels required for early Technicolor meant that the Pathé studio sets where *Becky Sharp* was being filmed, even with air conditioning, suffered from roasting temperatures. Director Lowell Sherman had been wearing shorts and an open-collar shirt to work. The shift between the hot studio and cool Los Angeles nights would have given anyone the sniffles. Sherman developed a cold, which led to the pneumonia that killed him on December 28, 1934.

Conniving, social-climbing Becky Sharp is one of the most famous characters in English literature—so much so, Margaret Mitchell went to some trouble after the publication of *Gone With the Wind* in 1936 to deny that she had even read William Makepeace Thackeray's *Vanity Fair*, let alone base Scarlett O'Hara on Becky. There are similarities in their manipulative attitude toward men, although Scarlett isn't reduced to singing in a music hall before a jeering crowd.

Mamoulian's adaptation, starring Miriam Hopkins, was based on the 1899 play by Langdon Mitchell. Screenwriter Francis Edward Faragoh had last adapted classic literature when he wrote the screenplay for *Frankenstein* (1931). The independent production released by RKO was the first feature-length film in three-strip Technicolor, a process developed in 1912 but not perfected until more than twenty years later. *Becky Sharp* is a demonstration picture, like a 1950s color TV program or *This Is Cinerama*. Producer Kenneth Macgowan hired Mamoulian within days of Sherman's death; filming was completed by mid-March 1935.

Mamoulian and cameraman Ray Rennahan wrestled with new technology in every possible way. The Technicolor camera, made even larger by its noise-deadening "blimp" cover, was about the size of a baby grand piano. It used three strips of black-and-white film. A prism behind the lens split the image into two beams; one passed through a green filter onto a single film strip, and the other through a magenta filter to two film strips with facing emulsion sides. The blue strip was on top, the red strip beneath. The three strips were developed as matrices, dyed, and printed onto blank stock.

Mamoulian's anecdotes obscure what he actually did when he reworked the color design by Robert Edmond Jones and also created the impression that he tossed out all of Sherman's footage. In 1971 to film historian Lewis Jacobs, he wrote,

> After reading the script and seeing all the footage shot by Mr. Sherman, I told them I did not like their script, nor the footage that was shot, nor the treatment of colors in that footage. . . . The film started with a bright red set, which to me, was blatantly wrong and undermined the color progression and dynamics of the film. [He wrote that he] moved red to the chromatic climax which went hand in hand with the dramatic climax of the film.

Actually, none of Sherman's footage was tossed out. Macgowan kept a chart showing that Sherman's scenes remained—mostly at the Crawley house with Alison Skipworth as Julia Crawley ("Beck-eee! Becky Sharp!"). That sequence, which does not have a red set, was the film's original opening, as it was for the play. In Sherman's version, Becky did not appear until after the first twenty pages of dialogue.

Mamoulian had Faragoh write a new opening in which Becky and her friend Amelia Sedley (Frances Dee) are leaving Miss Pinkerton's academy. That is from the novel's first scene, with one crucial difference. In the novel, Becky already is lined up to be the governess for Sir Pitt Crawley's family and has an invitation from the Sedley family to visit them. In Faragoh's version, Becky is quickly established as a young cynic: "We orphans must learn that the luxury of emotions is for our betters," she tells Laura (Viola Moore). Next she secures an invitation to the Sedleys by claiming that she's homeless and will have to take a public conveyance. Tom Milne observed, "The film thus not only short-circuits several chapters of the book, but brings its unwieldy wealth of characters under control by instantly pinpointing Becky as the puppet-master who will pull their strings."

Mamoulian designed the opening scene to show off blue. It appears mostly on Hopkins, who sports it on her dress and hat ribbon. The others are in brown, beige, gray, or lavender. "So I started practically in black and white [he was describing Miss Pinkerton's outfit] and I started intensifying colors. This being the first feature, you know, you had to accommodate your audience," Mamoulian recalled. Later, he draped Hopkins in deep blue and shimmering green; she is in bright canary yellow for her raucous turn on the musical stage.

Adhering to Thackeray's text was not a priority, and the film, in paring characters and subplots, omits Becky's young son and her bad maternal instinct. Historical accuracy was also ditched. For instance, everyone is waltzing in the ballroom scene. Mamoulian had research asserting that 1815 was far too early for that, and the characters should be doing the minuet. But he knew that waltzes move—minuets, not so much.

The waltz sets up the famed sequence in which wind and explosions evoke the terror of the approaching Napoleonic army. Mamoulian showed that the French emperor had escaped from exile in Elba with—what else?—his menacing shadow (George Sorel on horseback) edging along the streets of Brussels. The Duchess of Richmond's ball is interrupted by French cannon fire signaling the beginning of the Battle of Waterloo. A strong gale extinguishes candles, there's much running around by elegantly costumed figures, soldiers leave in a swoosh of cloaks—first blue, then red—their horses clatter across cobblestones, and finally the entire screen glows in a saturated red—Technicolor's best color.

Spectacular—but not Mamoulian's concept. It was already in Sherman's script. Mamoulian's idea was to extend the sequence, cutting it into thirty-nine takes to magnify the panic. There are about a hundred actors seen waltzing, but when they flee in terror, there are, in Mamoulian's account, five hundred. The effect is similar to a football stadium clearing out.

Mamoulian wanted to keep colors in sequence:

So I had to make a decision—which is stronger, the color impact or the logic? I picked the emotional, at my own risk. We had five hundred people there, and I told my assistant to divide them all in groups, start the first one in black and white, next one dark blue, dark green, then come to yellows and greens, then come to orange and at the end the officers in red.

Mamoulian, Nigel Bruce, and Miriam Hopkins on the set of *Becky Sharp*.

He said, "That doesn't make sense." I said, "I know it doesn't, don't tell me, I know it well." . . . So that's what we did, we divided them, and that's the way we did it, with the chromatic value ending up with the reds, and of course, that's the sequence everybody who's seen *Becky Sharp* remembers.

Hopkins was nominated for an Academy Award, even though *Variety* complained that she "at times fairly shrieks her way through the footage." She doesn't, although the combination of her alternately fluttery and brittle performance, alongside helium-voiced Billie Burke as Lady Bareacres and Alison Skipworth's braying Julia Crawley could leave that impression. In the New York *Herald Tribune*, Howard Barnes praised the color of *Becky Sharp* while finding Hopkins tiresome: "Too frequently she overacts as though afraid her radiant appearance in many hues will make one miss a gesture or intonation."

As soon as *Becky* wrapped, Mamoulian signed his Theatre Guild contract, some six months before *Porgy and Bess* rehearsals began. When he attended *Becky*'s Radio City Music Hall premiere in June 13, he had already been in town for two weeks. After months of anxious phone calls, letters, and missed connections, he got to hear George and Ira Gershwin play the score. He said it was "the first and only time in my whole life that I said over the phone, 'I will direct it' without having heard it."

CHAPTER 9

My Colored Brainchild

After the high drama of the saucer funeral in act 1, the second act of *Porgy and Bess* began on a rambling, cheerful note. At the Alvin Theatre, Jake (Edward Matthews) and nine other men sang "It Takes a Long Pull to Get There" as they repaired a fishing net while making plans to sail to the Blackfish Banks. Tired by this effort, five took naps at center stage, splayed out like the spokes of a wheel while another four dozed outside Porgy's window.

Porgy turned joyful, since Bess was finally his. Todd Duncan leaned from Porgy's ground floor window near center stage. As a banjo softly marked 2/4 time, he smiled and began to sing, "Oh, I got plenty o' nuttin'."

Mamoulian staged the number with the casual syncopation of a Disney cartoon. Four women in rocking chairs began to rock and sew in rhythm. The rest of Catfish Row—nearly thirty performers in windows, balconies, or the courtyard—sprang into action. Out of one window, Assota Marshall kept time with a dish rag; from another, Jimmie Waters created soap bubbles while Catherine Ayres beat a rug; Clarence Jacobs, on a ladder, tapped a hammer on a shoe; and Georgette Harvey, playing Maria again, sharpened a carving knife in front of her cookshop. A couple of others shook feather dusters while rugs were shaken from other windows.

Naida King was one of five children who usually were seen playing at the courtyard gate. She recalled, "George Gershwin told me to make my doll dance," which she did as Duncan sang, "De folks wid plenty o' plenty, gots a lock on der door." At one point, the hammer, dish rag, rockers, and sewing stopped. All movements resumed as Porgy's ecstasy increased and Duncan shouted, in the Gullah manner, "No use complainin'!" Bess (Anne

Brown) appeared at the window to give Porgy a drink. The sleeping men began to wiggle their feet and move their heads in time to the music, while tenors and basses hummed. Mamoulian's score annotation reads, "Everybody is working." As Duncan finished with "Got my gal—got my love—got my song!" Catfish Row returned to its movements, the women's rocking slowed, and two empty rocking chairs near Porgy's window, pulled by threads, began swaying. On Duncan's final note, the men rose in slow motion, stretching and yawning.

Olin Downes, the music critic of the *New York Times*, was a fan: "When did Isolde wave a scarf more rhythmically from the tower than those who shook feather dusters and sheets from the windows to accompany Porgy's song?" This undoubtedly was one of the scenes of which Hall Johnson, the famed African American choral director, complained, "Will the time ever come when a colored performer on a Broadway stage can be subtle, quiet or even silent—just for a moment, and still be interesting?"

The composer's intent? Yes. Before Gershwin wrote his music or saw brother Ira's lyrics, he had written in the margin of DuBose Heyward's libretto, "Entire stage affected by rhythm of Porgy's song." Mamoulian's attention to individual actions spurred Ruth Sedgwick to write in *Stage* magazine: "Each of the . . . people almost continuously on stage during the three acts of *Porgy and Bess* not only has a plausible and reasonable appearance and behavior but is an individual, with a life of his own and a purpose in living it. . . . You might see the opera a dozen times and still not grasp all the nuances of expression and movement."

Gershwin, who had an agreeable if narcissistic personality, had moved from composing Tin Pan Alley songs to Broadway shows and from there to concert works including "Rhapsody in Blue" (1924), "Concerto in F" (1927), and "An American in Paris" (1928). He was familiar with the work and ideas of Joseph Schillinger, Alban Berg, and Arnold Schoenberg; moved easily between pop and classical genres; and labeled *Porgy and Bess* a folk opera—but that's wildly inaccurate. Virgil Thomson, who had written *Four Saints in Three Acts* with Gertrude Stein, correctly called it "fake folklore." The "folk opera" question has since faded as audiences and critics shifted their attention to individual performances and the structure of the presentation. The debate over "authenticity" in George Gershwin's music and Ira Gershwin and DuBose Heyward's lyrics has never stopped.

My Colored Brainchild

Luigi Pirandello, Mamoulian, and George Gershwin in front of the Alvin Theatre during rehearsals of *Porgy and Bess*, September 1935. Photograph courtesy of Library of Congress.

When the show opened on October 10, 1935, there was respectful newspaper coverage and mostly positive reviews, but an opera, even with "folk" tacked in front, nonetheless has a limited potential audience. With an opening night cast of seventy-eight, a forty-three-piece orchestra, and a goat named Goo-Goo, *Porgy and Bess* ran just 124 performances. It began to show steep losses after the first month, and a brief national tour in 1936 lost money as well. Despite Cheryl Crawford's successful and streamlined Broadway revival sans recitatives in 1942 that toured through 1944, the work didn't truly go into the American repertoire until the Houston Grand Opera staging of 1976 and after the Metropolitan Opera finally staged it in 1985.

~

The Theatre Guild announced plans to produce an opera of *Porgy* on November 11, 1933; the next day, Heyward mailed Gershwin his outline for the opening scene of act 1. George, Ira, and Heyward worked on it throughout 1934; George reprised Mamoulian's summer visit to South Carolina to soak up local culture and spent the first half of 1935 orchestrating the opera. Theresa Helburn sounded confident about Mamoulian's possibilities: "I had lunch with [Gershwin] the other day and talked about the possibility of your staging it," she wired. "I told him you were interested and got him interested also. He is doing his most ambitious work on the score and feels the need of an experienced and musical director."

Her persuasion had its intended effect. "I spoke of possible producers and think the Guild leaned rather heavily toward Mamoulian," Gershwin wrote Heyward three days later.

> They feel that he knows more about music than any other producer and might do a beautiful thing with the musicalization of the book. They feel that John Houseman [Heyward's preference, who had directed *Four Saints in Three Acts* in 1934] is somewhat inexperienced to handle so huge a task . . . I told them that you are prejudiced a little against Mamoulian and that you would rather have someone else. They seemed surprised at that as they had thought the two of you had worked without friction.

Heyward wrote the lyrics of "Summertime" and the rest of the first-act lyrics and collaborated on ten other numbers, but Mamoulian ignored his changes to the libretto.

Mamoulian's contract brought him $3,500 for seven weeks of rehearsals, plus 1 percent of the weekly gross receipts over $8,000. In the early afternoon of May 29, the day after he arrived in New York, Mamoulian went to Gershwin's East Seventy-Second Street duplex to hear the score:

> George and Ira invited me to their apartment, and put me in a nice comfortable chair, gave me a highball, and George sat at the piano, and Ira stood by him, and he started off with this piano music ["Jazzbo Brown Blues"]. And he got through with that, and I jumped up, I said, "Great! Absolutely wonderful!"
>
> So and they went on, and Ira kept singing, then George couldn't resist the temptation, and he'd take over and he'd start singing. And every time George was singing or playing, he would look at me from the corner of his eyes to

see my reactions, you know. . . . They went through the whole score—it was the best performance of *Porgy and Bess* I ever heard—it usually is, you know, with the creators. Not much voice, but feeling. Style. I was absolutely delighted with the whole thing, and they lost their voices. For three days, they had to whisper. They went through the whole performance.

Mamoulian spent three straight afternoons and evenings with the Gershwins and attended one audition for supporting cast on June 8 before returning to California for a month for *Becky Sharp* postproduction. In July 1935, Gershwin shipped him the full score, inscribing it: "Dear Rouben: Here's my colored brainchild. I know you'll treat it well." Mamoulian responded with a letter complaining about the current lack of sun in Southern California: "But I hope this situation will improve because I want to come back to New York with a real tan—it will fit the color scheme better, don't you think?"

Rehearsals began August 26. Since Mamoulian hadn't cast the principals—composers had that privilege—and didn't know any of the performers other than Harvey and the members of her quartet, the first rehearsal had its share of difficulties. He learned that he had an unusually happy composer:

> George was there in the audience. I went home to the hotel and I just felt awful about it, I said, "It will never work." I was lying on my bed, you know, saying "I wish I weren't involved in this," and the phone rang and they said it was Mr. Gershwin . . . So I get on the phone and the voice came and he said, "Rouben, I had the most exciting time of my life watching that rehearsal. I think it is so wonderful." So I thought, my god, maybe I shouldn't feel so depressed. He said, "I just can't tell you how marvelous this music is. I don't believe I wrote it." That's all he had to say. He was thrilled by the music. But then he was really thrilled by the whole thing afterwards.

Anne Brown (Bess), born in Baltimore, was a twenty-one-year-old student at the Juilliard School when she auditioned for Gershwin in late 1933:

> I sang Brahms and Schubert and Massenet and even "The Man I Love." And then he said, "Would you sing a Negro spiritual?"

I was very much on the defensive at that age. I resented the fact that most white people thought that Black people should or only could sing spirituals. "I am very sorry," I said, "but I haven't any of that music with me." And then I broke out, "Why is it that you people always expect Black singers to sing spirituals?"

He just looked at me. He didn't say anything or do anything at all; he didn't appear angry or disturbed. But I saw that he understood my reaction. And as soon as I saw that, my whole attitude just melted away and I wanted more than anything else to sing a spiritual for this man. I said, "I can sing one spiritual without an accompaniment, if that's OK." He told me it was. And I sang "City Called Heaven." It's a very plaintive, very melancholy spiritual. And I knew when I finished that I'd never sung it better in my life, because I was so emotionally involved at that moment.

He was very quiet for some time. Finally he spoke: "Wherever you go, you must sing that spiritual without accompaniment. It's the most beautiful spiritual I've ever heard." And we hugged one another.

Todd Duncan, a thirty-one-year-old Kentucky native who taught voice at Howard University, took a train from Washington, DC, with his wife, Gladys, to audition at Gershwin's apartment in early 1934. He cherished the conversation:

"Well, where is your accompanist?"
"Can't you play?" (Duncan always roared at the memory of that question.)
"Well, I play a little bit."
"If you can't, I'll play for myself."

Duncan sang "Lungi dal care bene," an aria from Giuseppe Sarti's opera *Armida e Rinaldo*. Gershwin asked him, after he'd sung just twelve bars, "Will you be my Porgy?"

Thirty-three-year-old John Bubbles, cast as Sporting Life, had been a tap dancer since his teens and performed with a partner, Ford Lee "Buck" Washington, who played Mingo and pantomimed the role of Jazzbo Brown when that opening was still in the show. Bubbles couldn't read music. As the only name performer in the cast, he was accommodated, with conductor Alexander Smallens coaching. Mamoulian recalled the challenge:

I said to him, "Show me all the dance steps you know." So Buck sat down at the piano and Bubbles went through this terrific routine. Everything, you know? So I decided right then that Sporting Life would dance through the whole opera—never walk, never execute a pedestrian gesture, because Bubbles was so perfect. He could be described as a rather fey character, actually. . . .

At one time I remember that I wanted him to exit in a certain way. I said to him, "Look, it's one of your steps—I can't remember which one. Show me the variety of exit steps you used the other day." Well, he did one, another one, a third one. I said, "No, none of them are right." He said, "I can't remember which one you mean." I said, "I'll try to show you."

So I went on and tried to show him the kind of shuffle he showed me. And the whole cast stood around watching, and Bubbles was watching me, too, and when I got through, he said, "Mr. Mamoulian, you kill me."

After rehearsals were well under way, Mamoulian asked Bubbles, "How do you remember when to come in if you don't follow the music?" He replied, "When I get through, and the music goes on, I invent a dance in my head, and when I come to a certain step, I know that's my cue." In "It Ain't Necessarily So," Mamoulian gave Bubbles a ninety-second dance specialty, accompanied by guitars and humming. That interpolation became a subsequent tradition.

Naida King was seven years old, "and could sing and dance, I was told, well beyond my years." She joined Catfish Row after performing at an open audition for children. Her mother, Rosalie, was part of the Eva Jessye Choir, which filled out the chorus, and a cousin brought her to the audition. Gershwin, she recalled, was fond of her, and "he carried me everywhere he went. He'd put me on his shoulder. My mother didn't like that, you know. She didn't think it was ladylike."

Most of the time, she was part of a group of children near the Catfish Row gate, "playing jacks and stuff like that." They also sang an interpolated spiritual, "Sure to Go to Heaven," and because she was small, she had some special bits of unscripted business. When the policemen arrived after Crown is killed, "Everyone ran when the police were coming on stage. I jumped into a clothes basket. My rear end was sticking out. Then one of the police said, 'Oh, little girl?' and I jumped up and ran out screaming."

Before that, with a tiny parasol, she led the picnickers to Kittiwah Island as they sang "Oh, I Can't Sit Down."

Eva Jessye had some forty members of her choir in the show. She had been choral director of *Four Saints in Three Acts* and took pride in helping Gershwin make the ensemble numbers more authentic, particularly the saucer funeral and hurricane scene. "After all, being white, you can go only so far into the black," she said years later. Mamoulian enlisted Sergei Soudeikine to design a larger and much taller Catfish Row than the 1927 version.

The details of Mamoulian's original cuts during rehearsals, the show's Boston tryout, and the day after its New York premiere have long attracted academic interest, exploring whether the work "as originally heard by Gershwin" was a butchered version falling short of the composer's vision. The pioneer in this area was Charles Hamm, who used prompt scores and holograph manuscripts in various archives—but not Mamoulian's own score—and detailed every cut. Hamm got it right. His list, a significant monument of scholarship, matches all the cuts Mamoulian marked. However, "as originally heard" is still elusive for *Porgy and Bess*. 1935 was long before the days of the original cast album; prompt scores, the adage goes, are better for determining how a show sounded at the end of its run, not the beginning. For that matter, Mamoulian's annotations may be a better indication of how *Porgy and Bess* looked and sounded in Boston from September 30 to October 6.

Complicating matters further, the notes of the Theatre Guild board meeting of October 16, 1935, state that fifteen minutes were cut from the show after opening night, or at least that was the goal. The board had more interest in running time than in whether it might wreak havoc on a classic. Suggestions included, "crap game is too long; take out the trio ('Where's My Bess'); shorten Crown/Bess duet on Kittiwah Island." Langner "reported that there were two dawns and one of them might just as well be cut down." Warren Munsell, the Guild's business manager, complained of "repetition in business as devised by the director," which might refer to the "Symphony of Noise," now retitled "Occupational Humoresque."

Many Mamoulian cuts quite sensibly sped up the opera, as when he eliminated all the music from Porgy's killing of Crown (Warren Coleman) and nearly all the conversation in the hurricane scene. In the third act, Heyward's libretto had Bess take "happy dust" before Sporting Life sang "There's a Boat That's Leaving Soon for New York." Mamoulian directed Bess to reject the powder so Sporting Life took it himself before beginning to sing. Later, he leaves some on her doorstep, and while the orchestra continues his theme, she "comes out, looks around and hesitates; suddenly she grabs powder and goes in house, slamming door." That way, Mamoulian made the seduction vivid and complete.

Jazzbo Brown was Heyward's idea, based on "Jasbo Brown, an itinerant Negro player along the Mississippi, and later in Chicago cabarets" who gave jazz its name. Gershwin wrote 133 bars of piano jazz, to be accompanied by a half-dozen dancers "in a slow, almost hypnotic rhythm" and the singing of "wa-de-da" and "doo-da." A sliding panel near the top of Catfish Row opened as the show began to reveal Buck, who mimed at the keyboard. This lasted into the Boston run, where it was at first cut down, then eliminated before the New York premiere. Mamoulian's story matches both his diary and Hamm's speculation that the music simply didn't fit:

> From day to day I began to get the feeling that this opening was completely wrong, because the impression that one got when the curtain went up was Harlem, not Charleston, with all this jazz going on and this dancing. . . .
>
> One day, I told him, "You know, George, this music should come out." He said, "What do you mean?"
>
> I said, "We should start with 'Summertime,' because that's languid, it's the South, it's got the sunshine in it and it's Charleston. What you have now is Harlem." He was astonished, and said, "But when we played it for you, you jumped up and said it was great." I said, "I still think it's great. I just say I don't think it belongs in the show. It takes away from the beginning."
>
> Well, he took a pencil and cut the whole thing out. A week later, October 8, was my birthday and he came on the stage with a red ribbon around the piece of music and said, "Here's your present." I opened it and discovered the piano music we'd cut out of the show.

Music historian Joseph Horowitz asserts that the "operatic dignity and ceremony befitting royalty" marking Porgy's entrance is entirely the result of Gershwin's music, played here by "an upward flourish capped by a tingling trill," and not Mamoulian's staging. Porgy is more tragic than heroic here, though, as he sings "They Pass by Singing," which includes the line "When Gawd make cripple, he mean him to be lonely." He is welcomed into the craps game because he's had a successful day of begging alms.

For the play, Mamoulian limned Robbins's fight with Crown with flashing lights and shadows. Eight years later, he sent Catfish Row into kinetic spasms: "Crowd heaves in and out like a serpent, following them, coming in close and backing back to the walls again." He made the killing more daring for audiences. Crown used a knife, rather than a cotton hook; a red spotlight illuminated the stab. With Robbins (Henry Davis) dead, "All rush around body like a wall, hands up in horror." Then, "Serena screams, crosses to body and throws herself on it." Bess is still desperately looking for shelter before the police arrive, but this time, with the music swelling, Mamoulian directed that she "walks toward Porgy's door as going to an altar."

The saucer funeral had the mournful chant "Gone, Gone, Gone" (interrupted by the arrival of the detectives who arrest Uncle Peter), the faster "Overflow," Serena's heartbreaking "My Man's Gone Now," and the ensemble "Leavin' fo' de Promis' Lan.'" Mamoulian choreographed the sequences himself. Mourners were seated in a triangle of chairs and stools that rose against the back wall, with others on the floor, flanking the bed with Robbins's body. A writer for *Theatre Arts* described Mamoulian in rehearsal: "For one of Porgy's moments with Bess he wanted a gentle swaying movement from her as they sit back to back on the floor. Brown's movement was too vigorous, however, and Mamoulian aided her by saying, 'You're the accompaniment, not the melody. What we want here is an obbligato.'" The funeral included a movement that wasn't yet common. As the ensemble began "Overflow," Mamoulian's direction read, "All sit, slowly bringing hands down shimmering." The use of hands with splayed fingers, known as jazz hands, was not popularized until director/choreographer Bob Fosse used them in *Pippin* (1972) and *Chicago* (1975). Mamoulian was after shadows, though; the moving fingers cast hundreds of them on Serena's wall. All the performers then swayed during Serena's lament, "My Man's Gone Now."

"Leavin' fo' de Promis' Lan'" had more hand gestures, progressing to Mamoulian's signature shadows of 1927. On the line "Keep that driving wheel a 'rollin'," he noted, "All hands waving above heads. Serena raises arms to create largest shadow of all." It had the identical effect of *Porgy*'s act-closer and inspired the same patronizing descriptions that spur winces today. For example, Sedgwick saw "voodoo shadows begin their dance of death along the wall. At the end Lord Jesus has entirely gone, and the sultry soul of Africa broods over the room."

Duncan sang Porgy's "Buzzard Song," the character's only true aria (it precedes "Bess, You Is My Woman Now"), after Archdale scolded Frazier about selling phony divorces. Porgy's warning to the shadow of the buzzard that, if it lands, spells doom, was performed through the Boston tryout. Mamoulian never thought it fit; the A minor key is quite a shift in tone from what precedes it. Archdale's lecture was intricately timed comedy. Catfish Row was seemingly sleeping again, but it was only the reaction of a suspicious ghetto to an outsider's arrival. Every time Archdale glanced at the windows, all feigned sleep; when he wasn't looking, they eagerly watched his lecture.

In Mamoulian's version, he was diplomatically appealing to Gershwin's erudition:

> I was rehearsing the buzzard scene and again it bothered me. It's really subconscious, you know. Because it is very much like "The Song of the Viking Guest" in *Sadko* by Rimsky-Korsakov. . . . So we went to lunch and I was whistling the *Sadko* aria and George stopped eating and said, "Rouben, you're rehearsing one music, you come here and you're whistling this Russian thing. Why do you do that?"
>
> I said, "Well, I'm sorry George, I'm sorry. Go ahead and eat."
>
> Then he said, "I know why you're doing it. Because my parents were Russian." And then he was happy. Then finally, after three days, I told him, I said, "George, let's cut that out. It just doesn't fit." And he cut it out.

Mamoulian deleted "I Ain't Got No Shame," the ensemble number that was to begin the picnic on Kittiwah Island, instead dividing the cast into three groups dancing to drums before Sporting Life glided into "It Ain't Necessarily So." He also cut Serena's scolding rejoinder, the arioso "Shame on All You Sinners." That way, as in 1927, the emphasis remained on Bess encountering Crown. Crown whistled from the thicket because Mamoulian gave him a measure of the score, which the orchestra repeated. Bess didn't

They came . . . they sniffed . . . they went away . . . Gogol. The caricatures are of Lawrence Langner, DuBose Heyward and Theresa Helburn. The hand is Mamoulian's. The line is from *The Inspector General*, and the sprig of hay in Heyward's mouth may be an indication of how Sergei Soudeikine, the set designer who drew this during *Porgy and Bess* rehearsals, thought of him. Courtesy of Library of Congress.

get her "barbaric laugh"; instead, Crown led her in "a barbaric version of a fox trot" as they sang "What You Want with Bess" before he led her off for their sexual encounter.

The next day, Bess is in Porgy's room moaning and delirious with fever. Serena promises Porgy she'll be well and begins the touching "Oh, Dr. Jesus." The hurricane scene began quietly with "Oh, de Lawd Shake de Heavens," with Heyward's lyrics. "Then George decided he wanted to do six prayers to be sung practically simultaneously, so I wrote the additional five," Ira recalled. Each prayer has its own tune. Hamm observed that the number would today be called aleatoric—in which some element of the composition is left to chance and the performer's interpretation.

Gershwin's inspiration for the sequence came from an experience identical to Mamoulian's church visit of 1927. Because he had socialized with jazz musicians, Gershwin moved comfortably among African Americans in South Carolina and participated in singing with one congregation in 1934. At another, standing outside what Heyward called a "holy roller" church, they heard "Perhaps a dozen voices raised in loud rhythmic prayer. The odd thing about it was that while each had started at a different time, upon a different theme, they formed a clearly defined rhythmic pattern, and that this, with the actual words lost, and the inevitable pounding of the rhythm, produced an effect almost terrifying in its primitive intensity." Mamoulian cut nearly all of the accompanying dialogue to maximize the impact of the "many shrieks and wild yells" that came at the end, leading into Crown's unexpected arrival. He choreographed the resulting shock: "All fall back in a wave making a triangle beginning at Crown's feet to high spot on bed."

"There wasn't a single grouping that would happen accidentally, as in real life. That was just out of the question," he said. "Oh, Dr. Jesus" was sung with "all bobbing up and down" after Crown taunted the pious fearful of Judgment Day with "A Red-Headed Woman" and left in search of the doomed Jake.

After the women of Catfish Row consoled the newly widowed Clara with "Clara, Don't You Be Downhearted" (Bess is now taking care of Clara's baby), it's time for Crown to meet justice when Porgy kills him, shouting "Bess, Bess, you got a *man* now, you got Porgy!" Mamoulian said he had to argue for the "Occupational Humoresque": "I said to him, 'George, what's this? What made that scene was the music of noises. Now here you've put music under it—it's meaningless." He agreed, left the music out and we did it with just the noises."

Mamoulian also decided that for the opera, Porgy shouldn't plead for his goat. Now a knight on a quest, he orders his steed:

PORGY: Mingo! Jim! Bring my goat!
MARIA: What you wants wid goat, Porgy? You bes' not go anyplace.
PORGY: No! I'm going—Bring my goat! (commandingly)

In Mamoulian's recollection, Bubbles had the only opening-night mishap, during "There's a Boat That's Leaving Soon for New York."

Bubbles . . . did the whole scene with his back to the audience. I went backstage and asked the stage manager, "What's the matter with Bubbles?"

He was upstairs in his dressing room. He was crying. He was late for the cue. And he walked on the stage with his zipper open. George Gershwin and I attempted to console him. I finally said, "It's okay, we forgive you." He said, "Ah! That's the word I wanted to hear!"

Gershwin "had an innate aristocracy," recalled his friend Oscar Levant, a pianist and a celebrated wit of the age. "I'll never forget his opening bow . . . It was a beautiful one. And it should have been the last bow of the evening, but Mamoulian took that."

Mamoulian returned to California on November 8, taking a train from Grand Central Station. The cast gave an emotional sendoff:

As I started walking down the ramp, I saw a red runner of carpet leading to the train. Then I heard a band, playing the "Orphan's Band Theme" from *Porgy and Bess*. I thought I was crazy. I saw, as I came down to the coach, where I had my reservation, the whole cast of *Porgy and Bess* and the . . . band going to town and the goat and the cart. That's the way they saw me off to Hollywood.

I remember when the time came to get inside, I could see through the large windows on the side, nothing but a sea of black faces pressed against the window, and looking at me with such love that, you know, I broke down and cried for five minutes. I just couldn't help it. I loved them and love is reciprocated. You love something and you get it back. And unless there is love, you never get marvelous results.

In late November, as receipts dipped, the Theatre Guild trimmed the chorus. Bubbles obviously wasn't the only cast member to feel despondent, although he was quite a bit more visible about it. "Bubbles got on his high horse a week or so ago," Russell Crouse, then a Guild publicist, wrote Mamoulian in early December. "He apparently took up with the bottle, for the rest of the cast complained that he was interfering with scenes and making a general nuisance of himself. But for the last week he has been behaving and may have learned his lesson, for Warren [Munsell] threatened to replace him if there was any more trouble."

Just a week later, Jessye wrote to Mamoulian:

The other night, Bubbles missed his pre-picnic cue . . . all the sequence when he says, 'Lo, Bess, goin' to the picnic . . . on thru the refusal of dope by Bess. The guy was upstairs asleep. He was frantically rushed down and on stage, and though the music for his 'picnic is alrite' had long since passed, he bursted in like a house afire and began singing in his W. K. [William Keith] vaudeville manner. If he nourished the thought that "Papa" Smallens would so indulge him as to cut back, it was for one second only, for that worthy glowered and kept on keepin' on. Had it not been a serious matter, it would have been funny. Duncan saved the situation by advancing the 'Stay away from my woman' part.

Until he began his work on the motion picture for *Porgy and Bess* for Samuel Goldwyn in 1958, Mamoulian directed the opera only once more, in early 1938 in Los Angeles. The dialect has faded away, and so has the goat—an expensive item for such brief stage time. Porgy is usually now portrayed with a crutch.

CHAPTER 10

The Folks Who Live on the Hill

Jesse Lasky rescued a drifting Mamoulian in February 1936 when he came up with the musical spoof *The Gay Desperado*. Before that, Mamoulian spent a desultory couple of months trying to work out a script with a new Armenian American friend. Fresno-born William Saroyan, living in San Francisco, was unproven as a short-story writer when he wrote Mamoulian a long letter of introduction in 1931. He was just twenty-three, and three years away from his breakthrough *The Daring Young Man on the Flying Trapeze*, an autobiographical piece about a starving young writer.

"I have long cherished the desire to meet you someday, naturally . . . without forcing myself upon you," Saroyan wrote. "I have the viewpoint, I mean, that it is not quite enough for one to be simply an Armenian (though that in itself is a splendid thing) but that one should be making some conscious effort to be the finest sort of Armenian possible." That initial contact didn't lead to their meeting. Saroyan's next letter, from early November 1934, after *The Daring Young Man* was published and his promise was established, thanked Mamoulian for hosting him and introducing him to Virginie and Zachary. Saroyan piled on flattery: "You have vision, and your eye has the power to transform the drab into the beautiful, and to change the meaningless into the profound."

Having just completed an opera, Mamoulian's next goal was to get another on film. Albert Kaufman, who at Paramount had been his critic for overshooting, was now an agent for Myron Selznick. Mamoulian hoped to be able to return to Paramount through him. Kaufman tried to negotiate a deal to direct both *Carmen*—first filmed as a silent picture in 1915 and as recently as 1927 (with Dolores Del Río)—and the first full-talking version

Mamoulian with William Saroyan in Hollywood in 1935. They sometimes planned to collaborate on a film, but never did. Photograph courtesy of Library of Congress.

of *The Phantom of the Opera*, the famed Paramount silent of 1925 with Lon Chaney (a part-sound version had been released in 1929). Bizet's opera, not the remake of *Phantom*, was Mamoulian's preference.

Nothing came of that, so Mamoulian worked briefly with Saroyan on a treatment for a surrealistic film named *Love Immortal*. Saroyan tried to get work as a screenwriter, but was turned down. Mamoulian spent his free time involving himself in the organization of the Directors Guild of America. He joined core organizers King Vidor, Henry King, Rowland V. Lee, Lewis Milestone, Frank Borzage, Howard Hawks, William Wellman, A. Edward Sutherland, Frank Tuttle, and Irving Pichel.

"The unholy eleven were what the studios called them," Joseph Youngerman, by then an assistant director, recalled. "One of the group, Irving Pichel, was a commie [blacklisted in 1947] and except for Mamoulian, the other directors didn't go near him." (Mamoulian cast Pichel in the choice role of the priggish Mr. Stark in *High, Wide and Handsome*.) The impetus for actors and writers was a 50 percent pay cut the studios imposed in 1933. The directors were motivated by creative control; a new edict at Paramount notified directors there that their contracts would be voided if they didn't accept films assigned to them. "It was tough to get important directors in because they had a lot to lose, big salaries to lose," Mamoulian said. "The bigger the directors, the more reluctant they were."

Nino Martini and Ida Lupino in *The Gay Desperado*.

"Mexican gangsters are watching an American gangster film and they decide to modernize their methods and act like the gangsters." That was the simple pitch for the musical *The Gay Desperado*. The small-budget independent production kept both its producer, Jesse Lasky, and director, Mamoulian, afloat.

Lasky was in the midst of rescuing himself. He had been in partnership with Adolph Zukor since 1916, when they formed Famous Players-Lasky, but the studio's 1933 bankruptcy forced him and Zukor out of Paramount. Zukor returned after a few months, while Lasky began a joint venture with his old friend and business partner Mary Pickford. Pickford-Lasky Productions, releasing through United Artists, sputtered out after just two films, both comedies with Ida Lupino in 1936: *One Rainy Afternoon* with Francis Lederer, and *The Gay Desperado* with Nino Martini, a young Italian tenor. Mamoulian hired screenwriter Wallace Smith, a former colleague of Ben Hecht at the *Chicago Daily News*, to adapt "Senor Troubadour," a treatment by Leo Birinski. Filming began June 3, 1936, on the Goldwyn lot and was completed July 30 after a week of location shooting amid the saguaro cacti outside Tucson, Arizona.

Although its cleverness has faded, *The Gay Desperado* was highly acclaimed in its initial release, winning the best director award from the New York Film Critics Circle. Leading the praise was Howard Barnes of the New York *Herald Tribune*, who wrote, "It pokes fun at the musty mold of screen musical devised to introduce opera stars to filmgoers. . . . The gangster films have had their day . . . and so have the labored attempts to incorporate grand opera in program pictures." *The Gay Desperado*'s comic blurring of film fiction and reality is a close parallel to the mistaken-hero plot of *Three Amigos* (1986).

The film opens on an American gangster picture, *Give 'Em the Works!* A handful of crooks are punching a traitor in the back seat of a speeding car. "Give 'em the woiks!" one snarls, and the corpse is tossed onto a sidewalk. Mamoulian's camera pulls back. We're in a movie house in rural Mexico. Most of the audience watches impassively, except for Braganza (Leo Carrillo), the swaggering leader of the local bandits. "That's modern methods—you gotta learn!" he tells his partner Campo (Harold Huber). He shouts "Bravo!" at the use of a machine gun.

When other audience members start to shush the bandits, a brawl like the one on screen breaks out. The theater manager's solution for these occasions is to bring in Chivo (Martini), like a south-of-the-border Dick Powell, to sing "Adios, Mi Terra" while a travelogue screens. Braganza is a sentimental music lover, and he invites Chivo to join his band. When the tenor refuses, saying he wants to get out of the desert and sing on the radio, that's not a problem—Braganza and troupe storm a nearby radio station.

There, the close-harmony Vervo Sisters (Sophia Pedroza, Lupe Posada, Consuela Melendez) are trilling the year-old hit "Lookie, Lookie, Lookie, Here Comes Cookie." They're unflappable; after Braganza points his pistol and announces, "Stick 'em up!" they keep their hands waving in rhythm even with arms to the sky. Braganza introduces "Señor Troubadour" with "Such a voice what make you cry," and Martini launches into all five minutes of Verdi's "Celeste Aida." His listeners include Jane (Lupino) and her fiancé, Bill Shay (James Blakely) who are crossing the border in his expensive convertible. When police on motorcycles can't capture the bandits on horseback, Braganza orders the reluctant Chivo to overtake the couple. Chivo needs coaching just to say "Stick 'em up!"

Braganza has to lasso Chivo and Jane to end that discussion, setting up their eventual romance. Before that, he's delighted when Jane tells them she and Bill have just gotten married. That's not true, we learn later—they got to the justice of the peace too late. Braganza is only interested in seizing the car until Bill blurts out that his father is rich and important, so he switches his plan to demanding a $10,000 ransom. When Braganza returns from his dealings with Señor Butch, Braganza insists there's much to be learned from American gangsters and the movies. Campo doesn't think so: "I like funny moving pictures with whatcha call gags! And Mickey the Mice!" Braganza is enraged to learn that Bill has escaped and decides to shoot Chivo at sunrise. Chivo reminds him, "When I die, my voice dies, too!"

Finally, it's time for Diego (Mischa Auer) to make his move. One of Mamoulian's favorite images—he sketched this for decades—was a squatting sarape-clad Mexican peon, sombrero pulled down over his face for his siesta. He got this from Diego, the poker-faced, nearly mute counterpoint to the criminal hijinks. Diego tells Braganza that he's resigning:

> You see a movie picture and you want your banditos to become like the Americanos. What have these gangsters to teach us—except cowardice, unfair

methods, treachery? I have been very patient with you, Braganza, but today you should hide your head in shame! Today you would kill a man who is ready to give his life for love! . . . *por mis huesos*, you do not even permit him the courtesy of singing one little song before he dies!

Braganza relents. Lined up before a firing squad, Chivo sings "Lamento Gitano" (Gypsy Lament). Braganza weeps, since his ex-wife used to sing that to him. He proclaims, "I could kill the man, but I could not kill that beautiful voice!" Jane and Chivo break away and escape in the car, which sets up the final comic twist. The American gangsters headed by Butch (Stanley Fields) are parodies of movie hoodlums, including a coin-flipping George Raft lookalike and a cigar-chomping Edward G. Robinson mimic. They take over Braganza's gang and his Mexican village. The police apprehend Chivo, who promises to help them find the kidnappers.

The Americans, who have hiked the ransom to $100,000, are anxiously listening to the radio for news flashes with a response from Shay's father. What they hear instead is Chivo crooning a sumptuous "Estrellita" (Little Star). He speaks directly to Braganza, telling me that the only way to get his freedom is to send Jane to him; he reminds him that she's not married to Bill. Braganza regains his courage, offers to turn his gang in to the police for Chivo's freedom, and true love reigns to a reprise of "The World Is Mine Tonight" as the bandits gallop into the sunset, pursued by the wail of police sirens.

The film's weakness, besides Martini's wooden acting, is that he is the only performer in most of the musical numbers. Ida Lupino is given little to do. The Mexican gangsters are exceedingly good-natured ethnic stereotypes. They only kill in self-defense, and Braganza and Campo trade quips like Latino versions of vaudevillians Eugene and Willie Howard.

~

In May 1937, Mamoulian toyed with the notion of directing a musical version of Ferenc Molnár's *Liliom*, with music by Kurt Weill and James Cagney as the title character. It had already had screen adaptations, notably by Frank Borzage in 1930. Weill proposed to model Molnár's best-known work on his satiric 1930 opera with Bertolt Brecht, *Aufstieg un Fall der Stadt Mahagonny*

(*Rise and Fall of the City of Mahagonny*), which has a scruffy protagonist, a disastrous lust after wealth, and an appearance by God.

Weill wrote Theresa Helburn, "What we have to do, is to make him clear [*sic*] that it will not be an opera but a play with songs and music, like *Three Penny Opera* (which he adores), and that we would not change the play." Helburn wrote the composer, "I think Mamoulian would be an excellent person to direct if he were interested, and I should like to write to him about it." Weill met twice with Mamoulian. Molnár refused to meet. His possessiveness had more to do with *Liliom* being his most successful play. It's also his most personal. His biographers have found that Liliom's relationship with Julie—including the domestic abuse—mirrors the playwright's troubled first marriage.

Before *The Gay Desperado*'s release in October 1936, agent Charles Feldman returned Mamoulian to Paramount with a one-picture deal—a big-budget musical by Jerome Kern and Oscar Hammerstein to star Randolph Scott and Irene Dunne. *High, Wide and Handsome* had pedigree. Arthur Hornblow Jr., the producer, was married to Myrna Loy; *Ruggles of Red Gap*, which he had produced, had been a Best Picture Oscar nominee in 1934. Kern and Hammerstein were using Dunne, who had played Magnolia in the motion picture of *Showboat* in 1936. Mamoulian used cinematographer Victor Milner, who had filmed *Love Me Tonight*. Scott had recently begun his long string of memorable starring roles in Westerns.

In October 1936, Hornblow wrote Mamoulian enthusiastically: "You'll notice in the treatment that we call our hero Gary. It was originally my hope to get Cooper for the part but that has not worked out and I am accepting Scott in view of his growing popularity and his first-rate physical qualifications for the character. . . . The [Molly] part is presently set for Dorothy Lamour, a new girl we have here whom I think we'll like."

Decades later, though, Hornblow's remembered experience with the picture was less positive:

> It seemed to be born, so to speak, with a golden spoon in its mouth. But it didn't come off well . . . the casting of the roles was unsatisfactory. But basically the story was false, and it didn't come alive. It's not a picture I'm particularly proud of when it was all done. Also, the conditions of making it

Mamoulian with Elizabeth Patterson and Irene Dunne in *High, Wide and Handsome*.

were very acrimonious. . . . I would have liked to have taken Rouben Mamoulian off the picture.

Hornblow was referring to a number of rancorous circumstances. *High, Wide and Handsome*, scheduled for ten shooting weeks, stretched into four months; principal photography began January 6, 1937, after two days of rehearsals, and lasted until April 24. Bad weather was one factor; the manmade mountainside used in the spectacular finish was destroyed by rain and had to be rebuilt. Near the end of filming, a mishap during a chase sequence injured more than a dozen extras. The final cost of $1.8 million was about half a million dollars over budget. Part of that cost came from Mamoulian's $7,500-a-week salary, the most he would make for any film.

"He was kind of washed up in Hollywood because of that," said Paul Ignatius, who had a small part in the melee that ends the picture. Mamoulian only conceded that it "was a very difficult story to film about the war between the railroad and the landowners. Tough going, but it was interesting, because it had a great deal of Americana in it."

High, Wide and Handsome combines a fanciful love story with authentic history and manages to botch both, although Hammerstein had a questionable premise to work with: northwestern Pennsylvania farmers in 1859 take on greedy railroads charging confiscatory freight rates and, while sustaining violent attacks, build a pipeline to get their newly discovered oil refined. It has faint echoes of the historical sweep of *Show Boat* and can be seen—if one stretches some points—as a precursor to *Oklahoma!* Only here, the farmers and the railroad men can't be friends.

It begins with an old-time medicine show, segues to a blossom-filled romance and gushing oil wells, then builds to circus elephants and acrobats who take on the railroad-paid goons who are lashing the farmers with bullwhips. Sequences with the mechanics of oil-drilling are authentic down to the last bolt, contrasted with a barn dance with a whimsically querulous cow, horse, and owl. The bullwhip-fight finale looks exactly like what it is—an odd device.

Mamoulian enjoyed the challenge:

> What got me interested in it was, I didn't want to make a naturalistic film—I never do. And certainly with music, you can't, it would fail. Oh the other hand, I didn't want to make a fairy tale. But I thought, could those two things be combined? The earth and the sky. The music and oil—without hurting each other. The vision I had was a sort of phantasmagoria. . . . You've got this black oil versus blossoming flowers. The idea was kind of a super reality, kind of a dream. . . . I think the more you stylize it, the more vivid becomes the whole vision of this country at that period.

The film opens in rustic Titusville, Pennsylvania. Sally is singing the robust title number and dancing as part of her father Doc Watterson's (Raymond Walburn) traveling medicine show. Assisted by Mac (William Frawley), Doc is hawking an elixir that's really just "rock oil," the term for crude petroleum straight out of the ground. Peter, who knows rock oil is in every nearby creek, challenges Doc's authenticity; a brawl begins, but Sally's carelessness has set Doc's wagon ablaze. Naturally, they have no place to stay except with Peter and his grandmother (Elizabeth Patterson). Doc and

Mac stay in the barn while Sally's in the house charming gruff-but-lovable Grandma Cortlandt, who has a canary named Oscar (a Mamoulian in-joke). Peter (Scott) is ambitious, constructing a wooden derrick with a steam-powered drill so he can sell inexpensive energy to the masses.

Sally learns her way around the farm while Doc and Mac fix up a new wagon and prepare to hit the road again. Sally and Peter quarrel at first but realize at a barn dance that they're falling in love. They stroll through an orchard redolent of *Maytime*, and Dunne sings "Can I Forget You."

The film was Mamoulian's first work with Hammerstein and with Robert Russell Bennett, who had arranged the music of *Show Boat* and whose arrangements for *Oklahoma!* began his long collaboration with Rodgers and Hammerstein. Bennett's story about "Can I Forget You," mentioning a bit that was cut, shows how he learned to adapt to Mamoulian's personality after Kern suffered a heart attack and stroke that May:

> Jerome Kern fell seriously ill . . . so all the music we needed had to come from me. This is nothing new for a music arranger, but Mamoulian was very critical of the music all through the shooting. One morning my telephone rang and someone asked me when I could get the music ready for one of the songs. The answer was, "day after tomorrow." The following day the music supervisor assigned to our production by the studio came by and told me we were asked to go to Rouben Mamoulian's office.
>
> When we got there, Rouben made a speech about all orders having to come from his office and someone had scheduled a recording for Thursday with Irene Dunne and told him about it and we weren't going to work that day, and so on and so on. This was the time to put into words just what I thought about the motion picture industry, but I looked at the amused expression in the eyes of the music supervisor, Sigmund Krumgold, and suddenly saw how to get along in the movies.
>
> At the recording of "Can I Forget You," Rouben complained to me about the accompaniment. On the screen, Irene was in a rowboat as she sang, and Kern had given me a little waving figure that continued the refrain. With distaste in his face, Rouben asked me why that was in there. I told him what the composer had told me; it was to suggest waves gently tapping the boat. Whereupon Rouben asked a bit sarcastically, "Well! Which side of the boat are they tapping?"

At the wedding scene, Mac leads everyone in the polka "Will You Marry Me Tomorrow, Maria?" That's followed by Peter showing Sally the site on which he plans to build their house, and Dunne sings "The Folks Who Live on the Hill," the best song in the picture with its homey evocation of "You and I, shiny and new, a cottage that two can fill."

What more symbolic time for Peter's well to gush forth? The wedding guests rush from the celebration, everyone's soaked in oil, and the tone shifts from operetta to rustic adventure story. Peter gets too wrapped up in business to build the house, and next we see railroad baron Walt Brennan (Alan Hale), discussing his plan to keep raising freight rates to the refinery. "You gentlemen have certainly heard of a little game called freeze-out," he tells his chuckling companions.

The oil boom lowers community morals in the form of the shanty boat, a floating casino on which Lamour is a chanteuse. Mr. Stark and the others start to drive Molly out of town, but she finds refuge with Sally and Grandma Cortlandt. Peter dickers with Italian-accented saloon owner Joe Varese (Akim Tamiroff), who demands Peter's hilltop in exchange for land needed for the pipeline. Sally teaches Molly "Allegheny Al," a song about a steamboat dandy, which they perform at Varese's Hunky Dory Saloon. Sally longs to return to her performing roots, so when Bowers's carnival rolls through town, she runs after it. She becomes the next Jenny Lind, and even P. T. Barnum himself (Raymond Brown) comes to Harrisburg to hear her sing "Can I Forget You." The farmers have a contractual deadline with the refiner to deliver their oil; montages show the pipeline going up and raids by railroad gangs to tear it down. Just when it looks like the pipeline won't deliver, here comes Sally, acrobats, a strong man, elephants, and even a bearded lady in a surreal cavalry charge for the clash that ends the picture.

This sequence involved Mamoulian at his most dangerously disengaged. He had directed hundreds of extras before, but this was an outdoor wagon chase. The problem that day, Mamoulian explained decades later in what is surely one of his more fantastic accounts, was continuity. In his version, he wasn't present:

> They had to go left to right, because that's the way all the shots had appeared on the screen. In the arrival scene, they come in right to left. In order to

make that logical, you have to put in a shot where they change direction. Show them turning . . . and then you bring them in.

And I can't explain to you why—I didn't want to do it. I just had a very bad feeling about that. And I said, "I'm not going to take this shot." [When told he had to take the shot, he replied] "I don't know. I'll do something in the cutting room. Cheat somewhere, but I will not do this shot." And here I was feeling like an utter idiot, because I had no reason, other than the feeling that I'm not going to make this shot. Joe said, "I'll make it for you. Before you arrive, it'll be in the can."

[When he arrived on the set the next day, 116 miles from Los Angeles], as we came to that dirt road, I saw [assistant director Joseph Youngerman and the unit manager]. And they said, "Why didn't you tell us? Oh, we feel like murderers." [As the turn was made], one of the wagons fell off. Twelve extras and circus people were injured. One had his nose cut off by a branch of a tree, the other had a stick go through his chest. An absolute horrible tragedy. The fellow was lying in the hospital with this terrific wound, and . . . the first thing he said was, "Gee, I hope we didn't ruin this take for Mr. Mamoulian."

The "hope we didn't ruin this take" part of the story was used in publicity as Paramount touted the rough-and-tough adventure of the film. Youngerman told a different version of the mishap that had Mamoulian very much present:

The cutter was standing there, and said, "That's right, Rouben, it [won't] cut properly the way we are setting it up. Rouben said, "Oh, yes, it would." We argued, but he wouldn't give in. I finally said, "Look, Rouben. If I could come to work here at seven some morning and do a shot of the circus coming down the street and then turning so we get it straightened out, would you object to that?"

He said, "No, I wouldn't object to that at all. But I don't need it." I said, "Rouben, you do need it." He said, "Okay, go ahead and do it. You'll have the people ready for me at 9:00?" So we lined up five circus wagons, including the lion's cage, a cage with monkeys, a clown wagon and one of those tally-ho wagons with twelve or thirteen actors riding on top of it. We got ready to reverse the way that Mamoulian had been shooting them.

I wanted the drivers to come as fast as they could, but primarily I wanted them to stay as close together as they could. We started to do the shot, but one of the traces on the tally-ho—which was second in line—wasn't hooked up. The driver got off and hooked it. At the bottom of the hill, the first wagon was way ahead of the others. The others were racing to catch up with him.

As the tally-ho caught up and started to make the turn, the darn thing turns over and went through a barbed-wire fence. There were some people who were badly hurt and later we had to go to court. We did get the shot.

Mamoulian looked at me and said, "See, I told you we didn't need it." But we did need it, and we used it in the picture.

The orchard blossoms appeared to bother critics more than those rampaging elephants. In London, writing in *Night and Day*, Graham Greene called it "long, dumb and dreary" and spat venom at "The Folks Who Live on the Hill," ridiculing "masses of irrelevant Mamoulian blooms flowering at the right, the sentimental time; nature panting to keep abreast with studio passions, flowering for first love and falling for separation." The *Variety* review used a particularly cruel term in show business circles: "The story swings along with unabashed hokum, with crudeness in spots, but with a thoroughly becoming vigor in the battle between the Pennsylvania pioneer oil farmers and the railroad interests that tried to spike the first competing oil pipeline."

Mamoulian fired back in an interview: "Hokum simply means the stirring of the emotions of the populace in the simplest terms . . . the last reel of the picture was essentially true historically. If it did not happen, it should have." Paramount exhibited the film in the road-show format, meaning twice-daily reserved-seat showings instead of the all-day "grind" screenings. The public didn't respond to the studio's packaging of *High, Wide and Handsome* as prestige entertainment.

Mamoulian didn't dwell on disaster. On August 4, 1937, just after *High, Wide and Handsome* opened in New York, he sailed to Europe for a long-planned art vacation. This took him out of the Directors Guild's negotiations with producers; Frank Capra eventually took the lead on those. Paramount lashed back at Mamoulian in August 1938, during the DGA's hearing before the National Labor Relations Board in Los Angeles. He appeared alongside

Hawks, Herbert Biberman and J. P. McGowan to explain the role of the director and that no matter how well-compensated, directors still worked at the whim of studio moguls.

Milton H. Schwartz, who represented the studios, attempted to show that Paramount, under the terms of Mamoulian's first contract, would have paid him $658,000 for directing ten films in three years, even though Mamoulian made nowhere near that. For *High, Wide and Handsome*, Paramount claimed to have paid him a total of $178,750; Mamoulian put the figure at about $145,000. There was no explanation of the conditions that brought about this discrepancy; the studios were trying to embarrass the directors by showing that those who made as much as Mamoulian and Hawks were not in a position to represent assistant directors and unit production managers, some of whom typically earned no more than $150 a week.

In Paris, Léopold Marchand feted Mamoulian at the Paramount studio there, and he saw Maurice Chevalier perform. In London, he lunched with Randolph Churchill and chatted with René Clair, who was then directing *Break the News*, a musical with Jack Buchanan and Chevalier. Returning to Paris, he attended a performance of Marchand's operetta *Trois Valses* (*Three Waltzes*) and dined with Charles Boyer. At the Louvre, the El Greco exhibit gave him an inspiration for the Crucifixion art he later worked into the matador chapel in *Blood and Sand*.

Florence, visited on October 8, his birthday, was Mamoulian's most sensuous art expedition. His general reactions, which he carefully recorded in the outline of a book he intended to publish, are not unusual. The Uffizi Gallery, Palazzo Pitti, and Museo Nazionale del Bargello are overwhelming for lovers of painting and sculpture. For Mamoulian, there was transgression as well. He wrote of famous artworks as if tasting forbidden fruit while at the same time communing with the creators.

Mamoulian regarded the Renaissance masters not as religious icons to be kissed but as aesthetic icons to be touched. He brazenly plopped his hands on fragile centuries-old canvases, behaving precisely as he had directed Greta Garbo to do in *Queen Christina* when she "memorized" a bedroom. A sampling:

> Today I shall see and touch—actually touch with my hands—as many great masterpieces as I can. I shall gather enough beauty to last a lifetime.

> I have touched Carlo Dolci's "St. John Asleep" (what tenderness!), Perugino's "Mary Magdalene" (what mysticism!) and Raphael's "Madonna de Granduca" (what beauty!)
>
> Michelangelo's David: Touched him for strength. Could hold only the big toe in my right hand.
>
> Just touched the lips of Carlo Dolci's "Maria Maddalena"! She has been hanging over my bed in my youth for so many years!
>
> I have just touched—very delicately—the golden hair and the two exquisite nipples of Titian's Mary Magdalene. This is the most seductive combination of form and color I have ever seen. It is the very essence of overflowing womanhood, rich, warm and fertile, like the Earth itself.

In Rome, the Fascist government was his eager host. The hospitality included a tour of the Cinecittà studios. On October 24, Luigi Freddi, the Italian film minister, called Mamoulian "in great excitement" and arrived at his hotel, standing "transfixed" as he produced "the enormous envelope—Il Duce wants to see you!" The following Saturday at the Palazzo di Venezia, Mamoulian got a Mussolini autograph, but he didn't write anything about the experience.

He was far more impressed a couple of days after he attended an audience with Pope Pius XI. "Great day," he wrote. "Special permission from Vatican to go up the scaffolding in the Sistine Chapel." The ceiling, painted by Michelangelo in the early sixteenth century, was undergoing one of its periodic restorations. Others would have been content to simply gaze on Michelangelo's work up close. Mamoulian preferred to touch it. "Touched the woman in the deluge [Noah's flood], the face of the old man—the two lovely faces of father saving the son. Can hardly be seen from below—the amazing miracle of the perspective—lying on my back the way [Michelangelo] did—a thrilling experience."

He wasn't focused entirely on art. His romance at the time, Mary Anita Loos, the niece of screenwriter Anita Loos, arrived in Rome for an assignation. After graduating from Stanford University in 1935, Mary Anita was working as a movie publicist. She later became a successful screenwriter and novelist. Going by correspondence, her relationship with Mamoulian began shortly after the release of *The Gay Desperado*.

Mamoulian's attention inspired Mary Anita's colorful prose: "You gave me a keen appetite for beauty—and then you fed it on a banquet of superb courses conjured forth by the hands of a chef of genius," she wrote in December 1936. Lest that give the impression their relationship was platonic, the following June, she wrote him from the Santa Fe Chief, "It gives me great pleasure (almost approaching fetishism) to use your pen." Mamoulian used their time in Rome to draw the relationship to a temporary close. He extended his time in Europe simply because no work was available. Earlier that year, Mamoulian signed a contract with RKO involving nebulous plans for a picture with Charles Boyer. Boyer ended up fulfilling his contractual obligation with a film he liked quite a bit, as did his co-star, Irene Dunne—Leo McCarey wrote and directed the romantic comedy-drama *Love Affair*.

"The last picture you did at Paramount did not come up to expectations at the box office and hurt you rather than helped you," Neil McCarthy, his lawyer, bluntly advised Mamoulian. "Conditions at the studios have been very much upset and it has been impossible to negotiate a deal because of that." Mamoulian responded, "That silly contract with RKO that I signed seems to me practically non-existent."

Fortunately, he was about to land at another studio.

CHAPTER 11

Golden Holden

Mamoulian faced some challenges in 1938. An automobile mishap on April 25, when he rear-ended another vehicle, left him limping for a few weeks. He had lost out in his venture to become an impresario. In January 1937, he sponsored the American arrival of a fellow Georgian, Tamara Toumanova, who, with Tatiana Riabouchinska and Irina Baranova, were the teen "baby ballerinas" of the Ballet Russe de Monte Carlo directed by George Balanchine. As part of their contract, he paid her up to $175 a week for a year and paid for her training to become a dancer in motion pictures with the eventual goal of collecting a percentage of her earnings. He spent more than $9,500 on her, but Toumanova repaid Mamoulian by bolting to New York at the end of the year, and then to London, where she rejoined Balanchine.

Mamoulian ended up with *Golden Boy* (1939) because Frank Capra wanted a property he owned. On August 4, 1938, after a meeting with Columbia vice president Sam Briskin, Mamoulian recorded, "Goodbye to *Gentleman from Montana*." He had bought the treatment by Lewis Ransom Foster through his agency and sold it to the studio for just $1,500. Mamoulian was so nonpolitical, he never even registered to vote. So Foster's story about John Wilbur Smith, a "tall, angular Scoutmaster" with a "thin, piping voice," appointed to fill in a Senate seat from which he fought graft and defended Willets Creek, may have had uncertain prospects to his thinking.

Three days before the sale of the story, Mamoulian met with Capra in the run-up to the NLRB hearings on Directors Guild certification. Capra was nimble enough to combine that activity with professional ambitions. In his recollection, "Jesus, I wanted that story. I didn't give a damn whether whatchamacallim had that. I traded him *Golden Boy* for it." Mamoulian said Capra told him, "'I'd like to do it. Is there anything you'd like to do at the studio?' I went to Cohn and said, 'The one thing I like here is *Golden Boy*.'" After Capra failed to extract Gary Cooper from his contract with Sam Goldwyn, he persuaded the tall, angular James Stewart to play the scoutmaster, and they made the populist classic, retitled *Mr. Smith Goes to Washington*, a Best Picture nominee, the next year.

Rodgers and Hart were then at their peak with hit musicals such as *On Your Toes* (1936, 315 performances) and *Babes in Arms* (1937, 289 performances). In January 1938, their producer, Dwight Deere Wiman, offered Mamoulian the direction of *I Married an Angel*, the musical based on Hungarian Janos Vásáry's play *Angyalt Vettem Felesegul*. They thought Mamoulian would be perfect for this lightweight fantasy that introduced the melancholy "Spring Is Here." The initial offer—$500 a week for five weeks of rehearsal, plus 1 percent of the weekly gross—emphasized how much that 1 percent could bring: "As you are doubtless aware a musical of this size might gross between thirty and forty thousand for a long time, amounting to a not inconsiderable sum. These are the highest terms our office has ever paid to a musical director." Mamoulian withdrew from *Angel* because he got the nibble from Columbia.

He took on the task of transforming William F. Beedle, a scrawny twenty-one-year-old recently out of Pasadena Junior College with no professional acting experience, into the movie star known as William Holden. Mamoulian and producer William Perlberg had plucked him out of a screen test in which Holden was a supporting player. Certainly Holden was budget-priced, earning just $50 a week on his six-month Paramount contract; when Columbia Pictures chief Harry Cohn borrowed him, he had to only pay half of that. But even on those inexpensive terms, Cohn threatened his director: "If the kid isn't good, you're through."

Putting an inexperienced performer into the film adaptation of a major stage success just nine days before the cameras turned was a risk for all involved; Mamoulian insisted that Holden's casting had been his decision alone, since he thought youthfulness the deciding factor. "My main difficulty is to find the lead for it," Mamoulian wrote Seymour Obermer. "A young man of talent who could convincingly combine in himself the possibilities of being both a sensitive artist, violinist to be precise, and a fierce prizefighter." John Garfield, a stalwart for whom the part was written, hadn't played it on Broadway (Luther Adler did), was under contract at Warner Bros. and Jack Warner wouldn't loan him out.

The picture's success, then, rested on Barbara Stanwyck. She had spent years playing tough-talking, tenderhearted dames and wisecracking comediennes and was willing to take Holden under her wing so he would know where his marks were, camera angles and so on. The focus on Holden didn't make her a fan of Mamoulian, though. "He was like [Howard] Hawks, technically fine, you couldn't ask for more, but again, there was no affinity there, no joy," she told an interviewer. "To me, the essence of a good director is not to say, 'Walk to the table, then turn around and face to the left.' The good director will walk you through gently and give you some air."

Holden's screen test consisted of him with Margaret Young and Cheryl Lewis in scenes from *The Bride Comes Home* and *True Confession*; the director and producer were looking at actresses to play Anna, Joe's sister-in-law. Beatrice Blinn was finally cast. Holden's square jaw, sensitive eyes, and

On the set of *Golden Boy*: Mamoulian with William H. Strauss, Lee J. Cobb, Sam Levene, William Holden, and Barbara Stanwyck; at the piano, Beatrice Blinn.

deep voice gave him a nascent star quality, although he was far removed from the demonstrative Joe, whose mustachioed father (Lee J. Cobb on both stage and screen), speaks like Chef Boyardee ("Whatever you got in-a your nature to do is-a not foolish").

Mamoulian said Holden's was the seventh test he had seen: "There was this girl, and in front with his back to the camera—you could see his ear and cheek—was this boy. And somehow I forgot the girl and got interested in this boy. I said, 'Who is this guy?' Well, I couldn't find out. Nobody knew who the hell he was." When he interviewed Holden, "He was completely inarticulate, but somehow I felt he could do it."

Holden was thrown into lessons in violin and boxing. Columbia's publicity trumpeted that the ring scenes were "real," but Mamoulian knew a key truth—pugilistic and musical skills only have to look real enough for the two minutes or so of a take. The production schedule was arranged in the chronology of the play to allow time for whoever was cast in the lead to learn enough boxing and violin to get by. The scenes in which Holden fiddles were done near the end of filming on June 16.

Holden did well enough to get a long-term joint contract with Paramount and Columbia afterward, but the picture was a weak effort for Mamoulian, who was paid $50,000. The constraints of the Production Code, moreover, required that the script be watered down considerably from Clifford Odets's play, which featured ribald dialogue, a labor organizer, a suicide, and a gangster with a crush on Joe.

Odets's crackling twelve-scene Faustian parable contrasts the sensitive art of music with rapid success through violence. The play doesn't actually show violin playing, boxing, or suicide. Joe's musical skill and his fisticuffs, including the climactic bout in which he kills a fighter nicknamed Chocolate Drop stay offstage. When he and Lorna Moon (Stanwyck) decide to kill themselves in his Duesenberg with a high-speed crash on Babylon, Long Island, other characters discuss that revelation. It reflects the playwright's social conscience, earlier expressed in the one-act *Waiting for Lefty*, about a taxi strike, and *Awake and Sing!* (both 1935) which dealt frankly with the destructive effects of the Great Depression on families and economic security.

Some of its lines easily made the transition to the screen, particularly Lorna's rant at the transformed Joe: "You're not the boy I cared about! You murdered that boy with the generous face! I don't know you!" Quite a few more lines did not. The Production Code forbade portrayals of suicide. In their first draft, screenwriters Sarah Y. Mason and Victor Heerman had Joe, no longer able a concert violinist with his broken hands, but still a serviceable musician, serenading Lorna. When Mamoulian came up with his own treatment, he had Joe playing second violin—get it, second fiddle?—in a symphony orchestra performing Bach as Lorna looked on from a balcony seat. Odets demurred on adapting the screenplay, telling Mamoulian he had promised his wife Luise Rainer a trip to Europe.

Gangster Eddie Fuseli, as written by Odets, buys part of Joe's boxing contract from Moody because he has romantic designs on the youth. That was out for the film. Also out, along with the labor organizer: Fuseli calling Lorna a "nickel whore"; Joe buying a secondhand Duesenberg because Gary Cooper owns that model, then boasting, "In or out, nobody gets me! I like to stroke that gas!"; and Fuseli saying of Lorna to Joe, "Stop looking down her dress. Go out there and kill Lombardo." Adapted for the screen, Fuseli, played by Joseph Calleia, became just another oily gangster stereotype with a suspicious bulge in his breast pocket. The softening of Lorna's character—Stanwyck's relationship to Adolphe Menjou's Tom Moody is hinted at, but she's no "nickel whore"—was the priority, along with coming up with actual boxing. Harry Cohn, who had left school at age fourteen and had run the studio since 1923, was a famed bully, but those who knew him best saw the method behind it. Mamoulian insisted in later years that he liked Cohn: "One very simple reason. In spite of the fact that you couldn't quite believe his word, he was very honest, because he always said about himself, 'I am a son of a bitch.' And that disarmed you."

In January 1939, Mamoulian thought it best to take screenwriters Daniel Taradash and Lewis Meltzer and a secretary to Rancho Yucca Loma, a resort he favored in Victorville, far away from studio pressures, to draft revisions in five weeks. In the meantime, he ridiculed Cohn's limited vocabulary. He compiled a list of "pearls," most of which may have come from a couple of script conferences:

> The clux of the whole situation.
> If you play the song early in the picture, you can reprieve it at the end.

To screenwriter [of *Mr. Smith Goes to Washington*] Sidney Buchman: "You are nothing but a communist. All you think of is money." (Buchman was, in fact, a Communist Party member.)

I use literary language. I have no time to look for words.

[Discussing a plot development in *Golden Boy*]: Lorna goes back to the man because he needs her just like Joan of Arc. We want a Joan of Arc character.

Football—an intersexual game.

That character is not euphonious.

I want you to be the reactionary on that script—give me your reactions.

What happens after we die? I want you to prove it to me.

"Mamoulian never wrote anything, but he talked about it all the time," Taradash recalled. "He was so intelligent and he had a very private, very charming sense of humor." Mamoulian told the writers that the resort was known to be haunted by a ghost named Luke. Taradash and Meltzer once returned late after a night of drinking. "We slammed on the brakes, and we got out of the car. Out there in the desert, there was an apparition. Like ectoplasm. And a kind of pounding, like horses' hooves." It was Mamoulian, running around under a sheet.

The strangest script alteration—on the wrong side of history, although the United States hadn't yet taken sides on the matter—had nothing to do with Production Code restrictions. The Bonaparte family was earthy and noisy; Siggie (Sam Levene), Joe's brother-in-law, and sister Anna are fighting, and Siggie swats her with a rolled-up newspaper. Mr. Bonaparte admonishes, "Hit your wife in private, not in public," and neighbor Mr. Carp (William H. Strauss) adds, "A man hits his wife and it is the first step to fascism." A month before filming began, Ely Levy, head of Columbia's foreign distribution department, wrote Cohn not about "hit your wife," but about the fascism line: "This remark, naturally, will offend all those who believe in fascism as a form of government."

Cohn admired Mussolini and had released a documentary on his life; Mussolini had many American fans, including William Randolph Hearst (efficient strongmen tend to gravitate toward others of their ilk). Levy garbled his message a bit by talking about Italians in Argentina, adding, "there is [*sic*] a considerable number of people in South America who have fascist tendencies." The gist, without Levy having to be more specific, was the possibility of a Mussolini ban of the picture, which might have other dictators following his lead. Studios caved to many pressures, economic ones most of all.

So it came to be that Mamoulian filmed two versions of the scene—one for Americans, one for prints distributed in Europe. In the United States, the fascism line remained. In Europe, Mr. Carp was heard to say, "A man hits his wife, it is the first step to anarchism."

Golden Boy's ending is an unsatisfactory and abrupt resolution for a character whose violence has warped his soul. For starters, Joe's Duesenberg became a success gift, not a harbinger of doom. When Mamoulian takes Lorna and Joe to the viewing platform of the Empire State Building, she remarks, softly, "It's a big city and little people don't stand a chance." The line is echoed after Joe's bout with Chocolate Drop (James "Cannonball" Green), whom he kills in two rounds with a left uppercut. Chocolate Drop's father, a minister (Clinton Rosemond) tells him, "We're all small people, everybody wid a burden. You got yours, too—you gotta carry it—don't try to run away from it."

In the play, Joe does just that. Lorna advises him, "We speed through the night, across the park, over the Tri-Borough Bridge," and he understands exactly what that means. In the film, Holden is sad, then puzzled, then suddenly snaps back into being a bland All-American boy. "I've nothing to give you anymore," he tells Stanwyck. "I wanted to conquer the world, but instead smashed myself." She persuades him to take up the violin again when his hands heal, then there they are entering Poppa's parlor.

Mamoulian always insisted that the flavorless sentimental ending—Joe and Lorna turn up at his father's place, and he announces, "Poppa, I'm home!"—had no proscriptions on it: "So they are killed in a car; what does it mean dramatically? Nothing. It's an accident, and to end the thing on an accident is plain silly to me."

Later in 1939, Mamoulian did William Saroyan his biggest favor—he helped launch his Pulitzer Prize–winning Broadway play *The Time of Your Life*, produced by the Theatre Guild. Lawrence Langner and Theresa Helburn knew it was an important work, but they found parts of it confusing. Set in a San Francisco saloon with thirty characters, it sprawls across five sentimental, philosophical acts. Helburn and Langner took turns asking

Mamoulian to direct. Robert Lewis, the director they first hired, quit. Saroyan ended up co-directing the play with Eddie Dowling, who played Joe, the young loafer around whom much of the action revolves (The play helped launch Gene Kelly as Harry the hoofer, and William Bendix as Krupp, a cop).

Lewis didn't care for the Guild's methods, including having possible replacement actors watching rehearsals from the balcony. When he left during the New Haven tryout, he wrote, "Langner's last words to me were, 'After you and Orson Welles, no more geniuses.' 'Genius' was obviously a nasty word to Langner and served him as a substitute for the genuine dirty words he was afraid to enunciate."

Lewis failed to recall another part of the meddling. Mamoulian, while in New York in September, went up to the Langners' place in Connecticut to explain the plot and offer suggestions on dealing with Saroyan's truculence. After a preview in New Haven to administer late-night doctoring, he sent Helburn a facetious bill:

Expenses: $9.91
    Professional advice: $5,000
    PS. On account of because you and I is friends, I will let you overlook item 2. Item 1 I will let the Guild pay only if you insist.

Helburn responded with a $9.91 check (for the trainfare) and "ten thousand thanks. Your criticism was extremely helpful—to me, anyway. Whether we can get any of it through to Saroyan is another matter." Opening October 27, 1939; the play's original run was just 127 performances, but it was revived in 1940 and made into a 1948 film directed by H. C. Potter with James Cagney as Joe.

Mamoulian was about to plunge into the uncertainties of another independent film production.

CHAPTER 12

Mon General Zanuck

Mamoulian spent the remainder of 1939 in New York—many evenings in the company of Mary Anita Loos, with whom he had renewed his relationship the year before. She was now a fixture of Manhattan nightlife, famous for being on the arms of celebrities. Elissa Landi, on a lecture tour, encountered Loos on Fifth Avenue, then dropped Mamoulian a line: "May we not meet again? Perhaps the three of us. . . . In the meantime I write—and lecture—and feel grateful for my escape from Hollywood. It is a cruel place, I think." He added her to his schedule—Elissa for low-key lunches at the Plaza and Sherry Netherland hotels, Mary Anita to a performance of *The Philadelphia Story* and the opening night of the new Rodgers and Hart musical *Too Many Girls*.

At the end of the year, he met with Boris Morros, the former music director at Paramount, who had formed his own production company the year before; his only output so far was a Laurel and Hardy comedy, *Flying Deuces* (1939). Although Morros, born in St. Petersburg, was a Communist Party member and a Soviet agent (after World War II, he was a double agent for ten years), Mamoulian didn't record political discussions with him. He didn't like those conversations, anyway. At a New Year's party at King Vidor's at which the guest of honor was Charlie Chaplin, then making *The Great Dictator* (1940), Mamoulian recorded his impressions of Chaplin's ramblings: "Socialist—capitalist—anarchist—nihilist—acting Hitler—against organization and gadgets—despises science, Gandhi."

Mamoulian proposed to Morros a film of Aristophanes's comedy *Lysistrata*, in which Athenian women withhold sex from their husbands to end a war with Sparta. The original play is so specific to events in Athens in 411 BCE, it's always required a great deal of adaptation. Antiwar sentiment and isolationism hung heavily in the United States in 1940 after the German invasion of Poland set off war in Europe. Mamoulian was to receive $50,000 and half the profits.

There were Communist Party members involved, including a treatment from party members Oscar Saul and Louis Lantz, but that version adhered closely to Aristophanes's original story. Mamoulian's meeting with another party member, Donald Ogden Stewart, who won an Academy Award in 1941 for his adaptation of *The Philadelphia Story*, didn't go well. "Bored to distraction—slow-witted, dead mean (the face does not lie)," he wrote. A week later, he learned that Stewart asked Morros whether Mamoulian "had to direct *Lysistrata*—nice man!" Mamoulian asked Sergei Soudeikine to design the sets. Soudeikine thought he knew what the director wanted: "You want the Greek style simplified without too much architectural detail. (But not an Eddie Cantor musical comedy!)."

Mamoulian had another comedian in mind. His own treatment paired Carole Lombard and Jack Benny—a full year before Ernst Lubitsch did so in his anti-Nazi satire *To Be or Not To Be*. At the time, Benny's Sunday evening NBC broadcast was radio's top-rated program. An independent production was unlikely to be able to afford either star, even if they were free from their studio contracts, but Mamoulian let his imagination roam all the same. He opened with Lombard listening to Benny's program, which is interrupted by war news. During the interruption, Benny calls her to commiserate and mentions that a writer long ago had something to say about the misery of war, Aristophanes himself makes an appearance, and the story shifts to ancient Greece. There's a cigar-smoking Athenian general, Jacus Bennius, and Lombard plays the title role. When that idea went nowhere, Mamoulian tried to sign stage star Katherine Cornell, who had never made a film. Since he never had a completed script, Cornell wouldn't commit. He later pitched the film unsuccessfully to MGM, and by the end of May, he left Morros's studio. "It is really impossible today to have much comedy or laughter in connection with a war story," he wrote Soudeikine. "The actual reality is too strong and overwhelming." Mamoulian was horrified by the release of *To Be or Not to Be* in February 1942, calling it "wisecracking on the graveyard" with the German invasion of Poland a "background for bedroom farce."

That spring, Mamoulian found distraction with husky-voiced actress Kay Francis. Some years away from her descent into substance abuse, Francis had a reputation for sexual binging, which she carefully recorded in a series of diaries; her lovers eventually included Otto Preminger and Charles Feldman. Mamoulian, who took her on a month-long vacation to Hawaii, met her standards, such as they were: "A good lay," she wrote on April 6. Dinner at her place on May 21 became "an orgie [sic]."

Mamoulian had little time to nurse grudges, since Feldman secured him a one-picture, $1,500-a-week contract at 20th Century Fox. The film was a new version of the Douglas Fairbanks classic *The Mark of Zorro*, based on the 1919 novel *The Curse of Capistrano* by Johnston McCulley. Fairbanks was going to remake it himself, with son Douglas Jr. as Zorro, before his death from a heart attack in late 1939. Fox purchased the story from United Artists and had a script by John Taintor Foote, a specialist in horse stories.

Zorro, the Mexican nobleman who becomes a masked bandit on behalf of the poor and downtrodden, eventually forcing a corrupt governor to resign, was ideally suited for Fox chief Darryl Zanuck, going by the memory of Ben Hecht:

> Zanuck was a small boy with a tremendous excitement in a game he was playing, which is making movies. His mentality, when he was at his height, was about that of a 14-year-old boy, and it isn't too bad to be called 14 years, because that's the vivid age—the adventure, runaway, play Indians, play gangsters age. . . . I found him fast, quick, terribly loud, with at that time not the slightest concept of anything beyond a grade B movie . . . You could make a good movie with Darryl because he adored efficient work, and if you made your work efficient, he would go along.

Mamoulian addressed Zanuck in memos as "Mon general"—a reference either to Zanuck being a reserve colonel in the Army Signal Corps or his always speaking French to Mamoulian in the way only a thirty-eight-year-old from Nebraska would have enjoyed doing. Mamoulian's recollection of *Zorro* was, "I finished the film and had no interference from him at all." It would be more accurate to conclude that Zanuck had little interference from his director. Alone among the moguls, he had been a film editor, and his memos on casting, script drafts, and rushes were bluntly detailed. Going by those, it's easy to see why Zanuck had a reputation for being surrounded by obsequious yes-men. He didn't always get his way, but he never invited others' opinions.

The Mark of Zorro, in production from late July to early September 1940, was Fox's answer to the swashbucklers at Warner Bros. starring Errol Flynn and Olivia de Havilland. Tyrone Power, at age twenty-five, was cast in what would be the first of many similar roles as Don Diego Vega, the noble fop who dons a mask. Linda Darnell, a former child model, was not yet seventeen when she was cast as Lolita Quintero, her fourth co-starring role with Power.

While *The Gay Desperado* parodies screen action, *The Mark of Zorro* is all flash, dash and swordplay, with the romance almost an afterthought. Mamoulian adhered to the final set of notes from the studio chief: "Mr. Zanuck stressed the importance of keeping this story believable and gutty, with a melodramatic Robin Hood flavor, rather than the airy, tongue in the cheek *Monsieur Beaucaire* type of approach. This is most essential and Mr. Zanuck believes that the success or failure of this picture hinges on how we treat it."

Mamoulian didn't record his reaction when George Hamilton sent him a note in 1981 informing him that Hamilton's *Zorro, the Gay Blade* was being dedicated to him. Although Hamilton gave Diego a gay twin brother Ramon, who preferred to be called Bunny Wigglesworth, a discomfiting swishy stereotype, he was precise about showing the character's feyness as a revelation of his sexuality. It's in Mamoulian's film, too, but only as Diego's ruse. Alejandro (Montagu Love) calls him "this scented lily-fingers—this limp popinjay." Power's Diego sometimes carries a fan, loves scents, and announces, "I—I love the shimmer of satin and silk—the matching of one delicate shade against the other. Then there's the choosing of scents and lotions—attar of rose—carnation—crushed lily—and musk."

That's as far as the Production Code Administration and Zanuck were willing to go. After viewing rushes, Zanuck wrote: "I think we should retake one scene where he comes into the door at the cantina wearing the long black Japanese kimono. I know that we have to keep him in a robe at this time but this one looks like a nightgown . . . Can't we have a more dashing type of robe—something thrown over one shoulder or wrapped around? I am frightened to death that this will get a laugh." Mamoulian remade the scene with Power's kimono briefly over his shoulder.

Basil Rathbone, cast as Diego's rival, Captain Esteban Pasquale, had earlier matched swords in *Captain Blood* (1935), *Romeo and Juliet* (1936), and *Robin Hood* (1938). He was considered the best fencer in Hollywood—not for actual skill but because with his long arms and legs, he looked sensational in action. Flynn and Rathbone, in *Robin Hood*, fought across a massive castle set. Mamoulian preferred to set the Zorro climactic duel in a small room, "which makes it much more dangerous, and to me much more exciting."

Also, in the case of Power, it was more hazardous, going by Mamoulian's anecdote about the duel, which took two days to film:

> Now Basil, he's very proud of his fencing ability. On the day of the duel, [he] asked, "I have some friends here from England. . . . Do you think they could come and watch this scene?"
>
> Basil, you know, is bald. In the middle. So he wore a toupee. . . . The very first take . . . suddenly, Ty's sword hit the toupee and lifted it into the air. And Ty, who was a sweetheart, he died of embarrassment. And he stopped then! The camera stopped. Basil is looking at Ty, petrified like this, and Basil doesn't realize what happened! This silence lasted for a long time.
>
> So finally I said, "Basil, come on over, I want to tell you something." In the meantime, poor Ty got this toupee off and gave it to the hairdresser.

Mamoulian wrapped filming on September 13, 1940. *The Mark of Zorro* opened November 8 and was a hit, with a profit of more than $1 million. That won Mamoulian a two-picture contract for $2,500 a week, and another film for Power—a remake of the 1922 Rudolph Valentino silent *Blood and Sand*. Mamoulian was so preoccupied with that, he could barely respond when Miriam Hopkins sent him the script of *Battle of Angels*, her new play for the Theatre Guild, written by promising newcomer Tennessee Williams. "Somehow I think it would be lucky for us—if things come in threes," she wrote. "We've had two successes together and perhaps this is number three. Anyway, read it and call me."

The Battle of Angels, better known as *Orpheus Descending* after Williams rewrote it extensively for a 1957 Broadway production, was hardly Mamoulian's type of material. Hopkins thought it offered her a potential signature role: Myra, the sexually frustrated Mississippi woman who wears gardenias in her hair, dreams of dancing on the rooftop of the Peabody Hotel in Memphis, and is seduced and impregnated by a stranger. By then Mamoulian was engrossed in bullfighting. In Technicolor, his love of stylization and an immense selection of hues went raucously out of control.

Vicente Blasco Ibáñez, the most popular Spanish writer of the early twentieth century, acquired Hollywood heat in the 1920s, with his bullfighting novel *Sangre y arena* (*The Blood of the Arena*), published in the United States in 1911, and his World War I story *Los Cuatro Jinetes del Apocalipsis* (*The Four Horsemen of the Apocalypse*), published in 1919, made into films starring Rudolph Valentino. *The Blood of the Arena* is about bullfighting and not much else other than a love triangle: matador Juan Gallardo; his faithful wife, Carmen; and his mistress, socialite Doña Sol de Muira. In the novel, Juan's mother Augustias is forced to clean others' houses when her husband, Juan, a cobbler, dies. Young Juan is apprenticed to another cobbler before he takes up bullfighting. When he starts making money, he takes care of sister Encarnacion, but her husband, Antonio, Juan's occasional publicist, is a sponger.

Mamoulian supervised screenwriter Jo Swerling, who was Oscar-nominated for his screenplay of *The Pride of the Yankees* the following year, as he added characters to strengthen the theme of paths of glory leading only to the grave. Juan Gallardo (Tyrone Power) could be any famous athlete seduced by fame and wealth, his life spinning out of control. Swerling kept Juan's impoverished childhood, his mother (Alla Nazimova), sister (Lynn Bari), and parasite brother-in-law (William Montague, also known as Monty Banks) but made Juan's father a bullfighter who was killed in the ring. Garabato (J. Carrol Naish) is Gallardo's servant in the novel; Swerling wrote him as a famous matador reduced to begging before Juan hires him as his dresser. He also added fickle newspaper critic Natalio Curro (Laird Cregar) and compadre Manolo de Palma (Anthony Quinn), who becomes the new lover of Doña Sol (Rita Hayworth) when she tires of Juan.

Swerling introduces all the principals as children, emphasizing Juan's poverty, and his fearlessness as he sneaks into a practice ring at night. At a cantina, he smashes a bottle of wine over Curro's head when the critic mocks his late father's courage. Mamoulian introduces the adult Juan in a sequence set ten years later: Juan is becoming well known, but his friends are still struggling. He lowers a newspaper—which, being illiterate, he cannot read—to reveal his face surrounded by brilliant red silk. It's up to El Nacional (John Carradine) to observe the troubles ahead—mostly because of their illiteracy. The jealous Manolo observes that Juan has so far taken all the glory and most of the money for himself. Juan doesn't know that his first press notice from Curro calls him "fifth-rate" because the other passenger they ask to read it is too nervous to tell the truth.

After a hometown fiesta in his honor, the confident Juan hires a band to serenade Carmen (Linda Darnell), asks her to marry him and presents her with a wedding gown; before the night is over, he's hired Garabato. After a montage of posters in which Juan's billing becomes ever larger, Mamoulian shows Juan enthroned in his dressing room, surrounded by fawning hangers-on and an admiring Curro at his feet. Only Nacional has kept his bearings: "It's all ignorance and superstition—from not knowing how to read or write!" To Garabato, Juan confesses, "the feel of rust in my throat, the taste of death—fear!" The cape that Turro has tossed at his feet already resembles a bloodstain.

The film won an Academy Award for Best Color Cinematography for cameramen Ernest Palmer and Ray Rennehan. It marked the high point of Mamoulian's obsession with color and evoking artists of centuries ago. Mamoulian's indulgence in "art appreciation" didn't improve the acting and did nothing for the box office. He filled the dressing-room scene with colors he said were inspired by the sixteenth-century Italian painters Titian and Veronese. He decided to bring Carmen into the scene as well. After the men leave, Garabato gives Juan a long red sash, and he spins across the room in it to find Carmen holding the other end. Budd Boetticher, hired as a technical adviser on bullfighting, found that ridiculous: "And he never did anything right—like the sash that Tyrone Power had that was sixteen feet long and [made him look] like he was pregnant."

The Production Code was as strict about cruelty to animals as with sex and language. Instead, Mamoulian indicated the stabbing by a spectator spearing a sausage with his knife. For the fatal blow, the spectator stabs his wineskin, which bursts across the capes spread on the parapet. Boetticher, who had trained as a bullfighter in Mexico (he also directed *The Bullfighter and the Lady* in 1951), didn't find Mamoulian properly attentive. "I hated it.

Rouben Mamoulian was just awful. He was cruel. He had a bell, and if he rang twice, I'd have to come and stand behind him. He would ask about bullfighting, and bullfighting is like Catholicism—it's a religion. There's a right way to do it and a wrong way."

The styles of most of the painters Mamoulian evoked—Joaquín Sorolla in the marketplace, Francisco Goya in the bullring, Diego Velázquez for

Tyrone Power and Linda Darnell in the robing room of *Blood and Sand*.

Doña Sol's home—are noticeable if one knows to look for them, but they go by quickly. "It wasn't really imitating, but emulating their styles in design and color combinations," Mamoulian said.

The haunting chapel at the bullring, enshrouded in Alfred Newman's spectral music, is where Juan first encounters Doña Sol. In the novel, the chapel is squalid. Mamoulian had art directors Richard Day and Joseph Wright give it unexpected splendor. A giant crucifix and the wall behind it re-create a 1590 El Greco painting in the Louvre, "Christ on the Cross Adored by Two Donors," minus the two donors. Lighting casts a greenish pall on the actors. Mamoulian thought it a success: "With the green faces in the green chapel, everybody on the set would have said, 'Oh, God, what are you doing?' and I said to myself, too, 'This probably will be a dreadful thing.' But my theory was, if a painting can do it, shouldn't a painting on the screen do the same thing? A painter never uses a block of color for something; all El Greco faces are greenish; all cardinals' caps are not pure red." Boetticher, however, thought it ridiculous—and it is, especially when used for Power's death scene at the end. "He told us he wanted Tyrone to die with El Greco colors—the grays and the light greens and stuff. If you die, you don't die in a church, with a beautiful crucifix there; you die in a freezing hospital. But that's not how he wanted it. "

After their prayers, the matadors head down a dark tunnel into the roar of the crowd and blinding sunlight. Mamoulian described the effect: "I said to my two cameramen, 'I want you to pump so much light that you burn the celluloid.' So they lit it, and I . . . eventually said, 'Look, you don't understand. I want not only the matadors to blink, I want the audience to blink, too.' And that's what we did; we burned the film there. So technically it's lousy photography, but dramatically it's correct. It looks beautiful because it fulfills the intent of the scene."

There's little bullfighting in the film. All that's shown are daring passes by matadors as the bulls just miss their capes. Bullfighting, aestheticized by Ernest Hemingway in *Death in the Afternoon* (1932), consists of weakening the beasts before they are killed. Picadors on horseback stab the animal on its back to start the blood loss. After that, banderillos further weaken the bull by sticking barbed sticks in its neck, which forces it to lower its head before the matador begins to wield his cape and duck the bull's charges.

Finally, if the matador is not gored, he stabs the bull with a sword or two to kill it. The bull's ears and tail are often cut off as trophies.

Mamoulian filmed the bullfighting sequences in Mexico City between late December and the middle of January. Famed matador Fermín Espinosa, known as Armellita, doubled Power. Curro has the best line in the picture— Swerling's frisky reference to the Hemingway work. He gestures expansively to Doña Sol, seated nearby in the arena with her latest lover, Pierre Lauren (George Reeves) and proclaims, "If this is death in the afternoon, *she* is death in the evening!"

With her Mexican heritage and dancing ability, the twenty-two-year-old Hayworth, who had just appeared in *The Strawberry Blonde* at Warner Bros., would seem to have been a natural choice as Doña Sol. She wasn't. Her acting range at the time consisted mostly of a smile and the characteristic head tilt she used so effectively in her iconic *Life* magazine cover that year. (Bari was cast as Encarnacion after the studio failed to borrow Hedy Lamarr from MGM.) Even if Hayworth could sing, the thirty-eight-day shooting schedule wouldn't have allowed for rehearsal time and vocal coaching for the part that was the last to be cast, and by a loan-out actor at that. Graciela Párranga, whose soprano was completely wrong for Hayworth, dubbed her singing of Vicente Gomez's "Verde Luna."

Mamoulian, thinking like a painter, obsessed over small color elements. In one brief scene, Carmen, now married to Juan, tosses out the complaining Antonio and Encarnacion after they observe that Juan's houses, including the one he has provided for them, are not paid for, and he's fighting bulls as if afraid to get so much as a scratch. This segues to Angustias (Nazimova) discussing how she prays for Juan's safety:

> Well, [Carmen's] got a blue dress on and then she gets very angry with them and she grabs a sword and starts beating them out of the room. Well, now, through the first scene that's fine, but when she gets angry, blue is the wrong color. There's no anger in blue. It's an intellectual, spiritual color.
>
> I needed red. So, how do you bring in red? So I solved it by taking a long red scarf and I said, "Hold it in your palm and then when you grab a sword, let it out." But then, after she chases them out, the mother, Alla Nazimova, walks in, and the scene changes, becomes more serene and ends up with the

two of them praying, and then you don't want red, you want blue. How do I get rid of this scarf?

So I said, "When you get through, throw the scarf on a table. Well, it stayed on the table, still red. So I had weights on the end of the scarf, so she threw it on the table and the weights brought it on the floor out of the shot of the camera. You might think that's too much of a detail, but it isn't. Emotionally, it has a terrific effect.

Carmen prays to a bejeweled statue of Our Lady of Good Hope, which she asks for advice when she learns of Juan's affair with Doña Sol. She takes it in stride when the statue whispers back. First, it assures her Juan will "be safe and sound, my child," then, as Carmen edges toward explaining her crisis, it tells her, "I know what it is. I can read it in your heart. And you held it back—even from me." Carmen, dressed in black, confronts Doña Sol at her house. Hayworth, accentuated to full effect in a scarlet bra underneath a filmy white blouse, summons Juan to show Carmen that he is very much under her control.

For the scene in Doña Sol's lavish mansion where she first has Juan over for dinner, Mamoulian subdued tints, but not with lighting:

Now, where do you go, color-wise? I've exhausted it all with the red capes and all. So there's going to be a letdown. So after a while, the only thing to do is go the opposite way and do the whole thing black and white. So I always have meetings of all the departments before any set is built or costume or furniture, even, so I discussed this scene and I said everything has to be black and white—the set, the drapes, the table, the chairs, and all the guests—the women are in white, the men in black.

So I came on the set and everything was black and white except the white armchairs had golden frames around them and the flower piece in the center of the table was white roses, but green leaves. I said that's wrong. I always had a dozen spray guns for different colors on the set. They used to call it Mamoulian's palette. I could always pick one up and accent something, if I wanted...

So I said [to] spray all the gold black and then I took one and I sprayed all the green on the flowers black, and it looked awful. I said, "Oh, my God, maybe I've gone too far," and people thought, "What are you doing?"

Zanuck thought that, too. After he viewed the rushes of Hayworth's dubbed serenade, he laced into Mamoulian for excesses:

> I am absolutely disgusted by the manner in which the Doña Sol song in the patio was photographed. At most this should have taken a half-day. You used eight or nine angles to get over something that would have been sufficient with, and I guarantee it would be impossible to use, more than three angles.
>
> If you would stop making last-minute changes such as painting chairs and spraying ferns which all take time and your energy and would rely upon our competent department heads the same as other directors do on this lot, including John Ford, Henry King and others, I am sure that the final result would not offend you or anyone.

Two days later, he still raged: "I have worked with many directors who have a reputation for over-shooting but I must say that I have never seen such an example of over-shooting as you did on the Doña Sol song. Whatever possessed you to imagine that you could use 50 percent of the angles that you photographed is beyond me. One thing I do know and that is the next thing you do there will be no music in it—not even whistling."

Doña Sol, tiring of Juan, employs her usual excuse—a headache—and abandons him in a cantina where, in a crimson evening gown, she dances seductively with Manolo, trumpeted by Curro as bullfighting's next big star. Juan promises to return to Carmen after one last bout. This time, she is in the matador chapel, praying to the "man-god," who doesn't grant her wish. Clad in the white of martyrdom, Juan performs brilliantly and then is fatally gored. Carmen hears the shrieks from outside. The uncaring mob rains cheers and flowers on Manolo, there's a quick glimpse of Juan's blood on the bullring sand, and the gruesome cycle of fame resumes.

Mamoulian wrote Zanuck confidently in May: "At least, you must confess, there are no half-measures with me, and neither are there with you when it comes to elaborating on one single and unprecedented point. If you don't stop your series of notes on the theme of Doña Sol's song you will be as guilty of overwriting as I was of overshooting." The picture stumbled into overtime—a total of fifty-three shooting days—and at a cost of slightly more than $1 million, ran about $250,000 over budget. Despite Zanuck's discomfort at Mamoulian's methods, the film's beauty so seduced him, he approved its release at a longish 125 minutes without the usual previews.

That was a mistake. *Blood and Sand*'s initial release profit of $650,000 was lower than studio expectations. The *New York Times* complained, "there is too little drama, too little blood and sand in it. Instead the story constantly bogs down in the most atrocious romantic clichés, in an endless recital of proof that talented young bullfighters are apt to become arrogant and successful; that Curro, the critic, will sing their praises, and that thereafter their love life becomes very complicated. . . . This *Blood and Sand* has powder on its wrists."

Zanuck took the unusual step of dropping in on a showing at Grauman's Chinese Theatre in Hollywood after he heard that audiences were giggling. Afterward, he sent a withering memo to Mamoulian:

> It is my belief that you and I are jointly responsible. I am more responsible than you because all along I knew in my heart that this picture did not have the correct mood or tempo. Everything is played on the same level, with the exception of the bullfights.
>
> When I heard the audience snicker at some of the scenes, I could have died. The picture is the worst-edited film that I have ever been associated with. Instead of realizing we were dealing with a lustful and savage subject such as bullfighting, we cut our picture as if it were lavender and old lace, and in many places we produced our picture in the same lethargic style.

Nothing else went well that summer. A script Mamoulian developed with Daniel Taradash and Louis Lantz, *Bright Destination*, based on Darwin Teilhet's mystery novel, went nowhere. Zanuck's next offers were all B pictures, meaning that they were inexpensive, black-and-white, and went on the bottom of the bill of double features. Now known as a studio headache, Mamoulian learned that the studio would not pick up his option.

In late August 1941, Mamoulian took a leave of absence for illness. What was really bothering him was a torturous love affair that had begun in Mexico City. He identified the woman in his diary only as "Rabbit." She lived in Santa Barbara, was married with two young children, and occasionally made vague promises about leaving her husband, but mostly she strung Mamoulian along. At age forty-three, both his career and his romantic life were stalled.

He and Rabbit trysted in Van Nuys, and he spent whole mornings awaiting her phone calls. When she didn't call, he noted that it "felt like a century of silence." Eventually, Rabbit turned up at his house to report that her husband had given her an ultimatum: "leave or stay," and if she left, she must take the children. "She cannot leave, so she will stay." After that, "three longest days have gone by—unbearable. Must hear that voice." When he did again, they decided, "We'll go on talking and seeing each other. Get drunk as I never have. Woke up with one thought—to talk to Rabbit." About a week later, he recorded "hitting the bottom—in bed" wracked with "infinite and hopeless sadness."

He sent her a singing telegram for her birthday in September and spent his own birthday alone at Rancho Yucca Loma in a long, dark night of the soul: "All day on the rock—'Who are you.' For the first time trying to face myself and understand—the whole life in review—the world—the oneness. Very difficult."

He put his gloom aside when he returned to Fox in late October for the second picture under his contract. *Rings on Her Fingers* is a slight madcap

Gene Tierney, Mamoulian, and Henry Fonda aboard John Carradine's yacht on Catalina Island, December 7, 1941. Filming of *Rings on Her Fingers* ended early that day. Photograph courtesy of Library of Congress.

comedy starring Henry Fonda with a screenplay by Ken Englund. Zanuck originally assigned it to Irving Cummings before producer Milton Sperling sent it Mamoulian's way.

Zanuck kept him on a short leash, first demanding that fifteen pages be cut from the script. A subsequent memo laid out his vision of how to make cheap look expensive:

> Let it be understood, once and for all, and without equivocation, that this picture is considered by me and our company as a *cheater*. By this I mean that we are to cut corners in every conceivable direction and get out of it a splendid top bracket A picture, but one that because of the nature of the story and the slight cost of the cast as compared with other pictures we can make at a reasonable cost. . . .
>
> I will guarantee that I can take Irving Cummings or Walter Lang and make this picture for $600,000 or under. It is obvious to me that you have approached this production with the idea of making a classic, regardless of cost. . . . Do you realize that the budget on this picture as you now have it is a quarter of a million dollars more than the finished price of *Hot Spot*—and yet the cast in this picture only costs $30,000 more than the cast in *Hot Spot*?

Message received. This is why Mamoulian called *Rings* "the least important of my films" without anything resembling a signature touch. The blithe, fleece-the-rich storyline of *Rings on Her Fingers* seems better suited for the 1930s with Carole Lombard or Jean Arthur. It has nearly the same plot as Preston Sturges's *The Lady Eve* (made at Paramount earlier in 1941). In that, Barbara Stanwyck and Charles Coburn played father-daughter con artists out to steal from Fonda's naïve brewery heir. Of course, she falls in love with him.

Rings works off a similar premise, only with a middle-income scrambler. Spring Byington and Laird Cregar play grifters May Worthington and her partner Warren, looking for a pretty girl to serve as bait to a millionaire ripe for fleecing. Their last snare unexpectedly fell in love with the prey and is now honeymooning in the Catskills.

They find their new lure in Brooklyn shop girl Susan Miller, played by Gene Tierney. "Nature played a little trick on us," Warren burbles. "We should have been born with blue blood, so we have spent our entire lives correcting this biological error." He explains that there is no lawbreaking involved; Susan only has to be "beautiful and unobtainable—the queen bee." She acquiesces because she fears becoming a middle-aged saleswoman waiting on demanding matrons. On a beach visit, they quickly single out Fonda's John Wheeler, who likes to talk about yachts he wants to buy. He's a $65-a-week accountant with only two suits, but he has ambitions. The fun arrives as he admires Tierney in a bathing suit while he's on the phone using terms to describe a sleek watercraft: "I like her topside. Yes, nice and trim. Smooth and graceful. The overhang—yes, it's just about right for speed and stability."

Further amusement comes from Frank Orth as Kellogg, a private detective Wheeler has hired to learn who sold him a yacht that belonged to someone else. Kellogg dreams of buying a little cabin so he can go duck-hunting: "Bang, bang!" Susan, in love with John, eventually bribes a croupier so he can win at rigged slot machines and roulette wheels. Determined to keep their scheme alive, Warren intervenes. Kellogg tells John he's been played for a sucker, but he whisks Susan away for a happy ending all the same. "Ye gods, did you ever see anything so corny?" Warren sighs.

Filming was supposed to begin December 2, 1941, with the beach scenes on Catalina Island and a schooner rented from John Carradine; rain delayed that. To keep on schedule, Mamoulian had to film on Sunday, December 7, in Avalon Harbor on the eastern side of the island. Word of the Japanese attack on Pearl Harbor arrived that afternoon; "change of atmosphere—evacuation," Mamoulian wrote.

Nothing makes actors feel more useless than filming a comedy just as a war hits close to home. Frayed nerves settled in with the nightly blackouts in Los Angeles. Filming the final scene, set in a back room at a casino, "Laird Cregar goes fuming again—if he proceeds like this he will be impossible to handle within one year." Fonda, who starred in *The Ox-Bow Incident* in 1942 before enlisting in the navy, complained to Tierney, "This huge money they pay us; it just isn't worth it." Before long, Mamoulian noted antagonism between the stars; on December 31, he noted, "Talk to Fonda about not hating Tierney."

Zanuck, commissioned a lieutenant colonel in the Signal Corps in January 1941, was called to active duty within a few weeks of the Pearl Harbor attack, and he began appearing at the studio in uniform. Shortly before

Rings concluded filming on January 23, Mamoulian saw him striding across the Fox lot "in his full regalia and cigar. Compliments in French on my picture."

After filming wrapped, Mamoulian had time again for both Rabbit and Mary Anita Loos. On a drive, Rabbit complained about servants and "the crazy nurse whom the G-men want." At a dinner with Loos, he got "a generous measure of criticism," including "You with your money" and being a "perpetual guest, etc." Neither relationship went anywhere. Mamoulian busied himself working with Englund on a treatment for a film called *The Angels Weep*, a complicated drama involving a *New Yorker*–like magazine called *The Mad Hatter* and a paternity scandal. On May 3, he went to a luncheon at Tierney's house, where his life took a considerable turn: he met Azadia Newman.

At forty and twice married, Newman had been knocking around the fringes of Hollywood for five years. *Time* described her as a "comely, lynx-eyed socialite portraitist" notable for her red hair. Actress Coleen Gray, who met Newman when she performed in *Leaf and Bough* in 1949, observed of the red: "From a bottle, you know."

Newman considered herself American aristocracy. Her ancestry was supposed to have included a Quaker who arrived with William Penn, the founder of Pennsylvania, in 1682. Isaac Peirce, a descendant of the Quaker, bought up large tracts in Maryland and Virginia that eventually became part of the District of Columbia in 1791. As the federal government grew, so did the family's wealth, since they leased land on which government buildings were constructed. Until 1890, the family owned all of what became Rock Creek Park, and they had a mansion there near Peirce's Mill.

Thomas Newman, Azadia's father, was a lawyer and a Democratic National Committeeman during the presidency of Woodrow Wilson. She was the youngest of three sisters, and she sometimes claimed to be a distant cousin of Wallis Simpson, the Duchess of Windsor. Sister Helen stayed in Washington, while Artemesia married Arthur Drefs, a wealthy manufacturer in St. Louis. Azadia and Artemesia had artistic aspirations and painted; Azadia took classes at the Corcoran Gallery in Washington and the Pennsylvania Academy of Fine Arts.

In 1928, she married her first husband, William Herrmann, whose family was in the ginger ale business in Washington; she divorced him in 1936.

Two years later, she married actor Scott Kolk. He had been in films since the early sound era, with only one major screen credit as Leer in *All Quiet on the Western Front* (1930). When Azadia met Mamoulian, she and Kolk were separated. She split her time between Hollywood, where she painted portraits of Carole Lombard, Walter Huston, and Joan Crawford, and Washington, where she painted politicians, including Vice President John Nance Garner, and military officers.

Tierney told Azadia, "I think you two will have a lot in common." Mamoulian recalled his first words to her as, "You should be painted, not a painter." His diary records a couple of lunches with her; they were firmly a couple after that. Shortly thereafter, he bought his parents a place of their own in Beverly Hills.

On a November visit to Washington, Azadia wrote, "It is impossible for me not to be homesick for you—it seems a month already instead of a few days since you left." He responded in verse:

> I see your sulky lips and hear little sighs
> And think you are half woman and half child
> Perhaps a witch now fierce, now mild
> With smile and frown combined in every feature
> You very strong, you very lively creature.

Personal and professional happiness were about to combine in a spectacular way. Mamoulian hadn't heard much from the Theatre Guild since the previous year, when they proposed he direct Maxwell Anderson's *Candle in the Wind*, an anti-Nazi drama starring Helen Hayes. In summer 1942, Theresa Helburn sent him what she called "an extraordinary interesting Negro play" by Dorothy Heyward, *Set My People Free*, about the 1822 slave revolt in Charleston led by Denmark Vecsey. Mamoulian thought there was "something cardinally wrong" with the play. "That is, I (by I, I mean the audience) have not enough sympathy for the proposed revolt of the Negroes and the manner of their intended fight for freedom. I don't quite see, as you do, the analogy between the story of the play and the present-day situation of conquered nations in Europe. As a matter of fact, Vecsey and the voodoo doctor themselves seem dangerously analogous to Mr. Hitler and his lieutenants."

He engaged agent Arthur Lyons to explore film work, including an adaptation of *Porgy and Bess* at United Artists and anything he could find at Warner Bros., where Jesse Lasky was now a producer. Meanwhile, Mamoulian headed to Washington to see whether he could follow Zanuck into the Signal Corps, and to New York to find theater work. In 1935, he had treated *Porgy and Bess* as a one-off; now, for the first time since the early 1930s, he couldn't look at theater work as supplemental income. *Porgy and Bess* was snagged in contractual disputes with the Gershwin estate, but a Gershwin biopic, *Rhapsody in Blue*, was in the works. Lyons tried unsuccessfully to clinch a deal for Mamoulian to direct an English-language version of the Russian film *The Girl from Leningrad*.

Helburn sent Mamoulian the script of *Mr. Sycamore*, a fantasy by Ketti Frings about an unhappy mailman who decides to plant himself in his backyard like his favorite tree. In 1958, Frings won the Pulitzer Prize for her adaptation of *Look Homeward, Angel*. *Mr. Sycamore*, her first play, was as odd as it was lightweight. Mamoulian responded, "Sorry, the play, in spite of its charm, does not excite me enough to direct it. Have you got anything else?"

She did, as it turned out. Helburn thought *Green Grow the Lilacs*, a cowboy play by Lynn Riggs, had the makings of a full-scale musical and had begun her efforts in earnest after a 1940 staging at Langner's Westport Country Playhouse. Over lunch in New York, she and Mamoulian met in September 1942 to discuss its possibilities, although Mamoulian appears to have been the third choice after Elia Kazan, who turned it down, and Joshua Logan, who was about to go into the military.

In October, Lasky confidently waved the Gershwin biopic at Mamoulian again. But no movies emerged. The Guild eventually had a musical that transformed Mamoulian, the Guild and Broadway.

CHAPTER 13

A Bright Golden Haze

In the finale of *Oklahoma!*, Curly's killing of Jud has been ruled self-defense, Curly and Laurey start off on their married life together, and the surrey with the yeller fringe and brown upholstery rolls out as a dream realized. It's not far removed from Porgy in his goat cart.

Whether on Broadway, the West End, or in community theater, audiences still savor a Mamoulian "magic moment." Likewise in the first act, when Laurey puts her head on Curly's shoulder as he sings "Surrey with the Fringe on Top," as intuitive as that move may appear (Rodgers told a newspaper columnist he'd heard audiences let out a contented sigh), it began as a Mamoulian direction. Rodgers recalled:

> I remember, in rehearsal, when Mamoulian started to stage "The Surrey with the Fringe on the Top." I said to him, "How are you going to get a surrey in here?" And he looked at me as thought I were mad. And he simply had the boy and girl act out a surrey, and the relationship to each other, on the stage—the way they sang, the way they moved, and there was no prop at all, but it was the best-looking prop that's ever been on a stage. It was in the audience's mind.

Mamoulian's ideas about color for this musical have fallen into disuse—he insisted that Curly always wear an orange shirt, evoking a sunrise. But his other contributions to the staging and script remain. Even in the 1998 West End production directed by Trevor Nunn in which Josefina Gabrielle as Laurey wore dungarees instead of a ruffled dress in the first act and Hugh Jackman as Curly went shirtless in the second act, the surrey—by then, a gas-powered buggy with a fringed roof—still rolled out just where Mamoulian instructed.

At its St. James Theatre opening on March 31, 1943, *Oklahoma!* was not revolutionary in its elements, all rooted in stage comedy going back to antiquity, as well as operetta and vaudeville. There were, after all, a "stage Jew" (or wandering Gypsy) in peddler Ali Hakim, a soubrette with Ado Annie, and a conventional romantic subplot with Annie and Will Parker. Ballets had been incorporated in earlier shows, including in Rodgers and Hart's *On Your Toes*. As for Jud, the embittered pyromaniac farmhand, musicologist Tim Carter points out, "Every Arcadia contains its satyr, the lust-filled half man/half-beast who is a source of fear and a butt of jokes. Every Garden of Eden contains its snake." The wily peddler, a rapacious (but plain) Ado Annie, a "growly, bullet-colored" Jud, and square dancing were in Lynn Riggs's *Green Grow the Lilacs*, too.

What was stunning was how those elements combined. There are no specialty numbers—comic turns by a star comedian, stunts, broad comedy pieces, or dances meant to show off a single performer. That was remarkably advanced for a show where, as Mamoulian observed, "You realize that . . . there is no plot. Nothing moves. Nothing happens. It starts out with two people in love, and ends up with two people in love."

Before then—and as the early drafts of *Oklahoma!* reflect—Mamoulian pointed out, "musical comedy structure . . . was basically haphazard. You had a dialogue scene that was so simplistic it never could be taken seriously. You hardly had characters. Then a girl would break into song, and deliver it to the audience. Then they'd stop and say something else. Then there would be a dance specialty. It was really a series of vaudeville turns strung together very loosely."

The setting of this "folk operetta" begins with Laurey, an orphaned girl who lives in the Indian Territory with her Aunt Eller. She and Curly the cowboy are in love. He sets a mystical tone with a song about how beautiful the world looks ("Oh, What a Beautiful Morning"), and he promises her, to a clip-clop rhythm, a surrey when they marry. There's conflict from Jud, who lusts after Laurey and has a large collection of dirty (for their day) postcards in the smokehouse where he lives. Uncertain of her feelings for Curly, Laurey lets Jud ask her to the box social to be held that night.

A Bright Golden Haze

Celeste Holm performs "I Cain't Say No" in *Oklahoma!* At right, Joan Roberts. Photograph courtesy of Library of Congress.

Will, an impecunious and somewhat naïve cowboy, sings of all the newfangled improvements in "Kansas City" and Laurey's friend, the sexually adventurous Ado Annie, confesses to Laurey, "I Cain't Say No." Adding to the romantic merriment is Hakim, who lusts for Annie and any other naïve girl he finds on his travels. Annie's father, Andrew Carnes, learns of their involvement and forces Hakim at shotgun point to promise marriage. The peddler responds with "It's a Scandal—It's an Outrage!"

Laurey tries to tell her friends that she doesn't care about Curly in "Many a New Day," but she has less success when she and Curly sing "People Will Say We're in Love," a song that enumerates all the things they shouldn't do to tip off their friends and neighbors."

The solution to Jud, Curly thinks, is to persuade the farmhand to kill himself, and the resulting duet, "Poor Jud Is Daid," is the only funny Broadway hymn to suicide. Jud is immune to the suggestion, and his desire for Laurey only increases as he sings the grim "Lonely Room." The first act ends as Laurey, trying to sort out her feelings, buys a bottle of smelling salts from the peddler, then falls asleep under their harmless aroma. The ballet that follows, "Out of My Dreams" animates Laurey's fantasies as Jud's postcard dancing girls come to life and brings the chilling realization that Jud wants to kill Curly.

At the raucous square dance and box social that opens the second act ("The Farmer and the Cowman Should Be Friends"), Hakim buys Will's Kansas City souvenirs for $50. When Will bids that amount for Annie's picnic basket, Hakim bids a dollar more just so Will can have enough money to marry her. Curly outbids Jud for Laurey's basket by selling his valuable saddle and gun, and Jud then tries to kill Curly with a "Little Wonder"—a knife concealed in a pornographic viewing tube. Laurey angrily fires Jud, and he stalks away vowing revenge. Will finally gets Annie to promise fidelity with "All 'er Nuthin."

Weeks later, Laurey and Curly are married, everyone sings about the "Brand-new state! Gonna treat you great!" ("Oklahoma!"), and following the custom known as a shivaree—a pot-banging combination of salute to the newlyweds and fertility ceremony—Jud reappears with a knife, having set fire to the barn. He and Curly fight, and Jud falls on his knife and dies. A hastily convened makeshift trial finds Curly's act to be self-defense, and he and Laurey climb onto the surrey and begin their life together as the cast reprises "Oh, What a Beautiful Morning."

If audiences found an optimistic message about American pride during World War II, it would have been a matter of individual interpretation and not something overtly proclaimed from the stage. Settings and actions are perceived as realistic and homespun even though Mamoulian knew them to be as stylized as anything he had done. Although only "The Farmer and the Cowman" has an authentic thrum of the American West, no characters break into poetic verse beyond their station in life (the analytic expression for this is "within the diegetic").

Legends clung to the show from the morning after its Broadway opening, with most of the approbation going to the composers. Mamoulian consistently recalled that *Oklahoma!* was almost his undoing. "I became a tyrant," he conceded in 1964. "Nobody among my collaborators had a kind word for me as musical stage conventions were broken one after another. Although they were all my friends, they looked on me as the bête noire, the beast that threatened their very existence on the stage." (He was recalling the dispute over his personal publicity.) Agnes de Mille, who consistently minimized Mamoulian's contributions, called him "an autocratic dictator, accustomed to unquestioning obedience and complete authority."

The Theatre Guild's twenty-fifth season opened with considerable promise that November with Katharine Hepburn in a limited run in Philip Barry's *Without Love* (Hepburn made a bad film of it with Spencer Tracy in 1945). It was followed by *Mr. Sycamore*, costarring Stuart Irwin and Lillian Gish, which left the Guild Theatre after just nineteen performances and led *Time* magazine to conclude "the Guild is past its prime." Alfred Lunt sang and danced with Lynn Fontanne for 177 performances in S. N. Behrman's costume farce *The Pirate* (adapted into an overripe MGM musical with Gene Kelly and Judy Garland in 1948). A propagandistic work, *The Russian People* by Konstantin Simonov (a favorite of Stalin), adapted by Clifford Odets, lasted just thirty-nine performances.

Mamoulian hadn't gone east in September just to chat about plays. He had spent the previous week in Washington lobbying a friend of Azadia's family, Maj. Gen. Allen W. Gullion, the army provost marshal (she had painted his portrait), for a military commission. Just before the Helburn lunch, Mamoulian, classified 4-H (over age thirty-eight), had been turned down for a commission in the army or the Army Specialist Corps. With 20/600 vision, he had flunked his physical. He noted on one application that his experience as a director could be of use in psychology or criminal investigations. Pressing on, he sought a commission as a filmmaker in the Signal Corps.

In early January 1943, Mamoulian gave up on the military, writing Col. Richard T. Schlosberg, head of the Corps' Photographic Division, "my business commitment makes it impossible for me to enter the armed forces at this time." That commitment was still his hope of landing *Rhapsody in Blue*. If the picture wasn't scheduled to start for several weeks, Mamoulian thought he could squeeze in two months of rehearsal to launch the Guild's new musical. Jack Warner didn't see things that way. On February 2, Arthur Lyons wired Mamoulian, "His argument to Lasky was that he saw no reason for going outside for a director when they have what he termed important directors available on their lot." Irving Rapper got the job, and three days later, Mamoulian, his film plans in tatters, signed his Guild contract.

Even without a movie payday, Mamoulian's personal life became much happier. On January 14, Azadia wired from Reno, "Divorce granted 9:45

this morning. Leaving on Streamliner 11:30 tonight. Very much love." She joined Mamoulian at the Gotham Hotel two days later.

Many of the legends portraying the show as a long shot are true. The Theatre Guild board scrambled to come up with $90,000 in financing. Hammerstein, without a stage hit in ten years, had almost decided to join producer Arthur Freed at MGM if the show were not a success. His new songwriting partnership had uncertainties, since Richard Rodgers had only ever worked with the alcoholic and deeply troubled Lorenz Hart. Other producers thought a musical set on the American prairie, in which the female chorus—a given in all musicals of the era—doesn't appear for the first forty minutes, would have no chance. When it does, the gals are in modest nineteenth-century garb at a time when striptease had made its way into Broadway productions for war-weary audiences.

In revisions for his Columbia University oral history in 1958, Mamoulian began—but never finished—what he intended as his official account of his involvement in *Oklahoma!* He recalled that he was considering eleven scripts, with "the slimmest one," the rough draft of a musical version of *Green Grow the Lilacs*. The composers and the Guild, he added, "were flatteringly eager for me to direct this projected musical." "Flatteringly eager" sounds about right, if one also doesn't consider "desperate."

Mamoulian discussed the play with Rodgers on November 20, heard the partial score on December 1, and attended a backers' audition at Steinway Hall on December 21. The budget of $90,000 was austere, considering that a first-class musical at the time was budgeted at least $50,000 more. "They said I could do it any way I wanted to, just so long as I agreed to direct it," Mamoulian wrote. His contract, signed three days before the beginning of rehearsals, contains no such clause. It paid him $3,500 and 1 percent of the weekly gross. He collected 1 percent of the gross from any touring company without obligation to actually direct those productions. This gamble earned him an amount somewhere south of $2,000 a week for at least the next four years.

Hammerstein's initial ideas included the use of authentic cowboy music and a square dance caller; he and Rodgers also considered casting an established star, Mary Martin, as Laurey. "The most radical thing we did," Hammerstein recalled, "was to change what was the third act of *Green Grow the*

Lilacs. I think the author wrote a beautiful lyric play for the first two acts, and in the third act he went way off into some kind of Freudian darkness (the shivaree), which disappointed the audience."

From the outset, the script indicated at least some integration of music, lyrics, and dance, with specialty numbers included. The first draft contained twelve songs just in the first act, including some eventually cut, "She Likes You Quite a Lot," sung by Aunt Eller to Curly (in which she tells him the signs of women's desire), "I'll Be at Your Elbow," a song for Ado Annie to sing to the peddler, and "Peddler's Pack," Ali Hakim's description of life on the road. The essential structure, little changed from Riggs's play except for the addition of Will to compete with Ali for Ado Annie, was all there. "Oh, What a Beautiful Mornin'" was complete. "Surrey" and Ado Annie's comic lament "I Cain't Say No," were indicated only by cues in the script. The smokehouse scene with the "Poor Jud Is Daid" duet for Curly and Jud (a new name for the character in Riggs's play named Jeeter) and Jud's compelling solo "Lonely Room" also were indicated.

So was the integration of dance—the dream ballet for Laurey after she inhales the peddler's smelling salts. In Hammerstein's original version, which he specified as "bizarre, imaginative and never heavy," the surrey made its first appearance as part of Laurey's dream. Most flattering to Mamoulian probably was that Hammerstein provided the peddler, a nameless "wiry Syrian" in Riggs's play, with a name. Now he was Kalandarian [Kalantarian] Kalazian—"It's Armenian," Ado Annie explains.

The big second-act finish originally was a boot-stomping homage to marriage sung by Will (Lee Dixon), "It's Still Goin' On," with specialty dance routines, and Ali Hakim showed up not married to Gertie Cummings, the local girl, but to Lotta Gonzalez, a Mexican dancer Will had met in Kansas City. Since the songs advance the story, Mamoulian's paring of dialogue helped the first three songs tumble onto each other. Mamoulian also cut out several colloquialisms inserted by Hammerstein (they're not in Riggs's play). Out went two of Aunt Eller's lines about Laurey: "If she don't get you, Curly, she'll waste away to the shadder of a pinpoint" and "She's tougher'n a turtle's overcoat." Mamoulian and Hammerstein also sharpened comedy lines. When Ado Annie's father, speaking of Will and the fifty dollars he has to marry her, advises her, "Put it in yer stockin' or inside your corset where he can't get at it" the line originally continued, "or if them places ain't safe, think of a better place!" That was replaced with the punchier "or *can* he?"

As the second act was cut, out went both Lotta and her "barbaric Spanish song," replaced with the arrival of the peddler, now trapped in matrimony with Gertie and domestic life managing her father's store. Also deleted was a ballad for Curly and Laurey, "Boys and Girls Like You and Me," which everyone agreed was beautiful, but which Mamoulian thought didn't advance the plot and was difficult to stage. The song was replaced with a reprise of "People Will Say We're in Love" that made the verse a challenge: "*Let People Say We're in Love.*"

Singer Hayes Gordon remembered when Mamoulian made the decision on "Boys and Girls Like You and Me": "After one run of it, Mamoulian came onstage and said in his heavy Armenian accent, 'Years from now, when I am sitting in my padded cell, someone will come in and say "You are Rouben Mamoulian?" and I will answer "Yesss," and they will say, "You directed *Away We Go*?" and I will say "Yesss." Then they will say "And you staged the number 'Boys and Girls?'" And I will scream "Yaaaaaahhhhh!"'" The in-joke about the Armenian peddler didn't last. The peddler was renamed Ali Hakim, a Persian, although the character didn't otherwise change.

Backer auditions were difficult. The Guild had never put on a book musical. The closest it had come was a topical revue called *Parade* in 1935, and that had lost more than $90,000. Besides the uncertain wartime economy, there was an untested songwriting team, a director who had had nothing to do with producer Cheryl Crawford's recent successful remounting of *Porgy and Bess*, and the fatal stabbing in the second act didn't seem like musical-comedy fare. The financing plan involved selling 60 percent of the show, with the rest for the composers and the Guild and Mamoulian's percentage. The $54,000 arrived in bits and pieces, with Harry Cohn putting in $15,000, and Helburn strong-arming Behrman into coming up with $5,000.

The second act remained unfinished when rehearsals began on a chilly February 8 at the heat-rationed Guild Theatre. Dancer George Irving recalled, "I remember [Mamoulian] looking at the bare back wall with all those steam pipes running up from the floor, and he made a very touching speech, almost a monologue, about how much those pipes reminded him of the interior of a cathedral . . . that they were like organ pipes. 'For me, this theater is a holy place, and this work here in which we're involved in is a noble, holy thing.' We were all very moved."

Joan Roberts, a devout Catholic who had been unhappy at the coarse language in *Green Grow the Lilacs* when she read from it during her audition, was pleased to find that Hammerstein had removed that element, and she was impressed by the director's approach. "He injected an amazing amount of sincerity into the shaping of every scene—frowning, for instance, on such fetishes as swiveling in time to direct a punch line at the audience, instead of aiming it directly at the actor for whom it was intended."

Orchestrator Robert Russell Bennett recalled Mamoulian's mastery of crowd movement, when from the orchestra pit, he saw the director "instruct a stage full of people to suddenly stop short as Jud falls on his knife," which he compared to the work of Max Reinhardt (a more accurate comparison is to Catfish Row after Crown kills Robbins). He said of the script, some thirty years later, "It needed to be dug away at and Mamoulian was the only one capable of doing the digging."

Turf battles with de Mille broke out. Mamoulian banished de Mille's dance rehearsals to the lobby. Rodgers wrote that "at the beginning, [Mamoulian] did not have the security of command that I had remembered . . . from *Love Me Tonight*" although "gradually . . . he settled down." That was never de Mille's experience. She recalled his initial rejection of dancers Joan McCracken, Bambi Linn, and Diana Adams, all of whom went on to distinguished careers, as, "They're certainly not pretty. They can't act. Possibly they can dance. That's your department. They're useless to me."

Mamoulian managed to prevail in all the disputes, Roberts said, adding that when advice was coming her way from as many as six people, "I do remember Mr. Mamoulian standing up and saying, 'There can be only one captain of this ship and I am the director,' and it stopped." He developed what can only be called a fixation with getting animals on stage. In the opening, in which Curly sings "Oh, What a Beautiful Mornin'" while Aunt Eller (Betty Garde) works a butter churn, the original script called for only the sound of a gobbling turkey and a barking dog. But Mamoulian sought prairie verisimilitude. His rehearsal script notes, "sounds of animals: hoofs, dogs, turkeys, pigeons, cow, horse." The reaction of Rodgers and Hammerstein to a barnyard cacophony was never recorded. Another experiment with a live calf was quickly abandoned; "All it did was moo!" Roberts remembered.

Mamoulian wanted birds flying across the stage when the curtain opened. The concept was simple: on a platform stage left, a crate of white pigeons; stage right, a crate with birdseed. The one and only tryout was at the New Haven dress rehearsal on March 10. "Personally, I don't think I've ever been as excited and impatient to see the first curtain go up at any other dress rehearsal," Mamoulian wrote. Although the eighteen pigeons were supposedly trained—also expensive, at $15 a bird—disaster ensued. "Instead of flying across the stage . . . the perverse birds flew straight up like Roman candles, and landed on various scenic pipes on top of the stage. There they stayed, not only through the dress rehearsal but through the three days of our performing in New Haven." At another tryout performance, when Jud sets fire to Aunt Eller's place, Mamoulian, "to put a little more realism in the scene," Roberts wrote, "had a smoke bomb set off inside the farmhouse." The ensuing cloud nearly choked her.

In New Haven, Walter Winchell's secretary, Rose Bigman, left the theater after the first act to allegedly wire, "No legs, no jokes, no chance." Rodgers, who said the line originated with producer Michael Todd and was repeated by Winchell, insisted that Todd's quip was different: "The actual phrase was "No legs, no jokes, no tits, no chance." Winchell later ran the line his way."

Mamoulian and de Mille later jostled for credit for the staging of the title song. He recalled, "I told Dick and Oscar that what we needed in this spot was a rousing choral number." In remarks for Helburn's memorial service in 1959, Hammerstein wrote that she had suggested the song during a taxi ride to a backers' audition, saying, "I wish you and Dick would write a song about the earth." He added, "Now the strange fact is that, two days later, I had written a lyric which I had never intended to write." "Oklahoma!" was originally staged for Curly and Laurey, with a tap dance from one of the cowboys, not as a rouser for the entire cast ("Anything anyone does particularly well" read the stage directions in an early draft). During rehearsals, Mamoulian added a lariat twirler, an experiment dropped, Max Wilk wrote, when the rope hit his cigar and knocked hot ashes into his ear.

So how did the directions change to Bennett's "special and stirring vocal arrangement"? Holm recalled to Wilk that the arrangement originated with

Faye Elizabeth Smith, one of the singers, who suggested it to Rodgers. Langner's memoir backs up this account. Singer Vivian Smith told Wilk it was de Mille's idea to organize the singers into the flying wedge. Mamoulian claimed the wedge was his idea, and Roberts agreed: "He not only staged it, he came up with it. Agnes de Mille was sort of an aide, but he staged it."

"I staged it in half an hour and that's the way it stayed," Mamoulian said. "It stopped the show the very first time. By arranging the dynamics of the choral thing but starting them way up stage and gradually coming closer and closer to the footlights and then, at the end, almost stepping into the audience. Putting their feet on the footlights, leaning forward—which always brought the house down." That sure-fire "11 o'clock number" was perfected at nearly the end of the two-week Boston tryout. "All 'er Nuthin," which more or less resolved the romance between Will and Ado Annie, was polished just before that.

The show was a smash in Boston, with gross receipts of more than $50,000. "Rouben thinks they have a hit," Azadia wrote his parents, "but he says you never can tell." That same day, Hammerstein wrote Riggs: "The show is a solid success and now, if we can just make the hurdle over the first night grave diggers in New York, we will all be home." Mamoulian, faced with strong-willed collaborators, thought himself ostracized. "No one even spoke to me," he claimed. "Rodgers thought I was destroying his music. He couldn't accept the singers having their backs to the audience. Everyone wanted me to restage it as an ordinary musical comedy. I refused, and they didn't even invite me to the opening night party."

On opening night, Langner wrote, "as one beautiful song followed another, the audience took the play to its heart, and there was the most tremendous outburst of applause at the end of the ballet . . . During the intermission, I noted there was that electric thrill which passes through an audience when it feels that it is attending something of exciting import." The original New York run, closing in 1948, was a then-record 2,212 performances. The national company, first assembled in the fall of 1943 and shortly joined by a second company, toured for more than twelve years; the London production began a three-year sold-out run in 1947.

"One thing Mamoulian demanded—we were never allowed to acknowledge applause," said Roberts. "I only did it twice on opening night. After 'Many a New Day,' the applause was so thunderous we had to come out.

The finale of *Oklahoma!* At left, dancer George Church below Joan McCracken. At right, Lee Dixon and Celeste Holm. In the surrey are Joan Roberts and Alfred Drake.

After the reprise of 'People Will Say We're in Love,' I was backstage changing into my wedding gown. I had to hold the back of my dress and take a bow with Alfred!" After the title number, "people just stood up like they do at the opera. They thought the show was over at that point."

Critics were uniformly positive. In the *New York Times*, Lewis Nichols wrote, "It relies not on Broadway gags to stimulate an appearance of comedy, but goes winningly on its way with Rouben Mamoulian's best direction to point up its sly humor, and with some of Agnes de Mille's most inspired dances to do so further." Howard Barnes, in the *Herald Tribune*, applauded Mamoulian's "great taste and craftsmanship." In the *World-Telegram*, Burton Rascoe singled out Holm as "an astounding young woman," and Ward Morehouse observed in the *Sun*, "By the time they're singing the lusty title song near the finish, you're under the spell of it."

In its first eight days on Broadway, advance sales for *Oklahoma!* soared to $70,000. On April 9, Mamoulian recorded that the audience included

First Lady Eleanor Roosevelt. He hired publicist Ruth R. Maier, who used to work for Azadia, and embarked on a series of newspaper and radio interviews. The result of those was like tossing one of his lit cigars into gasoline.

Life-changing success creates new burdens. Two months into the run, everyone understood that *Oklahoma!* was a somewhat indefinable phenomenon. Audiences took it as an idealized reflection of the America they were fighting for overseas. That much the creators understood. The rest of it, not so much. For about two years, the show's success had no end in sight. Being the template for all subsequent Broadway hits isn't fun on the inside; everyone's happy they won the lottery, but they have no idea what comes next.

Rodgers and Hammerstein understood theatrical temperament; still, Mamoulian's publicity sent them into orbit. They called him down after a particularly hyperbolic press release in New York's *Daily Mirror* on June 13 (metropolitan newspapers at that time sometimes still ran press releases to fill out their issues). It asserted, "Mamoulian had his own ideas," and credited him with the play's quiet opening, the period of the costumes, the position of the first two songs, and the casting of Roberts and Drake.

Rodgers fired the first shot, demanding to the Guild on June 15 "That Mamoulian be stopped (and you will be able to stop him, unless you wish to continue your policy of appeasement)" and asking for a "vigorous campaign to rectify the harm already done." The diplomatic Hammerstein called Mamoulian the morning that letter arrived to lay out his version of the complaint. Langner, facing a threat to the greatest wealth he had known, panicked. He had a secretary record his phone call to Mamoulian:

As a matter of fact I am fed up with you and your lousy publicity. It's got to stop!

What publicity?

The stories you have been giving out in *PM*, *Sunday Mirror*, *Christian Science Monitor*, etc. You are just aggrandizing yourself at the expense of everyone else!

What do you mean?

And what's worse, you told a damn lie in *PM*, saying that you were going to direct *Porgy and Bess* in the pictures when this had fallen through, and also saying that I had tried to cut out a scene in *Porgy* and you told me I could either take it out or you would go. I have never been so insulted publicly in my life!

Why, I didn't say that!

Just read it! Your egomania is getting to be a disease when you have to say that no one else is any good in order to show how good you are.

What do you mean?

Saying you hired Alfred Drake and Joan Roberts in the *Mirror*, when you know that contracts were signed with them long before you were even asked to direct the play. Saying in *The New Yorker* that you had resuscitated the Theatre Guild!

Wait a minute!

I won't wait a minute! You can go right to hell! (*Slams down receiver*)

Right after that, Langner and Helburn, with additional signatures from the composers, sent a formally worded demand asking Mamoulian to "cease from these practices" and warning that if he kept it up, they would be forced to go public and prove otherwise. Mamoulian sputtered back about their "unfriendly and carping interpretation," but he didn't deny their assertion, either. "As the direction of *Oklahoma!* is my most recent work, it is perfectly obvious and natural that in any discussion of my professional activities with the press, *Oklahoma!* has its proper place." He also complained that the guild's publicity had minimized his contributions. Then he knocked over a bucket of poison: "Moreover, it has come to my attention from a number of sources that you have been making false, defamatory and derogatory statements about me generally, and in connection with my work on *Oklahoma!*"

The storm blew over fairly quickly between Mamoulian and the composers—he was having dinner with them just a month later. The damage with the Guild lingered. In his next two shows for the Guild, *Carousel* and *Arms and the Girl*, cordial exchanges were quickly followed with abrupt demands and arguments over money and credit. In August 1943, after an article about the show under Rodgers's byline had appeared, Langner wrote to thank the composer: "Terry is entitled to about 99.9 percent of the credit for *Oklahoma!* and under no circumstances do I want to pull a 'Mamoulian' on you, nor do I want any publicity about Agnes . . . Terry also thought of Agnes, and I know that your whole purpose in writing the article was to say nice things about the Guild in contrast to our lean and hungry Armenian." Langner didn't get around to apologizing to Mamoulian until October: "About the article in *PM*, I am perfectly willing to let bygones be bygones. We all lose our temper at times, and I am no exception to the rule. Nevertheless, it seems a shame to be able to work together amicably on so difficult a thing as production, then have to quarrel over publicity."

"It is sheer magic! Of course, it would take someone from the Caucasus to reveal the true beauty of this country of ours to us!" Anita Loos gushed to Mamoulian after she had finally been able to get tickets that fall. "Sam Goldwyn drooled to Dick for an hour, about every detail and department of the show," Oscar wrote to his son William, who was in the navy. "Then he got onto the music and said it was wonderful, finishing with a question. 'Do you know what you ought to do next?' he asked Dick. Dick said, 'No, what?' Sam said, 'Shoot yourself.'"

About a month after the opening, Hammerstein was making intermission speeches to urge audiences to buy war bonds. "Instead of dropping in just before my speech and leaving right after, I find myself standing through all the performances," he wrote William. "Much as I like the farm, I miss the show over the weekend. It's a lovable show. That is really the best description for it."

CHAPTER 14

Otto and Ethel

Otto Preminger, the mephitic scum.

—Undated Mamoulian note

Rouben and Azadia returned to California in June 1943 after he made his only contribution to the war effort—directing the first *Saturday Night Bond Wagon* radio program, with inspirational narration about Armenians fighting tyranny, for the Treasury Department. Film work was still difficult to secure. He wrote directly to Zanuck suggesting *Son of Zorro*. Zanuck didn't respond.

In fall 1943, he paid careful attention to his one-minute appearance in *Rhapsody in Blue*, which starred Robert Alda as George Gershwin. In a fascinating example of grasping for fame in someone else's biopic, Mamoulian rewrote his entire scene and talked director Irving Rapper into filming it that way at Warner Bros. He was shown emerging from the Alvin Theatre with Ernest Golm, who played Otto Kahn, chair of the Metropolitan Opera. Golm intoned, "Mr. Mamoulian, you handled George's opera as well as you did the original stage production." Mamoulian suggested that the Met stage *Porgy and Bess*, and Golm replied with something that Kahn never said, since the Met did not hire Black singers then: "We wanted it, but George felt it was a folk opera for all the people, not just the few that go to the Met." The scene was not used.

Oklahoma! became a turning point. Mamoulian only directed two more movies after this, both musicals. His embittering shambolic trip out of Hollywood's top ranks began with *Laura*, the elegant noir murder mystery at Fox that featured Gene Tierney's best performance and introduced Clifton Webb, a star of Broadway musicals, as a dramatic actor.

There are competing versions of what happened between him, Zanuck, and Otto Preminger, the Austrian-born producer who replaced Mamoulian as director. In Dana Andrews's recollection, supported by Zanuck's memos, Preminger, the studio insider, edged out Mamoulian, the perpetual outsider, in a conflict over how a single part should be played—Andrews's New York City detective Mark McPherson. Preminger contended that the dispute centered on Webb's effeminate performance as a newspaper columnist.

Mamoulian signed for *Laura* in March 1944. It was an agency package: Mamoulian, Preminger, Tierney, Andrews, and Vincent Price were all represented by Feldman-Blum. On March 20, he began work on the film for a $75,000 contract. Vera Caspary's novel may have struck Zanuck as a natural fit for Mamoulian, with its sophisticated New York milieu and powerful columnist Lydecker (who resembled Laird Cregar's critic in *Blood and Sand*)—so much so, Mamoulian wanted to cast Cregar. The point of the film is to keep the audience guessing about Laura's killer. Surely Preminger reasoned that Cregar, who had just played Jack the Ripper in *The Lodger* (1944) would have tipped the plot from his first moment on screen.

If Mamoulian sensed the studio politics at play, he didn't record it. The ambitious Preminger wanted to direct *Laura* all along. He had directed B pictures: the comedy *Margin for Error*, in which he'd also performed, and the wartime propaganda *In the Meantime, Darling*, which wrapped on March 7, a week before his first meeting with Mamoulian. Zanuck, just back from his war assignment in the Signal Corps, pushed out executive William Goetz, who had been running the studio in his absence, and didn't want Preminger directing an A picture. In Preminger's account, Zanuck told him, "You will never direct again as long as I am here at Fox."

Meanwhile, Mamoulian asked for script revisions and interviewed actors. Price played Laura's playboy fiancé Shelby Carpenter, Tierney was Laura, and Judith Anderson was Laura's socialite Aunt Ann Treadwell, who has been having an affair with Carpenter. "When he found out that I was not particularly in Zanuck's good graces, he started to ignore me," Preminger complained. "He started to rewrite the script, which I stopped. I said, 'You accepted the script; you've got to do it.'" Never mind that rewriting was routine to Mamoulian. He also added a deeply personal touch: Azadia painted the portrait of Laura, the murder victim with whom Andrews falls in love.

Clifton Webb was the last actor to fall into place. Preminger said he had to struggle through Zanuck's opposition and the lying of Fox executive Rufus LeMaire, who claimed that Webb, who was gay, had made a test at MGM in which he "flew" (meaning, he came off as mincing) off the screen. Preminger made his own screen test of Webb in which the actor performed a monologue from *Blithe Spirit*, the play in which he was appearing. Mamoulian's preference for Cregar may have had more to do with working with him twice rather than any particular hostility toward Webb. "He had that extra dimension," he said of Cregar. "There was something satanical in him, like John Barrymore had."

Andrews had talked his way into his role through Zanuck's wife, Virginia, whom he had met while filming *Purple Heart*. Zanuck had told Preminger to cast John Hodiak. Virginia Zanuck told Andrews, "I've never thought of you as a leading man. What's happened to you?" Andrews recalled that he laughed and told her, "They've never given me the chance. I guess it wouldn't do to have me take Tyrone Power's girl away." The next day, Preminger called Andrews to tell him he had the *Laura* part.

Mamoulian rehearsed the cast on April 25, 1944, and began filming on the set of Lydecker's apartment two days later. Zanuck worked in his gripes to Lew Schreiber in a May 1 telegram from New York:

> I am delighted with the *Laura* rushes from standpoint of photography, setting, camera angles and Clifton Webb's performance, but in my opinion Dana Andrews has been characterized completely wrong. I visualize a character like the role Dana played as the gangster in *Ball of Fire*. . . . In the opening scene Dana should have been standing in the apartment. . . his hat pushed on the back of his head, his hands in his pockets and an amused cynical look in his eyes as he wanders about the apartment of a fairy . . . This is not a role for a leading man. It is definitely a character lead: A cynical mug who falls for a girl who comes from a class he instinctively despises. I personally know that Dana has a fixation to be a leading man and he is probably influencing Mamoulian. I was afraid of this all along and that is why I wanted John Hodiak but stupidly listened to Preminger.

This corresponds with Andrews's memory: "Zanuck decided he didn't like the character played as a Princeton criminology professor, as I'd been instructed, but as a regular gumshoe like Pat O'Brien."

The rest of the story leaps into Preminger's self-aggrandizement: "Then Mamoulian started to direct the picture, ignoring me completely. He didn't even let me come on the stage, said I made him nervous because I also was a director. He behaved in a very silly way because I only could have helped him. I knew the script, and I knew where he was missing. And Mamoulian and Clifton Webb didn't like each other because Webb had heard that Mamoulian was against him."

So far, this is only the normal ego-driven course of filmmaking. Then Preminger's story went farther afield. He claimed Zanuck sent him a telegram reading, "This Dana Andrews whom you sponsored is an amateur without sex appeal, and Clifton Webb is flying. Judith Anderson should stay on the stage, and you should have stayed in New York or Vienna, where you belong." Zanuck's telegrams on *Laura* were routinely copied to Mamoulian. No such wire exists in Mamoulian's papers, and one like that he would have happily preserved.

Preminger said the Fox chief called them both into his office after he returned from New York:

[Zanuck] was ready to abandon the picture. Mamoulian had an alibi for everything. He said, "The script is bad. It cannot be directed differently." So I, being a director, played it for Zanuck. I said, "Now let's take this scene. This is the way it should be done." I knew the lines by heart. "This line was read this way by Miss Anderson. That's wrong—she has to throw it away." Zanuck was apparently impressed by it. He said to Mamoulian, "Well, I think he's right. Try again tomorrow. I'll give you another chance." Mamoulian tried again the next day, and again it was bad.

The following day at lunch, in front of eighteen people, Zanuck asked me, "Do you think we should take Mamoulian off the picture? It was a terribly embarrassing thing to do to anybody. And I said "Yes." Just like that. Zanuck said, "Okay." Then the whole group walked back to the administration building. Zanuck always walked in front with his [croquet] mallet. He called to me, "Come here." When we reached his office, he said, "You can start directing."

Mamoulian recorded a single meeting, undoubtedly stormy, between himself, Zanuck, and Lew Schreiber on May 14. "I didn't have to quit it," he said years later. "Zanuck was eager to fire Preminger, but I didn't want him to do it. I didn't want him to establish a precedent where you'd say producer engages Mamoulian and the first thing Mamoulian does is fire the producer. So I said, 'Look, to me, it's one of the pictures. To Preminger, it's die or live.' So I quit." Preminger threw out Azadia's painting, replacing it with a portrait of Tierney by studio photographer Frank Ponroy, which had a light paint wash applied.

Peter Bogdanovich's interview with Preminger, which included the *Laura* account, was published in the first issue of *On Film* in late 1970. The editors sent Mamoulian a copy with a letter inviting him to respond. Unusually for him, he did: "I wish to state that Mr. Preminger is a total, unmitigated liar and that everything he says in his piece pertaining to me is a fraudulent fabrication of a base and unscrupulous mind. Mr. Preminger's own answers to Peter Bogdanovich's incisive questions fully reveal his emetic self-portrait, both as 'man' and 'film maker.'" Those were the words of someone trying to bait a libel suit to finally tell the world about Preminger's duplicity. After his replacement on *Porgy and Bess*, Mamoulian could always reach a quick boil at the mere mention of Preminger's name.

The letter was never published. The first issue of *On Film* also was the last.

~

In every failed Broadway show, the creators point to a moment in rehearsal when they suddenly realized everything was going irretrievably wrong. For the musical *Sadie Thompson*, it came on September 18, 1944: "What the fuck is Mal Maison?"

Ethel Merman was a performing force of nature. On her first day of rehearsal in the title role, she was questioning a lyric in the opening number, "Fisherman's Wharf": "Put some Mal Maison on your lips." She wrote about it years later:

> There was a line that went like this: "You put some black pencil on your peepers and some Mal Maison on your lips." I hadn't an idea what Mal Maison was. I knew mal meant "bad" and maison meant "house," so I figured if you put those together they meant "bad house." But I couldn't see how you put that on your lips. The lyric writer [Howard Dietz] said it was a brand of lipstick, but I asked fifteen of my girl friends, and they'd never heard of it. I have to sing songs that make sense to me, and that "Mal Maison on your lips" stuck in my craw.

Dietz was being disingenuous. Sadie is Somerset Maugham's hard-edged prostitute who lures the Rev. Alfred Davidson, a South Seas missionary in the village of Pago Pago, into adultery and eventually suicide. "Mal Maison," a reference Dietz dropped later, meant a brothel, although Dietz told her it was a brand of lipstick. What other brand would Sadie wear? ("My Sin" was a perfume.)

Merman, a wisecracking, clarion-voiced comedienne in Cole Porter musicals, had reasons to feel insecure. Her version of sexual innuendo usually was no more than an ad-libbed "woo-hoo!" Her character in another Porter hit, *Panama Hattie* in 1940, was a harlot, but very much the good-hearted musical-comedy type. (A lyric from "I've Still Got My Health" went, "I knew I was slipping at Minsky's one dawn. When I started stripping, they hollered, 'Put it on!'") Sadie, made famous by Jeanne Eagels in *Rain* in 1922, on film by Gloria Swanson in 1928 and Joan Crawford in 1932, has a challenging, operatic personality. Merman was presumed to be guaranteed box office.

Upset as he would have been at losing a Hollywood salary over the *Laura* debacle, Mamoulian never let on to others. "Good news," he wired Dietz on May 14, 1944. "Am free to come to New York in two weeks, if it's possible to start on *Rain* at that time." Dietz (lyricist of "Dancing in the Dark") first approached Mamoulian in January with an offer to direct his collaboration with composer Vernon Duke ("April in Paris"). It was the third Dietz-Duke collaboration; in 1943, their musical for Mary Martin, *Dancing in the Streets*, closed in Boston just before *Oklahoma!* opened there. *Jackpot*, their war-themed musical starring Nanette Fabray and Buddy Lester, had just opened, but lasted just sixty-nine performances.

The 1922 play by John Colton and Clemence Randolph filled out Maugham's short story, "Miss Thompson," with supporting characters including US Marines, and Sadie romances Sgt. Tim O'Hara. The Rev. Davidson is well intentioned but sanctimonious; his wife is a prig. He's been enforcing church attendance and his dancing ban with a series of fines that can ruin those who oppose him. The Davidsons, along with Sadie, are stuck in a two-week layover in Pago Pago on their way to their intended island destination. It's raining nearly the entire time.

Maugham's Sadie was a slightly chubby "half-caste" prostitute from Honolulu's red light district by way of San Francisco. She's plying her trade with sailors on Pago Pago when Davidson decides to achieve her salvation. He prays loudly for her, she calls him a "low-life bastard" for getting the local governor to kick her off the island on the next boat to San Francisco, and pleads with Davidson to change his mind, since a return there will mean a prison term. Despondent, she asks Davidson to come to her room. After the first night, Davidson tells others, "A great mercy has been vouchsafed me. Last night I was privileged to bring a lost soul to the loving arms of Jesus."

He's been in her "loving" arms, of course, and he returns for the next three days and nights, coming back more haggard each time. Once, he tells his wife he'd been dreaming about the smooth, rounded hills of Nebraska—Maugham wrote that said hills resembled a woman's breasts. Overcome by his degradation, he slits his throat (in Mamoulian's production, Davidson threw himself into a shark-infested lagoon). He's not saved Sadie's soul—he's only reinvigorated her livelihood, and at the end of the story, she's unrepentant, back in her finery and spitting on Mrs. Davidson. Eagels built an entire career on Sadie's final line: "You men! You filthy, dirty pigs! You're all the same, all of you. Pigs! Pigs!"

Mamoulian suggested to producer A. P. Waxman that he hire Lenore Ulric to coach Merman in dramatic acting. That didn't come about, but if Merman learned of it, it would have increased her discomfort. Mamoulian signed for $1,000 a week for seven weeks' rehearsal, plus 2 percent of the weekly gross. The production was budgeted at $150,000, half of that coming from Paramount Pictures. He started working with Dietz on the book at the end of July, doing so much rewriting he ended up taking coauthor credit. Mamoulian again brought Azadia into his professional life; her sketches were the basis of Sadie's costumes designed by Elizabeth Montgomery, who went by Motley. Lansing Hatfield, a Metropolitan Opera baritone who bore a slight resemblance to Ronald Colman, was cast as the Rev. Davidson; Zolya Talma was the nonsinging Mrs. Davidson; Russian-born Edward Caton executed the lavish choreography.

Dietz stood his ground after Merman's "Mal Maison" blowup, writing Mamoulian, "At a late hour I have been forced to the decision that it would be impossible for the show to accede to Miss Merman's unprecedented and difficult demands . . . You have tried your best to save a situation caused by her attempts to dictate what the lyrics should be. But I can see no alternative but to stand on what I consider best for the play."

Three days later, Merman refused to rehearse Dietz's lyrics for "Poor as a Churchmouse" and insisted on using lyrics rewritten by her husband, newspaper advertising executive Robert Levitt. Merman left rehearsals on September 30; five days before that, agent Rex Cole wired Mamoulian from Los Angeles: "Young lady left tonight Sunday 8 p.m. United Air Lines. Through miracle, we were able to get her on plane."

That was June Havoc, who, as "Baby June" Hovick, had been a child performer in vaudeville with her younger sister, Rose Louise. She and Rose took diverging paths. Rose became the most famous stripper of her era, known as Gypsy Rose Lee; her life was the subject of the musical *Gypsy* in 1959, with Merman playing their domineering mother. June went into Broadway musicals in the 1930s and played conniving chorus girl Gladys Bump in Rodgers and Hart's *Pal Joey* in 1940; earlier in 1944, she appeared opposite Bobby Clark in Porter's long-running *Mexican Hayride*, in which she played a lady bullfighter. She had a reputation as a reliable professional, although she had never carried a show by herself. Dietz thought Havoc "talented, but lacked the voice." She didn't disagree. "This isn't a voice, let's face it," she told a columnist after the show opened.

For Duke, the real problem was Hatfield. He wrote that he thought Mamoulian took "a rather pontifically highbrow, Moscow Arty approach to Maugham's immortal strumpet which I thought somewhat misplaced." He "insisted on Rev. Davidson singing 'opera style' a la [Feodor] Chaliapin." Duke thought the cleric "would be best characterized as 'songless,' like the villainous whites in *Porgy and Bess*. As a result, Davidson's 'arias' . . . were synthetic as music and theatrically incongruous."

Mamoulian's extensive use of dance did little more than pad the story. The first act's nine numbers included an opening dance, a jungle dance, and a dance to the sun god, plus a choral number, "When You Live on an Island." The second act's nine numbers opened with a "dancing lesson" for native girls, and as the tragedy built to its climax, there was a six-part ballet to illustrate Sadie's "conversion" followed by another ballet, "The Mountains of Nebraska" in which Davidson (dancer Chris Volkoff) feverishly envisioned eight dancing Sadies.

"Dainty June" knew how to put her heart into opening-night notes. At the October 23, 1944 tryout in Philadelphia, she sent Mamoulian a classic of the form: "You have made my dream come true. You and you alone have lifted me out of the 'hack' class."

Sadie opened November 16 at the Alvin, putting in only sixty performances before closing the following January. Critics were unimpressed. In the *New York Times*, Lewis Nichols complained that the show was "neither play nor musical. . . . The mood of the story is lost in the orchestra, and the music is overwhelmed by the story. The result is that there are long stretches of talk which build up to the old tone of *Rain*, only to be broken by songs about ships that sail at midnight and by dances to the sun god." Back in Philadelphia, *Variety* had panned it, noting that Havoc "has no voice, but delivers her numbers fairly well and acts the dramatic scenes better than might be expected."

Havoc saved her rage for Waxman, whom she called "a little man; everyone loathed him." On January 6, closing night, "he called the cast onto the stage. I did not come out of my dressing room. Then he made the mistake of coming to my room. I don't know what it triggered in me, but he started toward me, I closed the door, locked it and let him have it. I beat him unmercifully. I was taken to the hospital."

Mamoulian had no time to lick his wounds. All the old fights with the Theatre Guild evidently had been forgiven. They had a second musical for him.

CHAPTER 15

A Real Nice Clambake

With his next Rodgers and Hammerstein production, Mamoulian's intoxicating grandeur, back to its earlier discipline, opened the show.

At the first measure of Richard Rodgers's "Carousel Waltz," delivered by a forty-piece pit orchestra, the curtain opens to reveal a scrim showing the New England coast. Awakening with woodwinds, over a tempo set by strings and a single tuba, there are six hesitant measures representing an old-fashioned mechanical organ on a merry-go-round. At measures 9 and 17, the arrangement by Robert Russell Bennett turns ominous with unusual pairings, first with flutes and piccolos in different keys, then joined with bassoons and horns in what amounts to a whole-tone scale. The ride is squeaky, the story ahead dark.

When the melody releases, the scrim rises to launch Mamoulian's painstakingly constructed pantomime with nearly fifty performers, more than he had used in either *Congai* or *Porgy and Bess*, and evocative again of Vakhtangov's "fantastic realism." This time, applied to luminously emotional American nostalgia and powered by the waltz, the source material, Ferenc Molnár's *Liliom*, becomes something magical. Dominating the stage, a twinkling nine-horse carousel spins on a nineteenth-century fairground. At stage left, a barker and three scantily clad "beauties of Europe." At stage right, Billy Bigelow, the star barker, luring riders to the carousel for five cents each. The carousel owner, Mrs. Mullin, takes tickets at center stage.

The eight-minute pantomime introduces the principal characters and their relationships. While the prologue of *Liliom* showed a Budapest street fair with Gypsies, soldiers, a strong man and a balloon vendor, the *Carousel* pantomime presented the coarse Billy (John Raitt); naïve Julie Jordan (Jan

Clayton), who worked at the local cotton mill; Julie's sweet friend Carrie Pipperidge (Jean Darling); stuffy Mr. Bascombe (Franklyn Fox); the owner of the mill, coarse Mrs. Mullin (Jean Casto); and supplementing the stage action, a juggler, an acrobatic clown, a ballerina with a small man in a bear suit, and a couple of fistfights.

Billy is irresistible to every woman he meets, including Mrs. Mullin. In *Carousel*, most of the girls are employed at the mill and live in the dormitory the company provides, with a strict curfew. Julie is immediately smitten when she pays her nickel, although Billy only gives her a patronizing wave. Billy and the barker for the "Beauties of Europe" compete for the attention of the crowd. Mamoulian's directions read, "Everyone on stage begins to sway unconsciously with the rhythm of his words except Julie, who just stands—looks at Billy, motionless." As Billy continues, "the eyes of the crowd follow his, focus on Julie." Billy begins to walk toward her before Mrs. Mullin pantomimes "Gonna let him take your crowd away? Hey!"

As soon as the carousel resumes spinning, Julie's return wave to Billy's casual one "means so much to her that she nearly falls off." As the waltz surges to its conclusion, the stage lights come up in full, the ballerina, dancing bear, juggler, and clown perform at center stage as "the entire stage in a bedlam of excitement, goes black" and the audience knows a doomed love affair will unfold.

When it opened at the Imperial Theatre on April 19, 1945, critics, realizing that it was a full integration of music, dance, and drama, struggled with their descriptions, ranging from operetta to musical play, which is what Mamoulian was calling it. The anonymous reviewer from *Cue*, who predicted that *Carousel* would be seen "as the beginning of our own American opera," was one of the few who correctly tagged the composers' intent. "We are writing it very nearly as an opera and everyone in the cast must be an exceptional singer," Hammerstein wrote to actor Dwight Marfield. Asked by a Boston music critic whether *Carousel* "was in degree operatic," Rodgers agreed, but quickly added, "We don't wish to scare people off by telling them so." Don Walker, who orchestrated most of the score, disclosed, "I always felt it was an opera. It should sound different from other shows." The waltz, though, is unique. Rodgers wrote it originally for *Hallelujah, I'm a Bum* (1933), in which it was not used. For *Carousel*, he found its perfect application.

Near the end of her life, Agnes de Mille tried to claim that the opening spectacle had been hers alone, although what she did was rework the pantomime for fewer performers. Virginia Moise Collins, a chorus member, recalled the details of the routine:

> And [Mamoulian] had little moments for a lot of us. Josephine [Collins] was my mother. Josephine was taller, and a bigger woman than I was, and a good friend, one of the singers, Bob Byrn was my father, and we came on, and I was supposed to be a little girl, and a dancer named Lynn Joelson was supposed to pick a fight with me, and I ended up in the floor on top of her, as if I was beating up on her, and [Mamoulian] was very, very particular about how that was done. . . . There were these little incidents going on all over, and it all had to look as if it were spontaneous—as if it really were happening.

Mimi Strongin was just seven, and the prologue was to be the only scene she was in: "As I remember, I can see what he was doing. He had everybody run around as they wanted to—and then he came up with stuff for us to do. One day he said, 'Okay, do everything, but don't talk.' He wanted something spontaneous, and that's what he did." With a womanizing protagonist who beats his wife and kills himself after a failed robbery, this is Rodgers and Hammerstein's darkest work—because it's Molnár's darkest, too—although with the memorable second-act uplift of "You'll Never Walk Alone."

As would become the pattern for the rest of his career, Mamoulian's involvement in this work began with acrimony. He got the *Carousel* job by default. Langner approached Elia Kazan while Kazan was filming *A Tree Grows in Brooklyn*, but Kazan was about to be drafted, and Josh Logan already was in the military. There is no record of the Guild approaching anyone else, which left "our lean and hungry Armenian."

A rapprochement was arranged for August 15 at the Barbery Room a month before *Sadie Thompson* went into rehearsals. Mamoulian's sour account:

> I came back here [to California] and they started writing letters and I wouldn't even write back. Then we were in New York a year later and Dick Rodgers and Dorothy called Azadia and said, "Will you come to dinner tomorrow?"

Azadia said, "How about it?" I said, "I don't want to have dinner with them." She said, "You're carrying it too far. You've been friends for years. Don't make it personal." So I said okay.

So we went to dinner and after dinner, Dick said, "I'd like you to hear a song we've written." I said, "No songs. I don't want to hear anything." Oscar said, "I'll play just one song," so they sat down and they played one song of *Carousel*, and then played another song. I said, "All right, I've had it. Forget it, I'm not interested."

But according to de Mille, "in that meeting, he apologized. Then they kept us apart, put us in separate (rehearsal) theaters. I was downtown, he was uptown."

With no discernible end to *Oklahoma!* audiences in sight, optimism for the new production's profits ran high, although William Fitelson, a Guild lawyer, warned Helburn during negotiations with the composers: "I think that it is important for you to bear in mind that your success with *Oklahoma!* is in the nature of a 'freak.'" Mamoulian didn't sign his contract until December 27, 1944, just before *Sadie* closed and after he had received word from his Hollywood agent: "The office has canvassed the industry and at the moment there is nothing for you." He was paid $3,500 during rehearsals and his percentages—1.5 percent of the gross until the production cost was paid off, 2 percent thereafter—would bring him usually more than $700 a week on top of his *Oklahoma!* payments. In addition, he was allowed to invest $3,200 in the show.

Rodgers and Hammerstein had moved quickly to capitalize on their new hit, both separately and together. In October 1943, Rodgers reunited with Hart long enough to mount a revival of *A Connecticut Yankee*, for which they wrote six new songs; Hart died of pneumonia after a drinking spree in November 1943. Hammerstein launched his long-planned *Carmen Jones*, an all-Black version of Bizet's opera in vernacular English. In 1944, they wrote songs for a musical film of *State Fair*, starring Dana Andrews and Jeanne Crain, that produced the classics "It Might as Well Be Spring" and "It's a Grand Night for Singing."

Liliom, a look at a carnival barker's chance to redeem himself in the afterlife, was a failure when Molnár first presented it in Hungary in 1909; the playwright recalled that the first-night audience had expected a comedy.

Disillusionment over the immense loss of life in World War I may have contributed to its 1921 Theatre Guild success in New York in its first English-language translation. Subsequently, it was made into films in Hollywood and France and successfully revived twice on Broadway (in 1940 with Burgess Meredith and Ingrid Bergman).

The Guild first asked Rodgers and Hammerstein about *Liliom* shortly after *Oklahoma!* opened. By then, Molnár's circumstances had changed from the time he had turned down Kurt Weill. He had fled Hungary in 1939 as a Jewish refugee from the Nazis; had separated from his third wife, actress Lili Darvas; and now lived with his secretary/mistress at the Plaza Hotel. Langner, as if to reassure the playwright of a potential hit, sent Molnár to an evening performance of *Oklahoma!* in October 1943. The following day, he and Molnár reached an agreement that included the sale of the screen rights to 20th Century Fox, provided Molnár could secure the services of Rodgers and Hammerstein or other composers he thought satisfactory. Molnár had sold the film rights to *Liliom* years earlier, but a musical version with a new title meant a lucrative new deal.

Hammerstein was skeptical of the original Hungarian setting and the type of music that entailed, so he introduced American themes from the outset. Rodgers suggested that Liliom's "entire dream of heaven should be identified with his dream of America." Helburn suggested moving the story to New Orleans and giving it a Creole setting. Then, at a meeting at Sardi's, Hammerstein wrote that Rodgers, who had a home in Connecticut, "rolled around with the idea of transplanting *Liliom* to the New England coast."

Mamoulian's challenge was to make Billy a sympathetic character, or at least not a one-dimensional villain. In *Liliom* and *Carousel*, Liliom/Billy and Julie, in different scenes, mention that he struck Julie. Once is all it takes for him to get a reputation as a wife-beater. There's justice in Molnár's play: Liliom is sentenced to "sixteen years in the cleansing fire"—either purgatory or hell, depending on one's interpretation—which he enters defiantly, an unlit cigarette between his lips. That mordant imagery, and Billy's second chance with the daughter he has never known, is what had made the work so appealing to Weill years earlier.

Liliom's odd popularity was discussed from the start. Helburn wrote the composers:

> I've asked a number of people about Liliom himself and they all say they liked him enormously. When I say "Why? He was such a bastard," their replies vary, but it's usually, "Yes, but he was so human," or "Such a cute bastard," or "Such an insolent or charming devil" or "I agree after you were married to him he wouldn't supply milk to the baby, but you couldn't help loving him." I'm sure he gets over much closer to Clark Gable than to Pal Joey.

Only in Billy's afterlife and in the final scene does the musical diverge from *Liliom*, and just as Mamoulian had done for Porgy, the changes give Billy's life transcendence. The largest problem, also discussed during that first meeting, "for musical purposes, seems to be what Mr. Hammerstein called 'the tunnel' of the gloomy scenes in the Hollander house where Liliom and Julie have a squalid room after marrying, followed by the culvert scene," where Liliom stabs himself with a knife. That was easy enough to fix. Hammerstein moved Billy and Julie's living quarters to a cheerful seaside spa operated by Julie's cousin, Nettie Fowler. Another consideration was that Hammerstein "may reconceive the heaven scene in quite different terms."

Auditions began in December 1944. The role of Carrie went to Jean Darling, a nineteen-year-old former member of the Little Rascals. She auditioned at the Rodgers and Hammerstein offices.

> I had finished singing "When I Marry Mister Snow" for Rouben, Oscar and Dick, who was playing the piano. I was asked to wait outside. So I waited while knitting. After awhile, Rouben came out and asked, "Will you knit me a scarf during rehearsals?" I never knew what happened to that knitting; it was lost when it dawned on me that I had the part of Carrie. . . .
>
> God, trying to read the verse from that ratty little piece of penciled lyric was very difficult.

Moise had been performing Gilbert and Sullivan at the Provincetown Playhouse when she auditioned for one of the eleven singing girls:

> Eight hundred of us auditioned for eight places in the chorus, because three of them already had jobs through agents. . . . Apparently I reminded Mr. Rodgers of someone he thought he was very much in love with when he was younger [she was, years later, told it was Gloria Stuart]. And I thought it was my

expertise, and my looks, and my ability, and that's why I got into *Carousel*. [At the final audition], he wanted—I guess he and Mr. Hammerstein and maybe Mr. Mamoulian wanted us to be graduated in height, so we found out that that's why he was standing us all up.

So there was a girl named Gloria Wills, and she was taller than I was, but she also had on high heels. So I had on flat heels. Fortunately, our shoe size was the same, so I got her shoes, and she got mine, so both of us got into the show. So it's not always your expertise at all.

For Strongin: "At one point, [Mamoulian] asked, "Can you do a somersault?" Of course, I couldn't do anything close—but I did it. I knew even at that age to say yes. I merely walked on hands and feet. Mamoulian was merciful or amused or in too much of a hurry to be bothered, but he hired me anyhow."

For the leads, the Theatre Guild found two who were struggling in Hollywood's lesser ranks. John Raitt had been Armina Marshall's find; Hammerstein also sent his daughter Alice to see him in a Los Angeles production of an operetta, *The Waltz King* in September 1943. Raitt had a powerful build; he had been a discus thrower and shot putter in high school and at Redlands College. As a pacifist Quaker, he was classified as a conscientious objector during the war, but his extremely poor eyesight would have disqualified him from military service, anyway. He had a $75-a-week contract to appear in westerns with a Poverty Row studio, Producers Releasing Corporation. The Guild bought out his film contract for $5,000, advancing $2,500 to Raitt, who repaid them in weekly installments. Marshall gushed in a memo to Helburn and Langner that Raitt not only did not think like an actor, he also was no "money grabber."

The leading lady had been signed less than a month before rehearsals began. Helburn had gone to California. At the end of January, Langner wired her: "Dick only has one song for Julie in first act and not too strong musically in second. Therefore good idea to look for dramatic actresses with singing voices, the singing being secondary." In early February 1945, Helburn announced the signing of twenty-seven-year-old Jan Clayton, a petite redhead. A native of Tularosa, New Mexico, she had won the title of Miss Southwest in El Paso, Texas, which got her a screen test in 1935. Nothing came of it, so she attended a two-year college in Mississippi. Returning to California, she sang at ex-boxer "Slapsie" Maxie Rosenbloom's nightclub in Los Angeles, and later took roles in westerns starring William Boyd, a.k.a. Hopalong Cassidy. That's where she met her first husband, cowboy star Russell Hayden, with whom she had a daughter in 1940. After she divorced Hayden and signed with MGM, Clayton appeared in B pictures such as *Airship Squadron 4* and *This Man's Navy*. She toured with the USO, and in her own account, developed a drinking problem during this time.

Another singing actress, Bonita Granville, told gossip columnist Hedda Hopper that she had been offered *Carousel* first, but "I know I couldn't sing the role." The difficulty of the role may not have been the issue. For a brief time, Clayton was a romantic partner of Helburn—something she made known to Darling, with whom she shared a dressing room. It is not known whether Helburn bothered to identify her sexual orientation. At the same time, Clayton was carrying on an affair with her MGM producer, Sam Marx, who eventually put her up in a Manhattan brownstone.

Singing in Hopalong Cassidy pictures, on radio, and in nightclubs didn't prepare Clayton for the vocal demands of the role. As Mamoulian told the story:

> The problem was that she was like a French soubrette. That would have made her very wrong for Julie. . . . So I said to them, "Look, I still have a hunch that she may work out all right. Let me work with her for three days and we'll hear her again at the end of that time . . . So at the end of that three-day period, I called them in and they agreed that she was perfect. We had changed her audition material and her approach completely.

"What a lovely job you did on Jan," stage manager John Fearnley wrote to Mamoulian near the end of Clayton's run in *Carousel*. "When I think what she was like on the day that she arrived from California, and then look at her now. She knows what you did for her, too."

Carousel was Mamoulian's working honeymoon. On February 12, a week before rehearsals began with the full cast, he and Azadia married before a justice of the peace in Peekskill, New York. No family members on either side were there; Boris Lovet-Lorski was the best man. Telegrams for personal news were restricted during the war, so Mamoulian let friends find out from the newspapers. "I must say I feel sort of like a Dan Cupid about the whole thing," Gene Tierney wrote. Elissa Landi cheered, "If the new Mrs. Mamoulian is the red-gold divinity Curtis and I met at the [Arnold] Weissbergers last winter, we both do indeed congratulate you."

Rehearsals began February 8. Clayton joined rehearsals a week later, followed by the final actor to be added, Murvyn Vye as Jigger Craigin, Billy's menacing sailor pal. "Mamoulian asked me if I could see myself as Billy," Raitt remembered. "I told him the idea frightened me because I was primarily a singer without much acting experience. He reassured me by asking, 'Johnny, do you think you look like the guy?' I said, 'I guess so.' He asked, 'Does the singing worry you?' When I said that it did not, he told me, 'Then you and I will work out the rest together.'"

Darling found Mamoulian to be a taskmaster:

[He] bawled me out about absolutely every move I made. It was all I could do to keep from crying. After about two weeks he took me into a dressing room and said, "You look so mad at every time I direct you, one of us is leaving and it won't be me!" At that the floodgates opened and, with eyes spurting like lawn sprinklers, I told him about how he kept bawling me out about everything when it wasn't my fault. He looked at me for a long moment, then his face softened and he put his arms around me. "But, Jeannie, I am only trying to direct the others through you. You are the only real professional in the cast. I'm sorry, I didn't understand." After that, we were friends. He still kept bawling me out but I didn't mind, as we now understood each other.

"[Mamoulian] didn't mingle with us," Moise recalled. "Now Mr. Rodgers did. Mr. Hammerstein, not quite so much." Rehearsals, Darling said, "could be difficult for everyone including Rouben, because each of the three Theatre Guildites tried to direct us behind his back. So the only thing to do was smile, say thanks and ignore their input."

As Mamoulian accomplished in *Oklahoma!*, the first three numbers spill onto each other while advancing the plot. The duet between Julie and Carrie, "You're a Queer One, Julie Jordan," reveals that Julie has felt herself in love for some time. The music turns into Carrie's ode to conventional married life, "When I Marry Mr. Snow." Carrie and Enoch Snow (Eric Mattson) are the musical incarnations of Marie and Wolf from *Liliom*, only Hammerstein made Wolf a New England fisherman who dreams of a fleet of sardine boats, not a Jew who only makes passing mention of his future plans. As in *Liliom*, Julie and Billy realize that they're in love while sitting on a park bench.

Julie already is out of a job by refusing Mr. Bascombe's offer to take her back to the girl's dormitory, and Mrs. Mullin has fired Billy for the time being. At that point, all they have are each other, but the haunting "If I Loved You" lets them express their emotions indirectly. That's followed by the ensemble's happy "June Is Bustin' Out All Over," anticipating the clambake. Billy and Jigger already are planning to rob Mr. Bascombe when Mrs. Mullin visits Billy to lure him back to his old job, insisting, "You're an artist type. You belong among artists." But Julie tells him she's going to have a baby, Billy ponders this sudden change in his life in "Soliloquy," his remarkable 253-measure psychological journey, in which he sings first with pride if it's a boy, and tenderly if the baby turns out to be a girl.

No ambition is too high, and Billy reflects on what his son might become. Two-thirds of the way through the song, Billy suddenly realizes he might have a daughter, and the number switches to tender thoughts of his relationship with her.

Mamoulian boasted of his staging of "It Was a Real Nice Clambake": "I used a gradual rise for what was, in 1945, probably the first time ever. The players are sprawled on the rocks—they have a good excuse, having been stuffing on clams and oysters—and are visible only as a gray mass. As the scene progresses they stir, sit up, stand up, climb up. It's quite an effect." He never mentioned the rest of the effect, with the performers standing up in sections: On the final "Ohhhhhhh" the grouping on stage left rose. On the final line, "We all had a real good time!" everyone rose and held their hands up high. Behold—the saucer funeral of *Porgy and Bess* again.

Billy loses what money he has in a card game with the cheating Jigger and dies in a panic when Mr. Bascombe overcomes them and the police arrive. He stabs himself and tumbles backward over a pile of crates. In *Liliom*, Julie is approached by a suitor after her husband dies. In *Carousel*, she is fully alone, with only Nettie (Christine Johnson, a mezzo-soprano) to offer comfort. Were Hammerstein adhering to the original story at this point, he would have adapted Julie's line "Sleep well, Billy" into something resembling an aria. He went instead for a universal message about not succumbing to the pain of loss.

NETTIE: Main thing is to keep on livin,' keep on keerin what is goin' to happen . . . 'Member that sampler you gave me? 'Member what it says?

There's no introduction to "You'll Never Walk Alone"—only a single verse. Although its original context, like *Oklahoma!* was in the midst of the loss of life during World War II, the lyric, reminding Julie to stay hopeful, since "at the end of the storm is a golden sky, and the sweet silver song of a lark," has proven to be a universal sentiment. When Nettie finishes, she and Julie kneel in prayer. Two heavenly visitors stroll in to take Billy to what he thinks will be what Jigger told him to expect—a celestial magistrate's court. No God, no throne for the likes of Billy. Billy's afterlife was the final *Carousel* problem to be resolved.

Liliom's afterlife had also been problematic for the Theatre Guild, with this exchange:

THE MAGISTRATE: Your name?
RICHLY DRESSED MAN: Forty-two, married, Jew
THE MAGISTRATE (with a gesture of dismissal): Religion does not interest us here—why did you kill yourself?

In 1922, before *Liliom* went on tour, Langner, himself a secular Jew, recommended a program note to Helburn: "I also suggest that the heaven scene be described as 'A courtroom in the beyond of Liliom's imagination.' Roman Catholics are simply furious and so are the narrow-minded provincial people until you tell them it is all imagination. They have no imaginations themselves. It is costing the show a couple of thousand a week in ill will."

Billy faces judgment defiantly, bellowing a demand, in "The Highest Judge of All," for "pink-faced angels on a purple cloud," as well as "organ music—let it roll out loud." In Boston, Billy got his organ music, but it wasn't what he demanded. There was a loud chord from "a mighty celestial organ" followed by the thin sound of a harmonium—a gentle Hammerstein joke. As Hammerstein described the following scene:

"Lights come up on a woman playing a harmonium. She is an old and very wise looking woman. Liliom is ushered in and they have a nice talk and then her husband comes in. It develops that God is a married couple. They talk over all problems together. A woman's viewpoint is needed as well as a man's. They decide that Liliom should be allowed to go back and see his daughter and prove that he is changed—though he is no more repentant than in the Molnar version.

The concept of a single deity in two sexes—Father God/Mother God—is used in Christian Science. Alice Hammerstein Mathias thought she knew where her father got the notion: "Oh! Milton Cohen! My father had a Christian Science friend, Milton Cohen. He used to spend the holidays with us. He was kind of an odd friend. He was very nice. He was . . . very strong about his ideas."

Neither He (Russell Collins) nor She (Kathleen Comegys) passed judgment on Billy. He became impatient with Billy's poor sense of what he needs to do to make things right on Earth and walked out after snorting, "If we were concerned with the foolish business of punishment we couldn't improve on what you are doing to yourself!"

Carousel opened in Boston on March 27, the Tuesday of Holy Week—not the best time for theological whimsy. Hammerstein knew enough about

Russell Collins as the Starkeeper tends to his sky in *Carousel*, April 1945. Photograph courtesy of Library of Congress.

audience reactions, and Mamoulian about repairing dialogue, not to need the advice of Elliot Norton, critic of the *Boston Post*, but Norton expounded all the same, calling the He and She scene "just plain silly." He ridiculed "a concept which is theologically and dramatically foreign to the New England of Billy Bigelow and alien to the whole tone of the play." Norton suggested a return to Liliom's police court.

That's sort of what happened when the Starkeeper (Collins again) came to be. There are different versions of how that occurred. Norton told it with a very convenient punch line: Rodgers and Hammerstein "took a walk through the Public Garden to try to work out how to fix the scene with God. God appears in a parlor and it was just awful. Oscar said to Dick, 'Well, where should I put God?' And Dick said, 'I don't care where you put him. Put him up a ladder.' He meant it as a joke, but Oscar put God on a ladder and turned him into a starkeeper hanging out stars in Heaven. It became a touching scene." Mamoulian, though, regarded the Starkeeper as one of his personal triumphs. The reality of theatrical collaborations and late-night sessions in hotel suites is complicated, but his account seems credible:

> But when we opened in Boston we had a flop, because in the second act we had a scene where Billy dies and he goes into Paradise and he meets Mr. God and his wife. And I told the boys even while we were working . . . I told them, I said, "There's a terrific hole here, because how the hell can you have God on the stage, especially when He's going to seem fifteen minutes long, and he's an actor we have to pay 70 bucks a week, and he's going to play God."
>
> And true enough, the first act went very well, the second act . . . we got very bad reviews. Including Elliot Norton—you know, he was the great Boston critic. So we had this long session at the hotel and I said to them, "Look, I have an idea and I'm not going to tell you about it. I have a rehearsal tomorrow morning, I'll improvise this thing, then we'll see it tonight." They said okay. So I went off and I cut out the God and Mrs. God, instead of that a janitor at the back entrance to Heaven, and improvised some dialogue. I even put in a joke about my wife's ancestors, you know. And that night we had a hit, because it was humorous, it was charming, and it kept moving, you see.

So it happened in the second week of the Boston run that the Starkeeper, atop a silver ladder and dusting five-pointed stars on a clothesline, greeted audiences. Just like the parlor, it's a scenario Billy had not expected, and it's essentially the magistrate court reworked in a gentle New England accent. The stage is bare except for a second clothesline of stars and an actor playing Brother Joshua, whom the Starkeeper tells, "This one's finished. Brother Joshua, please hang it over Salem, Massachusetts." Sometimes Mamoulian said Joshua was named after Azadia's ancestor Joshua Peirce.

The Starkeeper is dressed like a janitor but never identifies himself or mentions religion, which allows the audience to come up with individual interpretations. As far as he's concerned, he's somewhat short of a deity, and his best line is delivered as Billy realizes he's not in the part of Heaven he wanted to be: "The pearly gates are just in front. Those are the back gates. They're just mother-of-pearly." Although without the justice of the cleansing fire (the show isn't that operatic), Billy is given a chance to return to Earth to make things right with the daughter he's never seen, and he takes a star along with him.

Mamoulian found a way to nurse a grievance over the Starkeeper:

> So as we were walking out of the theater, I said to Oscar Hammerstein, "Now you go ahead and write that scene." He said, "What scene?" I said, "The new scene with the janitor." He said, "What do you mean, write? You wrote it. I wouldn't change a word of it."
>
> And that was it. But here is a little sign of, I guess, human frailty. So they decided we should ask Elliot Norton to come back and see this so that he could give us another review before we come to New York. So he came in and he saw the show, then as he came out of the theater there was Dick Rodgers and his wife, Oscar and his wife, myself and Azadia, and Elliot said to Oscar, "Oscar, you are a genius. What you did with that scene, you are a genius." And, you know, Oscar blushed and he said "Thank you."
>
> And my wife got so angry. I said, "Shhhh." So he was embarrassed. So later she said, "My God, this is terrible." I said, "Look, he was embarrassed." Because Oscar was a very nice guy . . . But that was the only trouble with *Carousel*. Otherwise it was a beautiful experience.

Billy gets to see his daughter grow up through an extended ballet in which he learns that his wife and daughter are now outcasts in the community because of his crime and the manner of his death. A subsequent scene shows Julie with the happily married Carrie and Carrie's now-large family, and Enoch Snow Jr. tells Louise that he can't marry her "because it'd be beneath my station."

Billy appears as flesh and blood to his daughter, Louise, and gives her the star, but the conversation doesn't go well. Billy suddenly slaps her on her right hand. After he leaves, she tells her mother that the slap felt like a caress and asks, "Is it possible for someone to hit you real loud and hard and not hurt you at all?" Julie replies, "It is possible, dear—for someone to hit you—hit you hard—and not hurt at all" (an improvement over the same line in *Liliom* where she says, "It is possible, dear, that someone may beat you and beat you and beat you, and not hurt you at all").

Liliom ends on that slightly ambiguous note. But Hammerstein was unwilling to let Billy fail. He has him ask his heavenly friends for yet another chance, which is granted, and as an unseen spirit, he gets to see Louise

Mamoulian and Azadia Newman shortly after their wedding in February 1945. Photograph courtesy of Library of Congress.

graduate from high school. Billy can't communicate directly with his family, but he can throw his thoughts to them. Afterlife communication and second chances back on Earth had been key elements of Thornton Wilder's 1939 *Our Town* and two films, *Here Comes Mr. Jordan* (1941) and *A Guy Named Joe* (1944). The town doctor, Dr. Seldon (Collins again) is giving the graduation speech, advising, "Jest keep yer faith and courage, and you'll come out all right." He begins to recite "You'll Never Walk Alone," which the students pick up in song.

First, Billy gets to finally help Louise, repeating part of the doctor's advice about parents: "And don't be held back by their failures. Makes no difference what they did or didn't do. You jest stand on your own two feet." She stands, and the woman next to her puts her arm on her shoulder. Next, Julie. Billy tells her, as the finale swells: "I loved you, Julie. Know that I loved you!" On the final "You'll Never Walk Alone," Julie stands. She and Louise are part of the community again. Billy's mission is complete.

Without the sunny appeal of *Oklahoma!*, *Carousel* came to a stop in 1947 after a still-impressive 890 performances. Mamoulian, who had sculpted the show's emotion into something eternal, had just one more successful project ahead.

CHAPTER 16

Come Rain or Come Shine

Later in 1945, Mamoulian's two smash-hit musicals landed him a $4,000-a-week contract with producer Arthur Freed at MGM to direct the musical version of Eugene O'Neill's *Ah, Wilderness!* With that came more Broadway work; Freed and Sam Katz, a studio vice president, asked Mamoulian to save a musical they had bankrolled. *St. Louis Woman* had music by Harold Arlen, lyrics by Johnny Mercer, an unwieldy book, an inexperienced director in Lemuel Ayers, and a cast in full skeptical rebellion. At the same time, the Theatre Guild wired Mamoulian that both *Oklahoma!* and *Carousel* needed cast tune-ups after actors were replaced. Mamoulian took a ten-week leave of absence from the studio to repair two shows and take over a third.

Producer Edward Gross, formerly a Hollywood production manager, was known for cheapie film fare such as *Hillbilly Blitzkrieg* and *Private Snuffy Smith* (both 1942). On Broadway, he found success in 1944 with *Chicken Every Sunday*, based on the novel of Arizona boardinghouse life by Rosemary Taylor. Casting about for his next hit, he came across *God Sends Sunday*, based on a novel about the African American demimonde of 1890s St. Louis. Written by Arna Bontemps, one of the literary lights of the Harlem Renaissance, and published in 1931, it had had a stage adaptation by the Federal Theatre Project in Los Angeles in 1938.

With saloons, prostitutes, gin guzzling, murders, and a jockey who loses his luck, then regains it with the right woman by his side, it echoed the milieu of *Porgy and Bess*. There was some expectation that it could fall into line with musicals such as *Cabin in the Sky* (1940), which became a hit MGM film directed by Vincente Minnelli, and Hammerstein's *Carmen Jones*. Gross commissioned Bontemps and poet Countee Cullen, neither of whom had ever written a play, for the book. Mercer and Arlen were skilled in pop and blues idioms and had written for Cotton Club revues. Arlen, whose music elevated *The Wizard of Oz* (1939), had recently composed "Stormy Weather," and he and Mercer had a huge success with "Blues in the Night."

The dialect-laden book of *St. Louis Woman* is long forgotten. Most of the score has endured with hits such as "Come Rain or Come Shine," "A Women's Prerogative," "Any Place I Hang My Hat Is Home," and a breathtakingly colorful ensemble number, "Cakewalk Your Lady." "I myself am immodest enough to think it is one of the best scores written for a colored musical," Mercer wrote in his unpublished memoir.

It was budgeted at $200,000, with hopes for an eventual film. For box office lure, Gross signed dancers Harold and Fayard Nicholas, the sensations of *Stormy Weather* (1943) and other Fox musicals, famed for their acrobatic splits. The show was the making of Pearl Bailey, a nightclub star who played barmaid Butterfly in the secondary comic romance with Barney (Fayard), a rival jockey. The title role of Della Green, a prostitute, was offered first to Lena Horne, the sultry breakout star of *Cabin in the Sky* and *Stormy Weather*, under contract at MGM. With her light skin, Horne was the rare African American performer whose appeal was believed to cross racial boundaries, even though films in which she appeared were structured so that her solo numbers could be easily snipped out by theater owners in the segregated South.

Horne's visibility put her in the uncomfortable position of representing the image and hopes of people of color. Although she already had successfully fought against being typecast as maids, she usually had controversies thrust upon her, with racial politics taking precedence over artistic choices. In September 1945, she turned down the role of Della. "I knew the book had been written by Negroes, but I still resented its pidgin English and the stereotypes they had written," she wrote. Eventually cast was Ruby Hill, a Virginia native who had performed on radio and in nightclubs since her teens. Her only stage experience had been in a touring edition of the Eubie Blake/Noble Sissle revue *Shuffle Along* in the 1930s. Gross sent her to California to audition for Arlen and Mercer, and although she passed muster, like Jan Clayton in *Carousel*, she hadn't had training in projecting in a theater.

Lemuel Ayers was pulling triple duty, designing the costumes and sets as well as directing. Mamoulian always indicated that he parachuted in for a rescue mission after *St. Louis Woman* tried out in New Haven, but documents show he was the de facto director all along. He discussed the show in Hollywood with Freed and Ayers and wrote detailed memos on the script starting in January 1946—two months before he left for Boston, the show's next stop. Mamoulian's presumed expertise with Black performers and *misé en scene*—the show also includes a funeral—was something to be consulted.

"I 'report' to (MGM) on the first of November," he wrote to Hammerstein. "*Jumbo* [the Rodgers and Hart musical Hammerstein thought he'd be directing] is not really set yet, and won't be until I can discuss things with them." The composers had begun producing and writing and were offering Mamoulian the direction of *Happy Birthday*, a comedy for Helen Hayes being written by Anita Loos. They promised a flat $5,000 fee and 3 percent of the gross—a generous triple-dip in the R&H income stream, made even more attractive a prospect since Hayes was the rare bankable star in straight plays on Broadway.

Meanwhile, his film work shifted to *Ah, Wilderness!*, a property MGM had owned since its 1935 film version. Comedy writer Irving Brecher was hired to punch up the script, and Harry Warren was slated for the music. By January 1946, Mamoulian was at work on the *St. Louis Woman* script, and he kept drafting suggestions for Ayers right up to when he signed to direct the show in late February. Instead of a fee, he received a complicated scheme of percentages of the gross receipts.

Panic set in when Countee Cullen, just forty-two, died of uremic poisoning on January 11, two days before rehearsals began. Bontemps sent in script changes from Nashville, where he was the head librarian at Fisk University. When Mamoulian took over, he replaced choreographer Anthony Tudor with Charles Walters, his dance director at MGM. After New Haven, the show headed to Boston for two weeks and Philadelphia for another two before opening at the Martin Beck Theatre on Broadway on March 30. From Philadelphia, Mamoulian wrote Brecher, "The show was a pretty sad mess and it is quite a Herculean task to get the thing straightened out and whipped into condition for the Broadway opening. It is a question of complete redirection, restaging and a great amount of rewriting, as well as adding musical material."

St. Louis Woman is set in the red-light district of that city. Promiscuity reigns, booze flows freely in the form of "sweeten' water"—gin poured over rock candy—and life often ends at the end of a gun or the flash of a knife. The hero, Li'l Augie, is a champion jockey whose luck never seems to run out. He has set his sights on winning Della (far less explicitly a prostitute in the musical than in the novel), who is the gal of oafish Biglow Brown, who runs a honky-tonk. Augie achieves his goal with his triumph in the Cotton Flower Cakewalk—a dance contest with a liquor-infused cake as the prize. Biglow later invades Augie and Della's cottage, where he is shot by Lila, his jealous former mistress.

Biglow curses Augie with his dying breath, after which the jockey's luck goes bad. Della, convinced it's her fault, leaves Augie and becomes the woman of Ragsdale, the new proprietor of the honky-tonk. Augie returns to St. Louis thinking that he's finally beaten the jinx, and in the finale, wins the race and takes Della back. Out of this squalid dross, Arlen and Mercer spun joyous, upbeat gold. Mamoulian took the unusual step of expanding the original two acts into three, giving each act an ending flourish.

The first act opens with a prologue—Mamoulian's concept—in which Badfoot (Robert Pope), a trainer, sings cheerfully of the jockey's virtues to a banjo's strum in "L'il Augie Is a Natural Man." At the saloon, after the men perform an ode to the beneficent effects of "Sweeten' Water," Ragsdale (Elwood Smith) asks Della if she's going to go on letting Biglow mistreat her, and she responds with the sublime "Any Place I Hang My Hat Is Home."

Augie arrives with his winnings, boasts of his luck with horses and the ladies in "I Feel My Luck Comin' Down," and buys everyone champagne. Biglow (Rex Ingram) arrives and argues, then leaves with Della, after which Lila (June Hawkins) sings the bitter "I Had Myself a True Love."

For the saloon scene, Mamoulian confronted delicate racial etiquette in rehearsals. Someone in the cast told him this exchange was offensive:

BADFOOT: I tell you Li'l Augie ain't studying no Della.
BARNEY: Oh yes he is, Badfoot. Every man what comes to St. Louis studies about Della. She's the prettiest gal on Targee Street.
LILA: Yeah, the prettiest because she's the yellowest. But that don't keep her from being the biggest hussy.

Later in that scene, Augie tells Della, "You yellow gals is my ruination," and he calls her "my yellow gal" in another scene.

The matter of light-skinned Blacks ("high yellows" was the term) looking down on those with darker skin is within the diegetic and written by two African Americans besides. Colorism was not, however, something the performers wanted discussed in front of white Broadway audiences. The lines were amended so Lila's mention of "the yellowest" was cut, and Augie's reference to "yellow gals" became "St. Louis women." Mamoulian's reaction: "I told them we had to change all that. I reminded them that we were all engaged in the struggle for equality. It is ridiculous to act with snobbery to someone who is darker than you are. Oh, I know, it appeals to an actor to play gentility, to look down on another character, but I insisted that this element be removed if I had to rewrite it myself."

The story takes a bawdy comic turn when Butterfly delivers Augie's light-blue suit to Barney so he'll have something to wear to the cakewalk. Barney asks her to come to his room. She replies that it's not "gal-like," to which he asks if that's not proper, how come it's fine when he goes to her room. She tells him, "That's different," and sings "Legalize My Name" in support of matrimony.

Mamoulian dispensed with the burlesque humor Bontemps and Cullen had inserted here. The scene originally ended with Barney and Butterfly, at the window of Barney's room, discussing silk underwear. Barney asked her to come inside to help look for his cuff buttons, and when she did, in the manner of a blackout sketch, she was heard shouting, "No, Barney, they ain't *there*!" He noted:

> The last line of the scene . . . is, of course, purely a matter of taste. As it stands in the reading, it is of course very raw, and no other line or situation in the course of the play comes within a mile of it in the quality of humor. If the whole play were treated in a broad Rabelaisian manner, the line would be easily acceptable. As it is now, though, the line stands out like a sore thumb. (It may also cause some criticism from the colored people.)

The line was changed to, "Oh, come on—we're going to the cakewalk!"

The high-strutting "Cakewalk Your Lady," in praise of "a full o' frolic, al-co-ho-lic pastry treat," ends the act on a rousing note, and was where

Harold and Fayard performed their splits. Augie and Della win and start to leave together. Biglow asks what this means, and Della replies, "Means me an' Augie is eatin' our cake together from now on!"

Mamoulian placed the show's love ballad, "Come Rain or Come Shine," in the second act. Harold Nicholas couldn't sing well by theater standards, so the number is mostly a solo for Della. A moral compass arrives in the form of the pious Leah (Juanita Hill), Augie's sister, who has her three children in tow so they can get some "learnin'" off the farm. She warns Augie, "God done made you lucky, but if you don't pay him some mind, he going to take your luck away!"

Della displays an unexpected maternal side and desire for family life when she sings the nursery song "Chinquapin Bush" with the children. Augie is so touched, he asks Della to marry him, and Piggie (Herbert Coleman), her youngest child, sings at Leah's urging, an a cappella spiritual, "We Shall Meet to Part No Never" as a wedding blessing. As performed by Coleman, a seven-year-old whose uncle Warren Coleman played Crown in *Porgy and Bess*, it "stopped the show on preem night," *Billboard*'s reviewer wrote. Biglow, trailed by the unseen Lila, arrives and tries to beat Della, but before he can land a blow, Lila shoots him and sings "Sleep Peaceful, Mr. Used to Be."

The act closes with Biglow's funeral. Augie's now in jail, accused of the murder, and when Lila arrives, Della, who knows the truth, accuses her of having no shame. The congregation sings the haunting "Leavin' Time," which echoes Preacher's (Creighton Thompson) sermon. Lila finally screams "I did it!" and police are summoned. Mamoulian staged the funeral in groupings similar to the saucer funeral of *Porgy and Bess*. This time, the arm movements created a cast uproar, in Bailey's recollection: "[In the] funeral scene in which June Hawkins (Lila) has killed her lover Biglow Brown . . . she was to fall on her knees and raise her hands to Heaven. That, in turn was to make everyone else sad enough to do the same. [The actors] felt it was too Negroid. We kept going over and over that scene, and Mamoulian was displeased with it because he sensed something lacking and didn't know what it was."

Finally, Bailey recalled, "I got so angry," and asked the cast, "Why don't you tell him what you don't like?" (Mamoulian recalled the remark as, "Wake up! Can't you see this man is for us, you fools?") "Again, no voice was raised. So I told him what the trouble was." Mamoulian "then assembled the cast and told them about *Porgy* and reminded everyone of the great contribution the Negro had made to America, giving the country its only original art: music. Then he dismissed us, and out of that came some new feelings and better relationships."

Bailey was unsurpassed at delivering winking double-entendre lyrics in her ambling Virginia drawl. She got her final comic turn in "It's a Woman's Prerogative," after Barney, now winning his races, admonished Butterfly that although she was stuck on him now, everything was different before. "Prerogative" lectures him right back, reminding him that if a man is "short on his talents, it's a woman's prerogative to change her mind!" With Della now Ragsdale's gal, Augie arrives at the saloon to announce that he's broken Biglow's curse. The Swanee Handicap is the next day. At the racetrack, Mamoulian conceived a brisk choral number, "Come On, Li'l Augie" with the cast watching the race through holes in the fence. Augie wins and leaps over the fence to rejoin Della. "Play Li'l Augie 'on top,'" Mamoulian wrote. "He is again the loud-talking little Napoleon."

Gross decided to open the show on March 30 because he was making a crude calculation. That was a Saturday night, and since entertainment sections of Sunday newspapers went to press before the rest of the edition, there would be no reviews until the Monday papers. What he got instead were critics who had taken some time to sharpen their observations. Lewis Nichols in the *New York Times*, who labeled the plot "a curse," took direct aim: "No doubt the basic trouble is that *St. Louis Woman* never fully decides what it wishes to be. Presumably the original design was to make a folk play of it, something on the order of *Porgy and Bess*. The scenes, being largely of saloons, cakewalk and carnivals, take it away from folk opera and put it in the classification of musical comedy." He identified the highlight: "A young lady named Pearl Bailey can sing a song so it stays sung."

In the proudly liberal *PM*, Louis Kronenberger served notice that the era of crass stereotypes for Black performers was in the past, questioning "whether the kind of glib characterization . . . the kind of stock humor and melodrama is in the Negro's best interest." He paid more attention to the score: "First-rate music may have yet turned the tide, but Harold Arlen's songs and orchestral tags and tid-bits are second-rate even for him." Echoing Nichols's criticism of the shape of the musical, Kronenberger wrote of the songs, "they lack musical urgency, they lack the excitement and cohesive power that folk drama demands. It is an agreeable score, but nothing more than that." The show ran for 113 performances, closing July 6.

Mamoulian had another fight to pick. In May, Howard Rheinheimer, Hammerstein's lawyer, wired Mamoulian that set designer Jo Mielziner's signed contract contained a clause that no one would receive credit on *Happy Birthday* as lighting designer, which Mamoulian had demanded for himself. Mamoulian indignantly wired Rodgers about it. Rodgers, perhaps weary of Mamoulian's tantrums but not wishing for the dispute to get into the papers, responded, "Believe best procedure is for us to agree in public that pressure of *Ah, Wilderness!* schedule forces you to relinquish *Happy Birthday*."

~

Summer Holiday delivered a brutal lesson about Mickey Rooney's postwar appeal. Audiences weren't as charmed with him as when he'd been at his adolescent peak in MGM's Andy Hardy series and with top-drawer

Mamoulian and Mickey Rooney on the high school graduation set of *Summer Holiday*, filmed in 1946, released in 1948. Photograph courtesy of Library of Congress.

musicals with Judy Garland, including *Babes in Arms* (1939) and *Strike Up the Band* (1940). Rooney wrote, "I sensed that I need to prove myself all over again in this musical, and I tried too hard." His trademark bumptiousness is light-years removed from Richard Miller, O'Neill's sensitive, poetic teen.

Rooney's performance wasn't the sole issue. In 1946, when filming of *Summer Holiday* began, Rooney was a twice-divorced (very famously from first wife Ava Gardner) twenty-six-year-old army veteran with a well-publicized romantic life. He gave the role of Richard his usual aplomb, but portraying a virginal high schooler was too much for audiences to accept. Never mind that opposite him as Muriel McComber was Gloria DeHaven, a married twenty-one-year-old with an infant daughter.

"I ducked seeing the beautiful musical mess derived from *Ah, Wilderness!* I hear and hope it is a financial flop of the worst sort," O'Neill wrote to screenwriter friend Dudley Nichols. His hope came true. Bloated with Mamoulian's excesses and with filming hampered by a studio strike in fall 1946, the picture was a substantial flop, going more than $400,000 over budget and losing nearly $1.5 million on its initial release. Preview audiences were so hostile, MGM shelved the film for a whole year. Before it was released in spring 1948, the studio slashed six of the fourteen numbers Warren wrote with lyricist Ralph Blane.

Summer Holiday is sometimes criticized for not being in the spirit of or being faithful to O'Neill's sentimental recollection of his adolescence. In the *New Republic*, Richard Hatch wrote, "It is so far removed from the source that the credit line is no more than a pleasant gesture and comparisons become ill-tempered." This is inaccurate. *Summer Holiday*, largely adapted from MGM's screenplay of the 1935 film version, not only adheres to the play but the score had songs such as "Spring Isn't Everything" with lyrics straight out of O'Neill's dialogue.

Ah, Wilderness! is O'Neill's only comedy, written in 1933 and first produced by the Theatre Guild. At MGM, Clarence Brown directed it in 1935 with Rooney as Tommy, the younger brother of Richard Miller (Eric Linden), Lionel Barrymore as Nat Miller, the patriarch and newspaper editor, and Wallace Beery as bibulous Uncle Sid. The play weaves in period songs such as "Waltz Me Around Again, Willie" and "Mighty Lak' a Rose," the same way *Green Grow the Lilacs* interpolated cowboy songs and square dances. So a musical version was a natural idea for producer Arthur Freed (it later had a successful Broadway musical incarnation in 1959 as *Take Me Along*, with Jackie Gleason as Uncle Sid).

Freed, a songwriter himself, "appreciated talent, he appreciated something new, he was tremendously enthusiastic, and of great help on anything you wanted as a producer, a great help," Mamoulian recalled. After *Oklahoma!*, *Carousel*, and his salvage job on *St. Louis Woman*, he found himself, as he had with *Love Me Tonight*, allowed to do nearly anything.

"Mamoulian's attitude and attention to detail were unusual for MGM, a producers' studio, but Freed gave Mamoulian his head," wrote assistant director Wallace Worsley Jr.

Mamoulian's ideas specifically called for "a musical play—integrated dialogue, song, dance and music." He wrote:

> As just one example let's mention the episode of Richard and the tart. Both in the stage play and the motion picture, this episode is shown with complete objectivity. It is a scene as we see it—sober and tawdry. Richard's feelings are only expressed through his spoken words. How much more interesting and imaginative it would be to see this scene as Richard saw it, to relive the whole adventure with him.
>
> [Muriel] . . . for instance is much too vague and monotonous. She can use more color and personality. The uncle should not be a gross, vulgar drunkard, but an appealing and engaging little man, in spite of his sickness, and endowed with touching pathos.

He also came up with Nat Miller (Walter Huston) introducing the cast in "Our Home Town" as he strolled through fictional Danville, Connecticut (the stand-in for O'Neill's boyhood home of New London), and a sophisticated five-part suite to illustrate Richard's drunken state of mind during his barroom encounter with chorus girl Belle (Marilyn Maxwell).

O'Neill's play takes place entirely over the Fourth of July in 1906; the two MGM adaptations fill out the action with Richard's high school graduation and the picnic at which Sid becomes joyously drunk. Richard is an overly earnest striver for knowledge, with affection for Karl Marx and fin-de-siècle favorites Omar Khayyam and Algernon Charles Swinburne. Muriel, his shy girlfriend, refuses to kiss him, and he sprinkles quotations from his favorite poets in his love letters. Uncle Sid is in love with Nat's sister Lily, but she's refused to marry him despite his many promises to quit drinking.

Richard's double date with the older Wint Selby turns out to be a sodden barroom encounter with a taunting chorine. Muriel's father confronts Nat with the letters, Nat and Richard have an awkward conversation about sex, and Richard finally gets a kiss from Muriel, but Sid's relationship with Lily is never resolved. As the play ends, Nat philosophizes, "Well, spring isn't everything, is it, Essie? There's a lot to be said for autumn. That's got beauty, too. And winter—if you're together." Meanwhile, the much wiser Richard has gone outside to look at the moon.

The problem with Mamoulian's adaptation is that he took it too seriously. Although he did what he was hired to do—turn O'Neill's play into a full-scale Broadway musical on film—there's not an emotional moment that doesn't bloom into song regardless of whether the audience is ready to accept or understand it.

Mamoulian suggested that the characters be introduced by an iceman making his rounds; this eventually became Nat Miller, something like the stage manager in Thornton Wilder's *Our Town*, proclaiming the virtues of Danville in "Our Home Town" and introducing each member of his family. It's a splendidly efficient compacting of the narrative. In the 1935 script, Sid and Lily didn't discuss their stalled romance for twenty-four pages; in Mamoulian's version, it's part of the opening that also includes Richard and Muriel, also in an uncertain relationship, at an ice cream parlor.

He filmed the appealing duet "Afraid to Fall in Love," in August at Busch Gardens in Pasadena. In his vanilla-colored suit, Rooney spins, twists, and lunges at DeHaven in his attempt to get a kiss. DeHaven, in frilly white and under the tutelage of Roger Edens, responds in the warbling style of Judy Garland (but with far less voice) right down to the exclaimed, "Oh!" in "Oh! There must be something else to do instead of it." This was supposed to be followed by the piquant "Never Again," a duet for Uncle Sid and Lily in which he pledges to stay sober, but it was later cut. The set, under original cameraman Charles Rosher, sweltered from the high candlepower. "It was especially hard on Frank (Morgan) . . . who was a heavy drinker and perspired like a waterfall," Worsley recalled. A simple scene showing Uncle Sid packing for a new job required twenty-three takes because Morgan kept muffing his lines. Mamoulian replaced Rosher with Charles Schoenbaum, who kept the candlepower and resulting heat under tighter control.

Richard's high school graduation was a simple enough event to film—students marching in to the school song ("Dan-Dan-Danville High") followed by the alma mater ("All Hail to Danville High") with reaction shots of Richard's family and other youngsters, and later Nat's quick intervention to prevent Richard's speech from becoming an attack on capitalism. Mamoulian embellished the sequence with some of the oddest patriotic imagery ever slapped into an MGM musical. High school graduations in the United States never have involved much flag-waving except during wartime, so Mamoulian's choices indicate his lack of familiarity with the ritual. He only acknowledged, "It amused me to be able to insert a painting . . . into the texture of the dramatic action so that they became an integral part of it."

As the students proclaim their love of the school and enduring friendship and the grownups dab at their eyes, Mamoulian added tableaux of famous paintings, beginning with Grant Wood's "Daughters of Revolution" (did he not understand that Wood intended his purse-lipped Iowa matrons as satire?), Wood's "Woman with Plant," the iconic farm couple of Wood's "American Gothic," and Thomas Hart Benton's farmer of "Ploughing It Under." Graduation over, new freedoms are celebrated with "The Stanley Steamer," an homage to vintage transportation. There's no connection to the plot. Intended as DeHaven's big solo, the song instead became an ensemble number that took six days to film.

Another cut number displayed Richard's poetic side: "We show what he and Muriel see in their imagination—so both of them become living illustrations of the Rubaiyat." Mamoulian thought "Omar and the Princess" would be "a sensational hit tune, full of atmosphere and dancing lilt."

This began with Rooney purring at DeHaven, "I see you clad in chemisette of green, with azure vest more ultra than marine." Heading off what would have been a convulsively dirty audience guffaw, Mamoulian cut a Rooney line: "Can't you see my golden sword?"

Uncle Sid "wins" a beer-drinking contest as a male chorus thunders "Independence Day" and the women, with their picnic, sing "While the Men Are All Drinking." Mamoulian was delighted with the sequence:

> There is a camera thing I love in *Summer Holiday*, and you can almost define it as a brushstroke—a bold brushstroke. [The picnic sequence] starts on one scene, then the camera whips to another scene, then whips and comes to a third scene, and so on. It's almost like a painter going, "Whoosh, whoosh, come over here." I don't cut, and it builds and builds, and it kind of combines the whole thing into one. . . . It's like an etching come to life, it's so stylized with the ladies playing croquet, and then you follow the ball to the children jumping in the pond.

The barroom suite required six days just for rehearsals and another six to film. The Production Code made it impossible for Belle to be a prostitute—in 1935, the script described her as "a typical college gold-digger"; as portrayed by Maxwell, she's a hard-edged chorus girl at the Danville Music Hall, which has a bar next door. Blane was prepared for the character to go either way. Originally, he wrote for a group of prostitutes at a brothel singing about "certain brands of kisses you can't get from the missus," but this was replaced with the milder cancan lyric, "If you've been dying for a chance to be elastic, and dance the light fantastic."

Marilyn Maxwell's finest moment in film was her duet of "Silver Bells" with Bob Hope in *The Lemon Drop Kid* (1951). She built a career portraying good-hearted sidekicks, but sidetracked herself during the 1950s by becoming known in show business circles as Hope's mistress, accompanying him on his overseas tours. For *Summer Holiday*, her film career still held promise, and Mamoulian remembered her as "a cute little thing."

The first four parts of the suite, still in the film, have Belle singing "The Weary Blues" and "The Sweetest Kid I Ever Met," in which she taunts Richard while changing her appearance. She transforms, in Richard's eyes, from a peach-colored dress and gaudily painted cheeks into a sequined scarlet gown with deep décolletage and ruby-red lips, Richard ripostes with "The Nicest Girl I Ever Met," in which he suggests she should settle down and "be a woman—be a wife!" Belle throws Richard over for a traveling salesman, and Richard sees Belle again in her cheap get-up. These effects were achieved by studio technicians operating red-and-white lights on Maxwell and green lights on the walls of the set as carefully as if manipulating a progression in Mamoulian's sound design.

Nat's frank discussion of sex with the remorseful Richard ran into censorship. The issue, MGM executive Robert Vogel wrote, was "the very bad phrase 'whited sepulcher,'" which in Britain was a slang term for prostitute. He advised, "Can only suggest briefer, more general speech in which Miller tells the boy to be careful of how he conducts himself so that the audience can really imagine what he means." As a result, Mamoulian remembered, "I had a new version written in which the father finds himself embarrassed with the subject of sex to such an extent that he is never able to finish a sentence. And with that the matter would be made perfectly clear to the audience without the use of one single censorable word."

Originally, Nat lectured about immoral women: "Here's what I'm driving at, Richard. They're apt to be whited sepulchers." Screenwriter Jean Holloway cut off the end of that line and had Nat stammering, "I mean—enough—that is to say—well—but heck, I'll admit I'm no authority, but I never had anything to do with such women, and it'll be a heck of a lot better for you if you never do!" While he's saying this, he's absent-mindedly smashing a clay bust of Abraham Lincoln.

Younger brother Tommy (Butch Jenkins) brings a missive from Muriel saying she's willing to make up with Richard, and they finally share a nighttime kiss after she extracts a promise: "Will it wipe off her kisses?" The last number to be cut (the first eight notes can be heard in the overture) was "Spring Isn't Everything," in which Nat quotes from the *Rubaiyat*. The film ends on Huston's mention of "Love's young dream," and a crane shot of Rooney outside the house gazing at the stars.

Without Nat's final song, there's no summing up. As a result, *Summer Holiday* lurches to a close. Two previews in January 1947 resulted in some suggested cuts, and three days later, Mamoulian was off the lot and the film completely out of his hands. It was not released until March 1948.

CHAPTER 17

Found in the Stars

The Carlton House, Mamoulian's hotel, and the Plaza Hotel were just twelve blocks apart in New York. In late April 1949, did he take a cab, or turn the journey into a pleasantly brisk walk?

He may have felt like sprinting. The day before, Kurt Weill wired, "Have been trying to reach you for several days because Maxwell Anderson and I would like to talk to you about our new play." Mamoulian instantly knew they weren't going with Agnes de Mille, with whom they had been discussing their new work—an opera, really, although the usual term is "choral play" and the program billed it as "musical tragedy"—based on Alan Paton's novel *Cry, the Beloved Country*.

Mamoulian had no film directing at hand, and his only Broadway project was a favor to Langner—the musical *Arms and the Girl*. Based on Langner and Armina Marshall's 1933 play *The Pursuit of Happiness*, it mixed authentic Colonial history with a romance and sexual leering. Another play, *Three Wishes*, an adaptation of Charles O'Neal's novel *The Three Wishes of Jamie McRuin*, was still in drafts, and he was exchanging tentative correspondence with O'Neal and producer Al Lewis. Badly needed prestige was falling into his lap. The previous two years had brought no more film work and just one play, *Leaf and Bough*, which closed after just three performances. "The joke was, it bowed and left!" said Coleen Gray, the play's star.

In spring 1947, Mamoulian treated Azadia to a delayed three-month honeymoon, which took in South America and New Orleans and a visit to the Hialeah race track in Florida with FBI director J. Edgar Hoover, a friend of Azadia's family, and his associate director, Clyde Tolson, before they returned to Los Angeles in July. He was receiving first-rate scripts for direction on Broadway, although he was less adventurous with source material, as in August when he rejected Tennessee Williams's *A Streetcar Named Desire*.

Agents still saw him as the top choice for directing "Negro plays." In 1944, Mamoulian was approached about *Polk County*, a folk comedy set in rural Florida by influential African American folklorist and novelist Zora Neale Hurston. In 1947, Anita Loos asked him about directing *Jacqueline*, her Americanized *Camille* with an interracial romance she had written with music by pop composer Alex Alstone and lyrics by Howard Dietz. Casting was troublesome: "We have considered all of the colored stars, from Lena Horne on down. Lena has gotten so stylized since her association with the white race that I don't believe she could act the part, even though she might be superb in the musical numbers. Muriel Smith could both act and sing the part, but she has grown so fat that her looks are gone." Despite Mamoulian's low opinion of Dorothy Heyward's slave revolt drama *Set My People Free*, the Guild staged it in November 1948, directed by Martin Ritt. It shuttered after twenty-nine performances; rehearsals went so badly that Arnold Weissberger, the agent for star Canada Lee, called Mamoulian two weeks before the opening to beg him to take it over.

Summer Holiday soured Mamoulian on musicals for a while, as he explained to Loos: "I have directed five musical plays in succession on Broadway and my last picture, which comes out in April, is a musical—so I'm most anxious to do a straight play. I've been reading scripts by the dozen, but unfortunately have not found one yet that excites me."

He took six months to decide on *Leaf and Bough*. In summer 1948, he went to San Diego to shape up the national company of *Carousel* before it arrived in Los Angeles and fired a series of harsh missives at the Theatre Guild for ignoring his billing in newspaper advertisements. Touring companies of *Oklahoma!* and *Carousel* had Mamoulian's original staging reproduced by Jerry Whyte, but contractually, ads had to say "Directed by Rouben Mamoulian." He drew up a lawsuit over his credit in 1953 in New York when *Oklahoma!* was revived at City Center. When you're not working steadily, six-point type in tiny newspaper ads can be a neon sign reminding the world you're still around.

Leaf and Bough's lure for Mamoulian seems mysterious. Critics compared it unfavorably to Tennessee Williams's short-lived *Summer and Smoke*, which had opened the previous October. Both plays have refined heroines in romances with wild boys, although at the end of *Summer and Smoke*, set in Mississippi, Alma Winemiller's sensual nature has taken over, and at the end of *Leaf and Bough*, set in a dystopian Indiana landscape, Coleen Gray's Nan Warren is sadder but no wiser. Joseph Hayes, a first-time playwright, was a native of Indianapolis. In January 1949, *Leaf and Bough* had a brief run in Dallas directed by Margo Jones, a pioneer of the regional theater movement. Producer Charles Heidt and his wife, Eidell, became Mamoulian's longest-lasting friends.

The Theatre Guild turned down *Leaf and Bough*. Heidt took it on himself and set about raising its $97,500 budget. Mamoulian arranged an agency package to cast three of the leads out of Hollywood: Richard Hart as the male lead, sensitive Mark Campbell; Dan O'Herlihy as Mark's bullying older brother, Glenn; and as Nan Warren, the female lead, Nebraska-born Grey. Grey's biggest film roles to that point had been as Victor Mature's wife in *Kiss of Death* (1947) and the doomed fiancée of John Wayne in Howard Hawks's *Red River* (1948).

Mamoulian's first memo on the script showed his enthusiasm for what he saw as lyricism: "I am excited by the throbbing humanity of the theme and of many of the characters involved, the appealing everyday humanity which comprises aspiration and failure, courage and frustration, beauty and pathos; in sum, the heaven and hell and purgatory in the souls of human beings." That's wildly overpraising Hayes's dreary little houses on the prairie. *Leaf and Bough* has two families, two kitchens, and one rolling hillside somewhere in the vicinity of Terre Haute. The Warrens, headed by father Bert (Anthony Ross) and mother Myra (Dorothy Elder) are warm and affectionate and operate a dairy farm. Myra has an embittered sister Attie (Louise Buckley) and an elderly father, Grandpa Nelson (William Jeffrey) who is dying and likes to talk of the true love he found in his marriage. Nan wears denim and men's shirts. She has a younger sister, Mary (Mary Linn Beller) and a sometimes-beau, Harlan Adams (Jared Reed) who is just out of agricultural college.

Nearby are the Campbells. In the South, they would be characterized as white trash. In Indiana, though, they're just rustic. Frederick, the father (David White) is a drunk who spends what little money he earns on prostitutes. Laura, the mother (Alice Reinheart) used to be attractive. Now she's just lusty, and the family was run out of Vincennes because she was chasing married men. Mark, their responsible son, works as a bank clerk and writes poetry in his spare time.

Nan's virginity, which she loses on a hilltop in a way now known as date rape, is key to the plot. Mamoulian thought Hayes had overdone that: "It appears rather as an anatomical detail made overly important." He advised the playwright, "Give Nan a touch of wildness, the wildness of a deer or bird. Make her fierce, passionate and pure. Like a baby leopard." In her first scene with Mark, she tells him, while crickets chirp: "I've always felt, why give up a small part of myself for a few hours? I'd only feel smaller afterwards." He asks her to marry him. Nan's Aunt Attie later tells her sex is dirty: "You imagine you're alone—but God is there, Nan. He sees." Nan and Mark's reverie is shattered by the offstage howling of a mentally disturbed woman. It's an omen of doom. Mamoulian noted, "the high point of the play is the soul-shaking cry of the mad woman in the night."

Azadia, whom Gray described as "a real character," also assisted. "Azadia took me to Bergdorf Goodman for my wardrobe. And I'm a JC Penney's girl... The clothes I wore in the play were very expensive. They didn't look it, but they were." O'Herlihy was taken out of the cast in Boston because he couldn't overcome his Irish brogue. Charlton Heston, his understudy, replaced him; Gray's recollection was that Heston was "much more formal and remote. I'd poke him and say, 'Hi, Chuck!' He barely spoke to me."

Gray recalled constant arguments between Mamoulian and Hayes. Glenn's sour final line foretold critics' reactions: "What the hell's the idea of anything?" *Billboard*'s review delivered a death blow: "Sends pew-sitters out of the theatre more or less deflated." *Time* called it "the worst sort of drivel—the pretentious sort," and hooted at *Leaf and Bough* as "kind of a Carryall Named Desire." Heidt lost his investment. Hayes had more success five years later with his novel *The Desperate Hours*, an escaped-convict yarn that became a 1955 film starring Humphrey Bogart, Heston moved into live TV dramas before getting his first film lead in *Dark City* in 1950, and Gray continued in films, including *Riding High* (1950) opposite Bing Crosby.

∼

Weill and Anderson based *Lost in the Stars* on an influential protest document. Alan Paton's *Cry, the Beloved Country* was published in February 1948, the same year apartheid became law in South Africa. The saga of Anglican

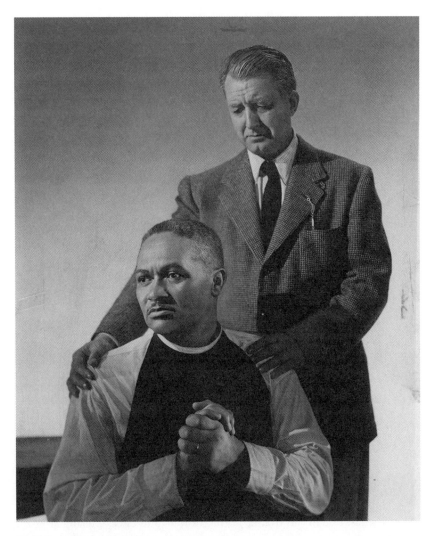

Todd Duncan and Leslie Banks in *Lost in the Stars*.

priest Stephen Kumalo's search for his wayward son Absalom in Johannesburg, Absalom's murder of a white man who was trying to help impoverished Blacks, his execution, and the minister's reconciliation with the father of the murder victim is unremittingly tragic.

Paton wrote about a landscape he knew well as a result of his work as a teacher in Ixopo and as principal of a reform school. Although he made no attempt to construct parallels between apartheid and American segregation, Anderson's script made the connection leap out by adding choral lyrics condemning racial hatred and questioning the role of government in abetting it.

The story depicts the evolution of racial attitudes in three generations: old men in Kumalo, a Zulu, and white planter James Jarvis; struggling young adults in Absalom and Arthur Jarvis; and children in Stephen's nephew Alex and Jarvis's grandson Edward, neither of whom have yet been affected by racial prejudice. Oscar Hammerstein may have written "You Have to Be Carefully Taught" as a condemnation of racism, but *Lost in the Stars* reflects that theme throughout. It was the second Anderson-Weill collaboration (*Knickerbocker Holiday* had been a hit in 1937) and quickly led to a third, a musical version of *Huckleberry Finn* that ended with Weill's death in April 1950.

Anderson saw *Lost* as an opportunity to work in themes and music they composed for their unproduced *Ulysses Africanus*, based on a 1919 novella about a former slave. They had pitched it to both Paul Robeson and Bill "Bojangles" Robinson. A song they wrote for that, "Lost in the Stars," became the title number of the new work. *Lost* replaced work on a "spaceship musical" idea Anderson had involving a spacecraft returning to Earth after a hundred years, with dialogue examining societal healing.

Opening at the Music Box Theatre on October 30, 1949, without a road tryout, *Lost in the Stars* struggled to find backers. There wasn't enough in the $100,000 budget, already stretched thin by its cast of forty-four, for a full orchestra (just twelve musicians) and very little to generate publicity. Mostly positive reviews (in the *New York Times*, Brooks Atkinson wrote, "We will be lucky this season if we have another scene as profoundly moving as the last one in this drama") brought it an audience. Closing after 281 performances, it managed a profit despite competition from happier musical fare, including *Gentlemen Prefer Blondes*. Broadway audiences accepted mentions of racial injustice, but the American heartland wasn't yet ready; the national tour lost money and shut down after eight venues.

The original choice as director, de Mille, had directed Rodgers and Hammerstein's *Allegro* (1947) and the Benjamin Britten–Ronald Duncan *The Rape of Lucretia* (1948), both of which, like *Lost*, had choruses commenting on interior action. They didn't find de Mille encouraging. After they met with Mamoulian, she wrote, "I do think there are basic difficulties—the chief one is that in certain ways the play is static, that too much of the action is carried by the chorus. The second difficulty is the aura of unrelieved tragedy." On April 9, Anderson noted, "It began to seem to Kurt and me that she's afraid of the form, doesn't like it, and thinks it will not go."

Weill had remained a Mamoulian fan ever since their discussion of *Liliom* in 1937. Anderson needed persuasion. The Theatre Guild had not asked Mamoulian about directing any of Anderson's plays for more than a decade, and the playwright, now part of his own producing organization, the Playwrights' Company, was enjoying a successful run of his latest drama, *Anne of the Thousand Days*, with Rex Harrison as Henry VIII.

Could Mamoulian hide his eagerness during his first meeting with Anderson and Weill in the Plaza's Oak Room? Two days later, they played the score, and Anderson wrote in his diary that Mamoulian was "moved and most intelligent about the whole thing." The director finished reading Paton's novel on April 27, discussed ideas with Anderson on May 1, and three days later over lunch with Weill, Anderson, and other members of the Playwrights' Company board, told them "it's on."

Mamoulian's next task was to push *Arms and the Girl*, slated for the fall, into the following year. He said the Guild complained of *Lost in the Stars*, "The show doesn't have a chance. Dick and Oscar have both turned it down." Eventually, an agreement was made with Nanette Fabray and Georges Gueteray, the stars of the new Guild production, to delay their compensation. Rehearsals were put off until November, with plans for opening the following January. Mamoulian dropped *Three Wishes* after O'Neal complained that he could not spend an additional six months working on the script without compensation.

Lost in the Stars had Mamoulian at his most engaged in any stage work since *Porgy and Bess*. In addition to suggesting new songs, he reduced the role of the chorus in favor of a strong lead singer, Todd Duncan as Stephen, and lightened the story line to make it more palatable. "Every laugh, chuckle or smile that can be honestly brought into our play will be like a drink of water in the desert," he wrote. Casting began immediately after he signed his contract: $7,500 for rehearsals, plus 2 percent of the gross on Broadway and from any touring company.

Veteran British character actor Leslie Banks was signed for the nonsinging James Jarvis, the father of the murdered Arthur. For Absalom, another nonsinging role, the Playwrights' Company relied on auditions. Ossie Davis read on June 2. A friend who came with him, who found an agent just in time to attend the audition, received a lot of attention. The muscular twenty-two-year-old, born in Miami, had grown up in the Bahamas. He was Sidney Poitier. "They liked his looks very much," a casting director noted. "He has a very sensitive face. Tall and lean, but a good figure. Soft warm voice. Excellent diction."

Poitier read twice more, but Anderson, Weill, and Mamoulian didn't decide on Absalom until the middle of August, and by that time, not having heard from them, Poitier's agent signed him with 20th Century Fox, where he made his feature film debut in *No Way Out* (1950). Poitier later played Absalom in the 1951 British film of *Cry, the Beloved Country*, directed by Zoltan Korda.

For Stephen, Mamoulian and the composers had a long list of classical recitalists pitched by agents. After casting stalled, Bill Fields, the company publicist, drafted a clumsy appeal that in 1927 for *Porgy* would have made sense; in 1949, it may have actually been counterproductive. Five copies, mailed over stage manager Eddie Brinkmann's signature, went to presidents of African American universities in search of an unknown performer.

"The Playwrights' Company is anxious to find within the great Negro population of America a person who fits these qualifications and who might possibly be able to interpret this fine part on the stage," it proclaimed. It added that Richard Harrison, who portrayed "De Lawd" in Marc Connelly's *The Green Pastures* (1930), had never acted before, and "We should like, if possible, to find a person like Mr. Harrison for this play." The reaction to this patronizing appeal is not known.

Mamoulian eventually proposed Duncan, who was extracted from an Australian tour. He arrived on September 15, just four days before rehearsals began. Mamoulian reunited with another friend as well. When contracts were being drawn up, Brinkmann wrote to the Playwrights' Company's business manager, Victor Samrock, about the casting of Georgette Harvey as one of the village women. "This is also not in the budget," he emphasized. "Mr. Mamoulian is fighting for this. I was told to call her and tell her it would be minimum salary. She said OK. She needs a job." Harvey was ill with the cancer from which she would succumb in 1952, and although she made the first week of performances, she was too ill for most of the rest of them.

The director's speech to the cast on September 19 made it clear that this was no "message" production:

> The meaning of the play—offhand, you might say it is about South Africa and about two races. But it is much more than that. Its real virtue is its final importance far beyond the class question. It is about brotherhood for human beings. No soapbox and no preaching. When it is over, it will not be about the English versus Zulus, but man versus man. It is the question of all of us—where do we go and where do we stop?
>
> The characters in the play are pretty clear. Stephen is a man of utter purity and simplicity. He reads the Bible and believes what he reads, and tries to carry out his beliefs. When reality offers conflicts, he is confused. It is not a pose, but the essence of his being and what makes saints. Jarvis is a purely decent and fine man and believes he is completely honest. He is open to justice and fair play. Absalom, when he leaves the country and people he is familiar with, is lost and goes wrong. Then there is the tragedy for Stephen when he has to decide what to advise Absalom—whether to plead guilty or not guilty. Stephen maintains if you are honest with yourself, you will be honest with the world. Simplicity is very important and cannot be stressed too much. If you have to, show less and *feel* more, but hold on to simplicity.

The choral number "Hills of Ixopo," drawn from the opening passages of the novel, describes the stark setting: the hills, green and "lovely beyond any singing of it," contrasting with the arid valleys. Kumalo's sitting room in Ndotsheni (EEN-dot-shane) introduces the priest, his wife, and a letter from John calling him "a faker in Christ." Son Absalom has been in Johannesburg for more than a year, and the Kumalos have had no word from him, so wife Grace (Gertrude Jeannette) suggests Stephen go to Johannesburg, which comes at a steep price—he has to use the money they were saving for Absalom's college education.

Mamoulian suggested "Thousands of Miles" for Stephen in keeping with his "starting out on a bright adventure." At the train station, the audience meets the three Jarvises. Arthur (John Morley), a lawyer who has been giving financial support to Stephen's congregation, goes out of his way to greet Stephen warmly. At John's tobacco shop, Stephen takes charge of his young nephew Alex (Herbert Coleman) because his sister Gertrude has turned to prostitution. John (Warren Coleman) coaches his political organization in how to obtain leverage with white politicians and has no respect for Stephen's work, calling him a "white man's dog, trained to bark and keep us in order." He demands to know why Stephen preaches the same Anglican faith of those who exploit Black people, to which Stephen meekly responds, "because all men do evil, I among them—and I wish all men to do better, I among them." John sneers, "Blessed are the chicken-hearted!"

During "The Search" montage, which condenses five chapters of the novel, Stephen, roaming across Soweto, gets progressively worse news about his son, finally learning that Absalom is no longer working in the mines; he's on parole for a petty crime, living with his pregnant girlfriend Irina (Inez Matthews) and keeping company with suspected thieves. That night, Stephen promises Alex he'll take him back to Ndotsheni in the soothing "The Little Gray House," another number from *Ulysses Africanus*.

The audience sees Absalom for the first time at a shantytown dive, where Linda (Sheila Guyse) is swaying on a table singing "Who'll Buy My Rutabagas?" The number is intended only as a relief from the story line. Absalom is a sullen observer, with his friends, John's son Matthew (William Greaves) and Johannes (Van Prince) doing all the talking before the women leave and they plan their robbery. Without a full-time choreographer, Mamoulian left the actors to work out their movements for "Rutabagas," mostly by tapping out rhythms on the table. With no firm structure, stage manager Andy Anderson complained in one weekly report, "the dance finish disorganized and too obviously improvised. This happens often."

That scene, which is not from the novel, also had the show's most controversial line. During a mock trial of Linda for licentiousness, Matthew scoffs, "Justice is when the black man digs and the white man carries his briefcase. Justice is when the black woman cooks and the white woman has breakfast in bed." Anderson reported, after the opening week, "Several objections through the mail to Matthew's line about the white woman having breakfast in bed." Shabby living conditions and racial injustice far away didn't have much impact, but maids serving breakfast hit many in the audience where they complacently lived.

Duncan found Mamoulian slyly sympathetic: "And, I think I said this to him once, I said, 'You have a very soft cotton hand, but don't you have a brick in your hand all the time?' He said, 'What do you mean by that, Todd?' I said, 'Aren't you at heart a revolutionary?' He says, 'You bet I am!'"

Matthew and Johannes want to rob a white man to get money to set themselves up in the gold fields; Absalom is pulled into their plot because he owns a gun. Absalom's parole officer, Eland (Charles Grunwell) introduces Stephen to Irina, and when she tells him Absalom has disappeared, he makes racist remarks about the Black poor: "They're like water. They live together, they get a child, they engage to marry, and the next day both have forgotten."

The bungled robbery isn't described in the novel; for Mamoulian, as in *Porgy*, there was no question over whether to stage an on-stage death. A servant confronts Matthew and Johannes, Arthur appears just long enough for Absalom's shot to ring out, the stage goes dark, and "Murder in Parkwold," another Mamoulian concept, uses a mixed-race chorus—an innovation in 1949.

Eland tells the grieving James that Johannes was one of the criminals. James vows revenge: "May he suffer as we suffer. As my wife is suffering now." Eland responds, "There are good and bad among them . . . Let us not blame the whole race." James asks what his dead son would have said, to which Eland replies, "He would have said, 'They live in such poverty and fear. They see no way out . . . and they grow desperate.'" This leads into the "Fear" montage, in which whites and Blacks sing of their fear of each other.

Mamoulian's staging left a deep impression on Greaves: "Mamoulian was for me a kind of idol. He had a unique sense of crowd management. His crowds had shape and personality; they weren't an amorphous mass. Very instructive. For example, to show fear, he would place all the people in an aversive slant away from the source of danger. They weren't perpendicular to it. They were at about 75 degrees, so that, looked at from a distance, they would almost seem to be starting to run away." Stephen has assumed the murder charge is false. Absalom, in prison, tells him he pulled the trigger. In the following scene, Stephen has put Alex to bed in their tiny shantytown room, and is attempting to write to Grace. He's adrift in anguish. "Lost in the Stars" in *Ulysses Africanus* was written for a freed slave, Nicodemus, who has been chased by the Ku Klux Klan. In the voice of an

Anglican priest, there's now the horror of shattered faith as he sings "And sometimes it seems maybe God's gone away."

The second act builds on the worth of Absalom's trial and the death penalty, leading to Stephen's soliloquy "Oh, Tixo, Tixo, Help Me," a plea to God (Teek-o) written originally for the choral leader (Frank Roane). Now given to Duncan, it was amended at Mamoulian's request:

> Let's have a sweeping, powerful aria, deeply emotional and of tragic dimensions.... The seventh [stanza] reaches an almost unbearable climax on "I shall lose Absalom then"—the cry of a loving, bleeding heart, biblical in stature.
>
> After the final line: "I see no other hope—no other hope," Stephen can sing out, "Oh, Tixo, Tixo, help me!" This should be a musical line of utter beauty, prayerful, humble and full of sorrow.... This line of prayer, repeated three times, could emotionally remind us of Christ's passion in the Garden of Gethsemane.

"Oh, I think once or twice in the theater, I touched the Lord with it, I think," Duncan recalled.

Stephen meets James to explore the possibility of a resolution. In his rage, James only barks white supremacist rhetoric: "Umfundisi, there are two races in South Africa. One is capable of mastery and self-control—the other is not. One is born to govern, the other to be governed. One is capable of culture and the arts of civilization—the other is not." He finishes with a demand for the death penalty: "Those who will not keep order must be kept in order! Those who lift their hands to kill must know that the penalty for death is death!"

Irina agrees to Absalom's request, made through Stephen, that she marry him so the child will have his name. At the trial the next day, Johannes and Matthew perjure themselves with a story about being elsewhere at the time of the murder, and they plead not guilty. Absalom, repentant, tells the judge that after the shooting, he decided he'd refuse to lie, so he confesses, although he says he fired his gun only to frighten the servant.

The hope for the future lies in the two youngsters, shown at play with Alex's homemade digging toy he calls "Big Mole." It was going to be a duet, originally, but with Herbert Coleman's powerful voice—the cast recording proves that he was, indeed, a tiny Ethel Merman—it became his solo.

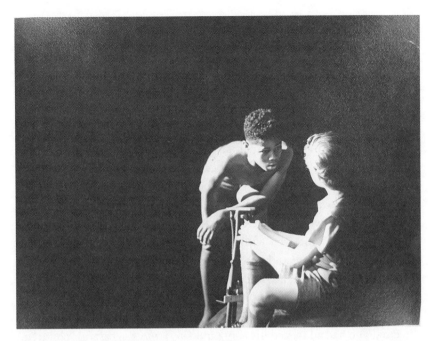

Herbert Coleman and Judson Rees in the "Big Mole" number in *Lost in the Stars*. Photograph courtesy of Library of Congress.

When he finished singing about "a digger of the fastest kind" who can "dig in the earth like you think in your mind," just as he had done with the spiritual in *St. Louis Woman*, he stopped the show.

James has his epiphany in the next scene, standing with Edward near a window of Stephen's church to hear the service. Stephen tells the chorus, now serving as his congregation, that he's leaving his ministry: "I had a sure faith that though there was good and evil I knew which was good, and God knew it—and men were better in their hearts for choosing good and not evil. Something has shaken this in me. I am not sure of my faith. I am lost. I am not sure that we are not all lost. And a leader should not be lost." His parishioners unsuccessfully plead with him to stay, singing "A Bird of Passage." As they repeat the final line: "Go forward into dark again," they are speaking to both Stephen and James and their grief at the loss of their sons.

In the novel, Stephen and James only exchange letters near the end of the story; for the musical adaptation, Paton and Anderson agreed that the fathers should meet. It's always the most criticized part of the show, since the transformation for both men is so abrupt. Duncan didn't think it quite worked, either: "But I never felt, I said then to Mr. Mamoulian, too, that it hit hard enough, that there was really homogeneity and oneness, and conformity. And believing in each other. And in the new."

At the scene opens, Stephen, praying before Absalom's early morning execution, is at his sitting-room table with Irina. James, deeply moved by what he witnessed at the chapel, arrives. At the time, just the sight of a white person in the home of a Black person had considerable impact. Paton advised Anderson, "If the story is to be true to South Africa it will be a strange and awkward friendship."

That's exactly what audiences got. James urges Stephen to stay with his congregation, "for even with all the horror of this crime some things have come that are gain and not loss." He also praises Absalom's bravery in court. "Let us forgive each other. Let us be neighbors. Let us be friends," he concludes.

Mamoulian's "paternalistic" remarks to the cast annoyed Greaves. The director, who had addressed his *Porgy* and *Porgy and Bess* casts as "children," hadn't realized that times were changing:

> I will always remember after the opening night he came back and said, "Children, I want to tell you I was deeply moved. And my wife . . . she cried." [Azadia] was a red-haired woman dripping in jewels. . . . Perhaps had he not started off with the word "children," my reaction at that moment would not have been negative.
>
> But unfortunately in those days, a lot of white people had a horrible habit of referring to adult Afro-Americans as boy, girl or children. The younger members of the cast were too nationalistic to accept that kind of patronizing, even though I'm sure Mamoulian meant no harm.

In the New York *Herald Tribune*, Howard Barnes wrote, "there is virtually nothing wanting . . . it is a harrowing theatrical experience, but one of deep satisfaction." John Chapman, in the *Daily News*, called Duncan "majestically impressive," but William Hawkins, in the *World-Telegram*, complained that the ending seemed "slick and arbitrary." The critical response and word of mouth stimulated the box office into a modest run. Just before the opening, the Playwrights' Company announced advance sales of about $130,000. The morning after opening night, *Variety* reported that most cherished sight, a long line of ticket buyers.

When the national tour began after successful runs in San Francisco and Los Angeles that fall, the cast fell victim to the indignities of racial segregation. In St. Louis, there were pickets from the NAACP because the American Theater was segregated, and the show went nearly $4,000 in the red. Brinkmann reported, "The Negro can sit way up in a gallery called Negers [*sic*] Heaven here. I went up there, you just can't see a thing." Just after arriving on October 10, "The cast is like a keg of dynamite right now. They can't eat in restaurants or sit anywhere in a theater but the very top gallery." Similar conditions prevailed in Kansas City. "The cast can only eat in railroad stations or their own Negro neighborhoods," Brinkmann wrote.

The tour was to include Cleveland, Pittsburgh, Baltimore, Washington, DC, Philadelphia, and Boston. It closed instead in Chicago in early November, where Brinkmann conceded the racial situation was no better than elsewhere: "There is an awful lot of hatred against the Negro in this city. It is close to a riot state. Even the theater bar [at the Great Northern Theatre] in the lobby charges fifty cents for a drink, [but] when a Negro walks in they charge him eighty-five cents. I have seen it with my own eyes." The last four performances there were sellouts, but with an $8,000 loss in Chicago, Samrock shut down the tour.

Mamoulian insisted to Duncan that he was opposed to such a tour all along and had asked that the show return to Broadway after its California appearances. "So, a beautiful work of art has to close long before its time because of shortsightedness and mistaken handling. It was a noble and important contribution to the American musical theatre. It will not be forgotten."

CHAPTER 18

Mamoulian Marches On

Arms and the Girl was a favor to Lawrence Langner and a quick Broadway payday from an unusually well-heeled backer. It turned out to be Mamoulian's last Broadway production.

In 1933, *The Pursuit of Happiness* had been Langner's most successful play, earning steady royalties from stock productions, and it was made into a Paramount film (1934) starring Francis Lederer and Joan Bennett. Its musical adaptation, with lyrics by Dorothy Fields and a book by her brother Herbert, and Mamoulian (he claimed he had to do all the rewriting.) combines physical comedy with historical accuracy. Winsome as that sounds, the show has a problem element that has kept it unperformed since its brief original Broadway run: the heroine's sassy sidekick, originally played by Pearl Bailey, is a runaway slave. That, plus a fusillade of "honey chiles" in one number, made it controversial then and an unplayable relic ever since.

In the *New York Times*, Brooks Atkinson called it "a spy-and-lover story that is not conspicuous for originality, skill or beauty. In craftsmanship and point of view it is closer to *The Student Prince* than they probably intended." In the *Herald Tribune*, Howard Barnes called it "a bountiful, if somewhat ponderous entertainment," and thought "stringent pruning" would have helped.

Arms and the Girl opened February 2, 1950, and folded after 134 performances. A close inspection of the book and Morton Gould's score reveals some vintage charms. It's very much a throwback—no integrated music and dancing with the story line, and mostly songs about the joy of being in love. It also was the rare three-star vehicle, with Nanette Fabray, Georges Guétary and Pearl Bailey. Herbert Fields treated it as he'd done with the 1925 Rodgers

Georges Guétary and Nanette Fabray in *Arms and the Girl*, Mamoulian's last Broadway musical, in 1950.

and Hart show *Dearest Enemy*, in which Helen Ford as heroine Betsy Burke made her first entrance "nude" in a barrel and later romanced a British general.

The colonial practice of "bundling" drives the plot of *Arms and the Girl*. In this tradition of courtship, a young couple would lie fully clothed (so it was claimed) in a bed at the house of the girl's parents, covers drawn up, with a jagged-top board chastely (more or less) separating them. On stage, an unmarried woman and man shown in bed together was risqué. The show defends bundling as practical while also leering at it.

Mamoulian kept a cranky distance from the production before rehearsals, writing a series of memos while working on *Lost in the Stars*. One of the dancers, Annabelle Gold, couldn't recall even recall taking directions from him; choreographer Michael Kidd handled all of that. The Fieldses and Gould produced one hit song for Bailey—the earthy "There Must Be Something Better Than Love." The show has the only comic Broadway appearance of historical straight man George Washington. It was almost as controversial as Bailey's role. She faced heat from a civil rights organization to drop out of the show, and Mamoulian's idea to have Washington make a grand second act entrance on a white horse caused fierce internal arguments.

Jo Kirkland (Fabray) is shown bundling twice—with Max (Guétary), the runaway Hessian soldier, to whom she reads from the Song of Solomon, and with a more-than-eager Col. Mortimer Sherwood (John Conte). Sheriff Thad Jennings (Seth Arnold) condemns bundling, while Jo's parents (Florenz Ames and Lulu Belle Clarke) are matter-of-fact about it and hopeful that their daughter will find a fellow and settle down. The Fieldses made Jo a plucky "ham patriot"—an overzealous, unauthorized participant in the Revolutionary War who forgoes skirts for knee breeches. When she's not plotting romantic schemes, she's blowing up bridges to halt the British advance. Audiences were supposed to find the type familiar. At one point, Jo proclaims, "I did it before and I can do it again!" echoing the popular slogan in the wake of the Pearl Harbor attack that launched the United States into World War II.

Langner had pushed *Pursuit* as a musical since *Oklahoma!* He had sent the script to Mamoulian in the summer of 1945, and for the next two years, wooed composers like Johnny Green, Harry Warren, Arthur Schwartz, and

Frank Loesser. By late 1948, Langner had commitments from the Fieldses, who had triumphed with Ethel Merman in Irving Berlin's *Annie, Get Your Gun* in 1946, and composer Burton Lane, who had written music for Yip Harburg's lyrics in *Finian's Rainbow* the year before.

Langner could afford the Fieldses because he landed a deep-pocketed producer in Anthony Brady Farrell, an Albany steel millionaire who owned the Mark Hellinger Theater. Farrell was an unusually generous Broadway "angel" in the postwar years; for *Arms*, he laid out $100,000 of the show's $200,000 budget. Of course, the material had to appeal to him, and his tastes were hardly Guild fare. Farrell preferred leggy chorines above all else, and the shows he backed fell along the lines of escapism for the tired businessman, with titles including *Texas, Li'l Darlin'* (1949) and *Ankles Aweigh* (1955). Most famously, he backed the musical version of *Gentlemen Prefer Blondes* (1949). "I went to see *A Streetcar Named Desire*, and I could not get to sleep for two days after," Farrell told a columnist in 1949. "What I like is pretty girls in pretty costumes and nice songs and dances. I like to relax and be entertained."

Arms certainly caters to that in the first-act double-entendre number "That's What I Told Him Last Night," an attempt to instill military discipline in the sprightly local girls, and "He Will Tonight," in which Jo finally dons female attire, changing clothes on stage—Mamoulian described that as a "modest striptease."

The presence of the remarkable sugar daddy made Mamoulian more than his usual obstreperous self when it came to his contract. His demands included Azadia's transportation and living expenses, being billed as lighting director, the right to direct any revival on the same financial terms as the original play no matter when produced, and most unusually, limits on when he could go into production conferences. "In view of the fact that Mamoulian's only successes that I can recall in the legitimate theatre for many years are *Oklahoma!* and *Carousel*, I can't see why he is entitled to impose such onerous conditions and terms upon us," William Fitelson sputtered to Helburn and Langner. He got none of that, settling for $5,000 and 2 percent of the gross. Armina Marshall reported to Helburn that Mamoulian "would try to work out some formula with [agent] Sam Jaffe to get Azadia's expenses covered, as he did not want his integrity questioned." She said she replied, "For God's sake, we would not question [your] integrity any more than [you] would question ours, and why make such a to-do about it?"

After battles with Dorothy Fields, Lane quit early on. Gould, hired that August, didn't have any easier a time. "Dorothy and Herb had very set approaches. They were concerned with me, that I would not be commercial enough, that I would write music that was too symphonic," he recalled to his biographer. "[Dorothy] would get violent and accuse me, saying that I'm destroying her lyrics, my music is 'mainly for Carnegie Hall,' that it's not for the stage."

The Theatre Guild board decided at one point that the sets should have the quaint New England look of Grandma Moses paintings and the artist herself should be approached. Anna Mary Robertson Moses, a lifelong resident of Vermont, had seen the value of her primitive paintings of country life, which she used to sell for only $10, soar after they became favorites of celebrity collectors such as Cole Porter and Louis B. Mayer. The Guild board thought she could make some drawings to be reproduced as sets much more inexpensively than an experienced set designer such as Jo Mielziner, whose fee was $5,000. After contacting her representatives, Fitelson reported they were "willing to compromise on $2,500" but also that the artist, at eighty-nine, was "sick and probably will not be able to execute new pictures." Horace Armistead, a veteran of the Metropolitan Opera, was hired to create the same nostalgic look.

Fabray, who later made her career in TV, had appeared steadily on Broadway since 1941 and had starring roles in *Bloomer Girl* (1946), *High Button Shoes* (1947), and Weill's *Love Life* (1948), for which she won a Tony Award. She had a star's temperament, Mamoulian recalled:

> There were two things she always liked to do. One was a whistle, where she'd put two fingers in her mouth, and whistle loudly. The audience would applaud, regardless of whether it fit the situation or not. They came to recognize it as sort of a trademark of hers. And the other was a regular old burlesque bump of the pelvis. So she just naturally went about to insert those in the show, because they were part of her.
>
> Well, I said that those were out. Both of them. Completely out. And she thought that I was killing her. Her husband at that time [David Tebet] was

a public relations guy, who put into one or two columns in the New York papers . . . how I was squashing Nanette Fabray's personality.

Fabray's version of her diva nature was even more colorful: "I was frightened of the stage spotlight beam being turned on me. Dave finally eased my spotlight psychosis by arranging for the beam to be turned on during the whole rehearsal period. That way I gradually got accustomed to it. In two months, we opened and did fine."

Guétary had one memorable film role as Gene Kelly's romantic rival in *An American in Paris* (1953). Born to Greek parents, he was a singing star in France and the cast member least acquainted with American history. Hessians were German soldiers who fought for the British in the Revolutionary War. This Guétary didn't understand. His agent wrote to Jerry Whyte, then working as a production manager for the Guild: "He is rather wondering why it was necessary for him to be a German and use a lot of German words which do not come naturally to a Frenchman."

Guetary's first number, "I Like It Here," was an immigrant's passionate hymn to New World freedoms. His first duet with Fabray, "A Cow and a Plough and a Frau," is the show's version of "Surrey with the Fringe on Top." With an infectious melody, it's exactly what an eighteenth-century German immigrant would dream about—a farm and a wife. As it unfolds, Franz expands his expected family from four to seven to eleven children.

Bailey had two bespoke numbers, the first-act ballad "Nothin' for Nothin'" and, performed in front of a drop curtain during a set change, the second-act "There Must Be Something Better Than Love," in search of "some practical plan that don't require the service of man," Like Lena Horne had been for *St. Louis Woman*, Bailey was pressured to drop out. The role of Connecticut was not written in Negro patois—Bailey simply made the part her own. Connecticut is neither idiotic nor childlike. She's running away, but so is Franz. Her line "All white people look alike to me" was taken out of the script.

Even so, the role and the first-act ensemble number "Philadelphia Plantation" came into the crosshairs of the Committee for the Negro in the Arts. The lyrics of that number end with a lot of "honey chiles" by different cast members, including Connecticut. In print, Connecticut's opening line about a "watermelon moon," and Jo's line about "where the Pennsylvania Dutch pickaninnies play" read like they're out of a minstrel show. In performance, they're sung briskly in a minor key, and the number is wildly out of character with the rest of the score.

After seeing a tryout performance in Philadelphia, Ruth Jett, the organization's executive secretary, wrote Helburn on January 19 that the way "Bailey and others are used left no doubt in our minds about the distasteful character of the show." Hammerstein allowed his name to be used on the committee's letterhead, so Helburn asked him for advice. He wasn't sympathetic. Hammerstein thought the charge "an example of the silly and screwball thinking that goes on in this connection. Everyone agrees that all portrayals of Negroes should not be of the stereotyped kind. It is, however, just as fallacious to maintain that they should always be heroic and saintly. I know of nothing else to do with this letter you received except to ignore it." She didn't. Instead, she issued a statement: "Miss Bailey's role . . . stands out in the show as a distinguished performance by a talented and well beloved artist and reflects the highest credit on her race."

Bailey came up with her own way of dealing with the controversy. On February 7, just five days after the Broadway opening, she went public with a complaint about racial harassment. The complaint varied, depending on the publication source. One version said white members of the cast were calling her Eurasian, another that she was being derisively called "honey chile." Mamoulian was the emissary. He held a noon conference with the Theatre Guild on February 10, followed by dinner that evening at Sardi's with Bailey and her husband, John Pinkett. Two days later, an article in the *New York Times* said the situation had been resolved, with Bailey telling the reporter that without Mamoulian's intercession, "I'd have walked out the door."

With the romance established and a subplot about possible spying tied up, all that remains in the second act is for Jo to give up her military ambitions and begin life as wife and mother. That requires the intervention of Washington (Arthur Vinton). Mamoulian thought up a way to pep up the scene: "What about General Washington making his entrance on an enormous white horse?" Already Washington arrived to the happy ensemble number "Mister Washington! Uncle George!" Now he would do it on horseback. Years later, Gould hooted at the memory: "So in Boston, when we didn't have any ending to the show, or a second act, they were going down to the stables—everybody walked the plank on this."

Audiences stayed away; with dwindling houses, on the week ending May 13, *Arms* turned a profit of exactly $30.50. The three stars bolted when their contracts expired at the end of May, and the show closed without plans for a road tour. *Arms* lost nearly $158,000. Helburn thought she knew why, writing to Dorothy Fields, "I must confess I have seen it coming for a long while. Actually, from the very beginning I never had a sense of the pulse which is necessary for a musical as costly as this to survive."

∼

Huckleberry Finn came out of Weill's idea to set classic American literature to music; he was also considering *Moby-Dick*. His five completed songs and Anderson's drafts of the script eliminated racial slurs and didn't explore any of the novel's racial commentary other than "This Time, Next Year," in which Jim speculates about his upcoming emancipation. The rest of his completed numbers: "River Chanty," "Catfish Song," "Apple Jack," "Come In, Mornin'" are all nonpolitical Americana. On March 17, two weeks after he turned fifty, Weill suffered a heart attack. A second attack, in a New York hospital on April 3, was fatal.

At first, Anderson struggled to complete the show. "Several times I have attempted to re-read and do a little work on *Huck Finn*—something seems to paralyze my brain when I approach that script," he wrote Mamoulian in July. The cancellation of a planned MGM musical of *Huckleberry Finn* in September 1951 ended Anderson's interest in his version.

∼

Hollywood continued to be unwelcoming. On October 22, 1950, Mamoulian was forced to defend his patriotism at a late-night meeting of the Directors Guild. Cecil B. DeMille, at the onset of the Hollywood blacklist of real and suspected Communist Party members, was insisting on a loyalty oath for the guild and attempting to recall Joseph Mankiewicz as the guild president. With careers on the line, the meeting became famous for its ad hominem rhetoric. DeMille tore into his opponents with, "Is it their object to split this guild wide open so that *The Daily Worker* and *Pravda* can gloat over the spectacle?" John Ford responded, "I don't think there's anyone in this room who knows more about what the American public wants than Cecil B. DeMille—and he certainly knows how to give it to them. But I don't like you, C. B. I don't like what you stand for and I don't like what you've been saying here tonight." Ford proposed that the entire board of directors resign, which occurred, and Mankiewicz retained the presidency.

The apocryphal part of the evening, recalled by Fred Zinnemann in his memoir, had DeMille deliberately mispronouncing William Wyler's last name as "Vyler" and Mankiewicz as "Mankiewitch." According to a stenographer's transcript, this did not occur. DeMille biographer Scott Eyman concluded that it could just be an urban legend. He also speculated that Mamoulian's words might have contributed to it.

Mamoulian took eloquent aim at DeMille's nativism. He acknowledged he was

> a little nervous standing up here tonight. It is my accent. I have an accent . . . I don't remember any time when a fellow director had to get up and before expressing what he had to say he had to declare himself to be an honest, reputable man. He has to mention how far back he goes of any generations to be born in this country. I came here and I am a naturalized citizen. I wanted to be an American, and I would not want anyone challenging my being a good American so I will forget the embarrassing feeling of being shy about my accent.
>
> I have known Mr. DeMille for a long time, not very well. He has always been most cordial to me . . . Tomorrow it is I who may be the subject of your remarks. I think it is wrong for a member of the Guild within the family to accuse anyone, even anonymously without actual data or actual direct knowledge, because it is that that suddenly sows seeds of a terrific mistrust, fear and anxiety and suspicion.

The awkward coda to that meeting was that after Mankiewicz kept his office, he reversed himself and requested a loyalty oath for directors. All guild members except Charlie Chaplin eventually signed.

Under those circumstances, Mamoulian would really have exploded with rage had he known the FBI had kept a file on him since 1943. He came under scrutiny not because of his attempt to join the Army Signal Corps in 1942 but simply because he was a foreigner who had helped found the

Screen Directors Guild in 1935. Labor unions and communist infiltration were one and the same in the FBI mindset of that time. Such files relied on secondhand information, rendering their accuracy spurious. Mamoulian's file does not include references to Boris Morros and the many Communist Party members involved in *Lysistrata* in 1940. Instead, it mentions that he met with an unnamed representative of the Soviet film industry in Hollywood (Sergei Eisenstein would have been one), attended National Council of American–Soviet Friendship dinners (his diary mentions one dinner with a Soviet film delegation in 1935), and he had taught writing in Hollywood under the auspices of the League of American Writers, identified as a communist front organization (not in his diaries, and unlikely).

The longest stretch of time Mamoulian spent in California from 1943 to 1950 was during the making of *Summer Holiday* in 1946, so FBI agents must have had to work energetically to track his phone calls and intercept his mail, as the file discloses. This might explain why they also began keeping track of Zachary and Virginie, who seldom traveled outside California. The file ends with a mention of a tapped phone call between two known Communist Party members who agreed that Mamoulian was not a communist—he only "held the Roosevelt view of things." Mamoulian's long association with African American performers never appeared to factor into suspicions about his work being in any way subversive.

~

Tiresome, anxious lapses between work opportunities and projects that stagnate without funding or commitments are the feared specter of show business. Mamoulian had some offers, though. He was busying himself, among other proposed projects, with an offer from the Metropolitan Opera and considering his own film version of *Carmen*. When Rudolf Bing, the Austrian-born impresario, was named general manager of the Met in late 1949, hiring Mamoulian was one of his first ideas to restore energy to the venerable stage. In January 1950, he took in a rehearsal of *Lost in the Stars* to offer Mamoulian a production of Verdi's *Don Carlos* that fall. Mamoulian suggested Bizet's *Carmen* or Puccini's *La bohème* instead, but Bing didn't want *Carmen* for his inaugural season, adding, "*Bohème* I admire. It is a lovely opera, but in my view, not quite important enough for the opening of a new season."

Despite the prestige, Bing's offer of a flat $2,000 was hardly Broadway money. He sweetened the deal with a second opera, Strauss's *Die Fledermaus*, but Mamoulian wouldn't commit. The following year, Bing relented on *Carmen*, suggesting a production for January 1952, in French, conducted by Fritz Reiner and starring Risë Stevens. By then, Mamoulian said he was "beginning two projects, making that impossible for me."

One of those was a repair job for David O. Selznick that began in March. In late 1949, Selznick co-produced *Gone to Earth* (released 1950), a Technicolor adaptation of Mary Webb's novel of a Gypsy girl in the Shropshire countryside, directed by Michael Powell and Emeric Pressburger. It starred Jennifer Jones, whom Selznick had married earlier that year. Selznick was unhappy with their initial cut of the film, which received tepid notices in Britain, although today it's regarded as a classic portrayal of nineteenth-century country life.

Selznick brought actors David Farrar and Cyril Cusack and cinematographer Christopher Challis from England and at considerable expense, reconstructed three interior sets—a bedroom, library, and parlor—on his lot, and used a storefront exterior and church interior for close-ups of Jones. *Gone to Earth* has Jones as Hazel Woodus, a gentle, free-spirited rustic. She marries the local parson, Edward Marston (Cusack), but a fox-hunting squire, Jack Reddin (Farrar) also pursues her. Selznick thought the film needed more emotion—specifically, from his wife. He asked Mamoulian to film a scene in which Reddin kisses Hazel while holding a brace of dead game birds, which horrifies her.

Mamoulian completed the retakes between March 12 and 16. Selznick had lost none of his manic energy that had marked his work of the 1930s. "I noticed that I'd rehearse Jennifer Jones and she'd be great, and then suddenly I'd make a take and something would happen; she wasn't there," Mamoulian said. "And it puzzled me. And there was David, you see, watching her, and she'd just go cold." Challis recalled that Mamoulian was perhaps "well aware of what was going on and had decided that discretion was the easiest course to take." Mamoulian prepared a list of suggestions for reediting the film but didn't take part in that when Selznick chopped it from its original 110-minute running time to just 82 minutes and added a prologue narrated by Joseph Cotten.

Carmen stuck with Mamoulian that year, and soon he was asking Anderson to come up with an English-language libretto. At the same time, they worked on an English-language *The Barber of Seville*, and (the second project Mamoulian mentioned to Bing) an adaptation of *Faust* to be called *Devil's Hornpipe* with music and lyrics by Harry Warren, starring John Raitt. It eventually became a 1959 musical film without Mamoulian's participation, starring James Cagney, called *Never Steal Anything Small*. Casting considerations for *Carmen* included Patricia Morison, who could sing, and Sophia Loren, who could not. By the end of 1953, their plan was to raise British and Spanish capital and make the picture in London and Spain, but they could never come up with financing or a studio.

The Theatre Guild planned to present *Porgy and Bess* in a limited run in late 1950, offering Mamoulian a whopping 10 percent of the profits. It did not come about after the Guild balked at the new Actors Equity weekly minimum of $100 for chorus members. So Mamoulian undoubtedly was pleased in January 1952 when he received a wire from producer Robert Breen asking simply, "Are you interested in directing *Porgy and Bess* again?" Breen was in partnership with Charles Blevins Davis, a former schoolteacher from Missouri who was a multimillionaire after his wife, railroad heiress Marguerite Sawyer Hill, died, leaving him $9 million. Breen and Davis were pioneering the international cultural exchange, sending, with help from the State Department, the best of American art and music to European nations rebuilding after World War II. Leontyne Price was signed as Bess, William Warfield as Porgy, and as Sporting Life, bandleader Cab Calloway.

In March, they offered Mamoulian a flat $5,000 with no percentage, since "operating losses on continental tour will be very heavy." Two weeks of rehearsals were to begin in May. Ira Gershwin and wife Leonore added encouragement: "Although the delays were unfortunate the problem is truly one of world significance. We hope you'll consider this both as a duty and an honor." Mamoulian balked at the short rehearsal period and turned it down.

After that came a bizarre Hollywood nadir. Adolph Zukor marked his eightieth birthday in January 1953. In an act of corporate fealty awarded only to the original moguls, Paramount executives planned a lavish dinner to celebrate the birthday and Zukor's fiftieth year in show business. Studio executives asked Mamoulian to plan and "direct" the banquet. For this, he got an office on the studio lot.

Some notions were bewildering in their presumption of who would show up and perform for Zukor, as if this were a royal command performance: Jeanette MacDonald and Nelson Eddy reuniting to sing a number from *Naughty Marietta* (1935); Fred Astaire and Ginger Rogers reuniting for a dance routine; and an idea of Mamoulian's in which Jack Benny would perform a scene from *The Horn Blows at Midnight* (1945), a flop he'd made at Warner Bros. and frequently kidded about on his radio program. Benny refused. As the January 7 date bore down, the elaborate plans fell away. The A-list performers mostly had Paramount contracts. Bob Hope was the master of ceremonies. Eddy sang "It's a Great Day" with a chorus after the fruit cocktail and salad were served, while Rosemary Clooney led the singing of "Happy Birthday" and "There's No Business Like Show Business." Dean Martin and Jerry Lewis, then the hottest team in show business, performed a routine.

"And the effects Rouben has achieved with the lighting tonight! I was carving on the shadow of my meat for ten minutes!" Hope cracked in his scripted remarks. "I've been to a lot of dinners, but this tops 'em all. This looks like *Quo Vadis*—with Tums. . . . He's auditioning for the next Marion Davies party. Three more parties like these and he can go to Copenhagen and come back as Elsa Maxwell!"

Mamoulian could have been stuck with directing more tributes. A few months later, Whitney Warren, a patron of the San Francisco Opera, was planning a fund-raiser and asked his friend George Cukor for assistance. Cukor had just the man to recommend, as he acidly wrote:

> I don't know who it was who suggested Rouben Mamoulian. You know who he is. He directed *Porgy and Bess*, *Oklahoma*, etc. At the moment he is rehearsing *Carousel* here for the Los Angeles [Civic Light] Opera. (He did the original production in New York.) A few months ago he staged a most brilliant show for the eightieth birthday celebration of Adolph Zukor. He would be the perfect person for this job. He's efficient, very knowledgeable musically, and is a good showman.

I've been trying to contact him but so far have not had any luck. I think, however, there might be a chance. I'll tell you why. Between us, Mr. Mamoulian is inclined to be impressed with uppercrusters, or bluebloods, or socialites—goodness knows why.

First I will find out whether he has the time to do your party, then I will broach the subject to him this way: I have been contacted by these great swells from San Francisco to ask Mr. Mamoulian—specifically—if he would undertake to do this as a "gesture" for the San Francisco Opera company. If I get a favorable answer then I will ask you to have your most distinguished and fancy patron contact him.

Mamoulian had begun to look inward by the time of that dinner. In September 1952, construction began on his contemporary one-story V-shaped house on two acres in Beverly Hills. He and Azadia wouldn't move in until the end of 1953. At a cost of $81,000, architect Burton Schutt designed a boxy structure more in keeping with new homes being constructed in nearby Trousdale Estates instead of the Mediterranean designs prevalent in the neighborhood. The house, sited to give a sweeping view of more than 300 trees, was a retreat for private contemplation. There was a single main bedroom, two rooms for maids, and a substantial dressing room for Azadia.

At its center was the thirty-by-twenty-foot garden room with white terrazzo floors. It had a large skylight, and its southern wall, entirely of glass, looked out on the trees. Dominating the room was unexpected kitsch—a Venetian statue of a white monkey playing a guitar. Just past the eleven-foot-high double front doors, Mamoulian installed a three-tiered copper and bronze Italian fountain, which he filled with colored stones he had accumulated on his travels. One wall of the dining room caught the attention of Dorothy Rodgers when she wrote her book about decor, *My Favorite Things*: "One of the most memorable things . . . is the *trompe l'oeil* Pompeian wall Azadia has painted for the living room; Rouben's delightful contribution is a group of fascinating portraits of Azadia made from shells, from pressed flowers, from semiprecious stones; there is even a *decoupage* one that incorporates luggage stickers and postcards from a South American trip they once took."

Design flaws became evident over time. The house had radiant heat built into its concrete pad, which failed when the coils rusted. Forced-air heating and cooling installed in the 1970s required cuts in the roof, which eventually leaked. Rain guttering built into the walls also leaked, which created mold. As a result, Rouben and Azadia began extended visits to New York and Washington.

Azadia could behave erratically when she was drinking, and word of that fact got around. Actor Michael Dante, only recently having arrived in the film industry, recorded his memory of a 1954 occasion:

> I was invited along with actor Gilbert Roland and his wife, director Rouben Mamoulian and his wife Azadia, Marlon Brando and attractive Greek actress Irene Papas, who were an item at the time. I was seated next to Mrs. Mamoulian and to her left was Gilbert Roland. About midway through dinner, Azadia was speaking with me while other conversations carried on throughout the table. I wasn't aware of it, but her husband, Rouben was in a heated exchange with Gilbert. She and I were talking and suddenly she excused herself to me and turned to her left and slapped Gilbert.
>
> "Don't you talk to my husband like that!" she scolded him. Everyone stopped talking and was in shock, especially Gilbert. His face on the one side was all red. He stood up, looked at her and the hosts. He excused himself and his wife got up and they left the table. Gilbert handled himself with self-control. The atmosphere in the room became uncomfortable. Mrs. Mamoulian was a slight, thin woman, but obviously very protective of her husband. Nothing more was said about the incident.

Hammerstein ended Mamoulian's fallow stretch with an *Oklahoma!* offer. He and Rodgers hadn't considered Mamoulian for the film version in 1955, directed by Fred Zinnemann, and didn't approach him for the 1956 film of *Carousel*, which was directed by Henry King. When it came to overseas prestige, however, they had only one choice. In February 1955, over lunch at the Plaza Hotel, Hammerstein asked Mamoulian to help prepare the upcoming European tour of *Oklahoma!* It was part of a US State Department project—show tune diplomacy to encourage pro-American sentiment. It was scheduled for Paris, with later stops in Rome and Milan and a side trip to a US military base in Germany. Mamoulian at first said, no doubt grumpily, he would be "available to help in pre-production work." Since no other employment was looming and both he and Azadia got government-paid travel and lodging out of it, off to Europe they went.

Shirley Jones and Rod Steiger were reprising their film roles of Laurey and Jud. Playing Curly was Jack Cassidy, whom Jones later married. None of them impressed Mamoulian when rehearsals began in New York in May: "Moody Rod Steiger. Precious Jack Cassidy. Inexperienced Shirley Jones." Steiger, an established movie star from *On The Waterfront*, went downhill from there. At first, he announced he was quitting because he didn't get billing on the posters. After being told he had to return, he found another way to break his contract at a rehearsal, when Mamoulian recorded, "flies off again—rewrite script—foul word." Three days later, thanks to Steiger's deftly placed "fuck," Mamoulian and the composers told him he was out, two weeks before the Paris opening on June 20.

Mamoulian enjoyed the bustle of the tour. "All the reviews in Rome without exception were great, the audiences are most enthusiastic, the 'Oklahoma' chorus stops the show every night, and we have to give them two encores after repeated final curtains," he wired Rodgers and Hammerstein on July 15. The happiness was cut short in Milan, where the show opened August 2. A week into the run, Jean Bradley, Jones's replacement, felt sick and couldn't go on. Two days later, she died from polio. Panic briefly swept the company as the theater was fumigated and some performances canceled, but no one else became ill.

CHAPTER 19

Breathtaking Cinemascope

All Mamoulian knew at first was that the phone call to his hotel in Rome was from California: "Worried me no end." The next day, he was in his room for a second call. It was Irving Lazar, whom Mamoulian had never met, about to bring his career back from the dead. He was offering representation for a musical planned by Arthur Freed at MGM.

Lazar and Lew Wasserman were the first of Hollywood's super-agents, known for their pugnacious ability to put together complex long-term deals with star actors receiving huge percentages of their film profits in the declining years of the studio system. Raised in Brooklyn and trained as a lawyer, Lazar was decades away from the caricature of his last years—a gnomish, name-dropping Oscar party habitué known as "Swifty" and peering through oversized spectacles. Mamoulian had been reluctant to sign with that type of dealmaker; in 1949, he canceled an agreement he had made with Wasserman after just six months. Lazar was more affable than Wasserman and, going by Mamoulian's diary, a skilled practitioner of the daily phone call designed to mollify egos and share gossip.

Lazar was out to land Freed an inexpensive director. Producers and actors were freelancers in the post–World War II world of movie financing, and Freed was now an independent producer within MGM—the famed "Freed unit" was a separate business entity, so the director was paid out of Freed's money, not the studio's. Mamoulian inked his contract for a flat $50,000—$1,000 a week during ten weeks of preparation, and $2,000 a week for a twenty-week shooting schedule—a comedown from *Summer Holiday*, but still considerably better than a risky Broadway assignment.

Freed's initial interest in Mamoulian was to see whether he could recoup his investment in *St. Louis Woman* with a film version starring Sammy

Davis Jr. as Li'l Augie. The project quickly shifted to *Silk Stockings*, the film of Cole Porter's stage musical. Based on a Melchior Lengyel story and the 1939 MGM movie *Ninotchka* starring Greta Garbo and directed by Ernst Lubitsch, the 1955 musical had been through several typewriters by the time Freed considered it.

Billy Wilder, Charles Brackett, and Walter Reisch adapted the film directed by Ernst Lubitsch. George S. Kaufman, Leueen MacGrath, and Abe Burrows updated it for the musical, adding the character of Peggy Dayton, an American swimming star. The French aristocrat (Melvyn Douglas in the film) who romances the humorless Russian was now Hollywood producer Steve Canfield (Don Ameche on stage), and Ninotchka's (Hildegarde Knef on stage) mission in Paris is not about selling jewelry for tractors—she attempts to get a new character, the famous composer Boroff, to return home. The three envoys—Bibinski, Popov, and Brankov—easily and happily seduced by the pleasures of Paris, remain the same. Mamoulian's version went through rewrites by Harry Kurnitz and credited screenwriters Leonard Gershe and Leonard Spiegelglass. One gem probably scripted by Brackett—a darkly comic reference to Stalinist purges—appears in all versions: a harassed Soviet commissar (George Tobias in both films) asks an apparatchik, "Does this office have a copy of *Who's Still Who*?"

Silk Stockings would be Mamoulian's only film in the stark rectangle of CinemaScope, the wide-screen process ideal for imaginative dance numbers. The Freed era of movie musicals, which began with *The Wizard of Oz* in 1939, was nearing its end—his last film as a producer was the sumptuous *Gigi* (1958). The only sense of a valedictory here, though, is Fred Astaire's "The Ritz Roll and Rock," a new number from Cole Porter in which Astaire bids farewell to his top hat, white tie, and tails.

For Cyd Charisse, who seldom had long appearances in films before *Brigadoon* (1954), it was the most screen time she ever had. Her accent, developed with a dialect coach, is immaculate. Astaire's devotees know this picture as the one in which he and his leading lady do the most kissing. Charisse, a screen dancing star for a decade, was cast first. The Broadway version didn't have much dancing in it, and Bing Crosby and Howard Keel were both considered before Freed sought a reluctant Astaire for Canfield.

Astaire had director approval, making Mamoulian's story about his persuasive lunch, held in early May 1956, somewhat misleading. In his version, Astaire complained, "Well, there's no dancing in this, that's number one, and number two, I'm too old to play a real romance with Cyd Charisse." In his last film, *Funny Face*, Astaire, at age fifty-seven, had been acutely aware of his thirty-year age difference with Audrey Hepburn. Charisse was in her midthirties and already had danced with Astaire in *The Band Wagon* (1953). Mamoulian said he replied, "'My whole emphasis is going to be on dancing, on rhythm and dancing. And the love scenes will be expressed to a dance, not through dialogue.' And that got him very excited."

That is, in fact, how the film operates. The plot is crisply artificial, its *Ninotchka* roots show, and the commissars are more cartoonish than *gemütlich*, as they are in the Lubitsch version, but the music and dancing overcome the occasional story flaws. David Thomson thought *Silk Stockings* "has some of the best intimate dances in the history of the musical."

In conferences with Freed, Mamoulian must have assured him that his penchant for excess was all in the past. Mamoulian's proposal for the first story conference emphasized softening key elements. For instance, he thought Canfield in the play was "very rough, rude and insensitive. Being a real artist, he should love great music, and what he feels about jazzing up the classics is that it's great to hear Tchaikowsky in the concert hall, but there is also no harm in having Tchaikowsky's 'Moon Love' in the jukebox—it all brings pleasure to the people." For "Ninotchka: The experience in killing with a bayonet during the war should be eliminated. A person of her young age, who has had the kind of past she describes, could not be transformed into what she is shown to be in the action of the story."

It worked. Clearly there was someone at the helm who wanted to breathe new life into the project. Astaire, about to leave for a European vacation with his daughter Ava, told Mamoulian he would now "be able to sleep at night" and "can't wait to come back."

Mamoulian completed *Silk Stockings* on time and on budget, without the extravagances that had plagued *Summer Holiday*. Lela Simone, a music supervisor at MGM, explained the efficient process: "As soon as the footage for a block sequence was in the can, a rough cut was made and it was presented to Mamoulian and Freed. Whatever changes or polishing were needed were done immediately, and the picture was mounted on completed reels." Simone dubbed footage while the production was in progress. By the time of "The Ritz Roll and Rock," the last number in the picture and the next to last to be filmed, the picture was dubbed.

For what would be his penultimate starring role in a movie musical, Astaire was working with his longtime choreographer, Hermes Pan. Eugene Loring handled everyone else's dances. That arrangement may have fortified Astaire's resistance. Only two of Mamoulian's dance concepts made it into the film—the hypnotic solo sequence in which Charisse does a slow striptease while changing into a pink negligee to "Silk Stockings" (in the stage version, it was a song for Canfield) and Astaire tapping out rhythm on bottle tops for "Too Bad" as the envoys sing of how they enjoy Paris. Mamoulian vetoed a dance that had Charisse twirling in the middle of a crowded restaurant ("I find it embarrassing and unattractive") and proposed that Astaire dance to a phonograph record for "All of You" (Astaire rejected that).

Filming began in November 1956. In Mamoulian's account, he used a rehearsal of "It's a Chemical Reaction, That's All"/"All of You" to remind everyone who was in charge. The anecdote is similar to the one he told about John Bubbles during *Porgy and Bess*:

> They go off, they rehearsed for two weeks and finally they called me up and said all right, will you come and look at it, and they also called Arthur Freed. So we went there and they went through the dance. . . . Of course, [Freed] said, "Fred, you're the king. You are the king. Cyd, this is just great, this is terrific," and he kept raving and raving and raving and I just sat there. Finally he ran out of words and Fred came over and said, "Well, what do you think?"
>
> I said, "Fred, anything you do is great, and Cyd is great, too. Hermes, beautiful choreography, but it's all wrong." He said, "What do you mean?" I said, "It's a dance. I don't want a specialty dance here. I want a love story dramatized through dancing," and I said, "At the risk of appearing ridiculous, let me show you," and Freed almost died, and I almost died. I mean, this is Fred Astaire sitting there.
>
> So I said, "First, you do this, this is better. Then you go say a line of dialogue, and there's no response. Then you take a chair, then you do this, and take a few steps. It builds and builds and builds until we know you're in love with each other."
>
> He sat there hating me, and there was silence. I said, "That's all I have to say, thank you, goodbye." I started walking out. Arthur Freed walks out with

me. The minute we leave the stage, he says to me, "You've done it! You've ruined it. For heaven's sake, Rouben! Are you going to tell Fred Astaire how to dance?"

I said, "Arthur, no, I'm not telling him *how* to dance. I'm telling him *what* to dance. There's a difference."

He said, "Well, you've lost him. Look, you can't tell him what to do. You've lost him. I don't know what's going to happen." I said, "I think you're underestimating Fred." . . .

Ten days went by, they called me again. We go in, and it was perfect. From then on, it was easy going.

Assuming Mamoulian's anecdote has veracity (his diary records only a single phone discussion with Astaire about the number), what he was describing was a way of conveying more emotion in the exchange. After Charisse explains that the relationship between men and women is only a chemical reaction, Astaire dances with a chair and rejoinders with "All of You," expressing his desire to tour "the east, west, north, and the south of you." As he dances, Ninotchka reminds him, "You go, go, go, but you don't get anywhere." Canfield responds, "You're telling me!" and dances with the chair some more until he pulls a surprised Ninotchka into his arms and they whirl into their own routine. Tom Milne compared this to "the same thrill of magic as that felt by Frankenstein in Mary Shelley's novel when he watched for that first spark of life which he felt would 'pour a torrent of light into our dark world.'"

Janis Paige as Peggy Dayton, when she's not tapping on a waterlogged ear, thrusts out her breasts as if they're fins on a Cadillac. She was cast after Mamoulian saw her nightclub act at the Cocoanut Grove. "I had seen [her] in *Pajama Game* and hadn't liked her. I thought her sullen and unpleasant in that. Then I went to see her in a nightclub and was amazed. Her own personality was altogether different."

Rubber-faced Jules Munshin was Bibinski, the first of the three envoys cast; Peter Lorre (Brankov) made the cut after Loring decided he could dance. Mamoulian evidently came up with Joseph Buloff (Ivanov). Lorre shows off comedy chops he had last used in John Huston's *Beat the Devil* (1954). Squat, pop-eyed, and Hungarian, Lorre's highlight is the deadpan Kastask during "Too Bad," with a knife held between his teeth as the envoys frolic with Tybee Afra, Betty Utti, and Barrie Chase. "Most of the time he seemed to be enjoying life hugely," Mamoulian said of Lorre. "He had a great kind of gusto when he felt happy." Charisse remembered another reason for Lorre's "gusto": "He was taking a little something he shouldn't have [a codeine-based cough syrup] . . . and we saw little drops of it fall to the ground as he walked across the stage."

As he had done in *Love Me Tonight* with the "exploding" vase, Mamoulian delved into sound effects to enhance the action. After arriving in Paris and detecting the corruption of the envoys by capitalistic values, Ninotchka swiftly begins typing a report to Moscow. It "spells some dire punishment to the three people standing at attention in front of her. The natural sound of the typewriter was too insipid considering the dramatic situation, so I substituted the deafening and ominous sound of a drill, the kind they use in boring through the concrete of city streets."

Charisse, a ballet dancer since age six, had one behavioral quirk, said dancer Roy Fitzell, who appears in the high-kicking "The Red Blues" after Ninotchka returns to Moscow's gloom. "She'd never talk to the other dancers. Some people thought it was rude. I just thought she was shy. She'd speak with Astaire, of course, and with Mamoulian, but not to the rest of us."

"She's not strong," Loring insisted to Fordin. "She's not a powerhouse—she just looks that way. In 'The Red Blues,' for instance, she looks like a dynamo."

And she really was, Fitzell recalled, and he knew because he had to catch her:

> The shot you see with the two of us in the picture is the second take. Cyd came in from behind the camera. On the first take, she came on like a locomotive. I'm not used to her power. So I dropped her. She crashed to the floor. Mamoulian says "Cut!" and I reached down to pick her up. She didn't say a word. She just looked at me. Not a word. When her back was turned when she went back to get into position, I looked at the other dancers and just raised my eyebrows, you know. They broke into silent applause!

Mamoulian's touch is far clumsier on "The Ritz Roll and Rock." At the end of "Ritz," which took three days to film, Astaire, sliding toward the camera, loses his top hat, wincing as it falls. It's a mistake with all the panache of a car wreck if you know to look for it. Otherwise, you're under the spell of the artist and the routine, assuming, as Mamoulian hoped you would, that nothing from this dance legend is accidental.

He insisted that the mishap improved the number:

> The whole thing is how [Astaire] gets out of it. Now if he had become confused, it certainly would have been no good, but the guy is a real dancer, a real professional the way he catches it and puts it back on . . .
>
> After the take, he said to me, "That was no good."
>
> I said, "Why isn't it?"
>
> He said, "I lost my hat."
>
> I said, "Sure, that makes it good because of the way you retrieve it. It seems like part of your dance routine, just like what you did with your cane."
>
> He said, "Oh, gosh, I wish I could do it perfectly."
>
> I said, "Look, I don't want you to worry about it. I'll make another take, we'll glue your hat on," which we did, and he did it all perfectly. And he said, "Well, that's the one." And I said, "No, the first take is the one."

Two weeks after filming, Astaire called Mamoulian to discuss the number. Mamoulian noted: "Discussed shot of catching hat with foot ("Roll and Rock"). Convinced him it is not serious—discussed cut to Cyd in beginning—discussed section where he loses hat (We both like it best—but it's not an issue.)." The lush orchestration and dancing of "Fated to Be Mated" is set to some of Porter's more overwrought lyrics about "burning bridegroom" and "yearning bride."

The second half of the number had Astaire and Charisse riding bicycles on the deserted movie set. Mamoulian said he never liked it: "I said, What on earth can they do with bicycles? They are wizards of dancing . . . And Arthur Freed said, 'Well, what have we got to lose? We've got the money, we've got the sets. Shoot it.' It took two days to shoot, and I looked at it and said, 'It doesn't mean a damned thing—let's forget it,' so out it went."

Freed agreed to a reshoot two weeks later. Charisse begins the number in a skirt, and in the retaken parts is wearing culottes. That's because she's doing knee drops and spinning on one knee—impossible to do in a skirt of the length she had, otherwise she would get snagged. Mamoulian had no expectation that audiences would notice or care if they did. Nothing takes away from the sheer joy of Charisse and Astaire's kinetic maneuvers, swinging under playground bars.

That era of movie musicals was at its clear end. Audiences were indifferent—the reality of the Cold War, with its constant threat of nuclear annihilation, made a musical-comedy melting of the Iron Curtain with negligee seem irrelevant. After *Silk Stockings* was released on July 18, 1957, it lost nearly $1.4 million. But as a completed film for a major studio, it made Mamoulian a viable commodity again.

Mamoulian nursed a new ambition, telling Lazar "[I] would like to direct a Western." Western series on TV were at their peak, but it seems an uncharacteristic aspiration for Mamoulian. No offers for such pictures were forthcoming, so instead, he embarked on a book about them. He didn't get very far, but he made a new friend—the former head of the Screen Actors Guild, Ronald Reagan, the future host of *Death Valley Days*.

Reagan was fully engaged and generous with his help. Mamoulian hosted the Reagans twice in his home in 1958, and evidently there had been a discussion of which characters on hit TV Westerns were based on real people, since Reagan called once to inform Mamoulian that "the more he investigates, the clearer it becomes that Matt Dillon is a fictional character." (Dillon, a federal marshal in Dodge City, was the lead character of *Gunsmoke*.) Mamoulian's diary records Reagan's occasional research help as late as 1961, when he called with a list of "good authentic Western writers."

Lazar knew all along that Mamoulian's dream was to make the definitive film of *Porgy and Bess*. It all ended in an unusually public humiliation.

CHAPTER 20

Perfidy and *Bess*

A lesson Mamoulian learned painfully: If you're going to battle with Sam Goldwyn over your dream project, it's better to be armed with more than a publicist.

The mercurial Goldwyn fired Mamoulian from *Porgy and Bess* in July 1958 and replaced him with Otto Preminger. Mamoulian's diary indicates that the final break came about over his demand for payment that was not in his contract. Goldwyn was able to conceal his motive behind the time-tested "we couldn't see eye to eye," and one of his malapropisms: "The trouble with these directors is that they're always biting the hand that lays the golden egg."

Mamoulian's reputation in Hollywood never recovered. He was briefly a hero among his peers—the result of Goldwyn's long-standing reputation for mistreating directors. Within months, however, his unsuccessful attempt to secure a co-director credit on the film transformed him into a professional victim looking for a vindication that would never arrive—in other words, a sore loser.

Mamoulian's bitterness was justified. He planned the picture, supervised the casting, persuaded Sidney Poitier to play Porgy, and supervised the soundtrack recording before a fire destroyed the Catfish Row set on July 1. It was the custom, long before directors were considered auteurs, for the replacement director to order a rewrite of the script, rearrange the set, and remove the fingerprints of the preceding director. Yet Preminger did almost none of that. He directed the film according to most of the details Mamoulian prepared, especially since the soundtrack required that scenes be played in specific ways. Mamoulian knew this because he was keeping track of events from afar, like a deposed Napoleon.

Released in 1959, the film was Goldwyn's last and a commercial and artistic failure. With Poitier's singing voice dubbed by Robert McFerrin, it is marred by Preminger's excess of boom shots and his astonishing failure to include even a single close-up. The best that can be said for it is Sammy Davis Jr.'s energetic performance as Sporting Life and the faithful score. The opera practically disappeared from sight for the next twenty-five years.

There's no question about Irving Lazar, though. He lied to Mamoulian. Mamoulian should have been more wary of Lazar, whom Goldwyn had offered a job in 1945 and even Milton Pickman, Goldwyn's production manager, who had tried to help arrange financing for Mamoulian's *Carmen* movie in 1954. Mamoulian also should have seen Preminger on the horizon. Preminger's 1954 film *Carmen Jones*, with Harry Belafonte and Dorothy Dandridge, had been successful, and he had approached the Theatre Guild about a *Porgy and Bess* film to be made at Fox in 1947. During *Carmen Jones*, Preminger began an affair with Dandridge, cast as Bess. That affair ended when he demanded that she get an abortion.

Goldwyn had done what no other producer had been able to do—cut through the complicated thicket of rights to buy *Porgy and Bess* in May 1957 for $650,000 and a promise to the Ira Gershwin and George Gershwin estate of 10 percent of the gross. Goldwyn's last two pictures had been musicals: *Hans Christian Andersen* (1952) with Danny Kaye and an original score by Frank Loesser, and Loesser's Broadway smash *Guys and Dolls* (1955) with Frank Sinatra and Marlon Brando. *Porgy and Bess* held a special allure, as an unnamed publicist (probably Marv Hauser) explained after Mamoulian was terminated: "Money he doesn't need. This is a love project with him."

Goldwyn's irascibility grew considerably after *The Best Years of Our Lives* (1946), directed by William Wyler, won seven Academy Awards, including Best Picture. With his legacy at the forefront, he no longer was the Goldwyn with whom Mamoulian's interactions were pleasant during *We Live Again*. Mamoulian didn't have a signed contract until December 1957, but he must have had some indication from Lazar that he was the front-runner, since in July, he went to Lena Horne's Cocoanut Grove opening to determine her potential as Bess. He didn't think favorably of her: "She's become hardened and bitterly aggressive—her act is vulgarized—never a sweet smile—not a single lovely number—walks as if she were ploughing the ground—stands with knees bent, wrapping herself around microphone."

Lazar arranged a meeting with Goldwyn in September. He called Mamoulian the next day: "Saw Goldwyn last night at dinner—Sam very enthused about my conversation with him—wants to discuss deal—told Irving to go do it and keep his powder dry." Anxious years later to add to the lore, Mamoulian told an interviewer that Goldwyn's reaction at that first meeting was "Good! That stylized! That means cheaper, doesn't it?"

Goldwyn announced Mamoulian's hiring in October 1957. The deal the director eventually signed was for $75,000 (Poitier got the same amount) and 2.5 percent of the net profits. Hollywood bookkeeping being what it was and still is, chasing a piece of the net was foolhardy, but Mamoulian didn't have the clout to demand a percentage of the gross. He certainly knew how to express his gratitude that Christmas. Most on his gift list received tchotchkes such as candles, and no item was more than $15. Except for Goldwyn's gift: a lemon tree arrangement priced at $55.

Mamoulian worked on casting even before signing his contract, attending auditions in New York. James Earl Jones didn't get a role, although Mamoulian noted, "Good face." The leads were problematic. Goldwyn preferred the soft-spoken Nat King Cole for Sporting Life, but told Mamoulian that Cole withdrew because he "wants to remain sympathetic." In that same conversation, Mamoulian brought up Sammy Davis Jr., but Goldwyn responded that he thought Davis "has no charisma."

Davis's campaigning for a film role was well known—in 1957, he recorded an album with Carmen McRae containing nine numbers from *Porgy and Bess*, although he sang Porgy, not Sporting Life. According to Goldwyn biographer A. Scott Berg, charisma wasn't the factor. He wrote that Leonore Gershwin, after seeing Davis in performance and finding him vulgar, pleaded with Goldwyn, "Swear on your life you'll never use him."

Davis was an unproven commodity in films. He had a leading role in an all-Black *Anna Lucasta*, which flopped in 1958, but had spent his career in nightclubs and TV, so Sporting Life would be his breakthrough role. He used powerful show business pals, including Frank Sinatra, to persuade Goldwyn to cast him. Davis wasn't signed until February 1958. Agent Martin Baum had signed Poitier before he'd had a chance to read the script. Mamoulian met with Poitier in early November in an attempt to iron out fears of racial stereotyping, offering to use Langston Hughes to collaborate with the screenwriter, N. Richard Nash, but the actor withdrew, saying, in a prepared statement, "Certain things I will play, but they must be constructive to my life as a Negro." A month later, Poitier was back in, following another conference with Mamoulian and Goldwyn. Mamoulian said he made his point by asserting, "Do you actually think I would tackle this film if I thought it was going to denigrate the Negro race in any way?" The acceptance called for a press conference, at which Poitier called his feelings about race his "sensitivity." He added, "I am happy to say that my reservations were washed away . . . I am happy that I met with Mr. Goldwyn and Mr. Mamoulian and I found them almost as sensitive as I am."

Pearl Bailey quickly agreed to Mamoulian's request that she play Maria, saying, "Before you open your mouth, anything you want me for, I say yes to." In New York the following month, Mamoulian met with boxer Sugar Ray Robinson, under consideration for Crown (the role eventually went to Brock Peters), and Diahann Carroll, who would be cast as Clara. She understood the drawbacks, writing in her memoir, "the racial stereotypes of Catfish Row held absolutely no attraction for me, and I was offended by the story."

Mamoulian focused his attention on the score and set design in early February 1958. On the music, he wrote to orchestrators André Previn, Ken Darby, and Gordon Sawyer that he had chosen recitatives to turn into dialogue. "I have chosen the ones that have a melodic lilt to them and that seem to be a natural extension of the Negro speech." He was willing to expand "It Ain't Necessarily So" into a large production number "with the trumpeter 'going to town' which I think, entertainmentwise, would be a great lift here. I think it belongs, and I don't feel at all that it would sin in the slightest against Gershwin's music, because I feel that if he were alive, he would like it." He kept racist imagery out of the parade to Kittiwah Island. Art Black, a Goldwyn assistant director, suggested watermelons. Mamoulian responded, according to the meeting transcript, "No watermelons—you ought to have a lot of children there."

Previn's memory of Mamoulian was of a director who would talk of his past triumphs at length, then suddenly display an unexpected litheness on musical matters.

> He liked to just sit and tell stories about *Oklahoma!* or *Carousel*. In this capacity, he was wonderful to be with. . . . His stories were always really good, fascinating, riveting. And yet he was a kind of loner. His whole way of working

was to be in the center; others made circles around him, but he didn't invite them in.

I admired him a lot for his willingness to consider new ideas. For instance, I had a far-out idea for "My Man's Gone Now." I asked him, "What if the orchestral interludes got more and more out of tune—a little sharp, a little flat—as a way of intensifying the piece?" Any other director would have said, "Behave yourself." But Mamoulian got it. He actually experimented on his own, with a phonograph, playing with the speed—and then decided no. Ultimately, things happened pretty much his way, or forget it. But he liked novelty, he was open to it.

Clashing with Goldwyn was inevitable even under the best of circumstances. Mamoulian behaved as one who went looking for trouble, since he kept Russell Birdwell as his publicist, and Birdwell, whose achievements had included organizing the publicity campaign for *Gone with the Wind*, was energetically getting Mamoulian in as many newspapers and magazines as he could. It had not yet become common for directors to use their own publicists, especially those whose screen hits were as far in the past as Mamoulian's.

Mamoulian later produced his own transcripts of his meetings with Goldwyn for Jerry Giesler, Hollywood's go-to lawyer at the time for scandals and difficult circumstances of any kind. Richard Nash vouched for the director's memory:

> He got into the habit of scoffing at everything Sam had to say. He didn't seem to be listening. One day Sam pointed his finger at Rouben and said, "You dunt listen to me!"
>
> Rouben said, "Here is what you said," and he repeated Sam's exact words. And Sam said, "You listen to de voids, and Richard listens to vot I *mean*!" which was absolutely true.

As he'd done with Harry Cohn, Mamoulian kept a list of Goldwynisms. They included:

> Concerning Ira Gershwin getting involved in casting: "Too many people in the soup spoil the soup!"

Who was the fella who said, "Forgive them, because they don't know what the hell they're doing"?

We don't want any overacting, except where we need it.

On June 3, after Mamoulian attended chorus rehearsals, Birdwell called to remind him to read Hal Humphreys's column in the afternoon *Mirror News*, since he'd written about Mamoulian's comments about movies shown on TV. Three days later, Mamoulian's studio secretary left him a note: "Peggy called—Goldwyn would like to see you."

What followed was the producer's first explosion. Mamoulian wrote that Goldwyn went into a tirade about "my attitude towards him which he said was lacking in respect and obedience." He asked Goldwyn why he was so enraged. The response: "You've been talking to the press, and you have engaged Russell Birdwell as your press agent. I want you to fire him immediately." He went on to call Birdwell "a dangerous, shady and villainous person."

Mamoulian attempted to remonstrate while Goldwyn attacked him with another blast, demanding that "all publicity while I am working for him can and will emanate only from himself, Mr. Goldwyn; that he is supposed to be the sole 'creator' of *Porgy and Bess*, and that I better give in to him or else." He didn't treat Goldwyn's outburst as a personal warning bell. Instead, he stepped up Birdwell's activities, and the day after, the publicist called him to suggest "would like you to dictate a hundred words on the fact that pregnant women shouldn't appear on TV."

Tony Curtis, starring with Marilyn Monroe and Jack Lemmon in Billy Wilder's *Some Like It Hot* (1959) on an adjacent soundstage, understood Mamoulian's need for recognition. As the beginning of filming neared, he noticed that Wilder's portable dressing room had a sign indicating it was Mamoulian's gift. "Mamoulian was one of the greats, but there had to be a sign on Billy's dressing room to let everyone know that Mamoulian had paid for it. In Hollywood, no one gives you credit unless you demand it."

At the next production conference, Mamoulian came up with an incredible image for Sporting Life—something Preminger used, since the film was scored for it: "I like to treat Sporting Life as if he were a cat. You know he lives like a cat; he likes darkness; he doesn't like the orthodox avenues of entrances and exits. He walks on the streets only when he has to, otherwise he has his own little byways and bypasses." Davis slides down a drainpipe to join the craps game. Goldwyn loved that image. Darby called Mamoulian to report "Goldwyn's reaction to soundtrack—tears after 'Clara, Clara' and 'Oh, you know I'm going to have Sporting Life walking on the roofs.'"

For all his sensitivity toward the lead actors and race, when it came to casting extras, Mamoulian's notes look antiquated. They include: "Louis Johnson—Not very Negroid; Harvey Huggins—Small—not Negroid enough." There's no way to finesse what he was doing. He was a white man deciding what characteristics Black actors should have.

On June 30, there was a second tirade after an article in the *Hollywood Reporter* that quoted Mamoulian on the use of the English language in advertising. This one turned personal, and Mamoulian's recollection of it more precise:

> "You know I love you, don't you, Rouben?"
> "Frankly, I don't, Sam. Sometimes, I think you hate me."
> "How can you say that? I love you very dearly."
> "I have the greatest respect for you. I think you are a man of tremendous talents and intelligence and taste."

A long speech followed,

> all about how dear I am to Goldwyn's heart, [then] the next section . . . was dedicated to the love of man and humility. . . . Then he got on the subject of publicity and said how much he scorns it . . . I sat there spellbound, fascinated, in a kind of horrible way, not believing my eyes and ears because to see Sam Goldwyn expounding such ideas would be to anyone that knew him even remotely an example of absurdity and farce carried to the utter extreme.

The conversation shifted to a malevolent finish.

> "You know, Rouben, that I am a very rich man."
> "I think I do, Sam. I haven't seen your bank book, but I am sure, as is everybody else, that you are a very rich man."

"That is a fact. I have many, many millions. Money means nothing to me. You know I am a very powerful man."

"Well, I suppose you are."

"Don't suppose. I am a very powerful man. I have great influence. I will tell you something. When I was last in Washington—that was a few weeks ago—the President of the United States wanted to see me to ask my advice on certain things. I talked to the president for twenty minutes and gave him advice."

"How nice."

"Don't interrupt me. Do you know how the President of the United States talked to me?"

"No, how?"

"He talked to me like he was a carpenter."

Goldwyn moved in for the kill.

"The point is, I am a very powerful and important man. Money means nothing to me. I have so much of it, I don't care. You know, once I took a director off a picture because I didn't like him. It cost me $600,000, but I could afford it. Whoever works for me must get along with me."

"Sam, I still don't understand why you are telling me all these things. I think we have gotten along splendidly on *Porgy and Bess*. You are very happy with everything I have done, so what is the point?"

"The point is, do you realize what it will mean if I take you off *Porgy and Bess*? It will have worldwide publicity. It will ruin your career. You are so much younger than I am, Rouben, you want to go on making pictures, don't you?"

"Yes, Sam, not only I want to, I intend to."

"You may not be able to do so unless you get along with me. I am a very influential man. People in the industry call me all the time. If I take you off this picture, or if I tell them all kinds of things as to how I couldn't get along with you, you will never work again."

"So?"

Goldwyn's face, Mamoulian wrote, "assumed an expression of ruthless ferocity." "While you are working for me, I am the only man who gives interviews or has publicity in the newspapers. There is only one man on this lot who is the 'creator' of *Porgy and Bess* and his name is Goldwyn!"

Filming was scheduled to begin July 21, 1958, on a sixty-three-day schedule that included ten rehearsal days.

Then, a stunning development: a July 2 fire destroyed the Catfish Row set—the day Mamoulian was to begin wardrobe and lighting tests. It was the only set on the Goldwyn lot that burned, and surely arson was considered. No one was charged, and Goldwyn made no accusations. He was reported to have taken the bad news calmly. He and Mamoulian had lunch that day, and made plans to begin filming in September.

Under the terms of his contract, Mamoulian's pay was suspended. He continued to work on the film, including plans for rebuilding the set. On July 9, he and Azadia attended a party at Goldwyn's house, at which all was cordial. That same day, there was another article in the *Hollywood Reporter*, generated by Birdwell, in which Mamoulian commented on the use of well-known and dignified actors in TV commercials.

A third Goldwyn eruption was looming, but if Mamoulian sensed it, he was too annoyed by not being paid to give that any attention. Marv Hauser called him to report, according to Mamoulian's secretary's note, "he was terribly upset because of the controversy your statement re actors doing TV commercials caused—said he didn't think it was good for you—said that Raymond Burr 'lashed back' at you (page 9 in today's *Reporter*)—and that you 'shouldn't be putting yourself on a level with this Burr person, whoever he is.'"

Before that, Mamoulian had lashed out at Pickman: "Officially brought to his attention that the word 'director' and 'directed' is applied to people involved in this picture who are not directors . . . Pickman assures me it was an oversight and it would be corrected in the future. Told him I didn't want to keep reminding him."

Mamoulian's last meeting with Goldwyn was on July 17. Four days later, he met with Lazar to discuss it: "In regard to the new 'no pay, no work' policy, Lazar said it would not fit what I told Goldwyn last. I told Lazar, 'I've changed my mind. I'm now unwilling to break my neck for free in view of the fact that it gets no appreciation whatsoever.'"

On July 23, Lazar visited Mamoulian in the afternoon. He had just come from Goldwyn's house. The final explosion had occurred, and Goldwyn fired Mamoulian. Lazar didn't tell Mamoulian this explicitly. Perhaps he resented being made the emissary of bad news. Mamoulian didn't record the contents of that conversation. Given the particularly detailed diary notes he made for the previous eight months, it would be odd had he not noted his dismissal, since he would have fired Lazar on the spot. He called Lazar the following day to tell him, "will see S. re production of P&B only." The day after that, Lazar called with "doubletalk about 10-week clause." He added that he was leaving for New York for three days.

Mamoulian's diary matches what he said in a later statement to the *Hollywood Reporter*. He said Lazar met with him on July 23 "merely to insist I capitulate to Goldwyn's demands I have no opinion of the picture and that I fire my publicist, Russell Birdwell. I said I'd think it over. The next day, Lazar called me and I told him I was sticking by my contract."

On July 27, Mamoulian's phone rang all day. His secretary, Violet Herschenson, recorded the important calls in order: Thomas Pryor of *the New York Times*. Louella Parsons. Hedda Hopper. Previn. Goldwyn had issued his statement: "He and I could not see eye to eye on various matters. Rather than go on with basic differences of opinion between us, I have relieved him and engaged Mr. Preminger to direct *Porgy and Bess* when production is resumed." Preminger signed his contract two days later. Through Birdwell, Mamoulian shot back: "Mr. Goldwyn's bland statement masks a story of deceit and calumny." He added that although there had been "no dissensions" regarding the film itself, there had been "other dissensions on his part" that were "trespasses upon my personal and professional life."

George Sidney, then president of the Directors Guild, called to report that there would be an emergency DGA meeting, with "[John] Ford on rampage." The DGA wanted Goldwyn to explain the firing, but he refused to meet with them. On August 3, the DGA announced a ban on union directors signing with Goldwyn. It would have had some effect, were not *Porgy and Bess* Goldwyn's last film and had Preminger not already signed.

"I felt betrayed," Sidney Poitier told Hedda Hopper. "I worked with Mr. Mamoulian for two months and there was rapport between actor and director, and that's the way we all felt. Now there'll be an entirely different approach. We don't know what will happen." Preminger diplomatically stated, "I knew nothing about the trouble before and it is not my business to know."

Goldwyn's July 31 cable to Lazar, who had made a quick excuse to fly to Europe, showed that he understood the problem with bad news not being delivered properly: "Vitally important you confirm immediately by cable fact I advised you Wednesday, July 23 Mamoulian being relieved from picture and that you advised Mamoulian accordingly same day. Mamoulian claims did not know this until he read it in papers." Goldwyn executive Kenneth Savoy hand-delivered Mamoulian's termination letter, with a check for $20,363.28—the balance of his pay. Lazar didn't issue his version of events until August 11 in a lengthy wire. He claimed he told the director "that Goldwyn wanted to settle his contract with Mamoulian that day . . . whereupon Birdwell orally composed the type of statement that he thought Goldwyn would like to have issued which would have merely stated that due to a difference of options that could not be reconciled it had been decided between RM and SG that they would part and I said that was precisely what Goldwyn had proposed."

Just before that, Birdwell and Mamoulian made a tactical error in attempting to gain public sympathy. They held a press conference with Leigh Whipper, then the head of the Negro Actors Guild—a professional organization, but not a union. Whipper, playing the Crab Man, announced he was withdrawing from the cast. He said, "I believe that the proposed *Porgy and Bess* is now in hands unsympathetic to my people," adding that he had "firsthand information" that Preminger was not sympathetic, but he didn't give details to support that. There was no exodus of cast members, and not a single word of support for Mamoulian. Davis told the *Chicago Defender* he thought Preminger "a very sensitive man. *Porgy and Bess* wold be as great even if it were done with Polish actors."

Mamoulian, helped by crew members, especially those who were fired, kept careful track of Preminger's progress—or lack of it—when filming began in September 1958:

> Called Helen [Ken Darby's secretary]. Sammy Davis had a blowup with Goldwyn on the subject of the dance, and the whole atmosphere is that of people sitting on a volcano. Ellie Fredericks [cameraman] fired, replaced by Leon Shamroy.
>
> Thaddeus Jones [Uncle Peter] fired, replaced by Clarence Muse. Leslie Scott said he thought it was terrible that they were taking the dialect out.

Ellie Fredericks here. Said that Preminger has tried to get off the picture three or four times but Goldwyn won't let him go.

Richard Nash would tell Mamoulian, "not a single change was made in the script, that shooting had to abide by the pattern of my recordings." In January, Oliver Smith came to dinner and reported that Billy Wilder, within hearing of Preminger, had told Goldwyn he was "replacing a great director with a plumber."

By this point, Mamoulian had begun his ill-fated attempt at getting a joint director credit. Pickman had written him asserting Preminger's single credit, to which Mamoulian appended, "(makes me sick!)." Mamoulian wired the Directors Guild to demand a co-credit. Two days later, director H. C. Potter (*Mr. Blandings Builds His Dream House*, 1948) called, and in Mamoulian's version, "hemmed and hawed, sputtered and stuttered about split credits being undesirable . . . Told him cannot see their point at all. Asked me if I wanted to forget the whole thing so they won't have to take it up with the board Monday—so 'the world would not know.' I set him straight on that one." Mamoulian made his case to the DGA in writing, specifying his eight months of preparations, the score, and the casting. The board turned him down. The detailed explanation came from George Stevens:

> After prolonged discussion, the consensus of the board was that at the very minimum, a director must have had directed scenes that appear on the screen. . . . I must tell you again, Rouben, because I know that the board talked to you before and after this meeting, that all of your good friends on the board—and that included all of those present—were very unhappy to have to rule on a matter unfavorably to you. The board had to rule the way it did, according to its best judgment.

Mamoulian sputtered out his rage in notes: "[On Goldwyn]: Perfidious and in my case predatory quality of his actions . . . the English language isn't the only thing he slaughters, he crushes the spirit of human beings under him. . . . Money in his veins—stop publicity and he will quickly wither."

The picture, billed as "Samuel Goldwyn's *Porgy and Bess*," sailed into the scorn of the civil rights movement, which directed its ire at the craps game and the dialect and organized boycotts at theaters, resulting in a disastrous reserved-seating engagement in New York. Back in California at a party, Mamoulian allowed a famous Gershwin pal to have *his* last word on the matter: "June Levant looking very pretty—doesn't want to be quoted, but tells me Oscar, after seeing *P&B*, said he's very anxious to hear Sam Goldwyn's next opera."

CHAPTER 21

Dulce et Decorum Est Cleopatra Mori

London in early November 1960 was not the ideal time to be a thinly clad Nubian slave.

On November 8—Election Day in the United States—Mamoulian's night shoot for *Cleopatra* began at 7 p.m. on a massive outdoor set and lasted until rain began to fall in the bone-chilling dawn. With 542 costumed extras, he filmed Mark Antony's arrival in Egypt after the death of Julius Caesar. Antony's galley alongside the quay was laden with Romans and horses. The extras' cheering made clouds of steam. There was a brief shot of Antony (Stephen Boyd) on the galley, then stunt rider Russell Forehead, astride a white steed named Shane, rehearsed the jump to the shore and gallop to Cleopatra's palace.

By then, it was 1:30 a.m. Before the first take, Shane slipped and tumbled into the icy water. An hour later, Mamoulian was told Shane wasn't coming back; it would take an additional half-hour to get the horse fully dry. A second horse fared no better. On the first take, it refused to jump; on the second take, its back foot slipped, by 3:45, rain fell heavily, and Mamoulian called it quits. The extras scurried to the warmth of a large tent, their overcoats, and hot tea.

The following night, from 7 p.m. to 5 a.m., he got Antony's "love ride" to Cleopatra's palace completed. This, time, 480 extras—Roman soldiers holding torches and townsfolk holding palm fronds and shouting "Hail, Antony!"—lined the way. A dozen "Nubian slaves" didn't have it so easy. The script called for Antony's horse to jump over the line of kneeling Nubians. Mamoulian's camera then panned to Antony's ride up the palace steps.

Stunt rider Russell Forehead and Shane leap from Mark Antony's barge during Mamoulian's night shoot of *Cleopatra* in London in November 1960. Photograph courtesy of Library of Congress.

A spectacular shot, considering that Mamoulian remembered, "I only did it because we wanted to show the insurance company that we were trying to shoot even with [Elizabeth] Taylor being ill." It took six takes. The Nubians kept flinching.

Having worked on the film for nearly two years, Mamoulian was up against an uncompleted script, a frequently ailing and permanently intractable star in Taylor, a producer in Wanger who couldn't keep anyone's anger from boiling over, and a studio chief, Spyros Skouras, who was trying to manage this catastrophe from California. Mamoulian quit in January 1961 after shooting nearly an hour of footage; edited, it would have amounted to about ten minutes on screen.

Mamoulian did not film a single scene with Taylor. Not only did he never have a finished script, he had no control over the writing because as it turned out, no one did. This was not the Fox of Darryl Zanuck, who inspected every word and every frame of film. Zanuck left in 1956 to work on independent productions; production chief Buddy Adler, the one person who might have clamped a lid on escalating costs, died of lung cancer in July 1960. After that, Skouras made recommendations from California, sometimes citing the advice of an unnamed "dear friend." Mamoulian could never announce that he was the captain of this ship; there was never a captain.

Before it bloated into a reputed $44 million monster overshadowed only by the intensely reported romance between Taylor and co-star Richard Burton, *Cleopatra* started out as a fairly modest historical picture. Based on a book by Carlo Mario Franzero, *The Life and Times of Cleopatra*, it was part of a six-picture deal Fox announced with Wanger in October 1958. Ludi Claire was hired for a first draft of the script in December 1958 and Nigel Balchin for revisions the following March.

Wanger was cresting on a comeback from scandal. In December 1951, stressed from accumulating debts associated with his 1948 film *Joan of Arc* and believing his wife, Joan Bennett, was having an affair, he had shot her agent, Jennings Lang. He received a light sentence—four months on a Southern California prison farm—and quickly returned to producing, including *Invasion of the Body Snatchers* (1956) and *I Want to Live!* (1958), a prison drama that earned Susan Hayward an Oscar for Best Actress.

Mamoulian had enough professional heat remaining from *Silk Stockings* to keep movie work viable. Agent Jack Gordean arranged meetings in May 1959 with casting director Lew Schreiber and Buddy Adler. "Very pleasant," Mamoulian wrote of Adler. "Said he and Skouras and Lew want me to be on the lot. If I like *Cleopatra*, good, if not, they will find another story or whatever property I may be interested in." Given the subject matter and with Wanger producing, there was no doubt of Mamoulian's interest—certainly not after he saw bulldozers on the back lot digging the sets for Rome and Alexandria, especially after Gordean and another screenwriter, Frank Davis, discussed the possible casting of Taylor, Marilyn Monroe, or Audrey Hepburn. If the budget became more modest, they had either Dana Wynter or Joan Collins in mind. The initial projected budget for a studio-filmed *Cleopatra* was about $3 million on a sixty-four-day schedule.

Wanger also was considering Gina Lollobrigida if Taylor wasn't available. Gordean reported that the buxom Italian "wants too much money." Wanger told Mamoulian that agent Charles Feldman "has a favorite candidate, his girlfriend," and that Skouras and Adler were trying to sell him on Hayward; Mamoulian agreed "she's completely wrong." In the meantime, they waited for Taylor to finish filming *Butterfield 8* at MGM.

When Taylor's signing was announced on October 15, 1959, the picture became an all-star epic on the scale of *Ben-Hur*. Mike Todd's twenty-seven-year-old widow knew how to drive a deal. Commensurate with her stardom, she was to be paid more than $1 million: $125,000 for sixteen weeks, $50,000 a week after sixteen weeks, and 10 percent of the gross. That announcement was just for show. Her real contract, which she signed June 28, 1960, contained the same terms plus the specification that the picture would be shot in Todd-AO, the wide-screen process developed by her late husband, from which she would derive royalties. Her third husband, singer Eddie Fisher, would receive $150,000 for nonspecific producer duties. Mamoulian's contract earned him $2,875 a week for not less than forty weeks.

Filming began September 28, 1960, in sunny autumn weather. November brought "unceasing cold, rain and fog," and Mamoulian called the subsequent attempt to film outdoors "undoubtedly one of the stupidest decisions in the history of motion pictures." Engrossed in preproduction, he had one brief phone conversation with Taylor in December 1959 while she was in New York, recuperating from pneumonia. In May 1960, he finally met her and took inventory of her family entourage: "Little Liza [Todd, 2], the two boys [Michael Wilding, 6, Christopher Wilding, 4], secretary, 2 Siamese and 2 Yorkshire terriers."

Mamoulian's first idea was to get his own screenwriter. In January 1959, he had been deeply impressed with a live *Playhouse 90* production, "The Velvet Alley," which starred Art Carney as a Hollywood screenwriter fighting studio interference. "Echoes of Goldwyn and the rest of it!" he wrote in his diary. He left a message with the teleplay's writer, Rod Serling, who turned him down: "Said he was too preoccupied with his TV and *Cleopatra* was not in his line, anyway." Serling had just launched *The Twilight Zone*.

Next up was Dale Wasserman, a few years before his from Broadway success with *Man of La Mancha* (1965). In his account, he and Mamoulian never understood each other. The director "wanted a love story, he insisted, the greatest love story ever put on film." He later wrote of the director, "Mamoulian's mind, brilliant in its own ways, was analytical and pragmatic, but not necessarily intuitive or creative." Wasserman worked a couple of months before being replaced by an odd choice—British poet and novelist Lawrence Durrell. Durrell had just published the first two parts of what became his Alexandria Quartet, a modernist experiment in telling interlocking stories from several perspectives. These were modern stories, nothing from the ancient city. He was a Wanger recommendation: "It's just a polish job and he's just what we need."

At first, Durrell agreed with that assessment: "It is pretty good, I think, as it is, and offers fairly convincing motivations for what is a very complicated story by any standards," he wired Mamoulian in April. A month later, anticipating the financial rewards of a prolonged rewrite, he thought differently of the Balchin-Wasserman version: "the more I looked at their wooden patchwork the more disgusted I became." Soon he was sending Mamoulian fifty pages at a time.

Durrell's writing process would have made any studio executive blanch. He wrote in longhand at his vacation home in France and shipped the manuscript for typing to his agent in London, who mailed the pages to Mamoulian in California. His goal was to give Cleopatra a profundity befitting her status as the last pharaoh of Egypt, although her soliloquy over Mark Antony's corpse likely would have spurred peals of laughter: "My shining one / Bright star of death / O famous jewel of love, beloved Mark Antony / What have they done to you, what have they done?" Wanger complained, "For every good speech there has been injected more silly speeches than we have ever had in the script before."

Mamoulian, revising the continuity, conceded that for his proposed scene in which Cleopatra flees Rome, "my pet ideas about the lions may prove impossible to accomplish." They were. Mamoulian, who knew all about the problems with goats pulling carts, suggested that four lions or four tigers pull Cleopatra's chariot during her escape after Caesar's death—something cats of any size won't do. Cleopatra's Temple of Sacred Cats, with two to three hundred felines, also didn't come about.

In the spring of 1960, Mamoulian headed to London and Rome to line up studio space and actors. Mamoulian and Wanger discussed Rex Harrison as Caesar, but Skouras thought him "poison, difficult to work with," so Peter Finch was cast. Stephen Boyd, who made Messala in *Ben-Hur* his breakout role, was a casting coup as Antony. Mamoulian had discussed Richard Burton as early as December 1959, and was told that Burton, as a

British tax refugee who had established residency in Switzerland, couldn't work in Britain before January 1961. Repairing the damage from World War II brought high tax rates on top earners, so Burton lived elsewhere.

Mamoulian's trip to Rome was discouraging (for Wanger as well, who noted, "Rouben, who was supposed to stay a week, stayed six"). At the studio, he learned that no stages there were soundproofed. Films were still being shot silently, with dialogue dubbed in later. An Italian studio executive estimated that it would take $3 million to bring soundstages there to Hollywood standards, and Mamoulian recommended that filming in Rome begin in August.

In May, Adler proposed a two-and-a-half-hour film with a budget of $4 million. By June, *Cleopatra* already had a $6 million budget, and Skouras accepted a British offer to shoot the whole picture in London. Producer Jerry Wald wrote Wanger, "From secret sources I hear Liz is irritated because the film is being made in England. She wanted to spend the summer in Italy." Because of the employment bonanza it would bring, British authorities offered Fox incentives to film all of *Cleopatra* there; the twenty-acre reconstruction of ancient Alexandria with four fifty-two-foot sphinxes, designed by John DeCuir, was the largest outdoor set ever built in London.

Wanger and Mamoulian tried to seize control of the production in July 1960 while Taylor headed to a vacation in Jamaica. Wanger wrote his lawyer, Greg Bautzer:

> Elizabeth is so susceptible to colds and bronchitis that from the enclosed chart you will see what weather conditions are liable to be in September/October/November here and you know what the delays, due to her health, cost this production. George [Skouras, Spyros's brother and a Fox executive] thinks the picture can be made for $6 million, make $50 million gross in Todd-AO. Spyros . . . argues with me that this picture has a ceiling of $20 million because it is not a biblical picture and that it has a limited appeal to adults.

Taylor knew how to drag her feet when she was unhappy. Mamoulian recorded a Wanger phone call: "She has read the 50 pages (thinks 'it's better, but still not right'!?) Says she is ready to report on August 15 (!!—working toward the $50,000 a week over 16 weeks!), feels hostile and bitter about the studio's way of handling her and is having her sweet revenge."

She had good reason. Taylor had starred in a smash-hit version of *Ivanhoe* (1952) opposite Robert Taylor, although she had not yet appeared in a wide-screen sword-and-sandals epic. Done right like *Ben-Hur*, it could be a commercial hit that won a raft of Oscars. Were the dialogue stilted, Taylor risked becoming a joke. Small unsuccessful dramas fade away; wide-screen stinkers linger.

Before then, intent on not being confined to London, Mamoulian sent Skouras a script that called for desert locations in Egypt. "I wish we could afford to incorporate Cleopatra's entrance into Rome," he wrote. "It's an expensive sequence, yes, but would be highly effective." Joseph Mankiewiz's final version had that: a spectacular parade to mark Caesar's ascension to dictator, choreographed by Hermes Pan with the bejeweled Taylor shimmering in gold atop a massive black sphinx. Mamoulian's script simply had Cleopatra in Caesar's palace the next day.

In July, Mamoulian enlisted a fifth screenwriter, Marc Brandel. Political intrigue and sexual allure are a difficult balance; in art and legend, Cleopatra's sexual prowess has long outweighed her political acumen. Cleopatra VII, who lived from 69 to 30 BCE and first ruled Egypt at age eighteen after the death of her father, Ptolemy XII, sought an alliance with Caesar, who was angry with her younger brother, Ptolemy XIII, for having engineered the murder of Pompey, his rival and son-in-law. In some accounts, Caesar regarded the murder as a personal insult. After Caesar's death, Cleopatra aligned with Mark Antony, and she had children by both him and Caesar.

Roman historian Plutarch was the first to write of Cleopatra's arrival in a rolled-up carpet snuck through enemy lines for her first meeting with Caesar—a moment as famous as her death allegedly from a self-applied asp. Brandel tried to mix history and humor. In all versions, Caesar first cuts the rope binding the rolled-up carpet, and after Cleopatra emerges, she and Caesar confront each other in silence.

Taylor's complaints prompted Brandel to rewrite the carpet scene six times. The history was Plutarch's, but the concept was Mamoulian's:

> I had an idea for a sequence when Cleopatra is brought to Caesar wrapped in a rug, and he opens it up and she looks like a hoyden, a little boy, full of smudges and she says she's Cleopatra, and Caesar can't help but laugh. So she goes to her apartment and she invites him to dinner that night—it's her

palace . . . and finally coming out as the most beautiful thing you ever saw in your life from this little hoyden ragamuffin boy.

Just how do an Egyptian queen and Roman emperor converse? In his second pass, Brandel had Cleopatra coolly displaying her intelligence, mentioning that she had read Caesar's history of the Gallic Wars. After she emerged from the carpet:

> CLEOPATRA: (*quietly*) Hail, Caesar! The queen welcomes you to her palace. (*Caesar slowly lowers sword and bows*)
> CAESAR: Your majesty . . . this is a charming surprise. And I congratulate you. You managed to obey my summons to meet me here in Alexandria after all.
> CLEOPATRA: A queen does not obey a summons. Cleopatra has accepted your invitation.
> CAESAR: (*gently*) We both know that I'm your last remaining hope, child.
> CLEOPATRA: (*cold dignity*) I haven't come to you for protection.
> CAESAR: (*pause, casually*) Your brother told me you were dead.
> CLEOPATRA: Not for want of his trying to kill me.
> CAESAR: And still, you don't need my protection?
> CLEOPATRA: (*imperious*) I came to demand that you proclaim me queen of Egypt.
> CAESAR: At the moment, your majesty scarcely looks like a queen. (*pause, thoughtfully*) But I can see that you are.

On September 28, 1960, production began with five scenes in Caesar's apartment. Two days later, Wanger noted, "Liz has a cold. We started shooting around her. 2 minutes and 28 seconds of sunshine. Temperature: 45 degrees." Mamoulian filmed twelve brief scenes, eight of them after dark, including a nighttime escape sequence with Forehead and Taylor's riding double, Dorothy Ford, galloping between the sphinxes. Taylor had something worse than a cold, though. Her ailment, first described as a low-grade fever or a respiratory infection, then as an abscessed tooth, eventually was diagnosed as meningism—a spinal cord inflammation at the base of the brain.

Perhaps the last moment of levity came with Brandel's October 3 rewrite of a dinner scene between Cleopatra and Caesar. He attached a sarcastic

"Thought for the Day": "Dulce et decorum est Cleopatra mori," a riff on the line from the Roman poet Horace's *Odes*: "It is sweet and right to die for your country."

On October 14, Mamoulian filmed the daytime arrival of Caesar in Alexandria. The costumed pageantry: 214 Roman infantry, 89 Roman cavalry, 86 Macedonian army, 94 horses, 400 townsfolk, and 1 stuffed eagle. Another night, royalty had to be served. Mamoulian, who arrived at 11:30 p.m. after a formal dinner of the Kinematograph Renters' Society, carried on, although he got nothing printable. He was in white tie, maintaining his aplomb at all costs, no matter the cost to the studio. Looking on were his guests, Prince Philip, the society's patron, and Lord Louis Mountbatten. Mamoulian found it inspiring:

> They said that the prince would like so much to see something shot on the set. So I said, well, I will cook up a little scene with Mark Antony and a stand-in for Cleopatra—because she wasn't there—and two horses. It was raining, the ground was frozen, everybody had blankets on. I had this enormous coat and muffler and hat on, and we were all shaking.
>
> We went out there a little ahead of time to get the whole thing set, and now comes Prince Philip followed by Mountbatten and a whole score of admirals. All of them in their uniforms, bareheaded, the prince with his hands behind his back, and it's freezing, and they're walking like this. It was inspiring—really a lesson, you know, in the Spartan quality—if it's royalty, this is no different, you see.... I thought that was brave, great style.

"There is nothing more we can shoot without Liz," Wanger wrote on November 18, as he sent layoff notices to four hundred workers. A week after she left a London hospital, Taylor and Fisher flew to Palm Springs. Outrageous rumors flew with Taylor in seclusion. On December 9, secretary Violet Herschenson wrote Mamoulian from Beverly Hills, "Jack [Hertz] called Jenny from work this morning to tell her that there was a horrible rumor going around where he works that Elizabeth Taylor died last night. Now who in the world starts rumors like that? ... It reminded me of the time in the commissary at Fox that they said that Jerry Lewis had died."

During that delay, studio machinations were under way in California that virtually guaranteed Mamoulian would quit or be fired. "Spyros Skouras

Lord Louis Mountbatten, left, and Prince Philip visit the set of *Cleopatra* in London, November 1960. At center is producer Walter Wanger with Stephen Boyd, who played Mark Antony when Mamoulian was directing. Photograph courtesy of Library of Congress.

and Bob Goldstein [Fox production chief after Adler's death], asked Nunnally Johnson to work on it. Rouben was not sold on the idea that Johnson was the right man to succeed Brandel. But this was one of Skouras's and Goldstein's impulsive telephone decisions. The studio's commitment to Johnson is $140,000," Wanger recorded.

Johnson, an Academy Award winner for his adaptation of *The Grapes of Wrath* (1940), wrote high-gloss comedies such as *How to Marry a Millionaire* (1953) and *How to Be Very, Very Popular* (1955), directed dramas including *The Man in the Gray Flannel Suit* (1956), and had just written *The Three Faces of Eve* (1957). The elegant Georgia native was the consummate Hollywood insider. Who can blame Mamoulian's scorn when Johnson's version of the carpet scene sounds like something grafted from a Marilyn Monroe comedy:

APOLLODORUS: Her majesty, the queen of Egypt!
CAESAR: Your majesty?
CLEOPATRA: Oh, dear gods, how dreadful! (*With a deep sigh, she seems to manage some sort of relief, and looks wearily at Caesar.*)
CLEOPATRA: If you have any choice at all, never travel in a rug.

Johnson twisted a dagger in his version of events, writing Groucho Marx:

Did you ever have anything to do with Mr. Mamoulian? Well, sir, he is quite a character. After a couple of meetings with him I managed the first successful prediction I have made in my whole life. I bet Walter Wanger that he could never go to bat. All he wants to do is "prepare." A hell of a preparer. Tests, wardrobe, hair, toenails. You give Rouben something to prepare and he's dynamite.

Elizabeth Taylor's costume test for *Cleopatra* was taken on a freezing set in London in December 1960. This outfit does not appear in the finished film. Photograph courtesy of Library of Congress.

But I bet Wanger two pounds (32 ounces) that he would never step into the batter's box. If you make him start this picture, I said, he will never forgive you to his dying day. This chap is a natural-born martyr. If you don't martyrize him he is going to be as sore as hell.

That was unfair. Mamoulian's costume tests were the required work of a costume epic. With dismal weather outside and without Taylor inside, often the tests were all the work he could do. Taylor and Fisher returned to London on December 23. Five days later, she made some costume tests under conditions that eventually led to her near-fatal illness the following March. Mamoulian recorded: "10 a.m.—Tests of Taylor's hair, clothing. Ice-cold stage, dressing room and makeup room (!) Elizabeth rightly angry—Nothing until after lunch—Eddie there (bought a new green convertible Rolls-Royce)."

On December 30, Mamoulian wrote, "Liz has laryngitis and cramps—feels worse, but goes through the day's work. Costume and wig tests." By then, Wanger realized he was caught in a scrap: "Mamoulian does not seem interested in conferring with Johnson over the script because he still doesn't think he is the right choice." Mamoulian *was* conferring—just unhappily: "Nunnally keeps rehashing same scenes over and over again, talking, reading and acting them out. Told him he should finish Caesar's section."

Finally, Taylor unleashed her rage. She and Fisher demanded a rewrite by Paddy Chayefsky, an Oscar winner for *Marty* (1955) and a friend of Fisher's. Over the phone from New York, Chayefsky said rewrites would take him six months, so the plan was dropped.

On January 10, 1961, Taylor and Finch raged about Brandel's carpet scene, asserting that "the scene they were rehearsing was unplayable," Wanger wrote. "Mamoulian, however, had approved it, even though I am sure he didn't consider it perfect. But he did want to get on with the picture and thought he would get something out of the scene on the set. . . . Liz said she wanted to see me later at the Dorchester. She was in bed, not feeling well, when I arrived. She was not happy with the script and insisted we call Skouras. She managed to upset him, too." Two days later, Mamoulian made Wanger read both versions of the scene: "A deaf man can see the difference!"

January 16 brought the final blow-up. One of the final arguments was whether the film could be moved back to Hollywood. "California out—

start shooting Thursday," Mamoulian wrote. In Wanger's account, "Mamoulian arrived at Rogell's office late—it was Azadia's birthday and he had been at lunch with her. . . . Rogell blamed Mamoulian for the delays; Mamoulian in turn blamed the executives. I tried to take some of the blame to pacify things, but the meeting ended with Mamoulian furious and sulking, and Rogell determined to start shooting, hot or cold, on Thursday—Liz willing." Liz was not willing. The next day, Wanger recorded, "Liz said it was terrible. Mamoulian, who had approved the script, ended up by siding with her and letting me take the blame for it."

In Mamoulian's London secretary's notes, after he returned to his rented townhouse, "Mr. Fisher telephoned and spoke to Mr. M. and asked Mr. and Mrs. M. to see them at 9 p.m." Mamoulian's next decision: "12:30 a.m.: Sent cable to Skouras—RESIGNATION—Drove home singing."

The cable read in part, "If you had listened to me Cleopatra would not be in the present mess. This is no longer the picture I was engaged for and for which I had great faith and enthusiasm in. The recent developments make it impossible for me to continue as the director and I am asking you to release me from this assignment." Wanger wrote that Mamoulian told him he had told Skouras he wanted to resign, not that he did. "I think he is maneuvering for complete autonomy, but I believe he made a bad tactical error."

Skouras accepted Mamoulian's resignation: "Record will show that up to this time I have complied with all your wishes and requests excepting your opposition that picture be produced (in) London, but when we secured Egypt you were satisfied to produce it in London and Egypt." Skouras quickly named Mankiewicz, who had directed *Julius Caesar* (1953) and guided Taylor through *Suddenly, Last Summer* (1959), as the new director, sweetening the offer by buying Figaro Productions, the company Mankiewicz co-owned with NBC, for $3 million. Mankiewicz arrived in London in early February 1961. Almost as quickly, he brought in screenwriters Ranald MacDougall and Sidney Buchman, although he ended up writing most of the scenes himself.

At dinner with Taylor and Fisher the night he told Skouras he was resigning, Mamoulian recorded, "Elizabeth won't do the picture if I leave. Told her she should do nothing—except what is best for her, and should follow her contract whatever it is." Wanger understood the situation as well:

"Mamoulian is looking for support from Liz, who likes to stand up for the underdog, but it is too late. Skouras knows she will quiet down if he brings in Mankiewicz."

On January 22, Taylor did, in fact, quit. "Had to order [her agent] Kurt Frings to do so—talked to her lawyer," Mamoulian wrote. "Skouras phoned her, said he would not release her for anything in the world." He seemed not to have understood the difference between any sympathy she had for her director and hard-nosed leverage with the studio for herself. But at least she could be very entertaining. That evening, they "dropped Eddie at the Dorchester—he had a headache. Elizabeth came to the house, sat talking until 1:30 a.m." Around midnight, the phone rang—reporters from the *Daily Express* and *Daily Mail*. Taylor "took the phone and pretended to be a most seductive French maid."

The day after Mamoulian quit, Wanger recorded a thirty-one-point list of complaints about the director, probably for Skouras's consumption. Most were grumbles about Mamoulian's blowups and autocratic behavior, such as "Rudeness to all and infuriated if anything didn't suit him such as office, his phones not answering, his mail not being properly presented to him." There was a sad description of a director past his prime: "Idiosyncrasies of the great master and repetition of anecdotes concerning his past," and "Preaching to everybody at production meetings quoting the value of *Becky Sharp* and other pictures of the past."

On March 4, Taylor, who thought she had been nursing a bad cold, was diagnosed with pneumonia, which sent her to the London Clinic, where she had an emergency tracheostomy. Some news outlets reported she had died. It is part of Oscar lore that her frail condition influenced the Best Actress voting that year, and her wan appearance at the April 17, 1961 ceremony, where she won for her role in *Butterfield 8*, is considered one of the all-time highlights.

The Mamoulians, who were running out their studio-paid lease, visited her two days after the operation and left for New York on March 21. Rouben momentarily found himself an in-demand figure with an eager audience for Taylor gossip. On April 2, publisher Bennett Cerf's wife Phyllis visited their hotel and invited them to that night's live broadcast of *What's My Line?* on which her husband was a panelist. At a party afterwards at the Little Club,

Arlene Francis regaled them with stories of the Theatre Guild school, and Marlene Dietrich, Milton Berle, Miriam Hopkins, and comedian Joe E. Lewis dropped by their table.

Mamoulian resolutely defended Taylor. On June 28, he called Hedda Hopper: "Told her we were great friends with the Fishers and how much we liked them, and told her Elizabeth used to consider her a second mother." At a party that night, "Many people asked me about Elizabeth Taylor's temperament. I set them straight on where the fault was with *Cleopatra* miseries." At William Wyler's dinner for Shirley MacLaine and Audrey Hepburn, Charles Feldman told him, "You survived, but I don't think Skouras will." The last he saw of Fisher and Taylor was at the Moscow International Film Festival in August. Mamoulian went alone to see Taylor introducing *Butterfield 8* preceded by her brief remarks about world peace.

When *Cleopatra* resumed production at Rome's Cinecittà Studios on September 25, 1961, with a half-completed script and for Taylor, a renegotiated contract that now included a fourteen-room villa, Mamoulian's footage was ditched and the principal cast replaced. Burton was now Antony, Rex Harrison now Caesar, Roddy McDowall was Octavian, and Cesare Danova was Apollodorus. Released June 12, 1963, after Mankiewicz cut it down from a six-hour running time to just under four hours, it turned a modest profit (depending on the interpretation of studio bookkeeping), was nominated for nine Academy Awards, and won four—none for writing—and only Harrison was nominated for acting.

Mankiewicz greatly improved the carpet scene, allowing Cleopatra to combine intelligence with unforced flirtation. Taylor, in a simple red and white gown, unrolls herself from the carpet, Danova announces "All hail Cleopatra!" and she responds with a simple "Thank you." After she reminds Harrison that he's in her palace, he retorts, "Only through me can you escape from the desperate straits in which you find yourself." They bicker some more, and Taylor observes, "We seem to have rubbed each other the wrong way." Harrison replies, "I'm not sure I want to be rubbed by you at all!"

Mankiewicz only made three more films after this, before retiring in 1972. Zanuck made a noisy 1962 return to the Fox boardroom, ousting Skouras after an internal audit revealed that Fox had bled $61 million over four years. Wanger, shut out of postproduction by Zanuck, kept developing projects until his death from a heart attack in 1968. Taylor and Burton married in Canada in 1964 while he was touring in *Hamlet* and made their best film together, Edward Albee's *Who's Afraid of Virginia Woolf?* a year later. They divorced ten years later, remarried the following year and divorced the year after that.

Mamoulian headed into a future in which Azadia stepped up her drinking and he never worked again.

CHAPTER 22

Leavin' Time

In 1962, Mamoulian maintained a household staff of five, including a gardener, secretary, and live-in housekeeper; his only lifestyle concession had been to start ordering cigars from Schwab's drugstore in Beverly Hills instead of his usual Uppmann's, now banned in the American embargo on Cuban goods. He never got a solid movie offer after *Cleopatra*, but Broadway producers still beckoned for a few years, usually with musicals—the happy legacy of *Oklahoma!*

By the time he died in 1987, his luxe existence had become a facade; his dream house, overrun by feral cats that bred with the pedigreed cats he and Azadia never had spayed or neutered, held squalor alongside the expensive antiques. He had no money for domestic upkeep. He had been painfully disabled with cancer and put under a Los Angeles County conservatorship, and Azadia slid into dementia from years of drinking.

A polite curtain might have been drawn over these circumstances, but Mamoulian's friend Eidell Heidt, upset at not being named his conservator, invited reporters to show them the condition of the house.

How had it come to this?

~

Shortly after his return from London in 1961, Mamoulian found he could enjoy, without the need for a publicist, the acclamation accorded filmmakers of Hollywood's Golden Age. A lengthy 1961 interview in the British publication *Sight and Sound* kicked that off, and as the reputations of *Love Me Tonight* and *Dr. Jekyll and Mr. Hyde* soared, he was honored at film festivals and university screenings, he happily sat for oral histories and interviews for dissertations, and he had an energetic champion in British critic Tom Milne. Mamoulian bought copies of Milne's compact 1969 appreciation, *Mamoulian*, in bulk to distribute to friends.

He recorded a final swipe at Wanger after *My Life with Cleopatra*, a compact version of Wanger's filmmaking diary, was published in 1963: "An elongated gossip column. Walter's literary style comes close to Louella Parsons, but in artistic taste and moral fiber he is a dwarf in comparison with her." In 1962, approaching age sixty-five, he energetically lectured his agent, Phil Gersh, about finding him some jobs. Knowing Mamoulian's appetite for gossip, Gersh produced a nugget: "Said he heard Elizabeth Taylor and Burton went to London and Elizabeth had a session with Sybil, at which time Sybil [Burton's wife] beat her black and blue. It's getting curiouser and curiouser."

Old friends were taking their leave, and Mamoulian was probably unwilling to take on any more stage work without them. Theresa Helburn died in 1959, Oscar Hammerstein in 1960, and Lawrence Langner at the end of 1962. Although Mamoulian avoided grief rituals and funerals when he could, for his oldest American friend, he insisted on placing a long-distance call to Armina Marshall. "Quite a wonderful way to go," he wrote in his diary. "They had just come back from a party at Dorothy Hammerstein's. While she was taking her gloves off, Lawrence called 'Armina' from the next room. As she walked in, he was already dead in the armchair. Heart infection which he had had for nine months. He knew what was coming and arranged for it methodically."

Among his recently acquired friends were Gregory and Veronique Peck, for whom Mamoulian threw an at-home black-tie dinner party—a vestige of old-time glamor—in 1958. But he passed up an opportunity to discuss with Peck what would be the actor's greatest role. In mid-December 1962, Peck called from Universal Studios to invite him to an impromptu party he was throwing for the publicity visit of Harper Lee on the set of *To Kill a Mockingbird*, which would be released on Christmas Day: "Told him we were having dinner and I didn't think we could manage to come over tonight."

Faint work offers turned up for a time. In June 1963, agent David DeSilva wired: "Have suggested you to David Merrick as ideal director for forthcoming Broadway musical of *The Matchmaker*. He's very interested in meeting with you." The meeting with Merrick that might have landed him *Hello, Dolly!* didn't come about because, as Mamoulian explained later, he was "feeling ill" and had to go to Paris for the opening of the Cinematheque, "and I said I couldn't touch anything for three or four months, so please forget me. Anyway, after seeing it, I'm glad I didn't do it. It's a very conventional musical."

He likewise had no interest in portrayals of shtetl life in pre-Revolution Russia. That August, he returned a script titled *Tevye (To Life)* that later became *Fiddler on the Roof*. In October 1966, agent Herb Tobias wrote, "I am talking to Jack Warner and Walter McEwen about your directing *Finian's Rainbow* for which Fred Astaire has already been set." The job went to Francis Ford Coppola.

In 1964, Mamoulian published a children's book, *Abigayil: The Story of the Cat at the Manger*. He had written it in 1959 as a Christmas gift to Azadia; it ended up at a tiny publishing house, New York Graphic Society. In just under 2,200 words, Mamoulian spun a story that's part fable in the style of a longtime cat devotee. It sold poorly. *Abigayil* tells the story of the birth of Jesus in a manager in Bethlehem from a cat's perspective—Abigayil was a kitten nursing a broken paw at the time, and since she couldn't sleep, she saw Mary giving birth to Jesus.

He spent his own money for book promotion and went to New York to sit for respectful newspaper interviews. He had some notion that he might be able to get booked with Johnny Carson on *The Tonight Show*; instead, he endured a taped interview with Joe Franklin for a daytime program, *Down Memory Lane*. Mamoulian also appeared on Long John Nebel's famed late-night radio program, popular for lengthy discussions of UFOs and paranormal phenomena. Another insomniac fan of that show was Irving Berlin, and one evening at his hotel, Mamoulian was surprised to find himself on the receiving end of a Berlin phone call. He thought Berlin "sounded lonely, anxious to talk." The songwriter disapproved of a recent TV appearance by Maurice Chevalier, who was approaching eighty. "Thinks he should stop public appearances (too old, too much strain)—time comes when one goes on living, but not in public."

Mamoulian never staged *Hamlet*, not even at the Eastman School. Having seen so many productions in his youth, on Broadway, and (going by his diary) never missing any TV performances of it, he developed strong opinions on how it should be performed. This led to a piece of quixotic scholarship, *Hamlet: A New Version*, published in 1965, in which he rewrote Shakespeare's play in the way he insisted it should sound.

Mamoulian thought Hamlet should always be played as a youth of twenty. Along with many scholars, he thought that had come about as Shakespeare's way of flattering the original Hamlet, Richard Burbage, who was thirty-four, to take the role. That was the only theoretical point taken seriously by critics, who scorned Mamoulian's version as amateurish. Had Mamoulian conducted original research into Shakespeare's use of language, he might have produced a useful reference work. Since all he did was change words around and add stage directions, the book was treated as a joke. "The thing is, predictably, an inconsistent and exasperating disaster," Phoebe Adams wrote in *The Atlantic Monthly*. "He also has a deficient understanding of the mechanics of poetry." In *The Saturday Review*, Philip Burton called the book "the work of a literalist, incapable of appreciating Shakespeare's brilliant double use of time, chronological and poetic."

Mamoulian nursed one final ambition in 1966. In 1962, Richard Rodgers had been named president and producing director of the Music Theatre of Lincoln Center. Mamoulian envisioned something similar for himself when he met with Roger Stevens, director of the new John F. Kennedy Center for the Performing Arts in Washington, DC. Early plans for the Kennedy Center involved resident opera and theater companies. Mamoulian proposed the Musical Theatre of America, with himself as head, staging operettas, musicals, and the occasional opera. He didn't receive an offer.

In November 1967, Mamoulian was diagnosed with colon cancer. The only treatment at that time was surgery and a colostomy. Although the operation didn't slow him down for public events—he attended film festivals in venues as far away as Sydney, Australia (which named an award after him), and Tehran—he quietly decided, at age seventy, that he should be more or less retired, and he stopped using agents to provide the flood of scripts that had been coming to him for the past forty years.

Public events without Azadia along made him lonely. One of these was an April 1969 Academy of Motion Picture Arts and Sciences reception for Ingrid Bergman, then making *Cactus Flower* and working in Hollywood for the first time since she made *Joan of Arc* twenty years earlier. Mamoulian carefully recorded the attendees, noting that Natalie Wood spoke Russian to him, and Gregory Peck "came over to talk to me!" He noted disapprovingly that Groucho Marx, then seventy-eight, was clad in a Nehru jacket.

Azadia had increased her vodka consumption and twisted ankles when she slipped off curbs, so she seldom traveled with him unless they were visiting her family in Washington or at film festivals that paid her way. One of the times her drinking became a public problem was at a 1970 New Year's party at the home of director David Bradley, a film lecturer at UCLA, at which the main attraction was a gathering of silent-movie actresses. It provoked a rare outburst. Celebrity biographer Charles Higham recalled that Azadia "slipped and fell on a mink-clad group of silent stars, all seated on the floor to see themselves on the screen as they were forty-five years earlier. He pulled her up and pushed her outside to the veranda, where we heard the unforgettable words, 'You have disgraced the name Mamoulian!'"

Sometimes his mask of affability slipped elsewhere. In 1971, after a screening of *Dr. Jekyll and Mr. Hyde* with Miriam Hopkins at UCLA, he lashed out at the student audience he thought had been snickering: "I can forgive mental denseness or lack of perception, stupidity. But I cannot forgive the dullness of the heart and the bluntness of emotional reactions. But, beyond that—stupidity and a lack of understanding—there is something that is primitive and that is called the law of politeness and hospitality . . . and yet there was a little bunch of you that kept giggling and laughing. At what—yourselves."

In summer 1972, Mamoulian used the occasion of an invitation from the Moscow International Film Festival to visit his childhood home for the first time since 1920. He had a Soviet government handler, although the only intent of his trip to Tbilisi, made in a three-car caravan, was reminiscence and a visit to family graves. "What a day," he wrote. "Full of feeling—some joy, but much sadness. So much beauty gone: national dress, horses, belts and daggers. New apartment houses all along!"

On the drive down, he noted "The Valley of Ararat—green—goats, sheep, pigs, two cats, one dog—how I missed them and what joy to see them!" His family home, which he could see from his hotel room, had been cut into two apartments. His old school and other buildings he remembered were "all as before, but crumbling." Mamoulian was suffering from a cold that turned into bronchitis, and that, combined with the small deprivations of Soviet life, made him melancholy: "How one misses the blessings of Kleenex, soft toilet paper, soap, etc." He was pleased to encounter people who still remembered Kato Babo. As for her dacha, "So sad—all gone. House, mill, gardens . . . yard gone, garden gone, big arched entrance gone, river gone, blacksmiths gone!" He offered up a prayer to his grandmother at her grave.

Miles Kreuger, a nephew of Broadway producer Cy Feuer, first met Mamoulian in New York in the mid-1960s. He made occasional visits to Mamoulian's home before he moved to Los Angeles permanently in 1979, when he turned his collection of scripts, recordings, and ephemera into the Institute of the American Musical. He was one of the few who got to know Azadia well during those years. At an evening at a restaurant in Beverly Hills, "There was a pinlight lighting the tables, and she was wearing a diamond ring that reminded me of the diamond in *Snow White*—it was enormous. I kept dodging the refraction. She asked me, 'Oh, is my ring disturbing you? It's a bit ostentatious, isn't it? Harry Winston sent it to me on approval.'" Azadia's taste for jewelry ate up Mamoulian's dwindling financial resources. As late as 1984, she went on a $20,000 shopping binge that included $10,000 for diamond earrings from Tiffany's. "She was a great, great expert on diamonds," Kreuger said.

Her decline eventually became apparent. Kreuger recalls one incident from the early 1980s at a restaurant. "Suddenly Azadia started acting out, crying, and throwing the food, and we quickly left. She was complaining that the food hadn't been served properly." Mamoulian, in Kreuger's account, "simply couldn't cope with chaos. He would not accept the fact that Azadia was going through this. The house began to smell terrible because there wasn't enough kitty litter. No one would work for them. I remember him saying, 'It will be all right, it will be all right.' He just could not allow himself to see it. He finally couldn't bear it anymore."

His final cancer diagnosis was made in the mid-1980s. Surgery was the primary option for prostate cancer then, and it typically resulted in incontinence. The prospect of that on top of the existing colostomy was too distressing to consider. Mamoulian chose to live at home with the disease as it steadily weakened him.

One of Mamoulian's final tributes was his most lavish. On August 15, 1982, accompanied by Azadia, he received the D.W. Griffith Award from the Directors Guild of America. There were tributes read from André Previn, Vincente Minnelli, Shirley Jones, and Fred Astaire. Hermes Pan told a story about rehearsing the "Stereophonic Sound" number from *Silk Stockings*; after it ended with Astaire and Janis Paige leaping off the conference table, Mamoulian's only comment had been, "Very good—but now what?" William Kaplan, assistant director on *Love Me Tonight*, reminisced about Mamoulian allowing him to direct a stuntman for Chevalier's high-speed ride on Solitude; before Mamoulian left the set, he advised Kaplan, "Make 'em funny!"

Finally, it was Mamoulian's turn. He rose slowly: "I was just wondering, could we do the whole thing over again? After all, it was only take one. I could listen to take two . . ." The audience erupted in laughter. "Sitting here tonight and listening and looking, I come very dangerously close to liking myself. I realize tonight that I've been a very, very lucky man." He continued, "I think we must face the facts that politics seem to fail, religions seem to fail, economics seem to fail, and I think that our last hope is in the fine arts." He urged other directors to "bring back faith in the future. There is plenty of goodness on this Earth."

In April 1986, Azadia was admitted to the mental health clinic at Cedars-Sinai Hospital, where she was confined for two weeks. Since the clinic didn't allow telephones in the rooms because of the risk of suicide with phone cords, her only contact with her husband was through a hallway pay phone. In 1987, when she was briefly put in the UCLA neuropsychiatric institute, she could not even sign her admission document. That June, to be discharged from a hospital where he had been admitted with various ailments, the county's Public Guardian Office placed Mamoulian under a conservatorship because of his poor health and lack of funds.

The first language Mamoulian heard in childhood was Armenian. It also was some of the last he heard. Arby Ovanessian, a documentary filmmaker, had met Mamoulian in London in the 1960s. In mid-summer 1986, he wanted to make a film on the director's career that stressed his Armenian roots and his time with Yevgeny Vakhtangov and the Moscow Art Theatre. He completed slightly more than an hour of filmed interviews.

Mamoulian, painfully shuffling in his bathrobe and pajamas, rallied to the task. "He was using a cane. He was frail. He remembered everything, he was brilliant." The cats, Ovanessian recalled, "were all around. He had an Abyssinian one named Nefertiti."

"I remember one time, he asked me, 'Have you seen my piano?' He got up with his cane and walked toward the big sitting room. It had a cupboard. Very expensive objects. A cat had given birth to three kittens in that little cupboard. He took it as a positive moment that the three white kittens were born."

On one visit, Ovanessian brought along Zaghik Gourjian, whom he had known from a theater group in Iran. Now she was teaching at an Armenian school in Los Angeles. She introduced herself, and when Mamoulian heard the name, he immediately warmed to her: "Zaghik! Oh! Flower!" Sensing that Mamoulian's time was growing short, and fearful of his isolation, Ovanessian asked Gourjian to start looking in on him.

"I'd bring him chicken, rice, and everything. Just like taking care of my grandfather," said Gourjian. He began to call her frequently at her school. She found herself writing his checks for bills and doing nursing chores. "He was in desperate need for someone, probably anyone. Physically, he was in very bad shape. He'd had a (private) nurse come by every single day. She (eventually) refused to come because he couldn't pay her." In Ovanessian's recollection, payment wasn't the issue. Instead, there was an old grudge. "The nurse from the county was named Laura. She was a very good nurse—but the name had cruel connotations."

Azadia's drinking led Gourjian to "hide all the liquor I'd find. Many times, she hit Mamoulian. And when he fell down, he couldn't get up. In the middle of the night, he'd call me: 'Come soon, I'm on the floor.'" Azadia "couldn't stand by herself. She didn't want to leave the house. That's why she stayed in that house. They couldn't afford servants." By her count, "That house had forty cats. Can you believe it? . . . Azadia and Mamoulian, they were in love with cats. You know what he said? 'In cats' eyes, everything belongs to them.' That's why."

Mamoulian made a rueful 1986 note: "One man to keep house and yard clean. The lawn in miserable shape." His last poem was a sad verse about the felines:

> The house we live in is quite nice
> with much upholstery to scratch
> attractive rugs to sharpen claws.

Gourjian found, "His brain was working . . . but his body was very bad. His mind, though, was just like the mind of a thirty-year-old." In that setting, she found him "a very, very private person. Even when I asked (about) Greta Garbo, he just smiled." By December 2, 1987, "He was in a semi-coma. I told the nurse I'd be back in the morning, but the nurse took him to the Motion Picture Hospital (in Woodland Hills)."

Mamoulian died on December 4. The Los Angeles County administrator's office briefly took control of his estate because no relatives had stepped forward. His funeral, attended by an estimated five hundred mourners, was held December 10 at St. Mary Apostolic Church in Glendale, arranged for by Gourjian and Joe Youngerman, now executive secretary of the Directors Guild of America.

Eidell Heidt had wanted to be appointed his permanent conservator but she was turned down. She invited reporters to the house because she accused the county of failing to pay bills. At that point, Mamoulian's estate, not counting the multimillion-dollar value of the house and property, had just $6,700. A reporter noted that paint was hanging in flakes. In the living room, "chairs, settees and every visible inch of the wall-to-wall carpet were shredded." Police officers were stationed at the house for a week to keep looters away. Animal control personnel rounded up all except one cat, which remained with Azadia, who was eventually moved to a nursing home, where she died in 1999.

Gourjian once promised Mamoulian that she would never leave him alone. "When I go visit my parents at the cemetery, I visit Rouben, also."

∼

In 1940, in the wake of the abandoned *Lysistrata*, Mamoulian began an essay about his challenges, placing himself in astonishing company:

> All other artists are allowed to do their ultimate in creation. No one and nothing can stop them from executing their highest concept in art, no matter

how advanced, prophetic or extravagant it may be. Mussorgsky could write his music though *Boris Godonov* was taken off the stage and the rest of his work was never played and he died in poverty. Still, he put it all down on the paper, and today it lives. Van Gogh in art. Veobel—Gallileus—Picasso. So many others.

Not so with a screen director. He needs big sums of money and he must please millions. His ultimate, which could be appreciated by many, even though not by millions, has to remain within his soul and his brain.

Mamoulian's favorite quote was from Leo Tolstoy: "Art is for life's sake." Tolstoy could have been articulating the director's innermost thoughts about his craft:

> In order correctly to define art, it is necessary, first of all, to cease to consider it as a means to pleasure and to consider it as one of the conditions of human life. . . . To evoke in oneself a feeling one has once experienced, and having evoked it in oneself, then, by means of movements, lines, colors, sounds, or forms expressed in words, so to transmit that feeling that others may experience the same feeling—this is the activity of art.

Joseph Horowitz noticed that "Bring my goat!" began as a director's way of controlling a recalcitrant animal but became an affirmation: "The epic dimension Mamoulian brought to Heyward's Catfish Row was a dimension previously unknown to Gershwin. Mamoulian and Gershwin amplified one another; something unanticipated, even unprecedented, resulted. Emboldened by ignorance, admiration and self-esteem, Mamoulian took a story about Gullah life and turned it into a parable about the human condition."

Mamoulian had the satisfaction of knowing that some of his work had permanence. David Thomson wrote, "At times, his ingenuity led him into preciousness, but much more often he succeeded on his own terms—the wish to blend movement, dancing, action, music, singing, décor, and lighting into one seething entity." He concluded, "More than any other director—more than Lubitsch, even—he should be known for his touch."

That touch included a lot of hopeful endings: Nan and the Kid find a Wagner overture on a car radio and see a happy flock of birds. Dmitri and

Katusha stride into Siberian imprisonment hand in hand. Curly and Laurey roar into a joyful prairie horizon. Billy Bigelow gives hope for redemption after death. Li'l Augie leaps over the racetrack fence into Della's arms. Grieving fathers Stephen and James awkwardly touch. As for Garbo's haunting gaze as Queen Christina—only she knew what she was really thinking.

Mamoulian firmly believed that his stylization would prove immortal: "You'll notice that in all art, naturalism is the first to die. Poetry lives on. You take something that may be successful in a given period; if its basis is naturalism, it is short-lived. Take all the painting from the eighteenth century, for example. It's dead as a mackerel now. It's the stylized artists that live on. I'd stick to style."

Acknowledgments

This book was the idea of Alice Lotvin Birney, cultural historian in the Manuscript Division of the Library of Congress. She had gone through a great deal of difficulty in getting Rouben Mamoulian's collected papers to their intended destination, which had been discussed with Mamoulian decades earlier. When they arrived, archivists accustomed to seeing water, sun, and mildew damage were faced with the additional challenge of removing the powerful urine odor from all the feral cats that overran Mamoulian's home in his final years.

Mamoulian lived during the Periclean age of business correspondence: secretaries (often the wisecracking kind) handling calls on black telephones, stenographers taking dictation in shorthand, pink "While You Were Out" slips, real long-distance operators, formally typed letters from typewriters with keys that skipped, onionskin carbon copies, carefully routed memos at the motion picture studios, postcards, telegrams delivered by young men on motor scooters, telegrams wired from transcontinental trains, overseas cablegrams sent to and from passenger liners, and vest-pocket notepads purchased at stationery stores. Yet the most fascinating part of his collection, other than his candid snapshots of Greta Garbo, consists of scraps that could easily have been tossed out.

Mamoulian's diaries, which he began writing in 1916, continued to nearly the last year of his life, when, having not even spiral notebooks at hand, he began to write on scratch paper—odds and ends of paper, cut-up posterboard, envelopes that bills came in, even the cardboard that came in pantyhose packaging. If his 1986 diary were spilled onto a tabletop, it would look like someone upended a wastepaper basket through a time warp. Laura

Kells, chief archivist for the Mamoulian collection at the Library of Congress, assisted by Tammi Taylor, Nicholas Newlin, Maribeth Theroux, and Lena Wiley, persevered and got what Laura dubbed "the pantyhose papers" into order. I am grateful to Alice for the number of times she said, "We might have that," to Laura for saying, "Try looking there," and to Mark Horowitz, senior music specialist of the Music Division, for all the times he said, "Yes, we have that," and for the time he played Richard Rodgers's original handwritten version of the "Carousel Waltz."

Mark Spergel, whose 1987 doctoral dissertation, published as a book in 1993, has been the only extant comprehensive biography of Mamoulian, provided cheerful support and comments every step of the way, perhaps because he understands how difficult it is to write a biography of a temperamental man, no matter how vast his papers.

The Rodgers and Hammerstein Organization is always interested in how original productions of their shows looked and sounded. Bruce Pomahac, then music director there, was helpful in providing information about *Carousel*. Dave Stein provided a very enjoyable day at the Kurt Weill Foundation.

Rob and Chris Bamberger graciously opened their home to me for movie viewings. Rob provided commentary from his vast knowledge of vintage popular music and Chris from her considerable expertise on dance generally and Fred Astaire specifically.

Special thanks to John Gallagher for his interview transcripts and copies of films not yet available commercially, and to Kevin Brownlow for his interview transcript and continued encouragement.

Amy Glover provided research at the Margaret Herrick Library and was generous with her knowledge of neighborhoods in Beverly Hills. Lee Lawrence, who makes my life so much more tolerable, offered suggestions on the text and, always willing to put friendship to the test, spent entire days at the Library of Congress and the Beinecke Library at Yale.

Milena Oganesyan, who provided translations, had insights into Mamoulian's character. "If you're an Armenian in the Caucasus," she told me, "no matter where you live, you're always being told by someone that you don't belong there."

Finally, my thanks to John Mulderig, who edited my film writing for Catholic News Service and whose lone directive in all the time I've worked with him has been simply, "Tell the truth." Also thanks to: Andrew Boose, Susan Brady, Sam Brylawski, Rev. David B. Collins, David Coppen, Patrick Curtis, Sebastian Fabal, Bert Fink, Samuel Goldwyn Jr., Barbara Hall, Katherine Harper, Charlie Ipcar, Brian Kellow, Dickran Kouymjian, Gregory Mank, Frank Rasbury, Dominic Symonds, Wayne Shirley, Charles Silver, Mary Skerrett, James H. Stevens, Andrei Malaev, William Mann, Nancy Martin, Zoran Sinobad, Josie Walters Johnson, John White, and Laurie Winer.

Responsibility for inaccuracies, shortcomings, and mistakes is mine alone.

Notes

Abbreviations

CU	Columbia University oral history
GGC	George Gershwin Collection, Library of Congress
KWF	Kurt Weill Foundation, New York
MAC	Maxwell Anderson Collection, Ransom Humanities Center, University of Texas, Austin
OHC	Oscar Hammerstein II Collection, Library of Congress
RMC	Rouben Mamoulian Collection, Library of Congress
SGC	Samuel Goldwyn Collection, Margaret Herrick Library
TGC	Theatre Guild Collection, Beinecke Library, Yale University

Introduction: Enjoy the Journey

3   "a concatenation": *Armenian Reporter International*, March 13, 1980.
4   "the ingenuity and vitality": Knight, *The Liveliest Art*.
4   "Mamoulian's tragedy": Sarris, reprinted in *American Cinema*.
5   *Carousel* review: Chapman, New York *Daily News*, May 11, 1945.
6   "In working with him": Hornblow, CU, 39.
6   "Professionally, I can't help": Joseph Adamson interview, 1979.
6   "He was a very brilliant man": Youngerman, *My Seventy Years at Paramount Studios*.
6   a phoetus: RM diary, January 27, 1959, RMC.
6   "the director's claims" and "The desperate ego needs": Eyman, *Speed of Sound*.
7   "Are you saying": Oberstein interview.
7   "in an atmosphere": From "*The Art of Gods and Monkeys*," the memoir Mamoulian contracted for in 1939 but abandoned in 1946, and which only covered his life through his arrival in London. He never explained that title.
8   "Monsters in *Rite of Spring*" and "Because we got tired": RM diary, April 19, 1940, RMC.
8   "personally, I'm religious": Greenberg interview.

315

Chapter 1. Tiflis to New York

10 "Strangely enough": Mamoulian, CU, 16.
10 Cable: Mamoulian told many versions of his job offer from George Eastman, but the telegram itself is missing from both his and Eastman's collected papers.
10 Met Rosing in 1915: Ruth Woodbury Sedgwick, "Mamoulian of the Movies," *This Week*, August 4, 1935.
11 "I went to the British Museum": Gallagher interview.
11 Zachary Mamoulian, 1866–1966; Virginie Mamoulian, 1876–1972.
11 "Not the wrong side of the tracks": undated lecture note, RMC.
11 "and all of my ancestors": "*The Art of Gods and Monkeys*."
11 honeymooned in Paris: *Armenian Observer*, August 9, 1972.
12 "rather imposing library": "*The Art of Gods and Monkeys*".
12 "She wasn't allowed": Mamoulian, CU, 12.
12 "I live for him": Quotes from Virginie's 1963 account are from Spergel, *Reinventing Reality*. Translation by Boris Murvis.
12 "She was dramatic": author interview.
12 "People gathered in large groups": "*The Art of Gods and Monkeys*," also published separately as "The Best Advice I Ever Had," dated September 16, 1957, RMC.
12 "Before I was six": "*The Art of Gods and Monkeys*."
14 "We stayed": "*The Art of Gods and Monkeys*."
14 "For a while": "*The Art of Gods and Monkeys*."
14 "if you listen": Guy Ramsey, (London) *News Chronicle*, August 25, 1937.
14 a visit to Tiflis: *Armenian Reporter International*, March 13, 1980.
14 Playing the inspector: Becvar interview.
14 Criminal law: *Armenian Reporter*, undated clipping, 1934.
15 "without blood and thunder": "*The Art of Gods and Monkeys*."
16 "a sea wave": "*The Art of Gods and Monkeys*."
16 "first kind of a taste": Becvar interview.
17 "Overnight, life became": the account from Essentuki is in "*The Art of Gods and Monkeys*."
17 "a stray bullet": "*The Art of Gods and Monkeys*."
17 "I will be kissing the pillow": from journal pages dated June 1919, RMC. This and all translations of Mamoulian's correspondence to his parents are by Milena Oganesyan.
18 "solid white wall": "*The Art of Gods and Monkeys*."
18 "There is, I believe": "*The Art of Gods and Monkeys*."
18 Makaroff: "*The Art of Gods and Monkeys*." Grigori Makaroff (1863–1940) was a star of early British TV in 1933 with Lady, his fox terrier, who performed tricks.

Notes

20　Style of the *Chauve-Souris*: Gallagher interview.
20　"What do you have to lose?": Gallagher interview.
20　"A toast!": "*The Art of Gods and Monkeys.*"
20　15 pounds a week: "*The Art of Gods and Monkeys.*"
20　"By the time the show opened": "*The Art of Gods and Monkeys.*"
21　"I remember": Gallagher interview.
21　"tall, slim, wiry": "*The Art of Gods and Monkeys.*"
21　"with the glorious name": Gallagher interview.
21　"bald, conservative man": "*The Art of Gods and Monkeys.*"
21　"So you know": Gallagher interview.
22　"So I started rehearsing": Gallagher interview.
22　Reviews from *The Observer*, November 12, 1922; *Sunday Express*, November 12, 1922.
23　"It was a totally realistic": Gallagher interview.
23　Jacques Hébertot: Adamson interview.
24　"it helped him think": Mamoulian, CU, 33.
24　"command performance": Mamoulian CU, 34.
24　"had a distinctly European look": Horgan, *A Certain Climate.*
24　"Like most": Luening, *Odyssey of an American Composer.*
24　"Baritones and tenors": Horgan, *A Certain Climate.*
26　"He was a dandified Armenian": Henry Clune, "Rochester Seen and Heard," Rochester *Democrat and Chronicle*, February 7, 1934.
26　"muttered and mumbled": Luening, *Odyssey of an American Composer.*
26　"I will show you": Horgan, *A Certain Climate.*
27　Corner Club: Bruck interview.
27　"Just a note"; "It helps me a lot": letters, Boonie Goosens to RM, November 16 and 23, 1923, RMC.
27　"Society of Unrecognized Geniuses": Slonimsky, *Perfect Pitch.*
28　"I realized it was utterly impossible": Mamoulian, CU, 19.
28　"failed miserably": Slonimsky, *Perfect Pitch.*
28　"Tell the film 'dictators'": letter, Rosing to RM, July 21, 1937; "When I look back": letter, Rosing to RM, July 31, 1937, RMC. Rosing (1890–1963) later directed opera sequences for films and produced operas for Lyric Opera of Chicago. In 1958, he directed Beverly Sills in *The Ballad of Baby Doe* for the New York City Opera.
29　"really the occasion": Mamoulian, CU, 21.
29　"in the style": Mamoulian, CU, 22.
30　"The final organist's score": Luening, *Odyssey of an American Composer.*
30　"My daughter slave to your son": Detailed accounts of the coroner's inquest were in *The Times* of London and a Bristol newspaper, *Western Daily Press*, March 16, 1926.

Notes

30 "Don't try to untie": letter, RM to father Zachary, September 25, 1925, RMC.
30 "Murder and suicide": *The Times* of London and *Western Daily Press*, March 16, 1926.
30 "I can only imagine": letter, RM to Zachary Mamoulian, March 27, 1926, RMC.
30 "If you give into your grief": letter, RM to Virginie Mamoulian, May 25, 1926, RMC.
31 That's what she believed: according to her grandson, Mark Godwin. Author correspondence.
31 "About the middle": Mamoulian, CU, 46.
31 "Martha, I'm twenty-eight": undated letter, Atwell to Mamoulian, fall 1949, RMC.
31 $75 a week: from a *Saturday Evening Post* profile of Mamoulian, "Sixteen Mamoulian-Dollar Story" by J. Lupton Wilkinson that was eventually given to another writer, Maurice Zolotow, and published as "Hollywood's Armenian Yankee Doodle Dandy" on December 13, 1947.
33 "You've got me here": Becvar interview.
33 "We were very enthusiastic": Langner's notes for Wilkinson's *Saturday Evening Post* article, RMC.
33 "It's very interesting": letter, RM to his parents, June 19, 1927, RMC.

Chapter 2: Catfish Row

34 "really like": In the New York *Herald-Tribune*, critic Arthur Ruhl thought so of *Porgy*, writing in his "Second Nights" column on December 4, 1927: "A play, in the conventional structural sense, it scarcely is, of course. It is a study in racial temperament, the authentic and imaginative reproduction of a certain milieu. Continuity is given by the fact that the various episodes are successive intervals in the life of one individual—the plucky and wistful Negro cripple of the Charleston waterfront—and but for the recurring waves of passionate emotion expressed in the singing and wailing of Negro spirituals, there would be almost no dominating emotional current at once to sweep the bits of 'character' together and carry them on."
34 "kind of Don Quixotean": memo, RM to Oliver Messel, who was designing the film of *Porgy and Bess*, March 2, 1958, RMC.
35 "very black": All quotes from *Porgy* are from Mamoulian's marked-up copy of the script, Box 115, RMC.
35 Bradford, introduction to *Ol' Man Adam an' His Chillun*.
35 Heywards contact Langner: letter, DuBose Heyward to Langner, December 4, 1926; Philip Moeller: letter, DuBose Heyward to Langner, December 22, 1926, TGC.
36 "it will give me a good name": letter, RM to his parents, June 5, 1926, RMC.

37 "nine-tenths DuBose's": New York *Herald Tribune*, January 1, 1939.
37 "When he saw a Negro": *Stage*, October, 1935.
37 *In Abraham's Bosom*: RM saw the play on May 31, 1927.
37 "a tall octoroon": Oberstein interview. An octoroon has one-eighth Black ancestry. Mamoulian might have felt comfortable using that term since one of the most famous examples was Russian poet Alexander Pushkin.
38 "taken to Folly Beach": Stiles, Martha Bennett, "*Porgy and Bess*: A Reminiscence," *Stereo Review*, April 1976.
38 "A Negro handles a hammer": *Charleston News and Courier*, August 16, 1927.
38 "Today is Sunday": letter, RM to his parents, August 14, 1927, RMC.
38 "it all seemed utterly hopeless": Mamoulian, CU, 33.
39 "I found out very quickly": Whipper interview in Hatch-Billops Oral History, City University of New York. Interviews in the collection conducted between 1970 and 1974.
39 Ella Madison: I am grateful to Charlie Ipcar, whose mother was cared for by Madison, for information on Madison and "All De Gold in De Mountains."
40 "I shall write it": *Musical Canada*, October 1925.
41 "Shutters bang open": From Mamoulian's marked-up copy of the script, Box 115, RMC.
42 "Mamoulian asked to have a lamp": Crawford, *One Naked Individual*.
43 Reviews from the *New York Times*, October 11, 1927; *Evening Sun*, October 11, 1927; *New York World*, October 11, 1927.
44 "I didn't want noise": Birdwell interview.
45 "one of the most moving": Sondheim in the *New York Times*, August 10, 2011. He was complaining about plans to "update" a production of *Porgy and Bess* starring Audra McDonald on Broadway.
45 "That goat doesn't know": RM interviewed in the New York *Herald Tribune*, October 27, 1927
46 "The end of *Porgy*": Bruck interview.

Chapter 3. From Eugene O'Neill to Burlesque

47 "Who is this Rouben Mamoulian?": *New York Herald Tribune*, October 23, 1927.
48 "So I did read the script": Oberstein interview.
49 "It was the court of Kublai Khan": Oberstein interview.
49 The plot of *These Modern Women*: Harold Haynes, a successful writer (Minor Watson) has a "modern" wife, Roberta Watson Coakley (Chrystal Herne), a feminist and a far less successful writer—who is having an affair with their visiting British friend Richard (Alan Mowbray). They have a young son, Bobby (Norman Williams), a strict governess, and an understanding French maid. Roberta says, "After all, my dear, we've got to change marriage to suit

people, not people to suit marriage." She doesn't realize that Harold knows of her own affair, which is slowing him down as a writer and destroying their marriage.

51 Lightfoot leaves the room: Oberstein interview.
51 "He dragged me out": Oberstein interview.
52 "I will not": Gallagher interview.
52 "will have a big future!": letter, RM to his parents, July 2, 1929, RMC.
53 "When I mentioned to you": letter, RM to J. P. McEvoy, March 22, 1929, RMC.
53 "I had to visit": Greenberg interview.
53 "walk around the studio": Gallagher interview.
54 "We'd walk ma-million miles": Such a cherished memory, Mamoulian made several notes about it over the years. RMC.
54 "Sam Harris was there": Chandler, *Hello, I Must Be Going*.
54 Mamoulian dealt: Oral history with Ronald L. Davis, August 1980.
57 "Nobody would do": Ardmore interview.
58 "There already were": Koszarski, *Hollywood on the Hudson*.
58 "So I walked through": Ardmore interview.
59 "I was overwhelmed": Ardmore interview.

Chapter 4. Finding Elissa

60 "made an outstanding fellow": Oberstein interview.
61 Ready for a large part: Edwards, *A Remarkable Woman*.
61 "When one of the major's windy stories": Davis, *The Lonely Life*.
62 "I met Scott Fitzgerald": Greenberg interview.
63 "One very simple thing": undated 1945 letter, Landi to RM, that mentions getting newspapers to read reviews for *Carousel*, RMC.
63 "She was really": All comments by Caroline Thomas in this chapter are from author interview.
63 "Don't dismiss": cablegram, RM to Woods, July 16, 1930, RMC.
64 "As you know": letter, RM to Obermer, June 20, 1931, RMC.
64 "There are many people": *Wall Street Journal*, September 25, 1930.
65 "To put into the role": *Brooklyn Eagle*, September 23, 1930.
65 "I've finally solved": Hemingway to MacLeish, November 22, 1930, published in *Ernest Hemingway: Selected Letters, 1917–1961*.

Chapter 5. Those Darn Cats

66 "Since I have met you": letter, Landi to RM, October 27, 1930. Landi's letters provided by her daughter, Caroline Landi Thomas.
66 "Do you play poker?": Mamoulian, CU, 87–88.
67 "Yes I have a 'pose'": letter, Elissa Landi to Karoline Landi, undated from 1931.

67 "I liked it very much": Greenberg interview.
67 "The story is trash": letter, RM to Horgan, April 28, 1931; "The story was originally planned": letter, RM to Sisk, April 28, 1931, RMC.
68 "There isn't a slight doubt": letter, RM to Sisk, April 23, 1931. RMC.
68 "mostly personality": Gallagher interview.
70 "all decked out": New York *Herald-Tribune*, April 18, 1931.
70 "I didn't like": letter, Sisk to RM, April 23, 1931; "I felt it was open": McKaig to Mamoulian, March 5, 1932, RMC.
71 "Today we would dub it": Adamson interview.
71 The combination of murders, gangsters, and bootlegging ran into bans from censorship boards in Canada, Ireland, and Great Britain. After one Canadian provincial rejection, Paramount executive George Arthur quipped to Mamoulian, "I understand *City Streets* is now being released as a one-reel picture owing to all the cuts being made by the various censor boards." Mamoulian responded, "The idea of releasing *City Streets* as a one-reel picture is a happy one, to say the least. May I take the liberty of suggesting that they put some peppy music to it, insert a snappy little chorus of bare-legged dancers everywhere where originally a murder had occurred, and add to the end a short scene (40 feet would do) of the Marx Brothers telling a joke." Arthur to RM, June 2, 1931; RM to Arthur, June 3, 1931, RMC.
72 "That's what it calls for": Greenberg interview.
72 "Lucile and I": letter, Guy Fraser Harrison to RM, May 4, 1931, RMC.
72 "The PA is deliberately in love": letter, Elissa Landi to Karoline Landi, undated, 1931.
73 "At 6:30 Mrs. Massie and Margel": letter, Elissa Landi to Karoline Landi, April 19, 1931.
73 "We suddenly discovered": letter, RM to McKaig, May 23, 1931, RMC.
73 "I am rather": letter, RM to Harrison, June 11, 1931, RMC.
73 The last time: "I would like to do one or two good plays next fall before I do anything else for the screen." letter, RM to Lawrence Langner, April 20, 1931; at least $1,000: telegram, RM to Langner, June 11, 1931. Mamoulian had received that rate earlier from McKaig (*Solid South*) and Woods (*A Farewell to Arms*); Paul Robeson: letter, RM to Walter Wanger, July 22, 1931; letter, RM to Theresa Helburn, August 31, 1931, RMC.
75 "Strengthens my faith": RM diary, September 12, 1941, RMC.
76 The only thing: Interview in *Filmfax*, No. 29, Oct.–Nov. 1991.
76 "the fiancée": Hobart, *A Steady Digression to a Fixed Point*.
76 "stylish cast" Stevenson, *The Strange Case of Dr. Jekyll and Mr. Hyde*.
76 "I had never met March": Ardmore interview.
76 "She said 'I don't want to play it'": Ardmore interview.

78 "It is not a nude scene": Greenberg interview.
78 "It was done": Prawer, *Caligari's Children*.
79 "To capture the feeling": *Film Journal*, Fall 1973, "Dr. Jekyll and Mr. Hyde: An Interview with Rouben Mamoulian," interview by Thomas R. Atkins.
80 "I didn't take a monster": Stevens, *Interviews*.
80 "So they just put": quoted in Weaver, *Double-Feature Creature Attack!*
80 "I had it raining": Atkins interview.
80 Dropped a kitten: memo, Jason S. Joy to B. P. Schulberg, August 10, 1931, Production Code Administration files, Margaret Herrick Library.
81 "I used to": Hobart quoted in Weaver, *Double-Feature Creature Attack!*
81 "Mamoulian had set up a camera": Quoted in Peterson, *Fredric March*.
81 "Well, I don't know" and "And I was just sobbing": Kobal, *People Will Talk*.
82 "Always photographed": Mamoulian, "Common Sense and Camera Angles," *American Cinematographer*, February 1932.
82 My greatest personal achievements: Letter, RM to McKaig, Aug. 29, 1931, RMC.

Chapter 6. Isn't it Romantic?

83 "The story": letter, RM to Langner, Febuary 24, 1932, RMC.
83 "We got along wonderfully": Rodgers, CU, 135; "fair-haired boy": Rodgers, CU, 143.
83 "The [Ernst] Lubitsch films": Harvey, *Romantic Comedy in Hollywood*.
83 Influences of René Clair: Cousins, *The History of Film*.
84 "I can't remember": Greenberg interview.
84 "deft, airy legerdemain": Milne, *Rouben Mamoulian*.
84 "Zukor said Paramount": Greenberg interview.
84 "said they had": Davis interview.
84 "A fat man": Higham and Greenberg, *The Celluloid Muse*.
85 "This was": R. Rodgers, *Musical Stages*.
85 "as I said, 'Action'": remarks following *Love Me Tonight* screening at University of Southern California, November 8, 1975.
87 "My assistant came to me": Ardmore interview.
90 "Let me tell you this, my dear": Richard Rodgers Collection, Library of Congress.
90 R. Rodgers, *Musical Stages*.
91 "It is our humble opinion": the *Hollywood Reporter*, August 5, 1932; "although he may not reveal": *New York Times*, August 19, 1932; "He has the artist's gift": *Times* (London), November 18, 1932.
91 "This morning's *Examiner*": letter, Landi to RM, June 6, 1932, RMC.

92 "Here I am": undated letter from 1931, Elissa Landi to Karoline Landi.
92 "the miraculous survivor": *Los Angeles Times*, January 22, 1933.

Chapter 7: Dietrich and Garbo

93 "Miss Dietrich is me": Bogdanovich, *Who the Devil Made It*.
94 "unsuitable": *New York Times*, January 5, 1933.
94 "rubbish": Aherne, *A Proper Job*.
94 "It was all right": Higham and Greenburg, *The Celluloid Muse*.
95 "They worked out": Greenberg interview.
95 "straight romantic lead": Aherne, *A Proper Job*.
96 "[Dietrich posed] fully clothed": Greenberg interview.
96 "She did *not*": Correspondence with author through David Riva.
96 "Marlene *did*": Correspondence with author.
97 Boris Lovet-Lorski: telegrams, RM to Lovett-Lorski, January 6, 12, 13, 1933, RMC.
97 "The action seemed to be treated": Hays Office report, Febuary 17, 1933, RMC.
97 "Care must be taken": Hays Office report, Febuary 17, 1933, RMC.
99 "A decent looking": memo, RM to Banton, December 17, 1932, RMC.
99 "To date you have lost twelve days": memo, Kaufman to RM, March 2, 1933; Mamoulian replied: memo, RM to Kaufman, March 4, 1933, RMC.
100 "Had two secret previews": telegram, RM to Dietrich, June 13, 1933, RMC.
100 "She was an immensely educated": Greenberg interview.
101 "I remember on one occasion": Owen, CU, 11.
101 "She said, 'You tell me'": Brownlow interview.
102 "I had to"; Brownlow interview.
102 "And he was subjected": Brownlow interview.
103 "The film was rolling": Behrman, *People in a Diary*.
103 "To my mind": Greenberg interview.
104 "She has just abdicated": Brownlow interview.
104 "Suddenly I remembered"; "So naturally"; "I said, 'Mr. Mayer'": Brownlow interview.
105 "I am so ashamed": quoted in Broman, *Conversations with Greta Garbo*.
106 "Just a little vacation trip": Associated Press, January 18, 1934.
106 Post-*Christina* jaunt: McClellan in *The Girls* maintains that Garbo went on the trip with Mamoulian to get away from her occasional lover, poet and playwright Mercedes de Acosta, and that she discovered afterward that she had contracted gonorrhea. Mamoulian's diaries, when he kept them, were meticulous about documenting doctor visits, and he didn't record any after this trip.

107 Joe Gerwitz: Associated Press, January 15, 1934.
107 "Do people who work in entertainment": Associated Press, Jan. 18, 1934.

Chapter 8: In Which Anna and Miriam Star

108 Sheilah Graham column, February 21, 1937. Other items linking Mamoulian to Michael include Walter Winchell, May 13, 1935 ("Rouben Mamoulian's poopsy is now Gertrude Michael") and Louella Parsons, March 17, 1936. On July 11, 1933, Winchell reported that the romance between Mamoulian and Maris was dying. Going by Hollywood columnists—admittedly not impeccable sources of information—Mamoulian alternated between Maris and Michael up through 1937.
109 "I was given": Kobal, *People Will Talk*.
110 "All melodrama": quoted in Kaneto Shindo's 1975 documentary, *Kenji Mizoguchi*.
110 "Mr. Goldwyn": Sturges, *Preston Sturges*.
110 "Good Boyle Heights types": studio casting memo, June 6, 1934, RMC.
113 "Gentlemen, I throw myself": letter, Thornton Wilder to Isabella N. and Isabel Wilder, August 25, 1934, *The Selected Letters of Thornton Wilder*.
113 "The public stayed away": Berg, *Goldwyn*.
114 "We started working": Brownlow interview.
114 "I am interested": telegram, RM to Helburn, December 10, 1934, RMC.
114 Pneumonia that killed him: United Press, December 29, 1934.
115 "After reading": letter, RM to Lewis Jacobs, July 5, 1971, RMC.
116 "short-circuits": Milne, *Rouben Mamoulian*.
116 "So I started": Gallagher interview.
117 "So I had to make a decision": Gallagher interview. The ballroom sequence includes a seated extra, Thelma Ryan, later First Lady Pat Nixon. Recognizable in the Brittania Hall sequence is Will Geer.
118 "at times fairly shrieks": *Variety*, June 14, 1935; "Too frequently she overacts": New York *Herald Tribune*, June 15, 1935.
118 "the first and only time": Bruck interview.

Chapter 9. My Colored Brainchild

119 "doll dance": This and all other comments from Naida King Rasbury in this chapter are from interview with author.
120 "When did Isolde": *New York Times*, October 11, 1935.
120 "Will the time": *Opportunity*, January 1936.
120 "Entire stage affected": libretto in George Gershwin Collection, Library of Congress (GGC).
120 "Each of the . . . people": *Stage*, October 1935.
120 "fake folklore": *Modern Music*, November 1935.

120 George and Ira Gershwin and Heyward's lyrics: In October 1971, Ira Gershwin, in a letter to Alfred E. Simon, editor of *Encyclopedia of Theatre Music*, gave a specific account of who contributed lyrics. He credited Heyward with all the first-act lyrics and "It Takes a Long Pull to Get There," "Woman to Lady," "What You Want with Bess?," "Time and Time Again," the street cries of the Strawberry Woman and Crab Man, "Oh, De Lawd Shake De Heaven," "Clara, Don't You Be Downhearted," and "On My Way." He credited George and Heyward with "I Got Plenty o'Nuttin,' "Bess, You Is My Woman Now," "I Loves You, Porgy," and "Oh, Doctor Jesus." He credited George with "Oh, I Can't Sit Down," "It Ain't Necessarily So," "A Red-Headed Woman" "There's a Boat Dat's Leavin' Soon for New York" and "Oh Bess, Oh Where's My Bess." Concerning "Bess, You Is My Woman Now," he wrote, "I worked out this duet with George while DuBose was in Charleston. Since, however, I used several of his lines from the libretto I thought it only fair to give him full credit as collaborator. Concerning "Oh, Doctor Jesus": "DuBose's script included a prayer that began with "Oh, Heav'nly Father" or "Oh, Doctor Jesus"—I forget which. Then George decided he wanted to do six prayers to be sung practically simultaneously, so I wrote the additional five. Concerning "Oh Bess, Where Is My Bess" he wrote: "This was worked out by George and me, including the interjected warnings and pleas sung to Porgy by Serena and Maria." Music Division, Library of Congress.

121 Goat named Goo-Goo: name provided by Naida King Rasbury.
122 "I had lunch": letter, Helburn to RM, December 14, 1934, RMC.
122 "I spoke of possible producers" and "They feel that": letter, George Gershwin to DuBose Heyward, December 17, 1934, GGC.
122 "George and Ira": Bruck interview.
123 "Here's my colored brainchild": inscription on Mamoulian's score, RMC.
123 "color scheme": letter, RM to Gershwin, July 18, 1935, RMC.
123 "George was there": Davis interview.
123 "I sang Brahms": *New York Times*, March 29, 1998.
124 Kentucky native: Duncan, interviewed by Robert Wyatt, in Wyatt, ed., *The George Gershwin Reader*.
125 "I said to him, 'Show me all the dance steps'": Oberstein interview.
125 "How do you remember": Bruck interview.
126 "After all, being white": *Michigan Today*, April 21, 1989.
126 Detailed every cut: Hamm, "The Theatre Guild Production of 'Porgy and Bess.'"
126 "crap game is too long": Theatre Guild board notes, October 16, 1935, TGC.
127 "Jasbo Brown": Heyward, *Jasbo Brown and Selected Poems*.
127 "From day to day:" Oberstein interview.

127 "operatic dignity and ceremony": Horowitz, *On My Way*.
128 "For one of Porgy's moments": *Theatre Arts Monthly*, November 19, 1935.
129 "voodoo shadows": *Stage*, October 1935.
129 "I was rehearsing": Davis interview.
130 "Then George decided": Ira Gershwin to Alfred E. Simon, October 25, 1971, GGC.
131 "Perhaps a dozen voices": Heyward in Armitage, *George Gershwin*.
131 "There wasn't a single grouping": Oberstein interview.
131 "I said to him": Oberstein interview.
132 "Bubbles . . . did the whole scene": Bruck interview.
132 "innate aristocracy": Levant, *Memoirs of an Amnesiac*.
132 "got on his high horse": letter, Crouse to RM, December 6, 1935.
133 "The other night": letter, Jessye to RM, December 13, 1935.

Chapter 10: The Folks Who Live on the Hill

134 "I have long cherished": letter, Saroyan to RM, December 28, 1931, RMC; "You have vision": letter, Saroyan to RM, November 3, 1934, RMC.
134 Kaufman tried to negotiate: letter, RM to Kaufman, February 25, 1936, RMC.
136 "The unholy eleven": Youngerman, *My Seventy Years*. Mamoulian's diary indicates that his first meeting concerning the Directors Guild was on January 16, 1936.
136 "It was tough to get": quoted in McBride, *Frank Capra*.
137 "It pokes fun": New York *Herald Tribune*, October 16, 1936.
140 "What we have to do": Weill to Helburn, March 20, 1937, TGC; "I think Mamoulian": Helburn to Weill, April 15, 1937, KWF.
140 "You'll notice in the treatment": letter, Hornblow to RM, October 5, 1936, RMC.
140 "It seemed to be born": Hornblow, CU, 39.
141 "kind of washed up": author interview.
141 "was a very difficult": Higham and Greenberg, *The Celluloid Muse*.
142 "What got me interested": RM remarks after USC screening, November 8, 1975.
143 "Jerome Kern fell seriously ill": Bennett, *The Broadway Sound*.
144 "They had to go": RM remarks at USC screening, November 8, 1975.
145 "The cutter was standing there": Youngerman, *My Seventy Years*.
146 Reviews: *Night and Day*, August 26, 1937; *Variety*, July 22, 1937.
146 "Hokum simply means": *Hartford Courant*, August 8, 1937.
146 Art vacation: RM diary entries, August 9–15, 18–22; September 1, 3–7, 9–29, October 6–30; November 7–22, 1937, RMC.
147 Florence: RM diary, October 8, 1937.
148 "in great excitement": RM diary, October 24, 1937, RMC.

148 "Great day": RM diary, October 23, 1937, RMC. Michelangelo didn't paint the ceiling on his back, but rather standing up using a scaffolding of his own design. The "on his back" version, believed for centuries, is shown in the 1965 film *The Agony and the Ecstasy*, which starred Charlton Heston as the artist.
149 "You gave me a keen appetite for beauty": letter, Mary Anita Loos to RM, December 16, 1936; "It gives me great pleasure": letter, Mary Anita Loos to RM, June 2, 1937.
149 "The last picture": letter, McCarthy to RM, December 7, 1937, RMC.
149 "That silly contract": letter, RM to McCarthy, December 19, 1937, RMC.

Chapter 11: Golden Holden

150 Automobile mishap: RM diary, April 24, 1938, RMC.
150 Tamara Toumanova: Contract dated Jan. 22, 1937, RMC. She never replied to Mamoulian's many letters demanding that she meet with her to discuss her progress. Toumanova (1919–1996) finally went into films in 1944 in *Days of Glory*, playing a Russian damcer rescued from the Germans by a Russian guerrilla played by Gregory Peck.
150 "Goodbye to *Gentleman from Montana*": RM diary, August 4, 1938, RMC.
150 "Jesus, I wanted that story": quoted in McBride, *Frank Capra*.
151 "I'd like to do it.": Mamoulian recalled the sale to McBride for *Frank Capra*.
151 "As you are doubtless aware": letter, Forrest Haring, business manager for Rodgers and Hart, to RM, January 20, 1938, RMC.
151 "If the kid isn't good": undated note from 1986, RMC.
151 "My main difficulty": letter, RM to Obermer, January 11, 1939, RMC.
152 "He was like [Howard]": *Film Comment*, Stanwyck interview with Bernard Drew, March/April 1981.
153 "There was this girl": Oberstein interview.
154 "One very simple": USC remarks, November 8, 1975.
154 "The clux": undated list by RM, RMC.
155 "Mamoulian never wrote": McGilligan, *Backstory 2*.
155 ghost named Luke: Taradash at the ceremony for Mamoulian receiving the D. W. Griffith Award from the Directors Guild of America, August 15, 1982.
155 "This remark, naturally": memo, Levy to Cohn, March 13, 1939, RMC.
156 "So they are killed in a car": Greenberg interview.
157 "Langner's last words": Lewis, *Slings and Arrows*.
157 "Expenses": letter, RM to Helburn, October 10, 1939; "ten thousand thanks": letter, Helburn to RM, October 12, 1939, TGC.

Chapter 12: Mon General Zanuck

158 "May we not meet": letter, Elissa Landi to RM, November 22, 1939, RMC.
158 "Socialist—capitalist": RM diary, January 4, 1940, RMC.

159 "Bored to distraction": RM diary, January 24, 1940; "had to direct": RM diary, January 29, 1940, RMC.
159 "You want the Greek style": letter, Sergei Soudeikine to RM, March 13, 1940, RMC.
159 "It is really impossible": letter, RM to Soudeikine, July 9, 1940, RMC.
159 "wisecracking on the graveyard": RM diary, February 20, 1942, RMC.
160 "A good lay": Francis diary, April 6, 1940, Kay Francis collection, Wesleyan Cinema Archives, Wesleyan University.
160 "Zanuck was a small boy": Hecht, CU, 726–27.
160 "I finished the film": Greenberg interview.
161 "Mr. Zanuck stressed": Fox conference notes, June 19, 1940, RMC.
161 Dedicated to him: note, George Hamilton to RM, August 11, 1981, RMC.
161 "I think we should retake": Memo, Zanuck to RM, August 8, 1940, RMC.
162 "which makes it": Greenberg interview.
162 "Now, Basil": RM remarks following screening of *The Mark of Zorro* at USC, November 8, 1975.
162 "Somehow I think": undated letter from 1940, Hopkins to RM, RMC.
164 "And he never did": Rausch, Andrew J., *Fifty Filmmakers*.
164 "I hated it": quoted in Rausch, *Fifty Filmmakers*.
166 "It wasn't really imitating": Greenberg interview.
166 "With the green faces": Greenberg interview.
166 "He told us": Rausch, *Fifty Filmmakers*.
166 "I said to my two cameramen": Atkins interview.
167 "Well, she's got a blue dress": Gallagher interview.
168 "Now, where do you go": Gallagher interview.
169 "I am absolutely disgusted": memo, Zanuck to RM, March 4, 1941, RMC.
169 "I have worked": memo, Zanuck to RM, March 6, 1941, RMC.
169 "At least, you must confess": memo, RM to Zanuck, May 5, 1941, RMC.
169 Fifty-three shooting days: Fox memo, May 2, 1941, RMC.
170 "there is too little drama": *New York Times*, May 23, 1941.
170 "It is my belief": memo, Zanuck to RM, June 4, 1941. A May 24 memo from studio executive Herman Webber to Zanuck indicated that the film was not performing well in New York.
170 "Rabbit": RM diary entries include August 1–5, August 9 to September 11, September 15, October 8, December 25, 1941; January 30 through March 11, 1942, RMC.
172 "Let it be understood": memo, Zanuck to Sperling and RM, November 18, 1941, RMC.
172 "least important": Greenberg interview.
173 Carradine's schooner: production of *Rings on her Fingers* is from RM diary, December 2, 5–7, 8–13, 15–27, 30–31, 1941; January 2–29, 1942.

173 "This huge money": Tierney, *Self-Portrait*.
173 Shortly before *Rings*: RM diary, January 23, 1942, RMC.
174 "a generous measure": RM diary, December 14, 1941, RMC.
174 Tierney's house: RM diary, May 3, 1942, RMC.
174 "lynx-eyed": *Time*, March 31, 1945.
174 "From a bottle": author interview.
175 "I think you two": Los Angeles *Herald-Express*, October 8, 1958.
175 "You should be painted": Los Angeles *Herald-Examiner*, August 30, 1976.
175 "It is impossible": letter, Newman to RM, November 12, 1942, RMC.
175 "I see your sulky lips": poem dated November 14, 1942, RMC.
175 "That is, I": letter, RM to Helburn, August 22, 1942, RMC.
176 "Sorry, the play": telegram, RM to Helburn, August 26, 1942, RMC.
176 Over lunch: RM diary, September 22, 1942, RMC.

Chapter 13: A Bright Golden Haze

177 "magic moment": Oberstein interview.
177 "I remember, in rehearsal": Rodgers, CU, 230–31.
178 "Every Arcadia contains": Carter, *Oklahoma!*
178 "You realize that": Oberstein interview.
178 "musical comedy structure": Becvar interview.
180 "I became a tyrant": *Ararat*, spring 1964. A quarterly publication of the Armenian General Benevolent Union in New York.
181 "an autocratic dictator": de Mille, *Dance to the Piper*.
181 "the Guild is past its prime": *Time*, November 23, 1942.
181 "my business commitment": letter, RM to Schlosburg, Jan. 11, 1943, RMC.
181 "His argument to Lasky": telegram, Lyons to RM, February 2, 1943, RMC.
181 "Divorce granted": telegram, Azadia Newman to RM, January 14, 1943, RMC.
182 "were flatteringly eager": RM's undated revision notes for CU oral history.
182 "They said I could do it": RM, CU draft notes.
182 "The most radical thing": Hammerstein, CU, 24.
184 "After one run of it": Wilk, *OK!*
184 "I remember": Wilk, *OK!*
185 "He injected": Roberts, *Never Alone*.
185 "instruct a stage": Bennett in Oberstein, "*The Broadway Directing Career of Rouben Mamoulian*."
185 "at the beginning": Rodgers, *Musical Stages*.
185 "They're certainly not pretty": de Mille, *Dance to the Piper*.
185 "I do remember": Secrest, *Somewhere for Me*.
186 "All it did": author interview.
186 "Personally, I don't think": undated RM account, RMC.

186 "to put a little more realism": Roberts, *Never Alone*.
186 Michael Todd: Rodgers, *Musical Stages*; "The actual phrase was": Rodgers, CU, 239.
186 "I told Dick and Oscar": Oberstein interview.
186 "I wish you and Dick": remarks written for Helburn's memorial service, August 20, 1959, RMC.
186 Holm recalled: Wilk, *OK!*
187 "he staged it": author interview.
187 "I staged it": Becvar interview.
187 "Rouben thinks they have a hit": undated 1943 letter, Azadia Newman to Virginie Mamoulian, RMC.
187 "The show is a solid success": letter, Hammerstein to Riggs, March 23, 1943, OHC.
187 "No one even spoke": Oberstein interview.
187 "as one beautiful song": Langner, *The Magic Curtain*.
187 "One thing": author interview.
189 Critics: all reviews published April 1, 1943.
189 "Mamoulian had his own ideas": New York *Daily Mirror*, June 13, 1943.
189 "That Mamoulian be stopped": letter, Rodgers to Theatre Guild, June 15, 1943, OHC and TGC.
189 called Mamoulian: Mentioned in RM diary, June 15, 1943, RMC.
189 Recorded phone call: transcript, June 16, 1943, TGC.
190 "unfriendly and carping": letter, RM to Theatre Guild board, June 23, 1943, RMC.
190 "Terry is entitled": letter, Langner to Rodgers, August 11, 1943, TGC. Mamoulian evidently got wind of this, writing Langner: "Believe me, Lawrence, I am not knocking you and am always referring to you as my friend. Your mystifyingly erratic and unfair attitude in New York I have forgotten. As to our long friendship—I am, I assure you, most conscious of it, and I hope and believe that in the future it will prove itself much more solid than it has in the recent past." Letter, RM to Langner, September 15, 1943, RMC.
190 "About the article": letter, Langner to RM, Oct. 25, 1943, TGC.
191 "It is sheer magic!": letter, Anita Loos to RM, October 5, 1943, RMC.
191 "Sam Goldwyn drooled"; "Instead of dropping in": letter, Oscar Hammerstein to William Hammerstein, April 22, 1943, OHC.

Chapter 14: Otto and Ethel

192 *Son of Zorro*: letter, RM to Zanuck, September 23, 1943, RMC.
192 *Rhapsody in Blue*: The scene was supposed to end with a montage of faces, including Black faces.

193 "You will never direct again": Preminger's account to Peter Bogdanovich appearing in this chapter is from his *On Film* interview published in fall 1970 and republished in Bogdanovich, *Who the Devil Made It.*
194 "He had that extra dimension": Greenberg interview.
194 "I've never thought of you": *San Mateo Times*, November 19, 1976.
194 "I am delighted": telegram, Zanuck to Preminger and Mamoulian, May 1, 1944, RMC.
194 "Zanuck decided": *San Mateo Times*, November 16, 1976.
195 Bogdanovich, *Who the Devil Made It.*
195 Bogdanovich, *Who the Devil Made It.*
195 Bogdanovich, *Who the Devil Made It.*
195 "I didn't have to quit it": Becvar interview.
196 Portrait: Tierney, *Self-Portrait.*
196 "I wish to state": letter, RM to *On Film*, November 29, 1970, RMC.
196 "What the": Kellow, *Ethel Merman.*
196 "There was a line": Merman, *Don't Call Me Madam.*
197 "Good news": telegram, RM to Dietz, May 14, 1944.
198 Leonore Ulric: RM diary, July 10, 1944, RMC.
198 "At a late hour": telegram, Dietz to RM, September 19, 1944, RMC.
199 "Young lady left tonight": telegram, Cole to RM, September 25, 1944, RMC.
199 "talented, but lacked the voice": Dietz, *Dancing in the Dark.*
199 "This isn't a voice": Earl Wilson column, November 30, 1944.
199 "rather pontifically highbrow": Duke, *Passport to Paris.*
200 "You have made my dream": Note, Havoc to RM, Oct. 23, 1944, RMC.
200 Reviews: All dated November 17, 1944.
200 "A little man": Bozeman, *Broadway Babylon.*

Chapter 15. A Real Nice Clambake

202 "as the beginning": *Cue*, April 14, 1945.
202 "We are writing it": Hammerstein to Marfield, November 14, 1944, OHC; "was in degree operatic": *Boston Post*, April 8, 1945.
202 "I always felt it was an opera": Walker to Ted Chapin, October 7, 1987, files of the Rodgers & Hammerstein Organization.
203 "Had little moments": This and other Virginia Moise Collins comments in this chapter are from author interview.
203 "As I remember": author interview.
203 "I came back here": Davis interview.
204 "in that meeting": *Newsday*, February 22, 1993.
204 "I think that": Fitelson to Helburn, August 30, 1944, TGC.

204 "The office has canvassed": telegram, Ralph Blum to Mamoulian, December 7, 1944, RMC.
205 "entire dream of heaven": Theatre Guild conference notes, January 20, 1944, TGC.
206 "I've asked a number": Helburn memo to Rodgers and Hammerstein, December 17, 1943, TGC.
206 "for musical purposes": Theatre Guild conference memo, December 17, 1944, TGC.
206 "I had finished": This and all other Darling comments in this chapter are from author interview.
207 "money grabber." Marshall memo, August 4, 1944, TGC.
207 "Dick only has one song": Langner to Helburn, January 29, 1945, TGC.
208 "I know": Hedda Hopper column, Feb. 14, 1945.
208 "The problem was": Oberstein interview.
208 "What a lovely job": Fearnley to RM, December 27, 1945, RMC.
208 "I must say": Tierney to RM, March 13, 1945; "If the new": Landi to RM, June 22, 1945, RMC.
209 "Mamoulian asked me": John Raitt, undated letter to Bennett Oberstein.
210 "gradual rise": Becvar interview.
210 Mamoulian intended to end the first act with a *Porgy and Bess* echo. Darling said a ringing buoy interrupted a reprise of "June" and as the curtain fell, the cast was supposed to be "frightened by the awful omen." Musical arranger Hans Spialek composed some storm effects. That would have been nearly identical to the dread provoked by the hurricane bell or maybe Porgy's buzzard. Since there isn't a storm or a shipwreck in the second act, the buoy wouldn't have made sense.
211 "I also suggest": letter, Langner to Helburn, March 8, 1922, TGC.
211 "The organ diminishes": Hammerstein outline for Act 2, Scene 5, OHC.
212 "Milton Cohen!": author interview.
213 "just plain silly": *Boston Post*, April 1, 1945.
213 "Well, where should I put": *Boston Herald*, June 11, 1999.
213 "But when we opened in Boston": Davis interview.
214 "So as we were walking": Davis interview.

Chapter 16: Come Rain or Come Shine

218 "I myself": Mercer's unpublished memoir is with his collected papers at Georgia State University.
218 "I knew the book": Horne and Shickel, *Lena*.
219 "I 'report' to the studio": letter, RM to Hammerstein, October 27, 1945, RMC.

Notes

219 "The show was a pretty sad mess": letter, RM to Brecher, March 6, 1946, RMC.
221 "I told them": Oberstein interview.
221 "The last line of the scene": RM memo, January 18, 1946, RMC.
222 "stopped the show": *Billboard*, April 6, 1946.
222 Funeral scene: Bailey, *The Raw Pearl*.
223 "He is again": RM memo, January 18, 1946, RMC.
223 Reviews: both dated April 1, 1946.
224 "Believe best procedure": telegram, Rodgers to RM, June 19, 1946, RMC.
225 "I sensed": Rooney, *Life Is Too Short*.
225 "I ducked seeing": letter, O'Neill to Dudley Nichols, December 4, 1948, published in *Selected Letters of Eugene O'Neill*.
225 "It is so far removed": *New Republic*, June 28, 1948.
226 "appreciated talent": Davis interview.
226 "Mamoulian's attitude": Worsley, *From Oz to E.T.*
226 "As just one example": RM memo, December 28, 1945, RMC
227 "It was especially hard": Worsley, *From Oz to E.T.*
228 "It amused me": Greenberg interview.
228 "sensational hit tune": RM memo, Dec. 28, 1945.
229 "There is a camera thing": Greenberg interview.
229 "cute little thing": Davis interview.
230 "the very bad phrase": memo, Vogel to Freed, July 17, 1946, RMC.
230 "I had a new version": RM in Fordin, *The World of Entertainment!*

Chapter 17: Found in the Stars

231 "Have been trying to reach you": telegram, Weill to RM, April 20, 1949, RMC.
231 "The joke was": This and the rest of Gray's comments in this chapter are from author interview.
232 *Polk County*: letter, Stephen Kelen d'Oxylion to RM, September 16, 1944, RMC.
232 "We have considered": letter, Loos to Mamoulian, December 7, 1947, RMC.
232 Arnold Weissberger: RM diary, October 29, 1948, RMC.
232 "I have directed": letter, RM to Loos, January 27, 1947, RMC.
232 Series of harsh missives: beginning with a letter from his lawyer, William Jaffe, July 27, 1948, RMC.
233 "I am excited"; "it appears rather"; "the high point": RM memo to Hayes, September 4, 1948, RMC.
234 Reviews: *Billboard* January 29, 1949; *Time*, January 31, 1949.
236 "We will be lucky": *New York Times*, October 31, 1949.

237 "I do think": letter, de Mille to Anderson, April 24, 1949, MAC.
237 "It began to seem": Anderson diary, April 9, 1949, MAC.
237 "moved and most intelligent": Anderson diary, April 23, 1949, MAC.
237 "it's on": RM diary, May 4, 1949, RMC.
237 "doesn't have a chance": Oberstein interview.
237 "Every laugh": RM memo, August 27, 1949, RMC.
238 "They liked his looks": auditions were held at the Imperial Theatre. RMC.
238 "The Playwrights' Company is anxious to find": draft of letter signed by Brinkmann, June 3, 1949, RMC.
238 "This is also": letter, Brinkmann to Samrock, Sept. 10, 1949, KWF.
239 "The meaning of the play": transcript of RM's remarks, RMC.
240 "This happens often"; "Several objections": Andy Anderson's weekly report dated November 6, 1949, RMC.
241 "I think I said this": Duncan oral history, KWF.
241 "Mamoulian was for me": quoted in Stott with Stott, *On Broadway*.
242 "Let's have a sweeping, powerful aria": RM memo, August 27, 1949, RMC.
242 "I think once or twice": Duncan oral history, KWF.
244 "But I never felt": Duncan oral history, KWF.
244 "If the story is to be true": letter, Paton to Anderson, June 22, 1949, MAC.
244 "I will always remember": quoted in Stott with Stott, *On Broadway*.
244 Reviews: all dated November 1, 1949.
245 "The Negro can sit": letter, Brinkmann to RM, October 14; "The cast is like a keg of dynamite," October 10; no segregated seating, October 17; "There is an awful lot of hatred," November 2, 1950.
245 "So, a beautiful work of art": letter, RM to Duncan, November 9, 1950, RMC.

Chapter 18: Mamoulian Marches On

246 Reviews: both dated February 3, 1950.
249 "I went to see": Jack Gaver, "Up and Down Broadway" *United Press*, January 3, 1950.
249 "In view of the fact": memo, William Fitelson to Theatre Guild board, June 17, 1949, TGC.
249 "would try to work": Marshall memo, June 20, 1949, TGC.
250 "Dorothy and Herb": Goodman, *American Salute*.
250 "willing to compromise": memo, Fitelson to Theatre Guild board, July 22, 1949, TGC.
250 "There were two things": Oberstein interview.
251 "I was frightened": Syndicated article under Nanette Fabray's byline, Dec. 9, 1956.

Notes

251 "He is rather wondering": letter, Foster to Whyte, April 26, 1949, TGC.
252 "Bailey and others": letter, Jett to Helburn, January 19, 1950, OHC.
252 "an example of the silly and screwball thinking": letter, Hammerstein to Helburn, January 31, 1950, OHC.
252 "Miss Bailey's role": published by wire services on February 7, 1950.
252 Noon conference: RM diary, February 10, 1950.
252 "I'd have walked": *New York Times*, February 12, 1950.
252 "What about George": RM memo, September 2, 1949, RMC.
252 "So in Boston": Goodman, *American Salute*.
253 "I must confess": letter, Helburn to Fields, May 10, 1950, TGC.
253 "Several times": letter, Anderson to RM, July 1, 1950, RMC.
253 "Is it their object?": transcript of Directors Guild meeting, October 22, 1950, as used in Eyman, *Empire of Dreams*.
254 DeMille's mispronunciations: Eyman, *Empire of Dreams*.
254 "A little nervous": Eyman, *Empire of Dreams*.
254 FBI file: Mamoulian's FBI record is File 100-HQ-361511.
255 "*Boheme* I admire": letter, Bing to RM, January 16, 1950, RMC.
256 "beginning two projects": letter, RM to Bing, February 16, 1951.
256 "I noticed that I'd rehearse": Greenberg interview.
256 "well aware": Challis, *Are They Really So Awful?*
257 "Are you interested": telegram, Breen to RM, January 28, 1952, RMC.
257 "operating losses": telegram, Breen to RM, January 28, 1952, RMC.
257 "Although the delays were unfortunate": telegram, Leonore and Ira Gershwin to RM, April 3, 1952, RMC.
257 Turned it down: Mamoulian wrote to Arnold Weissberger that he was "feeling in full honesty that the time allowed intended for preparation was inadequate" and that a production of that scope "surely requires more than two or three weeks preparation.": letter, RM to Weissberger, April 24, 1952, RMC.
258 Nelson Eddy et al.: RM note, December 20, 1952, RMC.
258 "And the effects": Bob Hope joke file, Recorded Sound Division, Library of Congress. The line including "go to Copenhagen" is a reference to Christine Jorgensen (1926–89), the first person in the United States to become widely known for having sex-reassignment surgery, performed in Denmark in 1952.
258 "I don't know who it was": letter, Cukor to Warren, May 1, 1953, George Cukor Collection, Margaret Herrick Library.
259 "One of the most memorable": Rodgers, *My Favorite Things*.
260 "I was invited": Dante, *From Hollywood*.
261 "pre-production work": RM diary, Feb. 25, 1955, RMC.
261 "Moody Rod Steiger": RM diary, May 19, 1955; Steiger was quitting; "flies off again"; he was out: RM diary, May 22, June 5, June 9, 1955, RMC.

Notes

261 "All the reviews": letter, RM to Rodgers and Hammerstein, July 15, 1955. At the June 28 performance, at which Jones lost her voice, RM recorded that one audience member shouted at her, "*Parley Francais!*" RMC.
261 Jean Bradley: RM diary, July 20, August 9, 11, 12, 1955, RMC.

Chapter 19. Breathtaking Cinemascope

262 "Worried me no end": RM diary, July 15, 1955, RMC.
262 Davis as Li'l Augie: RM diary, January 6, 1956, RMC.
263 "Well, there's no dancing": Davis interview.
264 "has some of the best": Thomson, *New Biographical Dictionary of Film*.
264 "very rough, rude" and "Ninotchka": RM memo, July 12, 1956, RMC.
264 "be able to sleep at night": RM diary, July 26, 1956, RMC.
264 "As soon as": quoted in Fordin, *The World of Entertainment!*
265 Dance concepts: RM memo, August 30, 1956, RMC.
265 "They go off": Davis interview.
266 "the same thrill of magic": Milne, *Rouben Mamoulian*.
266 "I had seen": New York *World-Telegram and Sun*, August 5, 1957.
267 "Most of the time:" Youngkin, *The Lost One*.
267 "He was taking": *San Francisco Chronicle*, March 19, 2004.
267 "spells some dire punishment": RM diary, January 2, 1957, RMC.
267 "She's not strong": Fordin, *The World of Entertainment!*
267 "silent applause!": author interview.
268 "The whole thing is": Greenberg interview.
268 "Discussed shot": RM diary, January 19, 1957, RMC.
268 "I said, What on earth": Greenberg interview
269 "[I] would like to direct a Western": RM diary, March 25, 1957, RMC.
269 "the more he investigates": RM diary, August 12, 1959. Mamoulian hosted the Reagans at dinner parties on June 21 and August 7, 1958, and his diary records that on September 11, 1961, Reagan called with a list of "good authentic Western writers."

Chapter 20: Perfidy and *Bess*

270 "we couldn't see eye to eye": Goldwyn statement of July 27, 1958, appeared in *Variety* and wire service articles; "The trouble with these directors": United Press, August 17, 1958.
271 Milton Pickman: letter, Pickman to RM, December 6, 1954, RMC.
271 $650,000 and 10 percent: the percentage breakdown: Theatre Guild 33⅓, Dorothy Heyward 15, the estate of DuBose Heyward 15, the estate of George Gershwin's mother Rose Gershwin 30, and Ira Gershwin 6⅔.
271 "Money he doesn't need": United Press, August 17, 1958.
271 "She's become": RM diary, July 5, 1957, RMC.

272 "Saw Goldwyn last night": RM diary, September 27, 1957, RMC.
272 "Good! That stylized!": Becvar interview.
272 Lemon tree arrangement: RM's gift list for 1957, RMC.
272 "Good face": RM note, November 6, 1958; "wants to remain": RM diary, November 6, 1958, RMC.
272 "on your life": Berg, *Goldwyn*.
273 "Certain things I will play": Poitier statement of November 10, 1958, RMC.
273 "Do you actually think": Oberstein interview.
273 "I am happy to say": press conference transcript, SGC.
273 "Before you open your mouth": Becvar interview.
273 Sugar Ray Robinson: RM diary, January 22, 1958, RMC.
273 "the racial stereotypes": Carroll, *Diahann!*
273 "I have chosen"; "with the trumpeter"; "No watermelons": production conference transcript, June 3, 1958, RMC.
273 "He liked to": Horowitz, *On My Way*.
274 "He got into the habit": Easton, *The Search for Goldwyn*.
274 "Concerning Ira Gershwin": Undated note, RMC.
275 First explosion: All quotes from Sam Goldwyn to RM for the rest of this chapter are from RM's August 20, 1958, transcript for Jerry Giesler, RMC.
275 "would like you to dictate": memo, Birdwell to RM, June 16, 1958, RMC.
275 "Mamoulian was one of the greats": Curtis with Vieira, *The Making of Some Like It Hot*.
275 "I like to treat Sporting Life": production conference transcript, June 16, 1958, RMC.
276 Darby called Mamoulian: RM diary, June 16, 1958, RMC.
276 "Louis Johnson": undated RM note, RMC.
278 "his name is Goldwyn!": from RM's transcript of August 20, 1958.
278 "he was terribly upset": note from secretary, July 11, 1958, RMC.
278 "Officially brought": RM diary, July 3, 1958, RMC.
278 "In regard to": RM diary, July 21, 1958, RMC.
279 "Will see S.": RM diary, July 24, 1958, RMC.
279 "merely to insist": *Hollywood Reporter*, July 31, 1958.
279 "He and I": various news outlets including *Variety*, July 28, 1958.
279 "Mr. Goldwyn's bland statement": Various news outlets including *Variety*, July 28, 1958.
279 "Ford on rampage": RM diary, July 28, 1958, RMC.
279 "I felt betrayed": Hedda Hopper column, July 30, 1958.
279 "I knew nothing": *Los Angeles Times*, July 31, 1958. Preminger signed with Goldwyn on July 29.
280 "Vitally important": telegram, Goldwyn to Lazar, July 31, 1958, SGC.

280 "that Goldwyn wanted to settle": telegram, Lazar to Joe Schonefeld of *Variety*, August 11, 1958, SGC.
280 "I believe that": news reports of August 6, 1958. Preminger appeared before the DGA board after this accusation, telling them, "I'm Jewish. I ran away from Hitler. How can they say I'm anti-Negro?" *Variety*, August 11, 1958.
280 "a very sensitive man": *Chicago Defender*, August 23, 1958.
280 "Called Helen": RM diary, September 8, 9, 12, 1958, RMC.
281 "replacing a great director with a plumber": RM diary, January 30, 1959, RMC.
281 Pickman had written him: letter, Pickman to RM, January 23, 1959, RMC.
281 "hemmed and hawed": RM diary, February 3, 1959, RMC.
281 "After prolonged discussion": Stevens to RM, letters dated March 3 and 11, 1959, RMC.
281 "Perfidious and in my case": undated RM notes, RMC.
282 "June Levant": RM diary, July 16, 1959, RMC.

Chapter 21. Dulce et decorum est Cleopatra mori

283 On November 8: The description of what was filmed and the nightly conditions in London are described in detail in the daily 20th Century Fox production memos. RMC.
284 "I only did it": Brownlow interview.
285 "Very pleasant": RM diary, May 27, 1959, RMC.
285 Bulldozers on the back lot: RM diary, May 29, 1959, RMC.
285 "has a favorite candidate": RM diary, September 2, 1959, RMC. Although it is impossible to know the name of Feldman's "girlfriend" with complete certainty, news articles from that time indicate it likely was the French actress Capucine; "wants too much money," "completely wrong," RM diary, September 8, 1959, RMC.
286 "unceasing cold, rain and fog": letter, RM to Olga Signorelli, March 6, 1962, RMC.
286 "Little Liza": RM diary, May 15, 1960, RMC.
286 "Echoes of Goldwyn": RM diary, January 22, 1959; Serling's teleplay "*The Velvet Alley*" starred Art Carney as screenwriter Ernie Pandish; "too preoccupied": RM diary, November 3, 1959, RMC.
286 "wanted a love story": Wasserman, *The Impossible Musical*.
287 "It's just a polish job": letter, Wanger to RM, March 14, 1960, RMC.
287 "It is pretty good": letter, Durrell to RM, April 3, 1960; "the more I looked": letter, Durrell to RM, May 2, 1960, RMC.
287 "For every good speech": memo, Wanger to RM, July 27, 1960, RMC.
287 "my pet ideas": revised continuity notes, RM to Durrell, April 11, 1960, RMC.
287 "poison": RM diary, December 14, 1959, RMC.

288 Before January 1961: RM diary, December 11, 1959; after RM looked at the 1956 film *Alexander the Great* and discussed Burton with casting agent Nora Roberts, RMC.
288 "Rouben, who was supposed to stay a week": Wanger with Hyams, *My Life with Cleopatra*.
288 "From secret sources": letter, Wald to Wanger, June 14, 1960, RMC.
288 "Elizabeth is so susceptible": letter, Wanger to Bautzer, July 20, 1960, RMC.
288 "She has read the 50 pages": RM diary, July 30, 1960, RMC.
289 "I wish we could afford": letter, RM to Skouras, July 20, 1960, RMC.
289 "I had an idea": Brownlow interview.
290 "Hail, Caesar!": Scene first submitted by Brandel on July 15, 1960, with revisions dated September 2, 13, 19, 21, and 28, RMC.
290 "Liz has a cold": Wanger with Hyams, *My Life with Cleopatra*. From this point on, unless otherwise noted, all of Wanger's comments are from this published work. A studio memo of September 29 says Taylor is "indisposed"; RMC.
290 Respiratory infection: Associated Press, October 19, 1960, quoting an unnamed spokesman for Taylor.
291 "Dulce et decorum": Note from Brandel to RM, Oct. 6, 1960, RMC.
291 "They said that the prince": Brownlow interview.
291 "Jack called Jenny from work": letter, Violet Herschenson to RM, December 9, 1960, RMC.
293 "Her majesty, the queen of Egypt!": Undated by Johnson, RMC. Tellingly, this was not part of Mamoulian's shooting script.
293 "Did you ever": Johnson, letter to Groucho Marx, February 7, 1961, Groucho Marx letters, Library of Congress.
294 "Tests of Taylor's": RM diary, December 28, 1960.
294 "Liz has laryngitis and cramps": RM diary, December 30, 1960, RMC.
294 "Nunnally keeps rehashing"; RM diary, January 3, 1961, RMC.
294 "A deaf man": RM diary, January 12, 1961, RMC.
294 "California out": RM diary, January 16, 1961, RMC.
295 "Mr. Fisher telephoned": RM secretary's note, January 17, 1961.
295 "Sent cable to Skouras": RM diary, January 18, 1961.
295 "If you had listened to me": cablegram, RM to Skouras, January 18, 1961, RMC..
295 "Record will show": cablegram, Skouras to RM, January 19, 1961, RMC.
295 "Elizabeth won't do the picture": RM diary, January 18, 1961, RMC.
296 "Had to order"; "dropped Eddie"; "took the phone": RM diary, January 22, 1961, RMC.
296 "Rudeness to all": Memo dated January 19, 1961, Walter Wanger collection, State Historical Society of Wisconsin.

296 *What's My Line?*: RM diary, April 2, 1961, RMC. The mystery celebrity on the CBS program that night was June Allyson.
297 "we were great friends"; "Many people asked": RM diary, June 28, 1961.
297 "You survived": RM diary, July 9, 1961, RMC.

Chapter 22: Leavin' Time

300 "An elongated gossip column": RM diary, June 14, 1963, RMC.
300 "Said he heard": RM diary, June 7, 1962, RMC.
300 "Quite a wonderful": RM diary, December 28, 1962, RMC.
300 Black-tie dinner party: Mike Connolly column, *The Desert Sun*, Sept. 10, 1958.
300 Impromptu party: RM diary, December 14, 1962.
300 "Have suggested you": telegram, undated, DeSilva to RM. They met on June 20, 1963, according to RM's diary.
301 "couldn't touch anything": Oberstein interview.
301 *Tevye (To Life)*: RM diary, August 5, 1963; "I am talking to Jack Warner": letter, Tobias to RM, October 26, 1966, RMC.
301 Taped interview: RM diary, November 2, 1964, RMC.
301 Irving Berlin: RM diary, December 12, 1964.
302 Hamlet reviews in *Atlantic Monthly*, April 1966; *Saturday Review*, March 5, 1966.
302 Roger Stevens: RM diary, July 29, 1966, RMC.
303 "came over to talk": RM diary, April 11, 1969, RMC.
303 David Bradley: RM diary, January 1, 1970, RMC; "slipped and fell": Higham, *In and Out of Hollywood*.
303 "I can forgive": Robert Bamberger, "Mamoulian's Cry for an End to the Dullness of the Heart," (UCLA undergraduate paper), November 29, 1971. Bamberger recalls, "I do not recall an inappropriate audience response, but there you are. I went up to Miss Hopkins and said what a great honor it was to have her join us, to which she replied. 'Thank you. Where's the drinking fountain?'" Author correspondence.
303 "What a day": RM diary, August 10, 1972. Other entries dated August 6, 8, 9, 1972, RMC.
304 "She was": All Miles Kreuger comments in this chapter are from author interview.
305 "I was just wondering": DGA recording, Recorded Sound Division, Library of Congress.
306 "using a cane": All Arby Ovanessian comments in this chapter are from author interview.
306 "of my grandfather": All Zaghik Gourjian comments in this chapter are from author interview.

307 "chairs, settees": Associated Press, December 11, 1987.
307 "All other artists": essay fragment dated April 5, 1940, RMC.
308 Tolstoy, *What Is Art?*
308 "The epic dimension": Horowitz, *On My Way*.
308 "At times": Thomson, *New Biographical Dictionary of Film*.
309 "You'll notice that in all art": Oberstein interview.

Bibliography

Published Sources

Aherne, Brian. *A Proper Job*. New York: Houghton Mifflin, 1969.

Alexander, Doris. *Eugene O'Neill's Creative Struggle*. University Park: Penn State University Press, 1992.

Bach, Steven. *Marlene Dietrich: Life and Legend*. New York: Morrow, 1992.

Bailey, Pearl. *The Raw Pearl*. New York: Harcourt, Brace & World, 1968.

Bainbridge, John. *Garbo*. New York: Galahad Books, 1971.

Baker, Carlos, ed. *Ernest Hemingway: Selected Letters, 1917–1961*. New York: Scribner, 1981.

Behrman, S. N. *People in a Diary*. Boston: Little, Brown, 1972.

Bennett, Robert Russell. *The Broadway Sound: The Autobiography and Selected Essays of Robert Russell Bennett*. Rochester, NY: University of Rochester Press, 1999.

Berg, A. Scott. *Goldwyn*. New York: Knopf, 1989.

Bogard, Travis, and Jackson R. Bryer, eds. *Selected Letters of Eugene O'Neill*. New Haven, CT: Yale University Press, 1988.

Bogdanovich, Peter. *Who the Devil Made It*. New York: Knopf, 1997.

Bradford, Roark. *Ol' Man Adam and His Chillun*. New York: Harper & Row, 1928.

Brayer, Elizabeth. *George Eastman*. Rochester, NY: University of Rochester Press, 2006.

Broman, Sven. *Conversations with Greta Garbo*. New York: Viking, 1992.

Bryer, Jackson, and Robin Gibbs Wilder, eds. *The Selected Letters of Thornton Wilder*. New York: Harper, 2008.

Carroll, Diahann, and Ross Firestone. *Diahann!* New York: Little, Brown & Co., 1986.

Carter, Tim: *Oklahoma! The Making of an American Musical*. New Haven, CT: Yale University Press, 2007.

Challis, Christopher. *Are They Really So Awful?* Concord, MA: Paul and Co., 1995.
Chandler, Charlotte. *Hello, I Must Be Going.* New York: Doubleday, 1978.
Cousins, Mark. *The Story of Film.* London: Pavilion Books, 2013.
Crawford, Cheryl. *One Naked Individual: My Fifty Years in the Theatre.* Indianapolis: Bobbs-Merrill, 1977.
Curtis, James. *Between Flops.* New York: Harcourt Brace Jovanovich, 1982.
Curtis, Tony, with Mark A. Vieira. *The Making of Some Like It Hot: My Memories of Marilyn Monroe and the Classic American Movie.* New York: Wiley, 2009.
Dante, Michael. *From Hollywood to Michael Dante Way.* Orlando, FL: BearManor Media, 2013.
Davis, Bette. *The Lonely Life.* New York: G. P. Putnam's Sons, 1962.
de Mille, Agnes. *Dance to the Piper.* Boston: Little, Brown, 1952.
———. *Promenade Home.* Boston: Little, Brown, 1956.
Dietz, Howard. *Dancing in the Dark.* New York: Quadrangle, 1974.
Duke, Vernon. *Passport to Paris.* Boston: Little, Brown, 1955.
Easton, Carol. *No Intermission: The Life of Agnes de Mille.* New York: Da Capo Press, 2000.
———. *The Search for Goldwyn.* New York: William Morrow, 1976.
Edwards, Anne. *A Remarkable Woman: A Biography of Katharine Hepburn.* New York: William Morrow, 1985.
Ewen, David. *George Gershwin: His Journey to Greatness.* Englewood Cliffs, NJ: Prentice Hall, 1970.
Eyman, Scott. *Empire of Dreams.* New York: Simon & Schuster, 2010.
———. *The Speed of Sound: Hollywood and the Talkie Revolution, 1926–1930.* New York: Simon & Schuster, 1997.
Fehl, Fred, and William Stott. *On Broadway: Performance Photographs by Fred Stehl.* Austin: University of Texas Press, 1978.
Fordin, Hugh. *The World of Entertainment! MGM's Greatest Musicals!* Garden City, NY: Doubleday, 1975.
Gaver, Jack. *Curtain Calls.* New York: Dodd, Mead, 1949.
Geist, Kenneth L. *Pictures Will Talk: The Life and Films of Joseph L. Mankiewicz.* New York: Da Capo Press, 1978.
Gelb, Arthur, and Barbara Gelb. *O'Neill.* New York: Harper & Row, 1974.
Goodman, Peter. *American Salute.* Portland, OR: Amadeus Press, 2000.
Gordon, Mel. *The Stanislavski Technique: A Workbook for Actors.* New York: Applause, 1987.
Hadleigh, Boze. *Broadway Babylon.* New York: Random House, 2007.
Hamm, Charles. "The Theatre Guild Production of 'Porgy and Bess.'" *Journal of the American Musicological Society* 40, no. 3 (1987): 495–532.
Harvey, James. *Romantic Comedy in Hollywood from Lubitsch to Sturges.* New York: Knopf, 1987.

Helburn, Theresa. *Wayward Quest*. Boston: Little, Brown, 1960.
Hemingway, Ernest. *A Farewell to Arms*. New York: Scribner's Sons, 1929.
Heyward, DuBose. *Porgy*. New York: George H. Doran, 1925.
———. *Jasbo Brown and Selected Poems*. New York: Farrar and Rinehart, 1931.
Higham, Charles. *In and Out of Hollywood: A Biographer's Memoir*. Madison: University of Wisconsin Press, 2009.
Higham, Charles, and Joel Greenberg. *The Celluloid Muse*. Chicago: Henry Regnery, 1969.
Hirsch, Foster. *Kurt Weill On Stage*. New York: Knopf, 2001.
Hobart, Rose. *A Steady Digression to a Fixed Point*. Metuchen, NJ: Scarecrow Press, 1994.
Horgan, Paul. *A Certain Climate*. Middletown, CT: Wesleyan University Press, 1988.
Horne, Lena, and Richard Schickel. *Lena*. New York: Doubleday, 1965.
Horowitz, Joseph. *On My Way*. New York: Norton, 2013.
Hutchisson, James. *DuBose Heyward: A Charleston Gentleman and the World of Porgy and Bess*. Jackson: University Press of Mississippi, 2000.
Johnson, Doris, and Ellen Leventhal, eds. *The Letters of Nunnally Johnson*. New York: Knopf, 1981.
Juchem, Elmar. *Kurt Weill und Maxwell Anderson*. Stuttgart: Metzler, 2000.
Kellow, Brian, *Ethel Merman: A Life*. New York: Penguin, 2008.
Knight, Arthur. *The Liveliest Art*. New York: Macmillan, 1957.
Kobal, John. *People Will Talk*. New York: Knopf, 1985.
Koszarski, Richard. *Hollywood on the Hudson: Film and Television in New York from Griffith to Sarnoff*. New Brunswick, NJ: Rutgers University Press, 2010.
Langner, Lawrence. *The Magic Curtain*. New York: Dutton, 1951.
Langner, Lawrence, and Armina Marshall. *Pursuit of Happiness*. New York: Samuel French, 1934.
Lazar, David, ed. *Michael Powell: Interviews*. Jackson: University Press of Mississippi, 2003.
Levant, Oscar. *The Memoirs of an Amnesiac*. New York: Putnam's Sons, 1965.
Lewis, Robert. *Slings and Arrows: Theater in My Life*. New York: Applause, 2000.
Luening, Otto. *The Odyssey of an American Composer*. New York: Scribner's Sons, 1980.
Macgowan, Kenneth, and William Melnitz. *The Living Stage*. Englewood Cliffs, NJ: Prentice Hall, 1955.
Mamoulian, Rouben. "Common Sense and Camera Angles." *American Cinematographer*, (February 1932).
Mank, Gregory W. *Hollywood Cauldron: Thirteen Horror Films from the Genre's Golden Age*. Jefferson, NC: McFarland, 1994.
McBride, Joseph. *Frank Capra: The Catastrophe of Success*. Jackson: University Press of Mississippi.

McClellan, Diana. *The Girls: Sappho Goes to Hollywood*. New York: St. Martin's Griffin, 2000.
McGilligan, Patrick, ed. *Backstory 2: Interviews with Screenwriters of the 1940s and 1950s*. Berkeley: University of California Press, 1991.
Merman, Ethel. *Don't Call Me Madam*. London: W. H. Allen, 1955.
Milne, Tom. *Rouben Mamoulian*. Bloomington: Indiana University Press, 1969.
Mosley, Leonard. *Zanuck: The Rise and Fall of Hollywood's Last Tycoon*. New York: McGraw-Hill, 1984.
Nolan, Frederick W. *The Sound of Their Music*. New York: Walker, 1978.
Paton, Alan. *Cry, the Beloved Country*. New York: Scribner's, 1948.
———. *Journey Continued*. New York: Scribner's, 1988.
Perlis, Vivian, and Libby Van Cleve, eds. *Composers' Voices from Ives to Ellington*. New Haven, CT: Yale University Press, 2005.
Peterson, Deborah. *Fredric March: Craftsman First, Star Second*. Westport, CT: Greenwood Press, 1996.
Prawer, S. S. *Caligari's Children: The Film as Tale of Terror*. Oxford: Oxford University Press, 1990.
Rausch, Andrew J. *Fifty Filmmakers: Conversations with Directors from Roger Avary to Steven Zaillan*. Jefferson, NC: McFarland, 2008.
Reinhardt, Gottfried. *The Genius: A Memoir of Max Reinhardt*. New York: Knopf, 1979.
Reis, Claire R. *Composers, Conductors and Critics*. Oxford: Oxford University Press, 1955.
Roberts, Joan. *Never Alone*. New York: Macmillan, 1954.
Rodgers, Dorothy. *My Favorite Things*. New York: Avenel Books, 1964.
Rodgers, Richard. *Musical Stages*. New York: Random House, 1975.
Rooney, Mickey. *Life Is Too Short*. New York: Villard Books, 1991.
Rose, Brian A. *Jekyll and Hyde Adapted: Dramatizations of Cultural Anxiety*. Westport, CT: Greenwood Press, 1996.
Sarris, Andrew. *The American Cinema: Directors and Directions 1929–1968*. New York: Da Capo Press, 1996.
Secrest, Meryle. *Somewhere for Me*. New York: Knopf, 2001.
Siegel, Marcia B. *Days on Earth: The Dance of Doris Humphrey*. Durham, NC: Duke University Press, 1993.
Simonov, Ruben. *Stanlislavsky's Protégé: Eugene Vakhtangov*. New York: DBS, 1969.
Simonson, Lee. *Part of a Lifetime*. New York: Duell, Sloan and Pierce, 1943.
Slavick, William. *DuBose Heyward*. Boston: Twayne, 1981.
Slonimsky, Nicolas. *Perfect Pitch*. London: Oxford University Press, 1988.
Spergel, Mark. *Reinventing Reality: The Art and Life of Rouben Mamoulian*. Lanham, MD: Scarecrow Press, 1993.

Stevens, George. *Interviews (Conversations with Filmmakers)*. Jackson: University Press of Mississippi, 2004.
Stevenson, Robert Louis. *The Strange Case of Dr. Jekyll and Mr. Hyde*. New York: Scribner's, 1886.
Stiles, Martha Bennett. "Porgy and Bess: A Reminiscence." *Stereo Review* (April 1976).
Stott, Willliam, with Jane Stott. *On Broadway: Performance Photographs by Fred Stehl*. Austin: University of Texas Press, 1978.
Sturges, Preston. *Preston Sturges*. New York: Simon & Schuster, 1990.
Swift, E. Anthony. *Popular Theater and Society in Tsarist Russia*. Berkeley: University of California Press, 2002.
Thomson, David. *The New Biographical Dictionary of Film*. 5th ed. New York: Knopf, 2010.
Tierney, Gene. *Self-Portrait*. New York: Wyden Books, 1978.
Tolstoy, Leo. *Resurrection*. New York: Dodd, Mead, 1899.
——— *What Is Art?* New York: Thomas Y. Crowell, 1899.
Turk, Edward Baron. *Hollywood Diva*. Berkeley: University of California Press, 1998.
Veeder, Willian, and Gordon Hirsch, eds. *Dr. Jekyll and Mr. Hyde After One Hundred Years*. Chicago: University of Chicago Press, 1988.
Waldau, Roy S. *Vintage Years of the Theatre Guild, 1928–1939*. Cleveland: Case Western Reserve University Press, 1972.
Wanger, Walter, with Joe Hyams. *My Life with Cleopatra*. New York: Bantam, 1963.
Wasserman, Dale. *The Impossible Musical*. New York: Applause Books, 2003.
Weaver, Tom. *Double-Feature Creature Attack!* Jefferson, NC: McFarland, 2003.
Wilk, Max. *OK! The Story of Oklahoma!* New York: Applause, 1993.
Worsley, Wallace. *From Oz to E.T.: Wally Worsley's Half-Century in Hollywood*. Edited by Charles Ziarko. Lanham, MD: Scarecrow Press, 1997.
Wyatt, Robert, and John Andrew Johnson, eds. *The George Gershwin Reader*. Oxford: Oxford University Press, 2004.
Youngerman, Joseph C. (interviewed by Ira Skutch and David Shepard). *My Seventy Years at Paramount Studios and the Directors Guild of America*. Los Angeles: Directors Guild of America, 1995.
Youngkin, Stephen D. *The Lost One: A Life of Peter Lorre*. Louisville: University Press of Kentucky, 2005.

Dissertations

Becvar, William J. "The Stage and Film Career of Rouben Mamoulian." PhD diss., University of Kansas, 1975.
Kilroy, David Michael. "Kurt Weill on Broadway: The Postwar Years (1945–1950)." Ph.D. diss., Harvard University, 1992.

Oberstein, Bennett T. "The Broadway Directing Career of Rouben Mamoulian." Ph.D. diss., Indiana University, 1974.

Interviews with Rouben Mamoulian

Adamson, Joe, for the Astoria Motion Picture and Television Foundation, 1979.
Ardmore, Jane Kesner, May 29, 1975, for *Photoplay*, May 1976.
Atkins, Thomas R., for *The Film Journal*, Fall 1973.
Becvar, William, March 20 and 22, 1973.
Birdwell, Russell, for unpublished book *The Western*, July 1958.
Bruck, Jerry, 1977.
Brownlow, Kevin, May 1969.
Davis, Ronald L., August 15, 1981.
Directors Guild of America recording, D.W. Griffith Award presentation to Rouben Mamoulian, August 15, 1982. Library of Congress Recorded Sound Division.
Gallagher, John, for the American Film Institute, January 8 and 10, 1978.
Greenberg, Steven, American Film Institute oral history, May 1973.
Kozak, Paul and Frank Merwald, University of Southern California, October 24, November 8, November 15, 1975.
Oberstein, Bennett T., August 1973.
O'Brien, Catherine, interview in London for Bill Batchelor Publicity for *Cleopatra*, December 1960.
"Painting the Leaves Black": Rouben Mamoulian interviewed by David Robinson, *Sight and Sound* (Summer 1961).

Author Interviews

Rob Bamberger, correspondence
Virginia Moise Collins, phone interview
Jean Darling, correspondence
Josephine Collins Breyfogle, phone interview
Roy Fitzell, phone interview
Annabelle Gold Gamson, correspondence
Mark Godwin, correspondence
Zaghik Gourjian, phone interview
Coleen Gray, phone interview
Paul Ignatius, phone interview
Charles Ipcar, correspondence
Miles Kreuger, phone interview
Mimi Turque Marre, correspondence
Alice Hammerstein Mathias, phone interview
Arby Ovanessian, phone interview
Bruce Pomahac, correspondence

Naida King Rasbury, phone interview
Maria Riva, correspondence through David Riva
Joan Roberts, phone interview
Lola Scarpitta, correspondence
Caroline Landi Thomas, correspondence

Archives
Columbia University (CU)

Reminiscences of Oscar Hammerstein II, 1957
Reminiscences of Ben Hecht, 1959
Reminiscences of Arthur Hornblow Jr., 1959
Reminiscences of Rouben Mamoulian, 1958
Reminiscences of Richard Rodgers, 1969
Reminiscences of Reginald Owen, 1971

Georgia State University

Johnny Mercer Collection, unpublished memoir

Kurt Weill Foundation (KWF), New York

Todd Duncan oral history, conducted by Peggy Meyer Sherry, May 2, 1991.

Library of Congress

George Gershwin Collection (GGC)
Bob Hope joke file, Recorded Sound Division
Oscar Hammerstein II collection (OHC), Music Division
Rouben Mamoulian Collection (RMC) Manuscript Division, Prints and Photos Division
"The Art of Gods and Monkeys," uncompleted autobiography, Speeches and Writings series, RMC.
Groucho Marx letters, Manuscript Division

Margaret Herrick Library, Academy of Motion Picture Arts and Sciences, Los Angeles

George Cukor Collection (GCC)
Production Code Administration files
Samuel Goldwyn Collection (SGC)

Ransom Humanities Center, University of Texas, Austin

Maxwell Anderson Collection (MAC)

State Historical Society of Wisconsin

Walter Wanger collection

Southern Methodist University

Oral History Collection on the Performing Arts in America

Wesleyan University

Kay Francis collection, Wesleyan Cinema Archives

Yale University

Theatre Guild Collection (TGC), Beinecke Library

Index

Abigayil: The Story of the Cat at the Manger, 301
Academy Awards, 75, 118, 159, 164, 271, 292, 297
Adler, Buddy, 285
Aherne, Brian, 94–95, 99
Ah, Wilderness!, 217, 219, 224–25
All God's Chillun Got Wings, 35
Alvin Theatre, 119, 121, 192
American Opera Company, 28
American Theater, St. Louis, 245
Anderson, Judith, 193, 195
Andrews, Dana, 193–95, 204
Animal Crackers, 48, 54
Applause, 4–6, 52–59
Arlen, Harold, 217, 223
Armenian Genocide, 114
Arms and the Girl, 7, 9, 190, 231, 237, 246–53. See *The Pursuit of Happiness*
Astaire, Fred, 5, 258, 263–69, 301, 305
Astoria studio (Paramount), 51, 76
Atkinson, Brooks, 43
The Atlantic Monthly, 302
Atwell, Martha, 29, 31
Atwill, Lionel, 96
Aufstieg un Fall der Stadt Mahagonny (Rise and Fall of the City of Mahagonny), 139–40
Ayers, Lemuel, 217, 219

Bailey, Pearl: in *Arms and the Girl*, 7, 246, 248, 251–52; in *Porgy and Bess* film, 273, in *St. Louis Woman*, 218, 222–23
Banks, Leslie, 238
Barnes, Howard, 118, 137, 188, 244, 246
Barry, Philip, 181
Barrymore, John, 73, 194
Barrymore, Lionel, 225
Battle of Angels / Orpheus Descending, 162–63
The Beating at the Door, 21–23
Becky Sharp, 5, 114–18, 123, 296
Behrman, S. N., 73, 100, 103, 181, 184
Ben-Hur (1925), 78
Ben-Hur (1959), 286–87
Bennett, Joan, 285
Bennett, John, 38
Bennett, Robert Russell, 143, 185, 201
Benny, Jack, 159, 258
Bergman, Ingrid, 75, 205, 302
Berlin, Irving, 301
Biberman, Herbert, 62, 147
Bigelow, Lucile, 27, 72
Billboard, 222, 234
Bing, Rudolf, 255–57
Birdwell, Russell, 274–75, 278–80
Birinski, Leo, 95, 137
Blane, Ralph, 225, 229

Blood and Sand, 4, 8, 147, 162–70
Boetticher, Budd, 164, 166
Bogdanovich, Peter, 93, 196
Bontemps, Arna, 217–19, 221
Borzage, Frank, 76, 136, 139
Boston Post, 213
Bow, Clara, 67–68
Bowen, Stirling, 64
Boyd, William (in *City Streets*), 71
Boyer, Charles, 147
Bradford, Roark, 35
Bradley, David, 303
Brecher, Irving, 219
Breen, Robert, 257
Brinkmann, Eddie, 238, 245
Briskin, Sam, 150
Britten, Benjamin, 236
Brooke, Tyler, 88
Brooklyn Eagle, 65
Brown, Anne, 123–24, 128
Brown, Beth, 53
Brown, Clarence, 108, 225
Brown, Jasbo, 127
Bubbles, John, 124–25, 131–33, 265
Buchman, Sidney, 295
Burbage, Richard, 302
Burke, Billie, 118
Burlesque, 55
Burton, Richard, 285, 287–88, 297–98, 300
Burton, Sybil, 300
Butterfield 8, 286, 296–97
Butterworth, Charles, 88
Byington, Spring, 172
By Pigeon Post, 21
Byrn, Bob, 203

Café Tomaza, 49
Cagney, James, 139, 157, 257
Calais, France, 18
Calleia, Joseph, 154

Campbell, Alan, 50
Campbell, Lawton, 60–61
Cantor, Eddie, 108, 159
Čapek, Karol, 60
Capra, Frank, 146, 150–51
Carlton House, 231
Carmen (Bizet opera), 28, 134, 255–57
Carousel, 3, 5, 63, 190, 201–16
Carradine, John, 164, 173
Carrillo, Leo, 137
Carter, Jack, 37, 41
Caspary, Vera, 193
Cassidy, Jack, 261
Cawthorn, Joseph, 89
Cedars-Sinai Hospital, 305
Cerf, Phyllis, 296
Challis, Christopher, 256
Chaney, Lon, 28
Chapman, John, 5, 244
Charisse, Cyd, 263–65, 267–69
Charleston, 33, 36–38, 127, 175
Chevalier, Maurice, 84–85, 86–87, 89, 109, 147, 301, 305
Chicago Daily News, 137
Chicken Every Sunday, 217
Christian Science Monitor, 189
"Christ on the Cross Adored by Two Donors" (El Greco), 166
City Streets, 4, 31, 63, 67–73
Clair, René, 3–4, 83–84, 91, 147
Claire, Ludi, 285
Clarke, Lulu Belle, 248
Clayton, Jan, 202, 207–9, 218
Cobb, Lee J., 152–53
Cocoanut Grove, 266, 271
The Cocoanuts, 54
Cohan, George M., 33, 49
Coleman, Herbert, 222, 240
Coleman, Warren, 126, 222, 240
Collins, Russell, 212–13, 216
Collins, Virginia Moise, 203

Columbia Pictures, 114, 150–51, 153, 155
Committee for the Negro in the Arts, 251–52
Communist ideology, 16
Communist Party members, 155, 159, 253–55
"Concerto in F" (Gershwin), 120
Congai, 50, 201
Connelly, Marc, 35, 238
Conte, John, 248
Cooper, Gary, 67–69, 93, 140, 151, 154
Corner Club, 27
Cousins, Mark, 83
Crawford, Cheryl, 42, 121, 184
Cregar, Laird, 163, 172–73, 193
Crouse, Russell, 144
Cry, the Beloved Country (film), 238
Cry, the Beloved Country (novel), 231, 234–36
Cukor, George, 52, 113, 258
Cullen, Countee, 218–19

Daily Express, 296
Daily Mail, 296
Daily Mirror, 189–90
Daniels, William (Bill), 104
Dante, Michael, 260
Darby, Ken, 273, 276, 280
Darling, Jean, 202, 206, 208–9
Darnell, Linda, 161, 164–65
Davis, Bette, 60–61
Davis, Sammy, Jr., 262–63, 271–72, 280
Day, Richard, 109, 166
de Acosta, Mercedes, 93
DeHaven, Gloria, 225, 227–28
de Mille, Agnes, 6, 180, 185–88, 203–4, 231, 236
DeMille, Cecil B., 31, 92, 253–54
DeSilva, David, 300
Die glückliche Hand, 61

Dietz, Howard, 196–99
Directors Guild of America, 136, 146, 150, 253, 279, 281, 305, 307
Disney, Walt, 8, 55, 119
Drake, Alfred, 188, 190
Dr. Jekyll and Mr. Hyde, 4, 63, 73–82; MGM film of, 75
Dorchester Hotel, 294, 296
Duncan, Todd, 119–20, 124, 129, 133, 235, 237–38, 241–42, 244–45
Dunne, Irene, 140–41, 143, 149
D.W. Griffith Award, 305
Dyall, Franklin, 21–22

Eagels, Jeanne, 49–50, 54, 197–98
Eastman, George, 10–11, 23–24, 28, 31
Eastman Kodak, 11, 23, 29
Eastman School of Dance and Dramatic Action, 28
Eastman School of Music, 10, 24, 31, 53, 72, 301
Eisenstein, Sergei, 255
El Greco, 8, 147, 166
Ellis, Evelyn, 37, 39, 41
Eltinge Theater, 49
El Tovar Hotel, 107
Englund, Ken, 172, 174
Essentuki, 17
Eyman, Scott, 6, 254

Fabray, Nanette, 237, 246, 250–51
Fairbanks, Douglas, 160
Fairbanks, Douglas, Jr., 160
Famous Players-Lasky, 31, 137
Fantasia, 8, 55
Faragoh, Francis Edward, 115–16
A Farewell to Arms, 62–65
Farrell, Anthony Brady, 249
FBI file, 254–55
Feldman, Charles, 108, 140, 160, 285, 297

Fields, Dorothy, 9, 246, 248–50, 253
Fields, Herbert, 246, 248–50
Fields, Stanley, 31, 139
Fisher, Eddie, 286, 294–96
Fitelson, William, 204
Fitzell, Roy, 267
Fitzgerald, F. Scott, 61–62
Fleming, Victor, 75
The Flute of Krishna, 29
Folsey, George, 54, 57–58
Fonda, Henry, 60, 171–73
Fontanne, Lynn, 36, 73, 181
Ford, John, 169, 253
Forehead, Russell, 283–84, 290
Fort, Garrett, 53
The Forty Days of Musa Dagh, 114
Four Saints in Three Acts, 120, 122, 126
Fox Studios (20th Century Fox), 60, 66, 92, 114, 160–61, 171, 174, 192–95, 205, 218, 238, 271, 284–85, 288, 291–92, 297
Frances, Arlene, 32–33, 297
Francis, Kay, 160
Franzero, Carlo Mario, 285
Fredericks, Ellie, 280–81
Freed, Arthur, 5, 182, 217, 219, 226, 262–65, 268
Freeman, Helen, 97

The Game of Love and Death, 60
Garbo, Greta: *Queen Christina* and, 4, 100–106, 309; vacation with Mamoulian, 106–7
Garland, Judy, 181, 225, 227
Garrett, Oliver H. P., 67
The Gay Desperado, 134, 136–39
Gentleman from Montana / Mr. Smith Goes to Washington, 150
Gershe, Leonard, 263
Gershwin, George, 3; first meeting with Mamoulian, 27; *Porgy and Bess* and, 34, 40, 44, 46, 114, 118–32, 176, 192, 271
Gershwin, Ira, 120, 271, 274
Gershwin, Leonore, 257, 272
Giesler, Jerry, 274
Gilbert, John, 102–4
Gogol, Nikolai, 14, 130
Golden Boy: film, 150–56; play, 154, 156; trade with Frank Capra, 151
Goldwyn, Sam, 151, 191; *Porgy and Bess* film and, 5, 133, 270–72, 274–81; *We Live Again* and, 108–9, 113
Gone to Earth, 256
Gone with the Wind, 114, 274
Goossens, Boonie, 27
Goossens, Eugene, 24, 27
Gordean, Jack, 285
Gould, Morton, 246, 248, 250, 252
Gourjian, Zaghik, 306–7
Goya, Francisco, 165
Graham, Martha, 28–29
Graham, Sheilah, 109
Grandma Moses (Anna Mary Robertson Moses), 250
Granville, Bonita, 208
Gray, Coleen, 174, 231, 233
Great Northern Theatre, Chicago, 245
Greaves, William, 240–41, 244
Green, James "Cannonball," 156
Green, Paul, 35, 110
Gross, Edward, 217–18, 223
Guétary, Georges, 246–48, 251
Guild Theatre, 36, 181, 184
Gullion, Maj. Gen. Allen W., 181
Guyse, Sheila, 240

Hamilton, George, 161
Hamlet: A New Version, 302
Hamm, Charles, 126
Hammerstein, Oscar II, 3, 34, 217, 219, 224, 236, 252, 300; *Carousel* and,

201–15; *High, Wide and Handsome* and, 140, 142–43; *Oklahoma!* and, 9, 182–83, 185–87, 189, 191, 260–61
Hammerstein, William, 191
Hammett, Dashiell, 67
Happy Birthday, 219
Harris, Sam, 49, 54
Harrison, Guy Fraser, 24, 72
Harrison, Rex, 237, 287, 297
Hart, Lorenz, 36, 83, 90–91, 182, 204
Harvey, Georgette, 37, 119, 238
Harvey, James, 83
Hauser, Marv, 271, 278
Havoc, June, 199–200
Hawks, Howard, 136, 146–47, 152, 233
Hayes, Helen, 91, 175, 219
Hayes, Joseph, 233–34
Hays Office, 97
Hayworth, Rita, 163, 167–69
Hecht, Ben, 137, 160
Heidt, Charles, 233–34
Heidt, Eidell, 233, 307
Helburn, Theresa, 36, 175–76; *Arms and the Girl* and, 249, 252–53; *Liliom* / *Carousel* and, 140, 204–8; *Oklahoma!* and, 176, 181, 184, 186, 190; *Porgy and Bess* and, 114, 122, 130; *The Time of Your Life* and, 156–57
Hemingway, Ernest, 60, 62, 64–65
Hepburn, Audrey, 264, 285, 297
Hepburn, Katherine, 60–61, 181
Herbertot, Jacques, 23
Herschenson, Violet, 279, 291
Heyward, Dorothy, 35; *Porgy* and, 35–37, 45; *Set My People Free* and, 175
Heyward, DuBose: *Porgy* and, 33–37; *Porgy and Bess* and, 120, 122, 127, 130
High, Wide and Handsome, 4, 136, 140–46

Higham, Charles, 303
Hill, Ruby, 218
Hobart, Rose, 75–77, 80–81
Hobbes, Halliwell, 77
Hoffenstein, Samuel, 75, 99, 113
Hofmann, Josef, 27
Holden, William, 151–53
The Hollywood Reporter, 91, 276, 278–79
Holm, Celeste, 179, 188
Hoover, J. Edgar, 147
Hope, Bob, 229, 258
Hopkins, Miriam, 297; *Battle of Angels* and, 162–63; *Becky Sharp* and, 115–18; *Dr. Jekyll and Mr. Hyde* and, 74–76, 80–82, 94, 303
Hopper, Hedda, 208, 279, 297
Horgan, Paul, 24, 26–27, 29, 67
Hornblow, Arthur, Jr., 6, 140–41
Horne, Lena, 218, 232, 251, 271
Huckleberry Finn, 4, 236, 253
Hurston, Zora Neale, 232
Huston, Walter, 108, 175, 226

Imperial Theatre, 202
In Abraham's Bosom, 35, 37

Jaffe, Sam, 111, 249
The Jazz Singer, 55
Johnson, Christine, 210
Johnson, Hall, 120
Jolson, Al, 55
Jones, Jennifer, 256
Jones, Margo, 233
Jones, Robert Edmond, 115
Jones, Shirley, 261, 305

Kahn, Otto, 192
Kalantarov, Georgy, 12
Kansas City, Missouri, 245
Kato Bobo, 12, 14, 304

Kaufman, Albert, 99, 134
Kazan, Elia, 176, 203
Kelly, Gene, 153, 181, 251
Kern, Jerome, 34, 140, 143
Khachaturian, Suren, 16–18
King, Henry, 136, 169, 260
King, Naida, 119, 125
Kolk, Scott, 175
Kreuger, Miles, 304

La bohème, 255
Landi, Elissa, 60, 63–67, 72, 91–92, 158, 209; *City Streets* and, 31, 63, 67–70, 72–73, 95; *A Farewell to Arms* and, 60, 62–65, 91
Lang, Fritz, 68, 96
Langner, Lawrence, 48, 83, 128, 176, 187, 203, 231, 246, 248–49; death of, 300, visits to Rochester, 29–30; *Liliom* and, 36, 211; *Oklahoma!* and, 187–91, 205; *Porgy* and, 33, 35, 126, 130, 189; Theatre Guild and, 29, 31, 33, 35–36, 47, 126, 156–57, 207
Lantz, Louis, 159, 170
La Quinta, California, 107
Lasky, Jesse, 108, 134, 137, 176
Laura, 192–96
Lazar, Irving, 6, 262, 269, 271–72, 278–80
Leaf and Bough, 174, 231–34
Lee, Harper, 300
Levant, Oscar, 132, 282
Levene, Sam, 152, 155
Lewis, Jerry, 258, 291
The Life and Times of Cleopatra, 285
Logan, Joshua, 176, 203
Lombard, Carole, 159, 172, 175
London, 5, 8, 10, 18–19, 21, 23–24, 29, 31, 34, 63–64, 75, 80, 82, 146–47, 150, 187, 257, 283–84, 287–89, 291–96, 299–300, 305

Loos, Anita, 148, 191, 219, 232
Loos, Mary Anita, 148–49, 158, 174
Lorre, Peter, 266–67
Los Angeles County Public Guardian Office, 305, 307
Los Angeles Examiner, 91
Los Angeles Times, 92
Los Cuatro Jinetes del Apocalipsis (*The Four Horsemen of the Apocalypse*), 163
Love Me Tonight, 3–5, 44, 63, 83–91, 140, 185, 267, 299, 305
Lovet-Lorski, Boris, 97, 208
Loy, Myrna, 89, 140
Lubitsch, Ernst, 3–4, 76, 83–85, 91, 159, 263–64, 308
Luening, Otto, 24, 26, 30
Lukas, Paul, 31, 70
Lunt, Alfred, 36, 48, 73, 181
Lupino, Ida, 136–137, 139
Lyons, Arthur, 176, 181
Lysistrata, 158–59, 255, 307

MacDonald, Jeanette, 84, 86–89, 258
Macgowan, Kenneth, 73, 115
Madison, Ella, 39–40
"Madonna de Granduca" (Raphael), 148
Maier, Ruth R., 189
Makaroff, Grigori, 18, 20–21
Mamoulian, Rouben: affair with Boonie Goosens, 27; affair with "Rabbit," 170–71, 174; Azadia Newman and, 8, 174–75, 181–82, 187, 189, 192–93, 196, 198, 203–4, 208, 214–15, 231, 234, 244, 249, 259, 261, 278, 295, 301–2, 304; childhood of, 12–14; death of, 307; Eastman School of Music and, 10, 24, 31, 53, 72; Moscow Art Theatre and, 11, 15, 61; relationship with Elissa

Landi, 60, 63–67, 72, 91–92, 158, 209; relationship with Gertrude Michael, 108; relationship with Greta Garbo, 106–7; relationship with Kay Francis, 160; relationship with Mary Anita Loos, 148–49, 158, 174; relationship with Theatre Guild, 29, 33, 47, 62, 73, 156–57, 175–76, 189–91, 203–4, 249–50; relationship with Vardanoush "Vava" Sarian, 17–18, 26; relationship with Vladimir Rosing, 10–11, 21, 23, 25, 28; Russian Revolution and, 15–16
Mamoulian, Virginie, 11–12, 14–17, 30–31, 111–12, 255; Mamoulian Dramatic Group and, 12
Mamoulian, Zachary, 11–12, 14–15, 17, 30–31, 255
Mamoulian (McQuaker), Svetlana, 8, 12, 16–18; death of, 30–32
Mankiewicz, Joseph, 253–54, 289, 295–97
March, Fredric, 92, in *Dr. Jekyll and Mr. Hyde*, 74–79, 80–81; in *We Live Again*, 110, 113
Marchand, Léopold, 84–85, 147
Marco Millions, 48–49
The Mark of Zorro, 4, 160–62
Marshall, Armina, 36, 207, 231, 249, 300
Martin, Mary, 182, 197
Martin Beck Theatre, 50, 219
Martini, Nino, 136–39
Marx, Groucho, 48, 293, 303
Marx Brothers, 54
Matthews, Edward, 119
Matthews, Inez, 240
Mattson, Eric, 209
Maugham, Somerset, 50, 197
Maxwell, Marilyn, 226, 229

Mayer, Louis B., 93, 101, 105, 108, 250
McClendon, Rose, 37
McCracken, Joan, 185
McEvoy, J. P., 52–53
McEwen, Walter, 301
McKaig, Alexander, 61, 70, 73, 82
McQuaker, Alexa, 30–31
McQuaker, Alexander, 30–31
Meltzer, Lewis, 154–55
Menken, Helen, 49–50
Mercer, Johnny, 217–18, 220
Merman, Ethel, 196–99
Metropolitan Opera, 4, 60, 109, 121, 192, 198, 250, 255
Michael, Gertrude, 108
Milestone, Lewis, 4, 39, 71, 136
Milne, Tom, 84, 116, 266, 300
Mirror News (Los Angeles), 275
Mr. Sycamore, 176, 181
Mitchell, Langdon, 115
Moeller, Philip, 36
Molnár, Ferenc, 36, 64, 139–40, 201, 203–5, 212
Monroe, Marilyn, 275, 285, 292
A Month in the Country, 60–61
Morgan, Frank, 227
Morros, Boris, 158–59, 255
Motion Picture Production Code, 4, 8, 77, 97, 153–55, 161, 164, 229
Munsell, Warren, 126, 132
Mussolini, Benito, 148, 155–56
My Life With Cleopatra, 300

NAACP, 245
National Labor Relations Board (NLRB), 150
Nazimova, Alla, 163, 167
Negri, Pola, 47, 94
"Negro plays," 5, 7, 34–35, 175, 232
New Haven, Connecticut, 157, 186, 219

Newman, Azadia, 8, 174–75, 181–82, 187, 189, 192–93, 196, 198, 203–4, 208, 214–15, 231, 234, 244, 249, 259, 261, 278, 295, 301–2, 304; alcoholism of, 260, 298–99, 303, 306; dementia of, 304–5, 307; previous marriages of, 174–75; sisters Helen, Artemesia and, 174
Newman, Thomas, 174
New York City, 10, 27, 29, 31, 34, 36–37, 46, 53, 55–56, 59, 62, 64, 92, 105, 107, 109, 122–23, 126–27, 146, 150, 157–58, 176, 187, 193–95, 197, 203, 205, 208, 214, 231–32, 251, 258, 260–61, 272–73, 279, 282, 286, 294, 296, 301, 304
New York *Daily News*, 5, 244
New York Herald Tribune, 47, 70, 118, 137, 188, 244, 246
New York Times, 43, 49, 91, 120, 170, 188, 200, 223, 236, 246, 252
New York *World*, 43
Nicholas II, Czar, 14, 21
Nicholas, Fayard, 218, 222
Nicholas, Harold, 218, 222
Nichols, Lewis, 188, 200, 223
Nichols, Robert, 50–51
Ninotchka, 263–64
Norton, Elliott, 213

Obermer, Seymour, 21, 23, 63–64, 151
Odets, Clifford, 153–54, 181
Oklahoma!: Broadway production of, 5, 177–91; as *Green Grow the Lilacs*, 176, 178, 182–83, 185, 225
Ol' Man Adam an' His Chillun, 35
O'Neal, Charles, 231
O'Neill, Eugene, 35, 47, 48, *Ah, Wilderness / Summer Holiday* and, 217, 225, *Marco Millions* and, 48–49
On Film, 196

Orth, Frank, 173
Ovanessian, Arby, 305–6

Paige, Janis, 266, 305
Panama Hattie, 197
Paramount Pictures, 4, 6, 51, 55, 57–58, 60, 63, 66–68, 72–73, 76, 84, 90, 92, 93–94, 99–100, 108–9, 134–37, 140, 145–47, 149, 151, 158, 172, 246, 257–58
Parsons, Louella, 279, 300
Paton, Alan, 7, 231, 234–35, 237, 243–44
Patterson, Elizabeth, 61–62, 89, 141–42
Pearl Harbor attack, 173
Peck, Gregory, 300, 303
Peers, Joan, 52, 54
Pennsylvania Station, 53
Philadelphia, 50, 61, 200, 229, 245, 252
Philip, Prince, 291–92
Pichel, Irving, 104, 136
Pickman, Milton, 271, 278, 281
Pirandello, Luigi, 36
Pius XI, Pope, 148
Playwrights Company, 237–38, 245
Plaza Hotel, 33, 231
PM, 189, 191, 223
Poitier, Sidney, 238, 270–73, 279
Porgy (1925 novella), 33, 35–37, 40–41, 43–45
Porgy (1927 Broadway), 34–46
Porgy and Bess (1935 Broadway), 119–33; 1942 revival, 20, 121; 1952 revival, 257
Porgy and Bess (1959 film), 270–82
Potter, H. C., 157, 281
Power, Tyrone: in *Blood and Sand*, 163–68; in *The Mark of Zorro*, 161–62

Praskins, Leonard, 110, 113
Preminger, Otto, 160; *Laura* and, 192–96; *Porgy and Bess* film and, 45, 270–71, 275, 279–81
Previn, André, 273, 279, 305
Production Code, 4, 8, 77, 97, 153–55, 161, 164, 229
The Pursuit of Happiness, 231, 246–53. See *Arms and the Girl*

Queen Christina, 4, 63, 93, 100–106, 108, 147, 309
Quinn, Anthony, 163

Raitt, John, 201, 207, 209, 257
Rancho Yucca Loma, 154, 171
Rapper, Irving, 181, 192
Rathbone, Basil, 162
Reagan, Ronald, 269
Reinhardt, Max, 5, 185
Rennie, Hugh, 33
Resurrection, 109–10
"Rhapsody in Blue," (Gershwin), 27
Rhapsody in Blue (1945 film), 176
Rings on Her Fingers, 171–74
RKO Pictures, 53, 115, 149
Roberts, Joan, 179, 185–88, 190
Robeson, Paul, 35, 73, 236
Robinson, Bill "Bojangles," 236
Rochester, New York, 10, 23, 26–27, 30, 72, 77
Rock Creek Park, 174
Rodgers, Dorothy, 203
Rodgers, Richard, 3, 36, 109, 143, 151, 158, 203, 302; *Carousel* and, 201–7, 209, 213–14; *Happy Birthday* and, 219, 224; *Love Me Tonight* and, 83, 85, 88, 90–91; *Oklahoma!* and, 177, 182, 185–87, 189–91
Rodgers and Hammerstein, 143, 185–86, 189, 201, 203–6, 213, 236, 261

Rodgers and Hart, 85, 88, 109, 151, 158, 178, 199, 204, 219
Roland, Gilbert, 260
Rolland, Romain, 60
Rooney, Mickey, 224–25, 227–28, 230
Roosevelt, Eleanor, 189
Rosing, Vladimir, 10–11, 21, 23, 25–26, 28, 30–31
Ruggles, Charles, 85, 88
R.U.R. (*Rosson's Universal Robots*), 60

Sadie Thompson / Rain, 50, 196–200
Sadko (Rimsky-Korsakov), 129
San Francisco, 134, 156, 197–98, 245
San Francisco Opera, 258
Sangre y arena (*The Blood of the Arena*), 163
Sarian, Vardanoush "Vava," 17–18
Saroyan, William, 134–35; *The Time of Your Life* and, 156–57
Sarris, Andrew, 4
Saturday Night Bond Wagon, 191
The Saturday Review, 302
Scarpitta, Lola, 96
Scarpitta, Nadia, 96
Scarpitta, Salvatore, 96–97
Schoenberg, Arnold, 60–61, 120
Schreiber, Lew, 194–95, 285
Schulberg, B. P., 66–68, 76, 108
Sedgwick, Ruth, 120, 129
Selznick, David O., 256
Serling, Rod, 286
Sherman, Lowell, 114–15, 117
Show Boat, 34, 54, 140, 142, 143
Signal Corps, US Army, 160, 173, 176, 193, 254
Silk Stockings, 5, 263–69, 285, 305
Sinatra, Frank, 271–72
Sister Beatrice, 29–30
Skipworth, Alison, 49, 95, 116, 118

Skouras, Spyros, 284–89, 291–92, 294–97
Slonimsky, Nicolas, 24, 27–28
Smallens, Alexander, 124, 133
Solid South, 60–62
The Song of Songs, 4, 63, 93–100
Soudeikine, Sergei, 109, 126, 130, 159
Stanislavski, Konstantin, 11, 23, 26
Stanwyck, Barbara, 152–54, 156, 172
Steiger, Rod, 261
Sten, Anna, 12, 109–11, 113
Stevenson, Robert Louis, 73, 75–76, 80
Stewart, Donald Ogden, 159
St. James Theatre, 178
St. Louis Woman, 7, 16, 217–24
Strand Palace Hotel, 30
Stromberg Carlson Hour, 72
Strongin, Mimi, 203
Struss, Karl, 78–79
Sturges, Preston, 110, 172
Sudermann, Hermann, 94
Sunday Express, 23
Summer Holiday, 4, 8, 224–30

Tamanouva, Tamara, 150
Tamiroff, Akim, 144
Taos, New Mexico, 106–7
Taradash, Daniel, 154–55, 170
Taylor, Elizabeth, 5, 284–86, 288–91, 293–98
Thackeray, William Makepeace, 115
Thalberg, Irving, 105, 114
Théâtre de Champs-Élysées, 23
Theatre Guild: organization of, 36–37
Theatre Guild acting school, 31–33, 297
These Modern Women, 47, 49
Thomas, Caroline, 63
Thomson, David, 264, 308
Throckmorton, Cleon, 38, 50
Tierney, Gene, 172–75, 192–93, 196

Tiflis/Tbilisi, Georgia, 7, 11–12, 14, 16–18, 303–4
Tobias, George, 263
Todd, George W., 11, 24
Todd, Michael, 186, 286
Tolstoy, Leo, 109–10, 113, 308
Turgenev, Ivan, 60–61

UFA studios, 93
Ulric, Leonore, 35, 198
Ulysses Africanus, 236, 240–41
United Artists, 137, 160, 176
Universal Studios, 62, 300
University of Moscow, 11, 14

Vakhtangov, Yevgeny, 11, 16, 44, 201, 305
Variety, 200
Vidor, King, 4, 8, 136, 158
Viertel, Salka, 100
Vogel, Robert, 230
Volkoff, Chris, 199
von Sternberg, Josef, 93–95
von Stroheim, Erich, 6

Wald, Jerry, 288
Wanger, Walter, 51–52, 60; *Cleopatra* and, 284–98, 300
Warner, Jack, 152, 181, 301
Warner Bros., 29, 152, 161, 167, 176, 192, 258
Warren, Harry, 219, 225
Washington, Ford Lee "Buck," 124
Wasserman, Dale, 286–87
Waxman, A. P., 198, 200
We Live Again, 12, 109–13
Webb, Clifton, 192, 194–95
Weill, Kurt: *Huckleberry Finn* and, 4, 236; 253, *Liliom* and, 139–40; *Lost in the Stars* and, 231, 234–45
Weissberger, Arnold, 209, 232

Welles, Orson, 53, 65, 157
What's My Line?, 296
Whipper, Leigh, 39, 280
Whyte, Jerry, 232, 251
Wilder, Thornton, 110, 113, 216, 227
Wilk, Max, 186
Williams, Tennessee, 162, 232
Wilson, Frank, 37, 41
Wiman, Dwight Deere, 151
Wings over Europe, 50–51
Wood, Grant, 8, 228
Woollcott, Alexander, 43, 47
World War II, 158, 173, 180, 211, 248, 257, 288
Worsley, Wallace, Jr., 226
Wyler, William, 68, 254, 271, 297

Xenia Alexandrova, Grand Duchess, 21

Youngerman, Joseph, 6, 87, 136, 145, 307

Zanuck, Darryl, 160, 170, 176, 192–93, 284–85, 297–98; *Blood and Sand* and, 169–70; *Laura* and, 193–95; *Mark of Zorro* and, 160–62; *Rings on her Fingers* and, 172–73
Zanuck, Virginia, 194
Zukor, Adolph, 52, 108, 137, 257–58; *Applause* and, 57–59; *Love Me Tonight* and, 84

WISCONSIN FILM STUDIES

The Film Music of John Williams: Reviving Hollywood's Classical Style,
second edition
EMILIO AUDISSINO

The Foreign Film Renaissance on American Screens, 1946–1973
TINO BALIO

Somerset Maugham and the Cinema
ROBERT CALDER

Marked Women: Prostitutes and Prostitution in the Cinema
RUSSELL CAMPBELL

Depth of Field: Stanley Kubrick, Film, and the Uses of History
EDITED BY GEOFFREY COCKS, JAMES DIEDRICK,
AND GLENN PERUSEK

Tough as Nails: The Life and Films of Richard Brooks
DOUGLASS K. DANIEL

Making Hollywood Happen: The Story of Film Finances
CHARLES DRAZIN

Dark Laughter: Spanish Film, Comedy, and the Nation
JUAN F. EGEA

Glenn Ford: A Life
PETER FORD

Luis Buñuel: The Red Years, 1929–1939
ROMÁN GUBERN AND PAUL HAMMOND

Screen Nazis: Cinema, History, and Democracy
SABINE HAKE

Peerless: Rouben Mamoulian, Hollywood, and Broadway
Kurt Jensen

A Cinema of Obsession: The Life and Work of Mai Zetterling
Mariah Larsson

Continental Films: French Cinema under German Control
Christine Leteux

Escape Artist: The Life and Films of John Sturges
Glenn Lovell

Colonial Tactics and Everyday Life: Workers of the Manchuria Film Association
Yuxin Ma

I Thought We Were Making Movies, Not History
Walter Mirisch

Giant: George Stevens, a Life on Film
Marilyn Ann Moss

French Film History, 1895–1946
Richard Neupert

The Many Lives of Cy Endfield: Film Noir, the Blacklist, and "Zulu"
Brian Neve

Six Turkish Filmmakers
Laurence Raw

Jean-Luc Godard: The Permanent Revolutionary
Bert Rebhandl, translated by Edward Maltby

The Cinema of Sergei Parajanov
James Steffen